AMERICAN
EVANGELICALS
and
·T H E·

MASS
MEDIA

AMERICAN
EVANGELICALS
and
· T H E ·

MASS

MEDIA

*Perspectives on the Relationship
Between American Evangelicals
and the Mass Media*

Quentin J. Schultze
Editor

Academie
Books Grand Rapids,
Michigan
Zondervan Publishing House

AMERICAN EVANGELICALS AND THE MASS MEDIA
Copyright © 1990 by the Zondervan Corporation
Grand Rapids, Michigan

Requests for information should be addressed to:
Zondervan Publishing House
Academic and Professional Books
Grand Rapids, Michigan 49530

ACADEMIE BOOKS is an imprint of Zondervan Publishing House,
1415 Lake Drive, S.E., Grand Rapids, Michigan 49506

Library of Congress Cataloging in Publication Data

American evangelicals and the mass media : perspectives on the
    relationship between American evangelicals and the mass media /
    Quentin J. Schultze, editor.
        p.   cm.
    Includes bibliographical references.
    ISBN 0-310-27261-0
    1. Mass media in religion–United States.   2. Evangelicalism-
-United States–History–20th century.   3. United States–Church
history–20th century.   I. Schultze, Quentin J. (Quentin James).
1952-
BV652.97.U6A46   1990
261.5′2′0973–dc20   90-34696
                                                                                        CIP

Edited by Jan M. Ortiz
Designed by Jan M. Ortiz

Printed in the United States of America

92   93   94   95 / CH / 10   9   8   7   6   5   4   3   2

To Cliff

CONTENTS

CONTRIBUTORS

Stephen Board is vice president and general manager of Harold Shaw Publishers. He has edited several major evangelical magazines.

Clifford G. Christians is research professor of communications at the University of Illinois. He is co-author of *Media Ethics: Cases and Moral Reasoning* (Longman) and *Responsibility in Mass Communication* (Harper & Row).

Mark Fackler is associate professor and chair of the communications department at Wheaton College. He is co-author of *Media Ethics: Cases and Moral Reasoning* (Longman).

John P. Ferré is associate professor of communication at the University of Louisville. He wrote *A Social Gospel for Millions: The Religious Bestsellers of Charles Sheldon, Charles Gordon, and Harold Bell Wright* (Bowling Green State University Popular Press).

Robert S. Fortner is professor of communication arts and sciences at Calvin College. He has conducted several major studies of international broadcasting and published dozens of scholarly articles on mass communication in the U.S., Canada, and around the globe.

Jeffrey K. Hadden is professor of sociology at the University of Virginia. He is the author (with Anson Shupe) of *Televangelism: Power and Politics on God's Frontier* (Henry Holt).

Stewart Hoover is associate professor of communications and Associate Dean for research in the School of Communications at Temple University. He wrote *Mass Media Religion* (Sage)

Mike Maus is visiting associate professor of communications at the City College of New York, reports on religion, and anchors network broadcasts for CBS radio news. He is a former senior correspondent and chief political correspondent, NBC radio news.

Marvin Olasky is associate professor of journalism at the University of Texas—Austin. He has written many journal articles and six books, including *Prodigal Press* (Crossway) and *The Press and Abortion, 1838–1988 (Lawrence Erlbaum)*.

Wesley G. Pippert spent nearly thirty years with United Press

International, where his assignments included three presidential campaigns, the White House, Congress, and the Middle East. He was a 1987 fellow at Harvard's Institute of Politics and Center for Press, Politics and Public Policy. He is director of the university of Missouri's Washington Graduate Program. He wrote *An Ethics of News* (Georgetown University Press).

William D. Romanowski is assistant professor of communication arts and sciences at Calvin College. He is co-author of *Risky Business: Rock in Film* (Transaction Books).

Quentin J. Schultze is professor of communication arts and sciences at Calvin College. He is co-author of *Youth, Electronic Media and Popular Culture* (Eerdmans) and author of a forthcoming book on religious broadcasting in the United States.

Dennis A. Smith has been a missionary to Central America for the Presbyterian Church U.S.A. since 1977. He is coordinator of the communication program for CELEP (Latin American Evangelical Center for Pastoral Studies).

Dennis N. Voskuil is professor and chair of the religion department at Hope College. He wrote *Mountains Into Goldmines: Robert Schuller and the Gospel of Success* (Eerdmans).

Robert Wuthnow is professor of sociology at Princeton University. His most recent books are *The Restructuring of American Religion* (Princeton University Press) and *The Struggle for America's Soul* (Eerdmans).

INTRODUCTION

QUENTIN J. SCHULTZE

This is the first book to address seriously the relationship between American evangelicals and the mass media. All of these original essays were written specifically for this volume. As a whole they significantly advance our understanding of how American mass communication and evangelicalism have influenced each other.

As this volume shows, evangelicalism has shaped the American system of mass communication. Evangelicals were often at the forefront of developing and using new media technologies, from the printing press to communications satellites. The American media, in turn, have influenced American religion, especially evangelicalism. This interaction between evangelicalism and the media continues to influence all aspects of American culture, including business, religion, the popular arts, government, and education.

Early American evangelicals largely established the tone and style of mass communication in the United States. As I point out in chapter one, American media are distinctly evangelistic enterprises hoping to attract new "converts." The radio advertiser, broadcast producer, magazine editor, and newpaper reporter are contemporary evangelists. They are hoping to "win" people to their medium, to maximize ratings, to increase readership, to double market share, to champion social causes, to report evil, and the like. This kind of goal-oriented communications strategy, though now commercialized, grows out of a historic evangelical desire to conquer geographic space and win souls with the Christian gospel. Evangelicalism has always been organized around the goal to bring new converts into the fold and to expand its power and influence in the surrounding culture. Rhetorically speaking, the modern media are inheritors of the evangelistic spirit so prominent in much of evangelicalism.

In chapter two, Marvin Olasky provocatively traces the historical origins of the concept of news in the early nation. While today's most popular media often seem to be primarily nonreligious, early American papers often were boldly religious. In fact, some of the most successful early newspapers reported news from an explicitly Calvinistic perspective. Reporters were like prophets and priests instead of like today's "objective" journalists. Most striking of all, Olasky claims that the very idea of news comes out of a Calvinistic worldview. News stories were originally seen as part of the "Great Story" of salvation.

As Olasky hopes to rewrite journalism history, Dennis Voskuil establishes in chapter three the importance of radio in the history of American Protestantism. He documents how evangelicals came to dominate religious broadcasting in the United States in spite of the efforts of other religious groups to secure their own place on the airwaves. Oddly enough, the federal government played a role in catapulting evangelicals to prominence in radio and later in television. Once again, however, it seems that evangelicals were naturals for the new medium. The so-called electronic church, which hit the newspaper and television headlines in the late 1970s and early 1980s, was hardly new. Evangelicals have long been the most successful religious broadcasters.

In the second part of this volume, well-informed observers examine four contemporary evangelical media: books, magazines, musical recordings, and radio. They document the incredible vitality and scope of these evangelical enterprises, reveal some of the common tensions between ministry and business in each of them, and discuss some of the problems such media have in common. The national evangelical community, made up of perhaps forty to fifty million Americans, often depends upon these media for information, entertainment, edification, and instruction. Moreover, these evangelical media influence the broader American culture.

As John Ferré says in chapter four, in the 1970s alone

evangelical publishers issued six books that each sold over two million copies—one of each title went to at least one out of every one hundred Americans. Some of them, like Billy Graham's *Angels: God's Secret Agents* and Hal Lindsey's *Late Great Planet Earth*, were widely available in nonreligious bookstores. Christian books are a billion-dollar force in the publishing world, and evangelical books are a sizeable part of that force.

In chapter five, Stephen Board concludes that about one out of every ten American magazines is explicitly religious. Here, too, evangelicalism has made its mark. However, few evangelical magazines can sustain a circulation of 200,000. Instead of pulling American evangelicals together, the many small-circulation evangelical magazines tend to amplify existing fissures and fractions among members of the faith.

William Romanowski is the first scholar to examine the fascinating world of contemporary Christian music. In chapter six he writes that the rock music of the Jesus movement, evangelicalism's own "counterculture" in the 1970s, led to a remarkable recording industry that creates religious versions of virtually every conceivable kind of nonreligious music, including hard rock. In recent years the process has actually reversed: now some performers who begin with religious recording companies "cross over" to the nonreligious market. Amy Grant's success in the popular music industry blurred some of the earlier distinctions between religious and secular entertainment. Nevertheless, such crossover marketing is not particularly new. American evangelicals have always exported their media products to the rest of society. Today that is simply good business for many evangelical companies and ministries.

In chapter seven, I turn to evangelical radio. Although televangelism gets nearly all of the publicity, evangelical radio is an important national and local medium for a small but loyal group of several million listeners. Day in and day out, hundreds of religious radio stations and a few networks serve diets of preachers, teachers, talk-shows, and musical recordings. Their audiences are rather small compared to those of the top-rated secular stations. Nevertheless, they help to maintain a national identity for the evangelical subculture in the United States. To the outside world evangelical radio is largely invisible, but to many believers it is a link with the wider religious community. The toughest challenges ahead for evangelical radio will be to forge closer ties with the ailing Christian music industry and to attract younger listeners, who now greatly prefer the secular rock music stations.

The third section of this volume is dedicated to the controversial subject of televangelism. All three essays offer their own provocative conclusions about this topic. Tens of millions of Americans regularly watch religious television, which is thoroughly dominated by evangelicals. There are over two hundred religious television stations in the United States, the vast majority being primarily evangelical. Cable and satellite communication has greatly increased the quantity of evangelical broadcasting in the United States. Many more evangelicals have access to the airwaves today than even a decade ago. While some nonevangelicals learn about evangelicalism from these programs, evangelicals also learn about nonevangelicals—or at least about televangelists' views of nonevangelicals. Most of the major public issues, from abortion to the United States' policy in Central America, are discussed on some of the major evangelical shows. Televangelism is not merely the business of evangelicals. It has become part of American public life.

In chapter eight, Robert Wuthnow challenges some of the common assumptions people have about the impact of evangelical television on the private and public lives of viewers. Wuthnow shows how evangelical television can serve the admirable function of bringing public issues and public figures to the attention of viewers. Certainly this happened with evangelical politics in the 1980s. Today many evangelicals who watch these programs feel that they are part of a national social movement and not merely part of a local religious group. Nevertheless, Wuthnow finds some potential dangers in television's power to change the relationship between religion and society.

In spite of M. G. "Pat" Robertson's sound defeat in his bid for the 1988 Republican presidential nomination, Jeffrey Hadden concludes in chapter nine that evangelicals may yet learn how to tap into the growing moral concerns of many Americans. He suggests that the so-called New Christian Right, represented by people such as Robertson and Jerry Falwell, is only one expression of a potentially powerful public movement that could include many nonevangelicals. In other words, Robertson's loss will not likely be the end of religiously inspired conservativism in America. To the contrary, Hadden believes that the movement needs only leaders who are not so easily stereotyped as the televangelists. Throughout American history religious leaders have both mobilized their supporters and elicited opposition leaders and groups. If the opposition can be minimized, Robertson's loss might yet be the gain of his evangelical cause.

Stewart Hoover's landmark study of the viewers of Robertson's "700 Club" program provides the most insightful observations yet of evangelical audiences. He finds that some people really are "converted to Jesus Christ" by these broadcasts. Moreover, Hoover documents the fact that many of the financial supporters of such programs are not viewers. These people sometimes support the show because they want evangelicalism to have a powerful and respectable presence in American society, not because the program edifies or educates them personally. In short, they hope that by sending money to the program they are helping to guarantee the ultimate triumph of their worldview over competing ones. Hoover's conclusions are further evidence that in today's world "spiritual" battles are often fought in and through the media.

In chapters eleven and twelve Mike Maus and Wesley Pippert offer somewhat opposing assessments of the quality of reporting about evangelicalism in American media. Since many nonevangelicals learn about evangelicalism through news stories, these are particularly important chapters about how to discern evangelical fact from fiction. Moreover, since both Maus and Pippert have extensive backgrounds as reporters, their insights are supported by personal experience.

Maus is not completely satisfied with evangelical news coverage, but he believes that the problem rests primarily in the nature of reporting, not in an anti-evangelical or even antireligious news bias. From his view, evangelicals have been treated just as fairly as other groups, although such "fairness" inevitably includes stereotyping. Modern news focuses on what people do, not on who they really are or what they fundamentally believe. The public will never learn much from the news media about who evangelicals are, but they will get periodic doses of how evangelicals are behaving, especially if these evangelicals are involved in politics or scandals. The problem as Maus sees it, is that evangelicals have had the most impact on American society as believers, not "behavers." In other words, reporters have missed the real evangelical story.

Pippert's views of evangelical coverage are far more critical. He sees a "worldly" bias among most journalists that is evident in their misunderstanding of and cynicism toward religion. Although the media began giving evangelicals more attention in the 1960s and 1970s, they did not report with significantly more understanding. For example, few journalists examined the impact of President Jimmy Carter's born-again faith on his executive actions. Journalists' cynicism is evident in the pejorative connotations given to words such as "born again" and "fundamentalist." Evangelicals are often treated in the news as caricatures. As a result, the public is often ill-informed if not misinformed about the nature and impact of evangelicalism on American life.

Most North Americans are unaware of the influence of U.S. religious broadcasting on other areas of the world. Dennis Smith and Robert Fortner address this topic in chapters thirteen and fourteen respectively. The most important question is whether international evangelical broadcasting is more North American or more evangelical. Like nonreligious broadcasting, religious programs create an image of America for the rest of the world. Other nations and cultures sometimes act upon those images rather than upon the underlying reality. Around the globe today many people believe that all Americans are like the wealthy oil barons of the "Dallas" television program. What might they think about American religion generally and evangelicalism specifically?

Smith has spent years studying the situation in Central America, and his conclusions should be troubling to most North Americans. From his perspective evangelical broadcasting is stirring up political troubles in the region and making it increasingly difficult for people to live in political peace and religious harmony. From the beginning, evangelical broadcasters there have mixed conservative and even reactionary politics with religion. Sometimes that meant refusing to address political issues while trumpeting an individualistic gospel of personal salvation in the midst of social disarray and political chaos. In the last decade, however, Central America has been the target of some explicitly ideological programming from North American evangelicals. Although there are growing numbers of local radio preachers, religious television is dominated by televangelists from the United States who have little understanding of the political or religious situation in the countries that receive their programming.

Fortner paints a considerably different picture of the situation in transnational or international evangelical broadcasting. Focusing primarily on shortwave radio, he finds that American evangelicals are probably more inept than they are constructive or destructive. Most international religious broadcasters, for example, use the kinds of culturally conditioned language and music that will not effectively communicate the essentials of evangelicalism to other cultures. Many American broadcasters ethnocentrically translate their domestic programs for international audiences. On top of that, many international broadcasters schedule programs at inopportune times for local natives. Although they receive a lot of mail, these international ministries have little information about the real impact of their broadcasts. No one knows for certain the effect of international religious broadcasting around the world—not even the broadcasters.

What, then, are the real effects of evangelical media? Clifford Christians boldly asserts in chapter fifteen that much evangelical mass communication is counterproductive to the cause of evangelicalism. "While claiming to save the world through mass communication," he writes, "evangelicals have merely adopted the techniques of the 'secular' culture they so deplore." Christians' point is not that evangelical mass communication is ineffective, but that it mimics the messages of the nonreligious world. Its effect—secularization—is nearly opposite that intended by evangelicals. Ironically, Christians locates the root cause of evangelicals' self-strangulation in their reading of the Bible. By focusing too narrowly on the "Great Commission" to proclaim the Gospel of Jesus Christ, evangelicals have turned their backs to the cultural calling presented in the first chapters of Genesis. "Hoping to convert others," says Christians, evangelicals "are reshaped themselves by the marketing ethos and stimulus-response mentality of the commercial broadcasting industry." Using television to illustrate his point, Christians contrasts the typical evangelical fare with the broader mission of humankind offered in Genesis.

In the final chapter, Mark Fackler presents an enormously helpful bibliographic essay that describes all of the major and many of the minor works related to American evangelicals and the mass media. Scholars, researchers, and students should find this chapter particularly helpful, but we hope as well that it will be used by others interested in this important topic. Fackler's annotations make the chapter suitable as an overall assessment of the state of scholarship. His work reveals how much—and how little—we know about the topic. This book is a significant addition to the field. Because of the large number of sources cited in Fackler's essays, it is not included in the outstanding index prepared by Gwyn Bersie.

American Evangelicals and the Mass Media was made possible by a grant from the J. Howard Pew Freedom Trust Institute. Joel Carpenter, former administrator of the Institute for the Study of American Evangelicals at Wheaton College, co-organized a conference on "Evangelicals, the Mass Media, and American Culture" at Wheaton in the fall of 1988. From the papers presented at that conference I and two reviewers, Robert Fortner and Mark Fackler, selected essays for this volume. During the late fall and winter I edited the essays. Kate Miller, secretary of the Calvin Center for Christian Scholarship, worked with me on some of the editorial details. Jan Ortiz of Zondervan expertly copy edited the book. Many people contributed to the final volume, both through the conference and through later advice. I thank them all.

Part I

THE HISTORICAL CONTEXT

1

KEEPING THE FAITH: AMERICAN EVANGELICALS AND THE MEDIA

QUENTIN J. SCHULTZE

American evangelicals have always had a love-hate relationship with the mass media. Evangelical theologican Edward Carnell captured this tension in his book *Television: Servant or Master?* published in 1950:

> The children of light will remain realistic about TV as long as they retain . . . an optimism with a pessimism. . . . Once the individual ossifies on the TV question the next step is to be either unwarrantably optimistic or unwarrantably pessimistic. . . . Even *teleleaguers* themselves ought to take heed. They will be defeated the very instant they allow their zeal at having the truth to be converted into an optimism that they can easily redeem history with that truth.[1]

In the evangelical imagination, the media have represented both a marvelous technology of hope and an apostate culture of despair. Such hope and despair have always come together in the present, as evangelicals reflected on the past and prayed for the future. Contemporary evangelicals share Napoleon's sentiments: "The old nobility would have survived if they had known enough to become masters of printing materials."[2] Perhaps Napoleon was right; he simply had the wrong medium. Evangelicals have created a new nobility on television every Sunday morning.

In the late 1980s evangelical critics stood before the mass media as Plato stood before the poets. Plato criticized the poets in the *Republic* for crippling the minds and spirits of listeners.

Then he exhorted readers to combat the wicked poets. Like the mass media in our day, the poets of Plato's time seemed to monopolize the cultural transmission of truth and wisdom. And Plato's students, like contemporary media audiences, uncritically drank from the poets' endless stream of stories. Eric Havelock has argued that Plato's attacks made good sense given the fact that few students habitually read books either for instruction or amusement.[3] In a society dominated by oral communication, and an academy tuned to arcane repetition, Plato's poets were the masters of truth and deception. Too many students, according to Plato, were moved emotionally rather than intellectually by the dramatic recitations of the poets; they simply absorbed the cryptic lessons through *mimesis*. Their education lacked a forum for building character and ethical judgment, precisely what the young guardians needed.[4]

Although we should not accept Plato's apparent disdain for the arts, we might consider seriously the implications of his critique for the world of popular culture today. The evangelical community, like the wider culture, similarly lives among poets, from advertising copywriters to film directors, who now use the mass media to recite their attractive shibboleths, which will supposedly open the door to cultural sophistication and personal happiness. Some fundamentalists pessimistically echo Plato's salvos against the poets. They recommend burning records, smashing television sets, and boycotting movie theatres. Other evangelicals cry out hopefully for a new breed of Christian poet who will seize the media for the glory of God. These prophets trade gloom and doom for marketing plans, satellite transponders, and audience ratings.

This chapter examines critically the love side of the love-hate relationship between evangelicals and the media. It looks at the long-standing affinity between American evangelicals and the communications media. After all, this is not a new or minor affinity. Evangelicals have always kept the faith partly by giving it away through every available medium. But the modern academy has greatly underestimated the crucial role that evangelicals played in the development of the American mass media. In turn, many evangelicals have overlooked the impact of American culture on evangelical media. Of course any claims about "evangelicals" could easily be countered with exceptions; evangelicalism is a large mosaic of disparate groups held together by a few fundamental beliefs and practices. In this chapter the term "evangelical" refers to the more public and popular expressions of the faith—a synonym for "popular evangelicalism."

The evangelical church throughout the ages and around the globe has always depended on communication to catechize its youth, evangelize the unsaved, defend the faith, and organize religious institutions. Even public executions were often a powerful forum for communicating the gospel. From one culture to the next, under various forms of ecclesiastical and congregational structure, through all of the historic changes in worship liturgy and personal piety, evangelical Christians have adapted the gospel to the latest medium. Sacred documents were collected, compiled, scrutinized, canonized, and propagated. Various apologia were written. Homilies and sermons were slowly formulated and institutionalized in worship services. Sacraments were celebrated publicly. The ritual of worship soon became the major medium for communicating the gospel, but the church never turned completely inward; it always had evangelists who looked beyond the existing media. From the first few decades forward, the Christian church was a dynamic organism expanding or contracting amid wide-ranging changes in political and economic power throughout Europe, Great Britain, Northern Africa, and the Middle East. Communication was often both the cement that held the church together and the wrecking ball that smashed it to pieces. But there were always new media, and there was always hope in new Christian poets.

The history of evangelical communication is impressive, but the American context is astounding. From the founding of the Plymouth colonies to the present, the United States has been an incredible laboratory in which evangelicals have been able to experiment with every imaginable form and medium of communication, from Bible and tract printing to tent revivals, gospel billboards, books, religious drama troupes, radio and television broadcasts, parade floats, motorcycle evangelism, periodicals, and even Rollen Stewart, the rainbow-wigged sniper who holds up Scripture signs in front of the TV network cameras during sports events.[5] American evangelicals were often leery of new media, especially those that provided "worldly entertainment," such as the stage and, later, film. But they also pioneered one form of mass communication after another. American evangelicals have long influenced the modes and styles of communication around the world.

From its beginning, the Christian church was a communicating church, and evangelicals were that church's naïvely hopeful pilgrims who repeatedly entered new media lands. Modern American culture has been an especially fertile environment for these media pilgrims. American evangelicals and the surrounding culture, although often antagonistic toward one another, share four essential traits: *a disinterest in tradition, a faith in technology, a drive toward popularization,* and *a belief in individualism.* Initially, these evangelical pilgrims turned to the media to keep their faith by giving it away, but their own faith and culture were increasingly shaped by the same media.

DISINTEREST IN TRADITION

American culture is remarkably free of the social and intellectual restrictions of tradition. Every year it becomes increasingly clear that practically any new values, attitudes, and ways of life will find adherents—and not just in California, although there is an incredible history of religious media started in California by various people, ranging from Aimee Semple McPherson to Charles Fuller, and from "Fighting Bob" Shuler to the founders of the Trinity Broadcasting Network. Instead of turning to the past for meaning and significance, instead of reestablishing historic institutions and social arrangements, Americans generally look to the future. Their identities are carved out of the conflicting, future-oriented values and beliefs of its many contending status groups. The past is largely nostalgia, that great American sickness spread by commercials and popular stories, while the future displays signs of the glory land to be ushered in through the fruits of prosperity and longevity. In this media supermarket, the Christian gospel is often merely one weak voice; there are many other, more appealing gospels in commercials, films, and popular magazines. Christianity becomes simply another lifestyle, another religion, or as they say in California, another trip. The faith shares all of the rather benign privileges of all of the other ways of life and paths to peace and happiness. In the early colonies, some Christian groups, most notably the Quakers, were viewed as cultural interlopers. In the 1980s, even bladder-healing, hurricane-rebuking charismatics were not worthy of persecution, only bad press, as the presidential campaign of M. G. "Pat" Robertson proved in 1988.[6]

Religious freedom is part of the cultural soil of modern

America, where liberty means freedom from tradition and hope in the future. Lacking any strong sense of their own tradition, evangelicals share the nation's optimism. As Allan Nevins has argued,

> . . . unity in American life and political thought certainly does not stem from general agreement on any body of [political] doctrines. . . . We are often told that we are held together as a people not so much by our common loyalty to the past . . . as by our common faith and hopes for the future. It is not the look backward . . . but the look forward that gives us cohesion. . . . The great unifying sentiment of Americans is hope for the future.[7]

This hopefulness partly explains why evangelicals and the advertising business have so much in common in North America: both are zealous communicators of visions of a bright future. Some of the fathers of modern copywriting, most notably Claude Hopkins and Walter Dill Scott, originally were destined for careers in the ministry.[8] Only their product changed. In 1924, advertising agency pioneer Bruce Barton wrote his best-selling book *The Man Nobody Knows*, arguing that Jesus was the greatest salesman who ever lived.[9] In America, Jesus is often little more than promoter or product. Like toothpaste or mouthwash, he is a means to the ends defined by the culture.[10] Is it really surprising, then, that the "health-and-wealth" gospel is building some of the largest audiences for religious television?[11] Hope springs eternal in a consumer culture, where identities are purchased in department stores, displayed on the streets, and stored in moth balls.

Americans celebrate the future through product consumption. Shopping centers, the modern shrines to this great vocation, are buzzing on Sundays. Daniel Boorstin has written that advertising copy is the most characteristic and remunerative form of American literature.[12] Indeed, mass-mediated religion is becoming the most characteristic form of religious expression in the United States. Historic liturgies are being abandoned in favor of variety shows and maudlin renditions of popular tunes. Amphitheaters and shopping-plaza churches are replacing traditional architectural forms. Today nearly all public communication, from news reports to political speeches, is dominated by hustle and hype. Not surprisingly, in American society political nominating conventions resemble religious revivals. Both public events imbibe gallons of the promotional ethos, which continually reinvents the past in order to sell an optimistic future.

Popular evangelicalism found a cultural home in the United States. As American culture became more evangelistic (in a secular sense), evangelicalism became more American. Each contributed to the other. We see something of this already in the nineteenth century as modern tract writers geared up for getting Christian literature into the homes of the nascent nation and into the hands of unsuspecting pagans. Even then there was a love affair between evangelism and mass marketing and promotion.[13] Throughout the 1800s, the commercial fires were stoked in the land of the free, and by the turn of the century the culture was permeated by a rhetoric of conversion. In that public language of salvation, it seems that practically anyone could be converted to practically anything new, and virtually every social and political movement adopted the linguistic and rhetorical style of the advertiser and the evangelistic preacher. The rhetoric sprouted in populism and blossomed in progressivism, which Clyde Griffen links in style and even in substance to earlier evangelical Protestantism.[14] It was used effectively in the campaign for prohibition, as in so many other moral crusades.

More recently, the rhetoric of conversion has been applied to the antismoking campaign: "I quit!" exclaim the jubilant sheep saved from the slaughter of tar and nicotine. "Datsun Saves," proclaimed billboards for the Japanese auto manufacturer who has certainly not saved the U.S. economy. Everywhere one turns in American culture after about the 1880s, the styles of public rhetoric are similarly fashioned out of an evangelistic passion to convert misguided or exploited people to the doctrines of the latest social, political, or religious movement or to the most recent commercial fad. This is the distinctly American rhetoric of social salvation, a semireligious postmillennialism that captures images of progress through faith in the future.[15] Evangelicalism, because of its disinterest in its own tradition, has contributed enthusiastically to this popular rhetoric of conversion.

There are exceptions, but evangelicalism is roaring ahead willy nilly into the consumer culture. Even fundamentalists and old-style Pentecostals, who once made a theological living out of cultural criticism, are adopting the mainstream culture of hope and success. Some of the more theologically conservative Christian colleges and seminaries promote themselves in advertisements and brochures as stewards of the latest educational fads and campus fashions. There is little in their ads about historic Christian education. They create an image of Christian colleges as occupational supermarkets or career-counseling resorts. Evangelicalism's disinterest in its own tradition makes it increasingly susceptible to commercial exploitation. Like the broader culture, evangelicalism seeks not to conserve the past, but continually to rewrite it in tune with the shifting values of the consumer culture and contemporary lifestyles. Even the get-rich-quick rhetoric and some evangelical promotional rhetoric have much in common.[16] After all, they are both the product of American culture, liberated from tradition and enchanted by the possibilities for the future. Evangelical poets have embraced enthusiastically the mass media, America's reservoir of symbolic hope.

FAITH IN TECHNOLOGY

American culture and evangelicals also share a remarkably uncritical faith in technology. This technological optimism has deep roots in European soil and especially in the Christian concept of linear history, which gradually replaced the classical view of cyclical history. From the fourteenth to the nineteenth century, the Western revolt against ecclesiastical and secular authority, along with the development of experimental science, gradually transformed the Christian doctrine of salvation into the modern idea of progress. Early technological utopianism is found in the writings of the pansophists, visionary and influential sixteenth- and seventeenth-century Christians who hoped to harmonize their faith with scientific and technological progress. In their minds, the Devil was Renaissance humanism, which secularized the technological imagination. Francis Bacon is the best-known pansophist; his New Atlantis (1627) included a scientific think tank called "the very eye of the kingdom." In Christianopolis (1619), Johann Andreae developed a similar concept he called the "innermost shrine of the city." These early and influential writers sanctified technology and technological progress. But it was up to the more pragmatic and optimistic Americans to transform the sanctification of technology into the popular veneration of particular communication technologies.[17]

Americans made technological progress equivalent to progress itself and enshrined the inventors of such things as the telegraph, the telephone, and the automobile. American public life was frequently organized around the veneration of technology as expressed in fairs, exhibits, museums, and celebrations.[18] Perhaps the best-known example is the Columbian Exposition held in Chicago in 1892. In addition to all of the nationalistic displays and technology exhibits were two statues described in the official guide to the fair as follows:

> Professor Sargent, of Harvard University, makes an interesting contribution in the form of two human figures, male and female, modeled after measurements of more than 25,000 American subjects. Over 60 measurements of each individual were made, from which composite photographs were produced for the figures, which were then modeled into clay. The result is a perfect type of American manhood and womanhood. In the opinion of the professor they are quite as perfect as were our original forefathers, and are named Adam and Eve.[19]

Americans have a natural romance with technology, investing the New World with both technological and spiritual significance. Walt Whitman captured this romance in "Passage to India":

> *A worship new I sing,*
> *You captains, voyagers, explorers, yours,*
> *   You engineers, you architects, machinists, yours,*
> *You, not for trade or transportation only,*
> *But in God's name, and for thy sake O soul.*[20]

American odes to technology are really arias to the technological sublime, for instead of simply secularizing technology, Americans have baptized it in popular religious imagery and sentiment. As historian Perry Miller argued, in the nineteenth century the "immense American missionary effort was presented as something basically *radical*, of a piece with the titanic entrance into the world of steam and electricity."[21] Missions and industry, evangelism and electronics, salvation and Silicon Valley—these were the emerging partners in popular evangelical optimism.

During the last half of the nineteenth century, the public imagination focused increasingly on communication technologies, beginning with the telegraph and shifting to the wireless. In part this simply reflected a gradual movement from mechanical to electric and eventually electronic invention and application. To many popular writers, the instantaneous transfer of written and eventually spoken words over great distances appeared magical, mysterious, and even supernatural. Americans in the nineteenth century attached spiritual significance to new communication technologies regardless of whether or not those technologies were used for specifically religious purposes. In the popular imagination, communication technologies seemed to be reversing the very effects of the Tower of Babel; they were seen as part of a new, national and increasingly worldwide pentecostal flame burning the fuel of technological progress. According to media historian Daniel Czitrom, popular writers saw a universal spirit in the new communications technologies, which were supposedly going to break down the walls of tradition, ignorance, ideology, and geography that separated human beings from each other.[22]

David Himrod has argued that American popular religion is a syncretism of technology and Protestantism.[23] This syncretism is apparent, says Himrod, "when human inventions replace the Lord's creations as the symbols which bind the present to the biblical past."[24] In his view, the symbols of Protestantism and technological activity have coalesced into a religious system that promotes republican technology. Regardless of the merits of his thesis about the religiosity of such syncretism, Himrod's analysis of the converging streams of religious hope and technological progress is highly provocative. Among evangelicals, Scripture is sometimes interpreted in terms of the apparent social benefits of technology. Moreover, evangelicals are prone to assess God's presumed actions in the world in terms of technological values such as efficiency and control. Jacques Ellul's concept of "la technique" has taken on religious significance as one of the governing values in the evangelical community.[25] Schneider and Dornbusch found that inspirational books in America tended to "instrumentalize" religion; popular writers viewed religion through the metaphor of technological activity. Religion was a "technique" for happiness.[26]

In the twentieth century, evangelicals created their own versions of the technological sublime. Evangelist William Foulkes wrote in 1937,

> There is something so uncanny and far-reaching in the persuasiveness of the radio waves that to the Christian it might well become another Pentecost—a potential Pentecost

at least. . . . Will the Christian church once again demonstrate its short-sightedness, and permit this swift-winged
messenger to become the permanent possession of forces
hostile to the gospel?[27]

More recently, Ben Armstrong, Executive Director of National
Religious Broadcasters, called the "awesome technology of
broadcasting" one of the "major miracles of modern times";
radio and television have "broken through the walls of
tradition" and "restored conditions remarkably similar to the
early church."[28] Armstrong predicted that this "electric church"
will become "a revolutionary new form of the worshiping,
witnessing church that existed twenty centuries ago."[29] He
concluded his book *The Electric Church* with Revelation 14:6:
"And I saw another angel fly in the midst of heaven, having the
everlasting gospel to preach unto them that dwell on the earth,
and to every nation, and kindred, and tongue, and people"
(KJV). That angel, writes Armstrong, could be a geosynchro-
nous-orbit satellite beaming religious programs to earth.[30] Of
course this type of writing is more exhortation and celebration
than it is critical analysis or even description. Douglas Frank
appropriately labels such rhetoric "cosmic hyperbole."[31] Nevertheless, imagery evoked by writers such as Foulkes and
Armstrong speaks significantly of the popular spirit of technological optimism found in evangelicalism today.

The technological sublime also exists in some popular
evangelical eschatology, which often resembles science fiction.
In both the literary and theological narratives, technology is
frequently linked to social upheaval and personal alienation, on
the one hand, and social advance and individual enlightenment, on the other. The genres share a technological imagination that interprets world events and personal experience in
terms of technologies of hope and destruction. During 1986,
televangelist Jimmy Swaggart told his viewers that it was "D-
Day or Delay." Either they supported his goal of communicating the gospel via television to all nations on earth, or they were
delaying the salvation of mankind. Pointing to his colorful map
of the world, Swaggart repeatedly told viewers that money was
the only obstacle to global evangelization; the technologies
were already in place. Like some science fiction writers, he
baptized communications technologies with metaphysical significance, claiming the technologies themselves held the future
of the world in their hands. In science fiction, people enter into

new realms of meaning and enlightenment through different technological devices, usually communication or transportation technologies. In the well-known television series "Star Trek," characters conquer space and time, although never completely; a popular joke in evangelical circles compares the Rapture to "beaming up" characters to starship *Enterprise*. Science fiction characters also flirt with omnipotence, like some televangelists, but usually are driven back to the reality of their humanness.

In both popular evangelical eschatology and science fiction, there is usually an underlying sense of the impending doom that awaits humankind. People are not omnipotent, but technologies are. Only evil spirits or corrupt people keep technology from saving humankind. According to the evangelical scenario, satellites and other media technologies hold both the promise of salvation and the threat of complete destruction or self-immolation. As in much science fiction, the future will be a war over the control of technology. In his book *The Hidden Censors*, for example, Tim LaHaye links the future of society to a secular-humanist media conspiracy emanating from the Trilateral Commission and the Council on Foreign Relations—the kinds of arguments often made by the Far Right, especially the John Birch Society. When the media are reclaimed from the liberals, says LaHaye, the kingdom of God will regain control of family, school, and nation.[32] Ironically, fundamentalists are most likely to decry media apostasy while simultaneously celebrating the technological sublime. There are many evangelical critics of the media, from media watchdog Donald Wildmon to psychologist James Dobson, but these critics usually rely on the media to effect social change. Their own belief in the power of the media is central to their work as popular media critics.

Evangelicalism has created a "mythos of the electronic church," a technological optimism that uncritically links the electronic media with the providential mission of God to preach the gospel around the world before the second coming of Christ. Research clearly documents the ineffectiveness of electronic media as agents of religious conversion, yet the popular mythology holds that spiritual battles can be won technologically.[33] An organization called World Mission Teams recently published a *Status Report on the Great Commission*, which offers a plan to win the world to Christ by the year 2000. After citing the impossibility of accomplishing the goal through traditional missionary work (10,833,000 missionaries would be required), World Mission Teams offers a film evangelism program to "increase the productivity of . . . mission agencies in reaching and teaching the unsaved . . . by *a thousand fold!*"[34] This type of outlandish technological optimism is a peculiarly North American phenomenon cultivated both by American culture and popular evangelicalism.

Every new communications medium has been interpreted eschatologically by popular American writers and religious observers. As a result, machines and electronics have become part of the American tradition of semireligious prophecy, from Patrick Geddes to Buckminster Fuller. One well-known evangelical ministry regularly launches new national and worldwide evangelism campaigns, each billed as the climax to the salvation of humankind. The fact that some Americans support every campaign says a lot about the power of the mythos to persuade believers in technology. Technological optimism, when tied to the futurism of American culture and popular eschatology, produces a compelling hope in the mass media. A few years ago the Genesis Project was launched to update Bible technology by transferring the Scriptures "directly" to film and video, supposedly without interpretation. In a book entitled *Mega Truth*, one author appropriately described the hope behind the project this way: "Imagine an international network for communicating the gospel of Jesus Christ that penetrates into the spiritual ambiguity of world systems and reaches across the lines of cultural diversity."[35] Somehow technology will overcome spiritual ambiguity.

The evangelical faith in technology depends on an optimistic hope in the future free of the sobering realities of the past. Communication technologies have probably secularized more than they have saved, commercialized more than they have consecrated, and propagandized more than they have proselytized. Nevertheless, the hope for the ultimate technological solution to the human condition lives on in both American culture and popular evangelicalism.

THE DRIVE TOWARD POPULARIZATION

As de Toqueville argued, Americans share a strong commitment to egalitarian principles, including the mass production and distribution of practically everything. This egalitarianism is not ideological or political per se, but a drive toward "popularization." Like product manufacturers or political candidates, evangelicals, too, hope to make all people true believers. Evangelicals want to keep the faith by communicating it to everyone. But popularization is something far different from the preaching of the gospel. Popularization focuses not so much on the message as on the "non-expert" audience; it defines success by the extent of distribution, not by the authenticity or fidelity of the message. In addition, popularization naturally simplifies and homogenizes messages, separating them from earlier social traditions and practices and plunging them into impersonal settings.

As Nathan Hatch has documented, the rapid popularization of a media gospel began in the early nineteenth century. Numerous preachers and Bible teachers challenged the existing social and religious authority of college-trained clergy by creating emotionally stirring messages for popular audiences. These new evangelists changed the standard conventions for proclaiming the gospel. First, they deintellectualized the message, simplifying it for mass audiences of common folk. Second, they replaced the genteel language of the educated clergy with vernacular speech delivered in easily understood oral styles, including storytelling and anecdote. Third, they dramatized the delivery of sermons with voice and body, transforming the pulpit (if there even was one) into a stage for popular religious drama in which the preacher was the main character. The effect of these changes was to create engaging messages and styles of delivery that both attracted large audiences and moved them emotionally. Religious communication became the property of what Hatch calls the "sovereign audience," although clearly the gifted popular preachers wielded considerable power and gained remarkable status in the new ecclesiastical order.[36]

During the same period, this process of popularization became the dominant marketing technique throughout industrial America. Only later was it appropriated and formally articulated by the business schools as the "marketing concept."[37] Marketing was deceptively simple and culturally revolutionary: produce what people are likely to consume in order to maximize the distribution and sales of a product or service. It encouraged all businesses to let themselves be driven by "the market," the industrial version of what politicians called the public. In the 1830s, the new penny press used the marketing concept to create modern reporting, which depoliticized and deintellectualized news for mass consumption. The penny press made news a popular commodity by transforming it into an odd combination of human-interest stories, reports of tragedies and other sensational happenings, statistical business summaries, and nonpartisan political coverage. These papers made news into popular literature—entertaining as well as understandable.[38] A similar process of popularization led to an explosion in religious publishing during the early decades of the nineteenth century.[39] In spite of the success of the secular penny press in the 1830s and the national consumer magazines in the 1880s and 1890s, religious mass media were the cutting edge of popularization. Secular media often learned from the successful marketing techniques of religious media.

Evangelicalism was well suited to the marketing concept. For one thing, the gospel was an excellent religious message for mass distribution. Cast in the form of an easily communicated narrative, the story of Creation, the Fall, Redemption, and the Second Coming could be summarized for even the most uneducated and illiterate audiences. This narrative structure provided inherent audience interest, especially compared with religious messages relying heavily on doctrines or systematic theology. Moreover, the tragic and comedic elements of the gospel story provided engaging dramatic appeal—as they still do for many radio and television preachers. When Christ's role in that story was personalized through the atoning blood of the Savior, the emotional appeal of the message was vicariously moving. Audiences might not have understood the theological complexities or doctrinal subleties of such biblical storytelling, but the messages moved people in the 1830s as they still do 150 years later. In modern evangelism, concepts such as the "four spiritual laws" are the latest formulaic distillations of the Christian faith designed to promote effortless communication to mass audiences. They are intended to make it easy for audiences to accept the faith as if it were the latest consumer product.

Popularization created new social authority founded not merely on the charisma of the messenger or the authenticity of the message, but on the sheer distribution of the message to a lay audience. Since the early 1880s, popularity has become increasingly significant in shaping public opinion and forming collective action in the United States. Best-seller lists direct readers to presumably worthwhile books, while television ratings influence both network decisions about programming and viewer preferences. This is precisely why so many television and film promotions emphasize the popularity of productions—"Everybody's watching it," or "Nobody should miss this one!" These are the slogans of what David Riesman called the "lonely crowd" of modern Americans who lack roots in traditional institutions such as the church and the family.[40] Amid the great personal insecurity and social alienation in America's consumer culture, popularity enables individuals to identify symbols of authority and to participate in geographically widespread and culturally diverse social movements.

The popularization of media messages among evangelicals has led to tension between evangelicalism as a market-driven enterprise and evangelicalism as an ecclesiastical structure. Evangelicals are pulled on one side by popular success and on the other by proper church organization and control. As congregants turn to media preachers and popular periodicals for their spiritual food and biblical interpretations, local pastors face increasingly difficult crises in their own professional authority. Some fundamentalistic and Pentecostal congregations have resolved this tension by granting authority over nearly all church matters to a popular, autocratic pastor who gives the congregation its vision and direction. In most situations, however, the evangelical emphasis on Scripture predictably raises new issues that challenge the authority of both parish pastors and media evangelists. Because they are usually para-church organizations, evangelical media can easily become market driven without a crisis in ecclesiastical authority; editors or producers might come and go, but the distant and impersonal market remains the key to popular success. The media have fueled the rise of popular evangelicalism, but they have also exacerbated tensions between local and national sources of authority. For this reason it is unlikely that media ministries will become the homes for new denominations.

SPIRIT OF INDIVIDUALISM

Evangelicalism also shares the individualistic spirit of the American liberal mythos, which encouraged entrepreneurial activity during the industrial revolution. The amazing growth of evangelical organizations and the development of commerce and industry in the United States have often been the result of individual enterprise and risk taking. Evangelical risks are usually translated as trust in God to finance the work of a ministry, while evangelical competition typically pits ministries against each other. Both American business and evangelicalism have succeeded—at least in the beginning—because of the amazing talents, contagious enthusiasm, and organizational prowess of tenacious and visionary individuals. These evangelical entrepreneurs have had as much impact on evangelicalism as capitalists have had on American business and culture, and their success stories have created a religious folk culture that encourages young evangelicals to take their own risks. Jerry Falwell, for example, grew up listening to Charles E. Fuller's "Old-Fashioned Revival Hour" and eventually even named his program after it.[41] Like corporate America, evangelical enterprise has not been marked by a spirit of cooperation. National Religious Broadcasters struggled during its early years to gain the support of radio evangelists who were kept off the networks by programming policies favoring "nonsectarian" broadcasts. In 1948, NRB treasurer James DeForest Murch lamented in a letter to members that "out of the millions of dollars that our constituency spends we receive only about $1,500 a year."[42] Forty years later, NRB membership has skyrocketed, but cooperation among religious broadcasters is still at a low ebb, as the "holy wars" among televangelists showed in 1987 and 1988.

As Max Weber argued, historic Protestantism may have been one of the seeds of entrepreneurial individualism.[43] Certainly Weber's thesis about the relationship between Calvinism and capitalism helps explain some of the dynamic behind contemporary media evangelism. The larger evangelistic organizations represent the middle ground between nineteenth-century family-firm capitalism and the modern era of large-scale corporate business. Within contemporary evangelicalism, the success of media ministries is often taken to be a sign of God's blessing. However, Weber's thesis hardly explains the rapid spread of pragmatic individualism in the United States. In this country, the church was not where the bishops or clergy resided, but where the congregants came together, where revivals took place, and especially where the Spirit of God was present. Lacking a state church, composed increasingly of a myriad of Protestant groups from throughout Europe, necessarily pragmatic in the face of many geographical and meteorological challenges, early American evangelicalism was predictably individualistic. Revivalism itself was individualistic, not communal. What Europe created, the United States amplified and extended—becoming a country of free-thinking, industrious, and risk-taking individuals. American evangelicals shared in that Enlightenment tradition regardless of their Calvinism or capitalistic desires. Their goal was not to fleece the flock, as popular writers too often mistakenly claimed, but individually to fashion successful media organizations out of available resources. Throughout the nineteenth century, individual evangelicals created thousands of media organizations, from the Bible and tract societies to publishing houses and religious newspapers. Some of these media were established by denominations, but the vast majority of the more popular ones were started by independent writers or businessmen. Hatch finds this to be the case with early American itinerant preaching and publishing, documenting how some of these individuals created enormous audiences and readerships within only a few years.[44] Modern individualism has encouraged evangelists to form para-church organizations outside of the ecclesiastical authority of particular denominations or specific church traditions.[45] It has also put a great premium on the potential role of individual religious entrepreneurs in establishing evangelical organizations, including mass media. Harrell's biography of television evangelist Oral Roberts is probably the best examination of the significance of entrepreneurial individualism in the creation of a large media organization. As Harrell shows, Roberts' talents included the ability to attract other gifted individuals who could handle much of the day-to-day decision making, enabling the Roberts' empire to expand to educational and medical ministries.[46]

The proliferation of evangelical media ministries is ample testimony to the folklore about American individualism. Many of the popular itinerant evangelists and writers were ordinary people driven by both a strong desire to spread the gospel and by the belief that no special training or skills were required. In the case of early nineteenth-century itinerant evangelism, this led to status conflicts between old-style, college-educated, New England ministers and the popular evangelists and writers, who often seemed to know little more than how to stir an audience and call for conversion.[47] Not much has changed: successful media ministers today frequently elicit public criticism from seminary graduates. An amazing number of successfull evangelical preachers and writers lack earned professional credentials, just as so many well-placed corporate executives lack college diplomas, let alone MBA degrees. The autobiographies and authorized biographies of media ministers often read like Horatio Alger stories. However, instead of luck and pluck, the theme chosen by evangelical media moguls is faith and opportunity.[48] In the corporate self-help literature, represented today by the writings and lectures of people like Tom Peters (e.g., *In Search of Excellence*), formal education is similarly unimportant compared with faith in the ingenuity and will of the individual person. Peters' books are parables of business success and failure told by an evangelist for common-sense free enterprise.

Like the readers of popular self-help literature, followers of evangelical media entrepreneurs are drawn to the individualistic spirit of the organizations. Again, this was evident in the early 1800s in religious publishing and itinerant preaching. It also holds true for turn-of-the-century urban revivalists, who often attracted audiences partly by the contemporary folklore that surrounded their ministries. Religious broadcasters have become the real champions, however. Beginning with Charles Fuller and Paul Rader, they used the airwaves nationally to tell the ongoing stories of their ministries. People tuned in to hear the message, which was presented simply and dramatically. But they also listened in order to follow the real-life narratives of their favorite broadcast evangelists. Before World War II, such on-the-air narratives were largely unplanned monologues about how well the ministries were doing. Often the broadcast evangelists read a few letters from listeners and made an unsophisticated appeal for funds. In the 1950s, as media evangelism merged with market research, the stories were scripted for maximum effect; financial crises and ministry "news" were used to build viewer interest and maximize donations. By the early 1970s, the veracity of the "gospels" of particular media ministries was nearly always associated with the accomplishments of the individual ministry leader. Robert Schuller's "possibility thinking" and Jim Bakker's "you can make it" philosophy are notable examples. A growing number of television evangelists based their experiential theologies on their own practical wisdom learned through building media ministries. The size, success, and status of their ministries supposedly validated their theologies. They were rewarded by God for their individual efforts—or so their rhetoric suggested.[49]

Taking its cue from revivalism, evangelicalism has also emphasized the atomistic nature of the church, which is often viewed as a collection of converts, not a dynamic, historic community of people who share a faith. Evangelical media similarly have tended to view unsaved souls as a mass audience. Converts are imagined as aggregates of numbers shifted from the lost column to the saved column, like TV ratings or baseball box scores. This individualistic perspective has generated some amazingly impersonal evangelistic strategies by which strangers are proselytized on street corners and also over the telephone when they respond to billboard advertisements. In a myriad of ways, individualism has challenged the authority of churches and religious traditions while energizing individual evangelical media owners and operators.

CONCLUSION

The evangelical faith has always had its media pilgrims. Because evangelicals shared with American culture a disinterest in tradition, a faith in technology, a drive to popularize, and a spirit of individualism, they found the media to be helpful conduits for establishing their own institutions and broadcasting their evangelistic messages. But the urge to communicate has not always served evangelicals well. As they ventured into new media, hoping to give away their faith, they also changed the very texture and substance of the faith. The American media were not neutral soil for planting religious messages. Without the anchor of its own historic tradition, evangelicalism could hardly test the spirits of its own media. Attracted to technological optimism, evangelicals frequently mistook the beauty of the machine for the authenticity of the message. Driven by the apparent authority of popular appeals, evangelicals often competed with the surrounding culture on its own terms. And breathing the individualistic spirit of American liberalism, evangelicals competed among themselves in the many common tasks they faced as cultural outsiders in their own land.

At the end of the twentieth century, the contradictory movements of evangelical media have become quite clear. Some of the media continue to formulate new messages and establish more institutions, from colleges and universities to political-interest groups. This *centrifugal* communication has led to continuous reorganization and fragmentation within the evangelical movement.[50] These specialized media celebrate their independence and fuel the decline of a cohesive, unified American evangelical culture. Much of this centrifugal force

reflected the frequent schisms within evangelicalism. Fundamentalists such as Carl McIntire and Bob Jones, Sr., used their
own periodicals and radio programs to build and maintain
small, national constituencies in the midst of tremendous social
disorganization and cultural flux. Their media kept them in
touch with followers and helped them to build specific identities that distinguished true believers from nonbelievers, fundamentalists from evangelicals, and even one brand of fundamentalist from another. Other specialized media have enabled
particular evangelicals to organize around social issues and
eventually to enter the public arena as various special-interest
groups and political organizations. The incredible variety of
values and beliefs within evangelicalism today is represented
by the thousands of media that claim the name.

At the same time, mass media have reorganized evangelicalism around a common identity framed by the most popular,
market-driven publications and broadcasts. The decline of the
evangelical consensus in the early 1800s was evangelicalism's
Tower of Babel dispersion; the rise of large-circulation national
periodicals and broadcast ministries since World War II is
evangelicalism's Pentecost. But this newer *centripetal* communication is deceptively shallow. Fueled by the pollsters, the
nation's general-interest media, and a few influential evangelical media, the latest round of efforts at evangelical reunification
is being constructed on the shaky ground of consumer semantics. Phrases such as "born again," "the infallibility of Scripture," and even "New Christian Right" are terms in the
mythical evangelical unification. In fact, evangelicals tend to be
separated by some of the most significant political and theological issues, as any reading of the spectrum of evangelical
publications will reveal. Like other forms of public consensus in
the United States, evangelical consensus is largely a product of
media oversimplification. As newpaper columnist Walter
Lippmann argued in the 1920s, individual Americans based
their perceptions of the world around them, not on personal
experience, but on the "pseudo-environment"—that collection
of symbols in our minds created by the mass media.[51]

If evangelicalism has suffered at the hands of its own
media, it has not been because of scandal or corruption, but
rather because of a misplaced hope in the techniques and
technologies of American culture and society. That naïve hope,
along with the preponderance of centrifugal over centripetal
media, has channeled evangelicalism's explosive and boundless

energy into short-lived and self-defeating enterprises. In spite of all of the evangelical media in existence today, giving away the faith has probably never been more difficult. Evangelicals have produced tens of thousands of their own poets over the years, but most of them have had to settle for relatively small stages and audiences. What sense would Plato make of this farrago of media dispensing words and images day and night? In Plato's day the poets were a monopoly medium for a captured audience. Evangelicals might look covetously at that arrangement. If only the poets of Plato's day had been evangelicals! Imagine the resulting spiritual condition of the modern university! If only CBS were in evangelical hands! Carnell wrote about such dreams in his book about television. "It is easy for the righteous to condemn history as wholly wrong," he said. "No particular skill is presuppposed to be a tabloid thinker."[52] In a nation where the *National Enquirer* is the best-selling paper, success is indeed a curious blessing.

NOTES

[1]Edward John Carnell, *Television: Servant or Master?* (Grand Rapids: Eerdmans, 1950), 194–95

[2]Laurence J. Peter, *Peter's Quotations* (New York: Morrow, 1977), 323.

[3]Eric A. Havelock, *Preface to Plato* (New York: Grosset & Dunlap, 1963), 37.

[4]Ibid., 23–24

[5]James Adair, "Football Teams Declare 'Gospel Banners' Out of Bounds," *Christianity Today* 17 (January 1986): 47–49.

[6]Quentin J. Schultze, "The Fundy as Fool," *Reformed Journal* 36 (November 1986): 4–5.

[7]Allan Nevins, "The Tradition of the Future," in *Now and Tomorrow*, eds. Tom E. Kakonis and James C. Wilcox (Lexington, Mass.: Heath, 1971), 398.

[8]Quentin J. Schultze, "Advertising, Science, and Professionalism," (Ph.D. diss., University of Illinois, Urbana, 1978), 37.

[9]Bruce Barton, *The Man Nobody Knows* (New York: Bobbs, Merrill, 1924).

[10]Virginia Stem Owens, *The Total Image* (Grand Rapids: Eerdmans, 1980).

[11]Bruce Barron, *The Health and Wealth Gospel* (Downers Grove, Ill.: InterVarsity Press, 1987).

[12] Daniel Boorstin, *The Americans: The Democratic Experience* (New York: Random House, 1973), 137.

[13]David Paul Nord, "The Evangelical Origins of Mass Media in America," *Journalism Monographs* 88 (May 1984).

[14]Clyde Griffen, "The Progressive Ethos," in *The Development of an American Culture*, eds. Stanley Cohen and Lorman Ratner (Englewood Cliffs, N.J.: Prentice-Hall, 1970), 120–49.

44 | Quentin J. Schultze

[15]Jean B. Quandt, "Religion and Social Thought: The Secularization of Postmillennialism," *American Quarterly* 25 (October 1973): 390–409.

[16]Randall L. Bytwerk and Quentin J. Schultze, "The Millionaire on the Beach," a paper presented at the Annual Convention of the Speech Communication Association, New Orleans, La., 6 November 1988.

[17]Howard P. Segal, *Technological Utopianism in American Culture* (Chicago: Universtiy of Chicago Press, 1985).

[18] James W. Carey and John J. Quirk, "The Mythos of the Electronic Revolution," *American Scholar* 39 (Spring 1970): 219–41, and (Summer 1970): 395–424.

[19] John Flinn, comp., *Official Guide to the World's Columbian Exposition* (Chicago: Columbian Guide Co., 1893), 38.

[20]Harold W. Blodgett, *The Best of Whitman* (New York: Ronald Press, 1953), 256.

[21]Perry Miller, *The Life of the Mind in America* (New York: Harcourt, Brace & World, 1965), 52.

[22]Daniel J. Czitrom, *Media and the American Mind* (Chapel Hill: University of North Carolina Press, 1982).

[23]David K. Himrod, "The Syncretism of Technology and Protestantism: An American 'Popular Religion,'" *Explor* 7 (Fall 1984): 49–60.

[24]Ibid., 54.

[25]Jacques Ellul, *The Technological Society* (New York: Knopf, 1964).

[26]Louis Schneider and Sanford Dornbush, *Popular Religion* (Chicago: University of Chicago Press, 1958).

[27]William Hiram Foulkes, "Radio Evangelism," in *The Message and Method of the New Evangelism*, ed. Jesse M. Bader (New York: Round Table Press, 1937), 230, 233.

[28]Ben Armstrong, *The Electric Church* (Nashville: Nelson, 1979), 7, 9.

[29]Ibid., 8–9.

[30]Ibid., 172–73.

[31]Douglas Frank, *Less than Conquerors* (Grand Rapids: Eerdmans, 1986), 27.

[32]Tim LaHaye, *The Hidden Censors* (Old Tappan. N.J.: Revell, 1984).

[33]Quentin J. Schultze, "The Mythos of the Electronic Church," *Critical Studies in Mass Communication* 4 (September 1987): 245–61.

[34]World Mission Teams, *Status Report on the Great Commission* (St. Petersburg, Fla.: World Mission Teams, 1987).

[35]David McKenna, *Mega Truth* (San Bernardino, Calif.: Here's Life Publishers, 1986).

[36]Nathan O. Hatch, *The Democratization of American Christianity*, (New Haven, Conn.: Yale University Press, 1988), chapter 4.

[37]Robert Ferber, Donald Blankertz, and Sidney Hollander, *Marketing Research* (New York: Ronald Press, 1964), 12–15; Paul D. Converse, "The Development of the Science of Marketing—An Exploratory Survey," *Journal of Marketing* 10 (July 1945): 14–23.

[38]Michael Schudson, *Discovering the News* (New York: Basic Books, 1978).

[39]Hatch, *Democratization*, chapter 4.

[40]David Riesman, *The Lonely Crowd* (New Haven, Conn.: Yale University Press, 1950).

[41]Jeffrey K. Hadden and Charles E. Swann, *Prime Time Preachers* (Reading, Mass.: Addison-Wesley, 1981), 81.

[42]James DeForest Murch to National Religious Broadcasters, Inc., mem-

bers, 14 December 1948, Herbert T. Taylor files, Billy Graham Center Archives, Wheaton College, Wheaton, Illinois.

[43]Max Weber, *The Protestant Ethic and the Spirit of Capitalism* (New York: Scribner, 1958).

[44]Hatch, *Democratization*, chapter 4.

[45]George M. Marsden, *Reforming Fundamentalism* (Grand Rapids: Eerdmans, 1987), 2.

[46]David Edwin Harrell, *Oral Roberts: An American Life* (San Francisco: Harper & Row, 1985).

[47]Hatch, *Democratization*, chapter 4.

[48]See, e.g., Oral Roberts, *The Call* (New York: Avon, 1973), and Jim Bakker, *You Can Make It* (Charlotte, N.C.: PTL Enterprises, 1983).

[49]I have addressed the "experiential" nature of the theologies of some of the major evangelical broadcasters in "Defining the Electronic Church," in *Religious Communication: Controversies and Conclusions*, eds. Stewart Hoover and Robert Abelman (Norwood, N.J.: Ablex Publishing, forthcoming), and in *Televangelism in America: The Business of Popular Religion* (Grand Rapids: Baker, forthcoming).

[50]My argument is adapted from James W. Carey, "The Communications Revolution and the Professional Communicator," *The Sociological Review Monograph* 13 (January 1969): 23–38.

[51]Walter Lippmann, *Public Opinion* (New York: Free Press, 1965).

[52]Carnell, *Television: Servant or Master?* 194.

2

DEMOCRACY AND THE SECULARIZATION OF THE AMERICAN PRESS

MARVIN OLASKY

The *Boston Recorder* was one of the outstanding newspapers of the early nineteenth century—and yet, even historians have rarely heard of it. The standard journalism history textbook, Emery and Emery's *Press and America*, does not mention the *Recorder*, even though it had the second largest circulation in Boston during its heyday and was known to contemporary editors throughout the country for its "interesting and useful matter."[1] The *Recorder's* success story—its integration of a Christian worldview with some of the techniques of human-interest reporting more frequently associated with the mass-circulation press—has vanished.

That is not surprising. Throughout the twentieth century, histories of American journalism have virtually ignored the influence of early Christian newspapers on the development of the American press.[2] But the blackout is unfortunate, and not only because it deprives us of some tales of journalistic entrepreneurship: when the births of the *Recorder* and similar papers are ignored, interesting questions concerning their fairly rapid demise also go unasked. The Christian journalism that the *Recorder* represented was strong in the 1820s; the New York *Christian Advocate*, for example, was a weekly that had the largest circulation in the country, with twenty-five thousand subscribers in 1828 and thirty thousand in 1830.[3] But the Christian newspapers that tried to establish more than a denominational base stood as firmly against the penny press onslaught in the 1830s and thereafter as do sand castles when the tide rolls in. Were these publications helpless in the face of social and theological changes? Did their failure in gaining a more lasting popular base stem from a refusal to democratize? Or was the problem democratization of the wrong kind?

In this chapter I examine attempts of the *Recorder* and its predecessors to combine journalism, Christianity, and democracy. First, I quickly review the *Recorder*'s record. Second, I place that history in perspective by showing how it fit into a Christian tradition of democratizing the press in two ways. Then, I suggest that a third type of democratization contributed to the demise of significant Christian journalism in the United States.

THE BOSTON *RECORDER*

Let's begin with the founder of the *Recorder*, Nathaniel Willis. Born in 1780 and trained as a printer, he came of age journalistically during the partisan political slashing that characterized the Sedition Act period and the Jefferson administrations (1798–1808).[4] As editor in 1803 of a Maine newspaper, the *Portland Eastern Argus*, Willis had no specific theological interests; as he wrote later, "I had not attended church for many months, but spent my Sabbaths in roving about the fields and in reading newspapers."[5]

At age 27, however, Willis' life changed. He went to hear what he thought would be a political speech by a minister, who instead discussed salvation. Willis, in his own words, "was much interested, and became a constant hearer." He wrote, "The Holy Spirit led me to see that there is an eternity; that it was my duty to attend to the concerns of my soul—that the Bible is the Word of God—that Christ is the only Savior, and that it is by grace we are saved, through faith."[6] The new vision changed Willis' life. First he "began to moderate the severity of party spirit in the *Argus*, and extracted from other papers short articles on religious subjects."[7] He wanted to make the *Argus* an explicitly Christian newspaper, but local politicians who had backed the newspaper were opposed, and Christians in Maine did not encourage him. Willis then gave up the *Argus* and moved to Boston. He opened a print shop there and investigated the journalistic marketplace.

Some newpapers, Willis found, were largely political and commercial, others largely church organs specializing in ecclesiastical news. Willis closely analyzed three religious weeklies in particular and would not even count them as newspapers, for "a proper newpaper . . . contains secular news, foreign and domestic, and advertisements."[8] With co-editor Sidney Morse, Willis soon produced the first issue of the *Boston Recorder*—on January 3, 1816. He had three goals in mind, according to the Prospectus published that day: to show theological truth; to put out a concise weekly *news*paper (including "the earliest information of all such events as mankind usually deem important") rather than a set of religious sermonettes; and to build circulation among churchgoers and nonchurchgoers alike.[9]

Willis' preference for detailed, lucid writing showed movement away from the tendency of some newspapers to emphasize long political essays and long-winded speeches. The popular success of the *Recorder* would be influenced heavily by its ability to avoid the hot-air tradition—and some of the stories succeeded wonderfully. For example, a *Recorder* story published in 1822, "EARTHQUAKE AT ALEPPO," included both a first-person account and a general report of destruction in Syria. Benjamin Barker, a missionary with the talent of a journalist, wrote that he was racing down the stairs of a crumbling house when another shock sent him flying through the air, his fall broken when he landed on a dead body. He wrote,

> [I saw] men and women clinging to the ruined walls of their houses, holding their children in their trembling arms; mangled bodies lying under my feet, and piercing cries of half buried people assailing my ears; Christians, Jews, and Turks, were imploring the Almighty's mercy in their respective tongues, who a minute before did not perhaps acknowledge him.[10]

The *Recorder*'s report continues the theme of sudden destruction. It began with a description of the poor but peaceful city of two hundred thousand that Aleppo then was, with "nothing remarkable in the weather, or in the state of the atmosphere." But "in ten or twelve seconds" the city was turned into "heaps of ruins," with "hundreds of decrepit parents half-buried in the ruins, imploring the succor of their sons," and "distracted mothers frantically lifting heavy stones from heaps that covered the bodies of lifeless infants."[11]

Other foreign correspondents of the *Recorder* also emphasized human interest and sensation. Poignant tales of the misery of an aged king of France[12] alternated with grisly and bizarre descriptions, as in this report of results of the Napoleonic War:

> More than a million bushels of human and inhuman bones, were imported last year, from the continent of Europe into the port of Hull. The neighborhood of Leipsic, Austerlitz, and Waterloo, and all of the places, where during the late bloody war, the principal battles were fought, have been swept alike, of the bones of the horse and his rider, and shipped to England, where steam engines have been erected, with powerful machinery, for the purpose of granulating them. In this condition they are sent chiefly to Poncaster, one of the largest agricultural markets, and sold to farmers to manure their land.[13]

A battle report from the Turkish war against the Greeks noted than many soldiers were "impaled alive and roasted. The whole town is destroyed, and the dead bodies, arms and legs scattered over the whole city."[14]

Willis also showed some willingness to examine domestic deeds of darkness. An article headlined "Shocking Homicide" gave grisly details on how a man had killed his own son after being "for a long time troubled with irreligious fears, and a belief that his sins were too numerous to be pardoned."[15] A story headlined "Infanticide" reported that "the body of a newly born infant, dead, and nearly naked, was lately found on the beach."[16] Overall, close to half of the *Boston Recorder* during its first fifteen years contained news not specifically church-related—such as information about accidents, crimes, marriages, deaths, and acts of Congress—while the other half concentrated on church activities. It would be a mistake to say, though, that part of the paper was secular and the rest religious, for all of it emphasized *God's* activity. For Willis, all kinds of stories provided "occasion to record many signal triumphs of divine grace over the obduracy of the human heart, and over the prejudices of the unenlightened mind." The *Recorder*, he wrote, was a record of "these quickening influences of the Holy Spirit."[17]

The *Recorder*, I should note, was not entirely immune to the hot-air tradition. It ran many long and preachy articles that covered events of little interest in a style of little interest. But the *Recorder* at its best was democratic both in coverage and style: it covered events of wide human interest in an easy-to-understand manner. At the same time, however, it was not democratic in theology: it did not praise all men, famous or infamous, nor did it define Christianity as whatever a majority of "Christians" believed at any particular time. Rather, the *Recorder* until the 1830s maintained a clear, classically Calvinistic theological vision by stressing God's sovereignty over all human activities. The Aleppo earthquake, for example, did not just happen: the *Recorder* viewed it as a heaven-sent general punishment for sin—one that would allow survivors opportunity for new reconciliation with God. The newspaper reported that in the destroyed city many people were seen "falling on their knees and imploring the mercy of God; and shortly after crowding the places of worship, eager to learn what they must do to be saved."[18] The *Recorder's* description of the earthquake culminated in an editorial plea.

> Should not these awful demonstrations of divine power cause us to fear Him who can so suddenly sweep away a whole city into destruction? Should not sinners tremble to think how awful it is to have such a God for an enemy? Should they not immediately seek reconciliation to Him through the Blood of the Lamb?[19]

Recoveries from illness also were reported as acts of God.[20] God was seen to answer prayers, not by making Christians feel better psychologically, but by actually transforming earthly situations.

In short, "news" in the *Recorder* included major and minor events that fit and authenticated a worldview that emphasized God's sovereignty over all aspects of life. Every news story was interpreted as part of what could be called "the great story," the story of God's holiness, man's sinfulness, and God's gracious redemption of sinners. *Recorder* editors and writers evidently believed they were more than journalistic scribes; they were doing God's work in communicating the great story. The *Recorder* prominently quoted one journalist's view that "a religious writer of popular talents, and of forcible style, could have no station of more extensive usefulness than the direction of a weekly newspaper. Neither the pulpit nor the senate house could afford him a more various or more ample field."[21] A minister wrote that a person desiring to teach about Christ "can spend a part of his time no better, than pleading the cause of religious periodicals."[22]

Because of the *Recorder's* coverage and analysis, circulation rose from five hundred for its early issues in January 1816 to eleven hundred six months later and thirteen hundred in

January 1817, apparently putting it in second place among Boston weekly newspapers at that time, just behind the *Sentinel*. Selling for the standard price of six cents for a four-page issue, the *Recorder* was said to have reached a circulation of thirty-five hundred in 1822.[23] Willis and Morse attributed success to God's blessings on their combination of theological insight and hard news coverage; as Morse put it, "The engrafting of religious intelligence upon the common newspaper" had gained "the attention of the public and particularly of newspaper editors."[24]

The *Recorder* continued to do well during the 1820s and into the 1830s—but then came the slump. Faced with competition from the new weekly and "penny press" daily newpapers of the 1830s and 1840s, the *Recorder* lost its sparkle, its audience, and soon its life. In 1849 its subscription list was bought up by the *Puritan*, a ten-year-old sheet that was more a public-relations organ than a newspaper.[25]

Why was the *Recorder* unable to do better? A number of explanations could be put forward. Perhaps Willis was a uniquely effective editor. None of the editors who succeeded him after 1830—including Calvin Stowe, Joseph Tracy, Ferdinand Andrews, Erasmus Moore, Richard Storrs, and Martin Moore—stayed with the newspaper for more than a few years, and none appeared to have the passion and ability Willis had brought to the task. Or perhaps the newspaper failed to make needed technological changes: while all around it the journalistic revolution was surging during the 1830s and 1840s, the *Recorder* stayed virtually the same in typography, size, frequency of publication, and so on. Maybe the *Recorder* failed to deal with challenges to Christianity from Unitarians (who dominated Harvard), Transcendentalists, and other assorted Rationalists, Romanticists, and Pantheists. The theological challenge from anti-Calvinist groups within Christianity was also growing. Perhaps to appeal to believers in faiths that emphasized man's goodness rather than his original sin, the *Recorder* had to water down its original stance; or if it did not, *Recorder* readership would decline.

A conventional and possibly accurate explanation of the *Recorder*'s decline could cite all three of these factors—changes in personnel, technology, and theology. A cultural historian concerned with the interplay of these ingredients might then hypothesize that the demise of the *Recorder* shows us something about democracy and the secularization of the American press; namely, newspapers that desired to appeal to the public generally had to "democratize" to survive, and to "democratize" meant to "secularize." The *Recorder*, then, died because it did not democratize far enough or fast enough. However, I am going to propose something very different. What if the *Recorder*—and perhaps other Christian newspapers of the time—failed, not because of insufficient democratization, but because of too much of the wrong kind? I will argue that evangelical newspapers may have died because they democratized in theology instead of continuing to democratize in coverage and style. In other words, the biblically orthodox newspapers died because they traded their distinctive perspective for a popular secular definition of news that was available in other publications. By attempting to soft-sell their own heritage, they entered the modern news world without their own particular perspective. They died because they secularized, not because they refused to secularize.

To make that statement understandable, we need to go beyond the case study and take a brief excursion into even earlier journalism history, beginning in England during the sixteenth and seventeenth centuries.

NEWS OF THE GREAT STORY

The primary journalistic vehicles in England during the late sixteenth and seventeenth centuries were not newspapers but "ballads"—quickly composed, event-oriented songs printed on single sheets of paper and sold in the streets. In the words of one historian,

> Ballads were not written for poetry. They were, in the main, the equivalent of modern newspapers, and it cannot well be denied that customarily they performed their function as creditably in verse as the average newspaper does in prose. Journalistic ballads outnumbered all other types. . . . In them are clearly reflected the lives and thoughts, the hopes and fears, the beliefs and amusements, of sixteenth and seventeenth century Englishmen.[26]

Often, the ballads were based on the great story of God's sovereignty, man's sinfulness, and the need for repentance. To cite a very early example, one report of a strange animal birth in 1562 first provided a description of the piglet whose head was shaped like that of a dolphin, and then the report gave "An Admonition unto the Reader."

> Let us knowe by these ugly sights, / And eke consider well, / That our God is the Lord of mights, / Who rules both heaven and hell. / By whose strong hand these monsters here / Were formed as ye see, / That it mighte to the world appere, / Almightie him to bee / Who might also us men have formde / After a straunge device.[27]

The emphasis on God's sovereignty in that stanza was followed by the corollary story of man's depravity in the next.

> And loke what great deformitie / In bodies ye beholde; / Much more is in our mindes truly, / An hundred thousand folde. / So that we have great cause in deede, / Our sinnes for to confesse, / And eke to call to God with speede, / the same for to redresse.

An account by another writer of the same incident drew a similar moral: "These straunge and monstrous things Almighty God sendeth amongst us, that we shuld not be forgetfull of his almighty power, nor unthankfull for his great mercies so plentifully poured upon us."[28]

Titles listed in the Stationers' Register, where new publications had to be registered during that era, suggest that explanations of events were based on a Christian worldview. For example, an April 6, 1580, earthquake was a relatively minor affair—only two lives lost and a small amount of property damaged—but within two days, five pamphlets or ballads about it were entered in the Stationers' Register for publication. More soon arrived, with titles like this: *A godly newe ballat moving us to repent by ye example of ye earthquake.* [29] Or this: *Alarm for London and Londoners setting forthe the thunderinge peales of Gods mercye.* Or this, by Henry Kyrkham: *A true and terrible example of Gods wrathe shewed by ye generall earthquake.* (One title sounds as if it has rock 'n roll potential—*Quake, quake, it is tyme to quake. When towers and townes and all Doo shake.*)

As these examples show, English journalism in the late sixteenth century was already democratic in both coverage and style; popular topics and readily understandable writing dominated the industry. Look, for example, at the dramatic reporting in 1586 of a fire in Beckles, a Suffolk market town:

> The flame whereof increasing still / The blustering windes
> did blowe, / And into divers buildings by / Disperst it to and
> fro; / So kindling in most grievous sort, / It waxed huge and
> hie; / The river then was frozen, so / No water they could
> come by.[30]

> And yet, amid this great distresse, / A number set theyr
> minds / To filtch, and steale, and beare away / So much as
> they could finde; / Theyr neighbors wealth, which wasted lay
> / About the streets that time, / They secretly conveyed away,
> – O most accursed crime!

Crucially, though, the balladeer-reporter went on to write
that the fire was part of God's providence. This did not mean
that the fire was punishment for the townsfolks' sins, although
the inability to rule that out made for a pointed moral.

> Wherefore, good Christian people, now / Take warning by
> my fall, / Live not in strife and envious hate / To breed each
> other thrall; / Seeke not your neighbors lasting spoyle / By
> greedy sute in lawe; / Live not in discord and debate, / Which
> doth destruction draw.

An emphasis on God's providence *did* mean that the disaster
served as a general reminder; the last stanza of the ballad
beseeched God that Beckle would "Remaine a mirrour to all
such / That doth in pleasure stay." God's judgment could come
any time, and Englishmen should have their spiritual affairs in
order.

Early journalists sometimes described their goal as creating
an awareness of how events communicated the great story. In
1595, when Thomas Wilcox wrote an account of a fire in the
town of Woodburne, he noted that his goal was to produce "a
short, yet a true narration of that pitifull spectacle, and
therewithall, some meditations of mine owne . . . I have aimed
at nothing but this, that . . . men might bee lead by the hande
to make some profitable use of it."[31] Concerning another
popular account, John Hilliard wrote, "My end in publishing
this Pamphlet, is not popular ostentation. . . . The only purpose I have, is to rouse up the sloathfull carelesse, and instruct
the filthy forgetfull, to behold the wonderfull works of the
Lord."[32] In 1622, John Reynolds provided one of the fullest
explanations of journalistic purpose when he wrote of his
desire to help readers understand the dangers of "the bewitch-
ing World, the alluring Flesh, and the inticing Devill."[33] His list
of what had to be guarded against is worth quoting at length.

The World . . . assailes us with Wealth, Riches, Dignities, Honours, Preferments, Sumptuous houses, perfumed Beds, Vessels of gold and silver, pompous Apparell, Delicious fare. . . . The Flesh presents us with Youth, Beauty . . . Perfuming, Powdering, Crisping, Painting, Amorous kisses, Sweet smiles, Sugered speeches, Wanton embracings, and Lascivious dalliance. . . . The Devil . . . will give us Pensivenesse, Griefe of minde and body, Affliction, Sorrow, Discontent, Choler, Envie, Indignation, Despaire, Revenge, and the like. Yea, he will watch us at every turne, and waite on us at every occasion: for are we bent to revenge, he will blow the coales to our choler: are we given to sorrow and discontent, he will thrust and hale us on to Despaire: are we inclined to wantonnesse, and Lasciviousnesse, he will fit us with meanes and opportuity to accomplish our carnall desires: or are wee addicted to covetousness and honours, he will either cause us to breake our hearts, or our necks, to obtaine it: for it is indifferent to him, either how or in what manner we inlarge and fill up the empty roomes of his vast and infernall kingdome. . . .[34]

Reynolds wrote of two ways to avoid citizenship in that infernal kingdom. First, readers needed to remember always that God was their Creator and Christ their Redeemer, and to pray for God's protection against the Devil's tactics. Second, readers needed to learn from the experience of others—and here is where journalism could play a crucial role. Reynolds wrote that his accounts of evil thought leading to evil action were

for our detestation, not for our imitation: Since it is a poynt of (true and happy) wisdome in all men to beware by other mens harmes; Reade it then with a full intent to profit thy selfe thereby, and so thou mayest boldly, and safely rest assured, that the sight of their sinnes and punishments, will prove the reformation of thine owne.[35]

Reynolds, like other journalists of his time, stressed a condemnation of sin and a proclamation of the need for repentance and future avoidance. His writing was democratic in coverage and style but not at all in theology; the great story proposed not that each man should be an oracle unto himself, but that sin was real, that all people were ensnared in it, and that some were captive to it.

By the last third of the seventeenth century, definite genres of journalism—crime reporting, disaster coverage, and so on—

had emerged. For example, "The Bloody Butcher," a ballad broadside of 1667,[36] began with an exclamation: "What horrid execrable Crimes / Possess us in these latter Times; / Not Pestilence, nor Sword, nor Fire, / Will make us from our Sins retyre." The report told of a husband and wife arguing, and then:

> She being with Child, and fretful too, / What he commands she would not do; / Which, with his drink, begat a rage, / Nothing but Murther could asswage.

> Words made his passion mount up higher / She was the bellows, he the fire: / Words are but wind, but yet they do, / Pierce through the Soul and Body too.

> The Devil had subdued him there, / And whisper'd Murther in his ear; / Which he impatient of delay, / Doth perpetrate the readiest way.

> With a strong long sharp-poynted knife, / Into the back he stabs his wife: / Flesh of his flesh, bone of his bone, / With one dead-doing blow is gone.

> She faltered, fainted, fell down dead, / Upon the ground her bloud was shed; / The little infant in the womb / Received there both Life and Toomb.

> Then was he Apprehended, by / Some Neighbours that did hear her cry / Out Murther, murther, and for this, / He judg'd and executed is.

> Let this a warning be to those, / Whose Passions are their greatest Foes: / And let all Women have a care, / To stir those that impatient are.

> Ten angry words with wrath and Knife, / Has kil'd a Husband and a Wife; / An Infant too, which makes up Three, / And ruin'd a whole Family.

The account ended with a final editorial comment: "Return to God, reform your Lives, / Men be not bitter to your wives."

A similar story thirty years later, "The Murtherer Justly Condemned,"[37] also spotlighting a man who killed his wife, points out the consistency of themes during this period.

> He had long been absent which made her suspect, / Both her and his business he did much neglect, / Which put her in passion, that streightway she went, / To know by this usuage what to her he meant.

> In Leaden-Hall Market she found him, and there / The cause of her grief she did freely declare. / Though justly reproved,

yet so Angry he grew, / That at her with violence his Knife he then threw.

The story continued with the man tried, found guilty, and awaiting hanging.

His Drunken Debauchries now swarm in his mind, / And how he to her and himself was unkind, / By spending his money so idley on those, / That Lewdly had brought him to trouble and woes, / And though for Repentance it is not too late, / Yet death now looks terrible on life's short date.

Finally, the practical application was rammed home.

Thus let all Rash men well consider his fall, / How innocence loudly for Vengeance do's call, / And govern their passions that bring them to shame, / For which when too late they themselves do much blame.

Consider how Rashness brings troubles and fears, / Shame, Ruin, and death, it oft for them prepares, / Then let all be warn'd how they rashly proceed, / Least trouble and anguish for them be decreed.

Hundreds of similar crime ballads sold in the streets during this period; they were thoroughly democratic both in content and style, but not democratic in theology. They showed a strong sense of biblical right and wrong and also emphasized God's sovereignty, particularly in stories of disasters.

One of the disaster genre's typical pieces was a 1684 ballad, "Sad News from Salisbury,"[38] which presented tragedies "incredible to believe, but that some who were in the same Storm are alive to justify the truth thereof." That stress on eyewitnesses was important because the purpose of the tale was not mere amusement, but testimony to be taken as important only if true; the story was to be a "warning to all, / Least greater Judgments on this land befall." The specific detail, rather than emphasizing the plight of nobles or gentlefolk, was thoroughly democratic.

Collins the Taunton Carryer, people say, / Upon the Douns did strangely loose his way, / Two of the Passengers were starv'd with cold, / A fearful Spectacle for to behold. . . .

And this for truth report us plainly tells, / The Carryer that belong'd to Bath and Wells, / His own dear Son was frozen unto death; / And on the Downs did loose his dearest breath. . . .

> And thirty more in Sometshire were lost / In this unusual
> Snow and cruel Frost, / Who littel thought when they went
> out of door, / Their wives & children they should see no
> more. . . .

Then came the crucial journalistic question—not just who,
what, when, where, and how, but *why*.

> This judgment came from god's almighty hand / For sins
> committed in our native land, / Lord grant that it to us a
> warning be / And teach us how to shun iniquitie.

> Our sins for vengeance do to Heaven cry, / Yet we like
> sinners live in vanity, / O grant that we our sinful lives may
> mend, / That we may live with thee when life doth end.

> From storms & tempests Lord preserve us still, / Teach us
> they holy laws for to fulfill, / So shall we gainers be by
> loosing breath, / And ride triumphant o're the second death.

Fires often provided the fuel for disaster stories, including
a typical one entitled "A Sad and True Relation of a great
fire."[39] Its lead showed this story's place within the great story:
"Give thanks, reyoyce all, you that are secure, / No man doth
know how long life may indure / Regard dear hearts, at the
truth the authour aims, / Concerning those that suffer in fiery
flames." The author, with superior artistry, then switched to
point-of-view from a neighboring woman who, while nursing a
sick child at night, saw the fire: "In the Merchants lower Rooms
she espied, / The Violent flames and then aloud she cryed / Fire,
Fire. . . ." Other stanzas vividly described what was found in
the wreckage, and then returned to the great story theme.

> Four lumps of flesh was after found. / About the bigness of a
> man's hand were they, / As black as a Coal, and a skull or
> two there lay; / O little did they think over night being merry,
> / That before morn in fiery flames to fry. . . .

> All you that are Masters of a family, / Govern well your
> house and fear the God on high, / For when to sleep that we
> do close our eyes, / The Lord doth know whither ever we
> shall rise.

The great story theme was taken across the Atlantic to
England's colonies. David Nord has shown how Increase
Mather was the first great American journalist, through his
preaching of "event sermons" such as *The Times of Men Are in
the Hands of God. Or a Sermon Occasioned by That Awful Providence
which Happened in Boston in New England, The 4th Day of the 3rd*

Month 1675 (When Part of a Vessel Was Blown Up in the Harbor, and Nine Men Hurt, and Three Mortally Wounded). As Nord points out, "The wellspring of Mather's journalism was his ardent devotion to the doctrine of providence. Like most New England Puritans, he believed that God's will could be read out of nature and history."[40] His news was always part of the Christian story of the Fall and Redemption. Mather preached and published parts of the great story for four decades. In the early eighteenth century he published works on storms, earthquakes, and fires; concerning the latter, he wrote in 1711, "All things whatsoever are ordered by the Providence of God. . . . When a fire is kindled among a people, it is the Lord that hath kindled it."[41] As Nord notes, remarkable events were not mysterious for Mather and other Puritans, but merely recent manifestations of types of events that had recurred through history; the Puritans were "obsessed with events, with the news. They could see all around them the providence of God. The great movements of celestial and human history were the prime considerations, but little things carried meaning as well."[42]

Coverage of little things, in a plain style, typified the democratized Puritan press. But the theology of journalism was theocentric rather than democratic; by theocentric I mean centered on God's sovereignty, and not on chance, popular will, or the clergy. Event sermons did not fawn on the common man, but criticized humanity's common sin. For example, the first published sermon of Increase Mather's son Cotton concerned the hanging of James Morgan, a murderer; rather than castigating Morgan as the one rotten apple in the barrel, Cotton Mather protrayed the murder as the result of sin infecting all New England.

Faithfulness to the great story continued into the eighteenth century, although sometimes less explicitly. John Campbell, editor of the first American newspaper to last more than one issue, the *Boston News-Letter*, had low-key coverage of events but still provided this obituary notice concerning a suicide: "She was esteemed to be a Person of Pious and Sober Conversations: And we hope the Inserting of such an awful Providence here may not be offensive, but rather a Warning to all others to watch against the wiles of our Grand Adversary."[43] The *News-Letter*'s second editor, Bartholomew Green, wrote that his newspaper would help readers to know "how to order their prayers and praises to the Great God."[44] Green tied local news to the great story.

> The Water flowed over our Wharffs and into our streets to a very surprising height. They say the Tide rose 20 Inches higher than ever was known before. . . . The loss and damage sustained is very great. . . . Let us fear the GOD of heaven, who made the sea and the dry land, who commandeth & raiseth the stormy wind, which lifteth up the waves; who ruleth the raging of the sea, and when the waves thereof arise, He stilleth them.[45]

Late in the eighteenth century newspapers were less devoted to clear exposition of the great story than their predecessors. Yet, in response to the French Revolution and domestic pressure from Deists, a new wave of Christian publications emerged after 1790. Some were academically theological, but others, like the *Boston Recorder*, included reports that were democratic in coverage, democratic in style, but theocentric in belief.

COMPETITION FROM THE SUPER STORY

The mixture of democracy and theocracy was eventually challenged by the new humanism (man-centeredness) of movements that grew out of or in reaction to the Enlightenment's emphasis on reason apart from revelation. In 1830s America, some of the challenges came from Transcendentalists (who tried to take away God's transcendence) and Unitarians (who tried to eliminate God's immanence). The strength of those movements among writers and intellectuals pushed many journalists away from the great story's emphasis on man's depravity and God's righteous anger.

The new theological movements had a political dimension as well. A sober Christian view of politics, based on the concept of man's original sin with its implication that governmental action could not lead us to utopia, gave way to a view of man as possessing unlimited potential that a strong and benevolent state could help to liberate. Soon many newspapers were crusading for governmental involvement in the development of state schools and a stronger economy. Many thinkers and writers began yearning to bring state power to bear on the side of perceived righteousness.

Under the innovative leadership of editors such as Horace Greeley—and later in the century, Joseph Pulitzer—a new view emerged to challenge the great story of Christian journalism. The twentieth-century development of that view has been well summarized by Joseph Sobran.

In the progressive myth, there is no Good or Evil, as traditionally understood: The ultimate categories are Past and Future. The world is broadly divided into the forces of the Past versus those of the Future, reactionary and progressive, politely termed "conservative" and "liberal" when necessary. . . .

The progressives' own value judgments don't have to be stated. They're built into the form of the stories themselves. The forces of the Past come equipped with a discernable set of traits: bigotry, greed, hate, selfishness, ignorance, zealotry, extremism—terms that by now all have a "right-wing" whiff about them. Ever heard of a liberal or left-wing bigot or hate-group?

By the same token, the forces of the Future can be discerned by their compassion, idealism, hope, intelligence, openness to new ideas. (Who ever heard of being open to *old* ideas?). . . .

The mythology determines the tone of just about any specific story on South Africa, "social" spending, the Pentagon, "civil rights," disarmament talks, Chile, abortion, and various other perennial topics. . . .[46]

Just as the Puritans paid careful attention to small events because they could see in them God's providential story, so many reporters today fit everyday facts into their larger story. Walter Lippmann noticed this in the 1920s when he wrote of news stories reflecting the "pictures in our heads"; William Rivers and other observers have noticed the same phenomenon in recent decades.[47] Just as, to the Puritans, strange occurrences were "intelligible because they represented types of events that had occurred before in an intelligible pattern, a pattern drawn by God,"[48] so for many of today's journalists tales of a feminist's election triumph in Kansas or the establishment of a day-care center in Washington are part of the intelligible pattern drawn by progressive humanity.

Those conservatives who try to root out conscious bias on the part of many mainstream journalists today may be wasting time. The morning after a New England earthquake in 1727 (or 1728), Cotton Mather preached the last of his event sermons; his first sentence was, "The glorious God has roared out of Zion." I doubt if Mather, before composing his lead, had to sit and ask himself, "How does the earthquake fit into the great story?" Similarly, many reporters today do not stop to think how particular events fit into the new view that conditions their thinking; the honest ones merely "call 'em as they see 'em." Deadlines leave little time for reflection.

From the 1830s on, many publications began to praise their readers, not criticize them as sinners needing God's grace. The classic *USA Today* story of democracy triumphant is easy to parody: "*USA Today* Poll—What Kind of People Are We? Response of Readers—250 Million of Us Are Great." This "morning in America" theme is sometimes associated with conservatism, but it is far from the earlier, properly conservative emphasis on man's sin and the slow gains that are possible as we work amid thorns. That tradition held that God may choose to overlook our sin, but we should not.

Perhaps the *Boston Recorder* tried to attract new readers in the 1830s and 1840s by coddling its readers. Instead of preserving and further developing democracy in coverage and style while maintaining its theocentrism, it tried to quasi-democratize in theology as well. Year after year through the 1830s, fewer stories covered instances of human sinfulness. Editors began pledging to cover "all subjects proper for a religious paper" and to "omit many things which some other papers publish."[49] In practice, this meant that *Recorder* articles increasingly depicted individuals who seemed overwhelmingly decent, cooperative, responsible, and benevolent. Happy talk of that sort hardly left the impression that man is a fallen creature desperately in need of Christ. The refusal to cover evil also led to a certain dullness of copy—without real villains there is little real drama. Sensational penny press newspapers were embracing what the Christian press had known, that bad news makes good copy. Meanwhile, newspapers such as the *Recorder* were contending that no news is good news, but they were finding out that to many readers good news is no news.

The change in theology led to a change in coverage and style—and that change wounded the *Recorder*. Public relations for well-meaning organizations tended to replace coverage of ill-spent lives. For example, in 1840 a *Recorder* report on a benevolence society designed to aid widows and orphans quoted one beneficiary as saying about contributors, "I feel as if I could take my fatherless babes, and fall down at their feet in thankfulness."[50] Twenty years earlier the *Recorder* would have been embarrassed to report a person's bowing before man in thankfulness rather than before God; perhaps it would even have quoted one of the apostle Paul's lines from the Book of Acts, "We too are only men, human like you."[51] But the

Recorder in decline quoted widows and orphans as "with united voice they said, *we thank you.*"[52] The biblical gratitude to God from whom all blessings flow was gone. The *Recorder*, in short, did what many ministers of the period began to do: attempting to appeal to those who wanted more of an upbeat religion, rather than one firmly distinguishing between God's holiness and man's depravity, they stopped etching portraits in black and white and started coloring much of life gray. Instead of maintaining their theological edge and working harder on coverage and style, many began emphasizing churchly goodness rather than natural corruption.[53] But when those ministers adulterated their positions, there was no reason left to take their work seriously; citizens might as well go directly to those who believed that men and God were co-rulers of the world. The *Recorder's* efforts may have produced similar results among Boston newspaper readers: Why purchase a minor-league version of man-centeredness when a better-produced and more consistent version was available down the street?

In short, secularization in early-nineteenth-century America is sometimes confused with the democratizing of the press. That is misleading in two ways. First, there was nothing "secular" about the tendency: a humanistic religion was being substituted for Christianity, with its great story. Second, publications did not need to democratize in most ways, because from the balladistic origins of English and American journalism the products of the press had been democratic in both coverage and style. The secular democracy embraced in the press of the 1830s held that each person could be his own oracle. That was a far cry from the theocentric news democracy of the early ballads, event sermons, and other forerunners of the modern newspaper.

Some journalists still contend that the only way for evangelical publications to build popular audiences is to cast the net wider, minimize theological distinctives, and hide certain facts of the great story in order to cozy up to potential readers rather than to criticize them. History suggests that Christian publications might most effectively address modernity, including some of the horrors of the twentieth century, not by avoiding an emphasis on God's holiness and man's sinfulness, but by embracing the great story. Certainly times have changed from the days of the *Boston Recorder*, and the Bible for most Americans is no longer the cornerstone of interpretation concerning the news of the day. Yet, hard-hitting Christian publications, democratic in coverage and style but theocentric in belief, could still have an impact. Gripping presentations of the bad news could still make recognition of the good news of Christ more likely.

Besides, believers in the biblical perspective know that God blesses those who honor him but lets those who move away from him reap the consequences of their own actions. The human factors behind the death of the *Boston Recorder* might all add up to a central theological message: Perhaps the *Recorder* died because God removed his blessing from it. If so, there is a message in that history for today's jounalists as well: Those who honor God will face immense challenges but will be blessed as well, perhaps in circulation, certainly in significance.

NOTES

[1]*Southern Intelligencer*, March 29, 1822, 105. Edwin and Michael Emery, *The Press and America*, 6th ed. (Englewood Cliffs, N.J.: Prentice-Hall, 1987), is the major textbook.

[2]For more on this see Marvin Olasky, "Journalism Historians and Religion," *American Journalism* V. 1, 1989:1, 41–53. The revised edition of Frank Luther Mott's *American Journalism* (New York: Macmillan, 1950) does have one paragraph on page 206 about the "religious newspapers" of the 1801–1833 period. According to Mott, about one hundred such publications, scattered across the country, covered both secular events and church activities: the newspapers were "a phenomenon of the times" and "often competed successfully with the secular papers." Mott noted that "many of these papers were conducted with great vigor and ability." Mott did not go into detail, but his brief mention was more than these newspapers have received in other journalism history textbooks written in the twentieth century, such as Willard Bleyer, *Main Currents in the History of American Journalism* (Boston: Houghton Mifflin, 1927); Robert W. Jones, *Journalism in the United States* (New York: Dutton, 1947); Sidney Kobre, *Development of American Journalism* (Dubuque, Iowa: Wm. C. Brown, 1969); and Alfred M. Lee, *The Daily Newspaper in America* (New York: Macmillan, 1937).

[3]Roberta Moore, *Development of Protestant Journalism in the United States, 1743–1850* (Ph.D. diss., Syracuse University, 1968), 237.

[4]Willis had worked in a print shop from the age of seven and had served his apprenticeship in the same room where Benjamin Franklin had worked.

[5]*Boston Recorder*, 21 October 1858, 167.

[6]Ibid.

[7]Ibid.

[8]Ibid.

[9]Ibid., 3 January 1816, 2.

[10]Ibid., 29 March 1822, 49.

[11]Ibid.

[12]Ibid., 10 July 1819, 116.
[13]Ibid., 16 January 1823, 11.
[14]Ibid., 17 August 1822, 131.
[15]Ibid., 11 September 1819, 147.
[16]Ibid., 25 January 1823, 15.
[17]Ibid., 23 December 1817, 202.
[18]Ibid., 29 March 1822, 49.
[19]Ibid.
[20]Ibid., 15 March 1823, 41.
[21]Ibid., 15 December 1830, 200.
[22]*New York Evangelist*, 20 December 1834, 204.
[23]*Recorder*, 29 March 1822, 49.
[24]*New York Observer*, 23 June 1849, 1.
[25]The death of the *Recorder* officially was described as a merger with the *Puritan*. Examination of one advertisement in the last issue of the *Recorder*, though, shows how the *Recorder* closed its office and offered "the type and other printing materials which are now used in this office—the whole comprising all the fixtures of a weekly newspaper establishment" (4 May 1849), 71.
[26]Hyder E. Rollins, ed., *A Pepysian Garland: Black-Letter Broadside Ballads of the Years 1595–1693* (Cambridge: Cambridge University Press, 1922), xl.
[27]*A Collection of Seventy Nine Black-Letter Ballads and Broadsides, Printed in the Riign of Queen Elizabeth, Between the Years 1559 and 1597* (London: Joseph Lilly, 1867), 45–47.
[28]Anon, *The description of a monstrous pig, the which was farrowed at Hamsted* (London: Garat Dewes, 1562).
[29]This and other titles cited in M. A. Shaaber, *Some Forerunners of the Newspaper in England* (New York: Octagon, 1966), 164.
[30]*A Collection of Black-Letter Ballads, 81–84.*
[31]Thomas Wilcox, *Short yet a true . . . narration of the fearefull fire that fell in the towne of Woodburne* (London: Thomas Man, 1595).
[32]John Hilliard, *Fire from Heaven . . .* (London: John Trundle, 1613).
[33]John Reynolds, *The Triumphs of Gods Revenge Against the crying and Execrable Sinne of (Wilfull and Premeditated) Murther*, 2nd ed. (London: Edward Griffin/William Lee, 1640), ii.
[34]Ibid.
[35]Ibid., 211.
[36]*The Euing Collection of English Broadside Ballads* (Glasgow: University of Glasgow, 1971), 26–27.
[37]Ibid., 360. The murder took place May 5 1697.
[38]Ibid., 251–52. The storm struck on December 23, 1684.
[39]Huder Rollins, ed., *The Pack of Autolycus, or, Strange and Terrible News of Ghosts, Apparitions, Monstrous Births, Showers of Wheat, Judgments of God, and other Prodigious and Fearful Happenings as told in Broadside Ballads of the Years 1624–1693* (Cambridge: Harvard University Press, 1927), 103–6.
[40]David Nord, "Theology and the News: The Religious Roots of American Journalism, 1630–1730" (paper presented to the History Division, Association for Education in Journalism and Mass Communication, Portland, Oregon, July 1988), 12.
[41]*Burnings Bewailed* (Boston, 1711), cited in Nord, "Theology."
[42]Nord, "Theology," 11.
[43]*Boston News-Letter*, 6–13 August 1705.

44Ibid., 21 January 1723.

45Quoted in Lee, *Daily Newspaper*, 27.

46Quoted in William Rusher, *The Coming Battle for the Media*, (New York: Morrow, 1988), 21.

47Walter Lippmann, *Public Opinion* (New York: Harcourt, Brace, 1922), 21; William Rivers, *The Opinionmakers* (Boston: Beacon Press, 1965).

48Nord, "Theology," 22.

49*Recorder*, 2 January 1835, 2.

50Ibid., 30 October 1840, 173.

51Acts 14:15.

52*Recorder*, 30 October 1840, 173

53See, for example, Sydney Ahlstrom's discussion of Horace Bushnell, in Ahlstrom, *A Religious History of the American People* (New York: Doubleday, 1975), 2:48–49.

3

THE POWER OF THE AIR: EVANGELICALS AND THE RISE OF RELIGIOUS BROADCASTING

DENNIS N. VOSKUIL

Radio exploded in America during the 1920s, a disastrous decade for evangelicals and especially for fundamentalists who had failed to purge the major Protestant denominations of liberalism. When the Scopes trial of 1925 showcased fundamentalism as a defensive antimodern movement, it appeared that evangelical Protestantism had moved to the very fringes of American culture. It is debatable whether evangelicals or even fundamentalists were really "religious outsiders" in America, but during the 1920s they "began to step self-consciously into outsider roles."[1] They believed that they were on the outside looking in—a faithful remnant of Bible-believing Protestants among apostatizing liberals.

Evangelicals certainly considered themselves to be "outsiders" to religious broadcasting. They repeatedly charged that the liberal Federal Council of Churches had engineered self-serving compacts with the radio networks, limiting evangelical access to the airwaves. Moreover, liberal Protestants received free air time whereas evangelicals had to purchase time to broadcast the gospel of Christ. Convinced that they were being discriminated against because of their alleged sectarianism, evangelicals organized their own ecumenical council, partly to show radio executives that they represented a significant and unified segment of American Protestantism.

The story of religious broadcasting in America is largely a tale of how evangelicals eventually came to dominate the airwaves. The complex story involved various constituencies: the federal regulatory agencies that laid the ground-rules for broadcasting, the owners and managers of local stations and national networks who controlled the airwaves, the ecumenical advisory committees that assisted the broadcasters and lobbied the agencies, the religious broadcasters, and the listeners and viewers. In spite of all the battles among these contending groups, by the 1940s the evangelicals had secured an amazingly strong position in American broadcasting.

There are no comprehensive historical studies of religious broadcasting. However, Harold Ellens and Ben Armstrong cursorily examine early radio and television ministries in books published in the mid-1970s.[2] Quentin Schultze has written the only scholarly article on the rise of evangelical radio in the 1920s and 1930s.[3] In that article Schultze convincingly demonstrates that evangelical radio represented a significant religious and economic force in the United States. Fortunately more recent studies of televangelism include sections on the historical development of religious broadcasting. Among the best are Horsfield's *Religious Television*, Hadden and Swann's *Prime Time Preachers*, and Hadden and Shupe's *Televangelism*.[4] Horsfield offers a penetrating critique of the ways the electronic media shape religious messages. Hadden, Swann, and Shupe address the political and social impact of televangelism. Others include Fore, who provides a mainline Protestant evaluation of evangelical broadcasting, and Voskuil, who has written a study of the relationship between mainline and evangelical broadcasting.[5] "Mass Communications," a helpful survey of religious broadcasting, has been penned by Martin.[6] Perhaps the most arresting analysis of the broadcast ministries is Schultze's article "The Mythos of the Electronic Church,"[7] which argues that evangelical confidence in communications technology is grounded in a Christian doctrine of progress and nurtured by American technological optimism.

THE BIRTH OF RELIGIOUS BROADCASTING

Electronic broadcasting officially began in 1912 when President Taft signed the first Radio Act. The first wireless voice broadcast had been achieved just six years earlier by Reginald Aubrey Fessenden, a Canadian scientist who successfully transmitted a Christmas Eve service from Brant Rock, Massachusetts, to ships off the East Coast of the United States. In addition to a selection from the Gospel of Luke, the ships' wireless operators picked up the voice of a woman singing Handel's "Largo" and a violin solo of Gounod's "Holy Night," played by Fessenden himself.[8] The first nonexperimental regular radio broadcast began when Westinghouse established Pittsburgh station KDKA, which went on the air on November 1, 1920, just in time to broadcast the Harding-Cox election returns. Only two months later KDKA carried the first radio broadcast of a church service from Calvary Episcopal Church. The Sunday worship bulletin informed the congregation that a "wireless telephone receiving apparatus" had been installed in the chancel and that the "incomparable service of the prayer book" would be "flashed for a radius of more than a thousand miles through space!"[9] Years later, the church's senior pastor reflected upon the occasion:

> The whole thing was an experiment, and I remember distinctly my own feeling that after all no harm could be done! It never occurred to me that the little black box was really going to carry out the service to the outside world. I knew there was such a thing as a wireless, but somehow I thought there would be some fluke in the connection, and that the whole thing would be a fizzle![10]

The experiment was anything but a fizzle. The service was aired without a hitch as two Westinghouse engineers, one Jewish and the other Roman Catholic, dressed in choir robes, monitored the equipment. Following the broadcast, the radio audience responded with appreciative letters and phone calls. KDKA recognized the popularity of the church broadcast and added Calvary's morning service to its regular Sunday programming schedule.[11] It was the birth of broadcast ministry.

RELIGIOUS RADIO STATIONS

KDKA's success was quickly emulated, and radio transmitters soon filled the airways across America. In 1922 there were already 382 stations in operation; by 1927 the number had mushroomed to 732. During the same five years, the number of receiving sets jumped from sixty thousand to 6.5 million. Most of the early stations operated on low power and reached audiences within only a few miles. These small transmitters were generally owned by electrical companies, radio shops, colleges, chambers of commerce, and other organizations "seeking to capitalize upon the novelty of radio."[12] Considering the relative ease of obtaining a federal license and the low cost of operating a transmitter, it is not surprising that religious groups were among those that got in on the ground floor of radio broadcasting. Of the six hundred stations operating in 1925, more than sixty were licensed to religious organizations. Already in 1922, those receiving licenses included the Bible Institute of Los Angeles (KJS); the YMCA of Denver (KOA); the First Presbyterian Church of Seattle (KTW); the Trinity Methodist Church of El Paso, Texas (WDAH); the Church of the Covenant, Washington, D.C. (WDM); the Broad Street Baptist Church of Columbus, Ohio (WMAN); the Unity School of Christianity, Kansas City (WOZ); Glad Tidings Tabernacle, San Francisco (KDZX); and the First Baptist Church of San Francisco (KQW).[13]

It appears that most of the early religious radio stations were owned and operated by evangelical Protestants, especially the Baptists. While all Protestant groups regarded radio broadcasting as a means of advertising and enhancing local ministries, evangelicals seem to have more eagerly embraced the radio as a tool for mass evangelism. Evangelicals may have regarded station ownership as the best way to secure unencumbered access to the unsaved. Whatever motivated evangelicals to enter the market, few of the religious stations licensed during the early- and mid-twenties would survive for more than a few years. The Radio Act of 1912 delegated the Department of Commerce the responsibility for licensing radio stations, but it did not give the Department of Commerce power to require stations to broadcast on assigned frequencies or to limit their hours of operation. As the number of stations multiplied during the mid-twenties there followed a frenzied frequency free-for-all. "Stations competed for the airwaves all across the frequency band, drowning one another in a bedlam of squeaks, whispers and disjointed words."[14] Finding it necessary to control the chaos in the radio industry, Congress created the Federal Radio Commission (FRC), which was empowered by the Radio Act of 1927 to assign frequencies, establish broadcast hours, require standard operating equipment, and license radio stations "as public convenience, interest, or necessity requires."[15] By 1928 many religious stations were reassigned low-powered frequencies to be shared with commercial stations. Unable to afford the newly required equipment or personnel, many religious stations either ceased operating or sold off their licenses to private owners. By 1933 fewer than thirty religious stations remained on the air.[16]

One of the evangelical stations directly affected by the licensing procedures of the Radio Act of 1927 was KGEF, owned by "Fighting Bob" Shuler, controversial pastor of the Trinity Methodist Church in Los Angeles. Although KGEF maintained a broadcast schedule of barely twenty-four hours per week, it attracted one of the largest radio audiences in the Los Angeles area during the late 1920s. Undoubtedly Shuler was the main attraction. In addition to Sunday sermons, Shuler scheduled Tuesday and Thursday evening broadcasts in which he frequently accused city officials of corruption and malfeasance. Criticism of Shuler's crusading broadcasts mounted, and in 1933, the FRC held public hearings in Los Angeles to determine whether Shuler's station was broadcasting in the public interest. Although the original FRC report supported Shuler, the FRC reversed its decision after a subsequent hearing, and KGEF was ordered off the air.[17] Shuler's problems were unique, but many religious stations succumbed to the increased operating costs resulting from the FRC's new technical guidelines. Only twelve of the religious stations licensed during the halcyon days of the twenties are still on the air today. Ironically, more than 1,370 religious stations are on the air today, and an increasing number of so-called secular radio stations have been adopting full-time religious formats because those formats have proven to be immensely profitable.[18]

Two of the flagship evangelical stations that overcame depression-era obstacles to serve as models for religious broadcasters were KFUO, a ministry of the Lutheran Church— Missouri Synod, which is operated by Concordia Theological Seminary in St. Louis, and WMBI, a ministry of the Moody Bible Institute in Chicago. KFUO was the brainchild of Walter A. Maier, a visionary young professor of Old Testament at Concordia. Convinced during the early 1920s that radio broadcasting was ideally suited for communicating the Christian faith, Maier felt that religious groups should purchase their own transmitters, in the event that commercial stations refused to carry religious programs. He quickly marshaled financial support from a group of Lutherans, obtained an operating license from the Federal Radio Commission, set up a make-shift studio in the attic of the seminary building, and on December 14, 1925, KFUO (Keep Forward Upward Onward) was on the air. The 500-watt station was soon receiving letters from across

America. From the beginning, KFUO broadcast a mix of religious and nonreligious programs, relying on listener contributions rather than commercial advertising. Maier took responsibility for two of the weekly programs: a Sunday vespers preaching service and a Thursday evening feature called "Views on the News," in which he provided commentary on the major news stories of the week. As it turned out, KFUO served as a training center for Maier,[19] whose "Lutheran Hour" would become one of the most popular national and international religious programs.

As early as 1921, soon after KDKA went on the air in Pittsburgh, supporters of Moody Bible Institute began discussing the possibility of operating a station in Chicago. It was not until 1925, however, that donations were adequate for the Board of Trustees to authorize a 500-watt radio station. The Institute aired programs on stations WGES and WENR during late 1925 and early 1926 and did not broadcast under the call letters WMBI until it received a license from the FRC. WMBI officially came on the air on July 28, 1926, operating under the provisions of a three-month license.[20]

Like other religious stations, WMBI soon faced license challenges from commercial stations, and the FRC scheduled public hearings to determine whether WMBI was operating "in the public interest." It remained on the air largely because of the tireless efforts of a Yale engineering graduate who served as an assistant to the president of the Institute. This engineer, Henry Crowell, made numerous train trips to Washington, where he presistently and effectively argued the case for WMBI. Few stations had such a well-educated, tenacious advocate. Although it was unabashedly fundamentalist, WMBI consistently broadcast a rather well-rounded schedule of news, educational, musical, and children's programs in addition to evangelistic programs. It quickly became the flagship of fundamentalist stations in the Midwest and beginning in 1930 was receiving as many as twenty thousand letters annually. It also became a national center for religious radio productions. In 1942 WMBI released transcribed programs to 187 different radio stations, thus demonstrating that there was a broad market for full-time religious programming in the United States.[21]

LOCAL EVANGELICAL PROGRAMS ON
COMMERCIAL STATIONS

During the late 1920s the FRC determined that no new licenses were to be issued to religious groups and that existing licenses were to be reassigned to "part-time or inferior channels." Now classified as "propaganda stations," religious stations supposedly violated the FRC's principle of "non-discrimination." The FRC officially favored commercial stations offering "well-rounded" programs. "In such a scheme there is no room for the operation of broadcasting stations exclusively by or in the private interests of individuals or groups," wrote the FRC. "As a general rule particular doctrines, creeds, and beliefs must find their way into the market of ideas by the existing public-service stations."[22] Schultze suggests that these "discriminatory" regulations turned out to be "a blessing in disguise for evangelical broadcasters." Rather than operating their own low-power, time-shared stations, evangelicals increasingly sought air time from the commercial stations. Because both the FRC and its successor, the Federal Communications Commission (FCC), identified religious programs in lists of public-service requirements to be considered in granting and renewing licenses, most commercial stations provided time for religious broadcasts.[23] A survey in 1925 of five high-powered stations in New York, Chicago, and Kansas City revealed that about 4 percent of their programming was devoted to church services and sacred music.[24] According to DuBourdieu, an early student of religious broadcasting, more than 8 percent of all radio programming was religious by 1932.[25] During the 1920s, local commercial stations generally provided free time for religious programs to meet the obligation to serve the "public interest." It is also true that, during the nascent years of radio, when air time was relatively inexpensive and programming was not readily available, station managers eagerly filled open time slots with religious programs. As radio became more profitable, and as larger numbers of religious groups sought air time, some stations began to demand payment from religious broadcasters. DuBourdieu estimated that three-fourths of all religious programs were broadcast on a free, or sustaining-time, basis in 1932.[26] While the percentage of religious programs receiving free time dropped somewhat during the late thirties, there seems to have been relatively little change in the figure well into the 1940s.[27]

Nonetheless, evangelicals generally did not obtain an equal share of the free time offered by local stations. A Federal Council of Churches study published in 1938 revealed that while evangelical groups broadcast more programs over a larger number of stations for a higher number of hours than Roman Catholic and mainline Protestant groups, they were twice as likely to be charged for access to the air. While Baptist, Gospel Tabernacle, and Holiness/Pentecostal broadcasters purchased about two-thirds of their air time in 1948, Methodist and Presbyterian broadcasters purchased only one-third of their air time. During the same year, nearly 70 percent of Roman Catholic air time was free.[28] It appears that all evangelical broadcasters suffered because of the outrageous programs of a few fringe groups. Some fundamentalists, in particular, offended station owners and audiences with their shrill, sectarian messages.

Whatever the reasons for these discriminatory practices, they shaped the future of evangelical broadcasting. Forced to buy time, "evangelicals learned early how to produce programming that would attract audiences and garner financial support."[29] Thus, when stations began to cut back on sustaining time for religious broadcasts during the late forties, evangelicals were prepared for the commercial challenges.

Evangelicals have consistently dominated local religious broadcasting. A January 1932 issue of *The Sunday School Times* ran a "Directory of Evangelical Radio Broadcasts" that included more than 350 broadcasting periods carried over seventy-eight stations in thirty-two states and provinces. Certainly this was not an exhaustive listing, but it reveals the extensive network of broadcasts that stood "without reservation for the fundamental doctrines of the Christian faith." Among the leading doctrines: an infallible and inerrant Bible, the lost condition of man since the Fall, the substitutionary atonement, the deity of Christ, the Virgin Birth, and the resurrection of the body.[30] Included in the Directory were programs produced by Lutherans, Presbyterians, Methodists, and others associated with mainline denominations. These apparently passed doctrinal muster. Although fundamentalists failed to gain control of the mainline Protestant denominations during the 1920s, many theological conservatives remained members of these churches and supported evangelical broadcasters.

The 1932 *Sunday School Times* radio directory was almost exclusively a guide to local religious broadcasts. It included programs that were or were becoming national broadcasts, such as the one by Donald Grey Barnhouse, pastor of the Tenth Presbyterian Church of Philadelphia, which was aired on over one hundred stations. Walter Maier's "Lutheran Hour" and Charles Fuller's "Old-Fashioned Revival Hour" were listed as well. The great majority of the listings, however, had a distinctly local flavor. The extensive line-up of Sunday offerings included the following programs:

7:00–7:30 A.M. (E.T.)	Morning Watch Hour, The Reverend and Mrs. M. J. Bouters, Evangelists, Orlando, Florida, *WDBO*
8:30–9:00 A.M. (E.T.)	"Sunday School of the Air," First Baptist Church, Pontiac, Michigan, *WJR*
9:00–10:00 A.M. (C.T.)	John Steenhoven, Yankton, South Dakota, *WNAX*
10:00–11:00 A.M. (E.T.)	Columbia Businessmen's Bible Class, Jefferson Hotel, Robert C. McQuilkin, Teacher, Columbia, South Carolina, *WIS*.[31]
10:45–12:15 A.M. (E.T.)	C. H. Churchill, Pastor, morning service, Buffalo, New York, *WKBW*

Also included in the *Sunday School Times'* directory was Paul Rader's popular worship service from the Chicago Gospel Tabernacle over station WJJD in Chicago. One of the pioneers of evangelical broadcasting, Rader produced "The Breakfast Brigade" over the CBS network for a time in 1930, but he is best remembered for innovative programs that were broadcast over a variety of local Chicago stations.

Rader began broadcasting on June 15, 1922, from the roof of Chicago's City Hall. William Hale Thompson, Chicago's mayor, had secured a transmitter that operated under the call letters WHT—the mayor's initials. Finding it difficult to fill the air time, he invited Rader to do a broadcast. With characteristic vision and confidence that radio could be an effective means of communicating the gospel, Rader accepted the invitation and, accompanied by a brass quartet, took to the air from the mayor's studio.[32] Clarence Jones, a member of that quartet who later became the moving force behind the World Radio

Missionary Fellowship and station HCJB in Quito, Ecuador, remembers the occasion.

> On that first broadcast, we had no studio—the mayor's men had set up a crude shack on the roof of the City Hall. So, out on the open air, we unpacked our instruments, and at the signal of the operator, pointed our trumpets and trombones at what he called a "microphone." It was literally an old telephone mouthpiece with a fearful array of wires, tubes and gadgets behind it called a "transmitter."

As Rader preached and the quartet blew their horns, none of them really expected that anyone could hear them over the "contraption" in front of them, but to their amazement a barrage of telephone calls came from listeners.[33]

Rader quickly capitalized on the new technology, inviting his growing audience to attend services at the Gospel Tabernacle. Soon he got his broadcasts on other Chicago stations, including WBBM, which let Rader use its idle studios for fourteen hours every Sunday. This one-day-a-week station went on the air as WJBT ("Where Jesus Blessed Thousands") and carried a wide range of religious programs: orchestra, band, and organ concerts, song services, preaching, the "Healing Hour," the "Bible Drama Hour," and the "Back Home Hour."[34]

While Rader built a large audience of radio listeners, he rejected the concept of a radio church: "The church revealed to us in the Bible is made up of Christians who gather for worship, baptism, communion, marriage, funerals, Bible teaching, prayer, faith testimony, song and Christian fellowship, bearing of sorrows, joys and burdens. None of this can be done well by radio." According to Rader, broadcasting was, above all, a powerful means of evangelism, as the "gospel message has a most supernatural grip over radio."[35] Even if radio religion could not substitute for the gathered church, it was anything but the "tool of the devil," as some of his early critics charged. "There's nothing in the Bible that tells the world to come to the church," Rader argued; "but there's everything in the Bible that tells the church to go to the world. Radio takes the Gospel to the unchurched. That's why I'm using it!"[36] Over the years the listings of local evangelical programs fluctuated drastically as new programs replaced those that went off the air. Evangelical broadcasting, however, remained strong. As a parade of evangelicals were to follow Rader to the microphone, they also would be motivated by a desire to reach the unsaved with the gospel.

PIONEERS OF NATIONAL EVANGELICAL BROADCASTING

Local evangelical broadcasts generally served as the seedbeds for national network programs. Some of these local programs attracted regional audiences after sunset. High-power stations reached half the country under the right atmospheric conditions. For example, R. R. Brown's "Radio Chapel Service," broadcast from WOW in Omaha beginning in April 1923, attracted an estimated audience of one hundred thousand people by 1925. Listeners were invited to join the World Radio Congregation, which issued membership cards, raised funds for disaster relief, and prayed for the world to know Christ. Even those broadcasting from relatively weak transmitters could reach huge audiences in densely populated areas. This was true of John Roach Stratton, who broadcast the services of Calvary Baptist Church in New York City from his own 250-watt facility, WQAQ.[37]

However, the electronic church emerged with the rise of coast-to-coast evangelical broadcasts on the radio networks. The first religious broadcaster to purchase network time was Donald Grey Barnhouse of Philadelphia. When he arrived in 1927, the officers of Tenth Presbyterian Church agreed to install radio equipment and regularly broadcast Sunday evening vesper services. After a year of local broadcasting and a net balance of eleven cents, Barnhouse signed a $40,000 contract with CBS. From 1928 to 1932 Barnhouse was heard across the nation every Sunday evening over that network.[38]

Other significant national evangelical broadcasters using early radio were Theodore Epp of "Back to the Bible"; M. R. DeHaan of "The Radio Bible Class"; Paul Myers of "Haven of Rest"; T. Myron Webb of "The Bible Fellowship Hour"; Clarence Erickson of "Heaven and Home Hour"; H. M. S. Richards of the "Voice of Prophecy," sponsored by the Seventh-day Adventists; and Henry Schultze and Peter Eldersveld, early speakers for "The Back to God Hour," a ministry of the Christian Reformed Church. Without a doubt, however, the most influential early evangelical broadcasters were Walter Maier of "The Lutheran Hour" and Charles E. Fuller of "The Old-Fashioned Revival Hour."

Maier was the driving force behind radio station KFUO in St. Louis. In 1929, under Maier's prompting, the radio committee of the Lutheran Church—Missouri Synod, explored the possibility of broadcasting a program over one of the emerging national networks. Maier and his supporters soon raised nearly $100,000 from the Lutheran Layman's League and the Walther League to purchase one $4,500 half hour every week on CBS. The Thursday evening program, known as "The Lutheran Hour," gave Maier a national, prime-time audience. His broadcast of "The Lutheran Hour" originated from Cleveland on October 2, 1930, to accommodate the city's Bach Chorus. CBS was pleased with the Chorus but fretted over the planned preaching format, convinced that it would never hold a Thursday evening audience. At the last minute network officials advised Maier to reduce his sermon to ten minutes. Maier obliged, but stayed with his planned theme from Psalm 14:1, "The fool hath said in his heart, there is no God."[39]

Maier's program elicited appreciative letters from across the nation, but the financial burden was extremely heavy. The lack of contributions from listeners and supporters led to the program's cancellation in June of the year after it began. Four years later it returned—on the new Mutual Broadcasting System, quickly becoming one of the most popular religious broadcasts of all time. In 1945 "The Lutheran Hour" was being broadcast over 224 mutual stations and was being transcribed to another 450 stations in twenty-six countries. *Time* estimated that twelve million people listened regularly to Maier's program, which received approximately three hundred thousand letters per year. Labeled a fundamentalist who preached a literalistic version of biblical truth, Maier was identified in *Time* as the "Chrysostom of American Lutheranism."[40]

A successful businessman and church worker, Charles Fuller rededicated his life to Christ in 1916 after hearing Rader speak at a church in Los Angeles. Shortly afterward, Fuller organized an adult Bible class at the Placentia Presbyterian Church in Orange County, California, and began preparing for the ministry while studying at Biola—the Bible Institute of Los Angeles. Ordained in 1925, Fuller was called to be the pastor of Calvary Church in Placentia, a congregation newly organized around the nucleus of the Bible class Fuller had formed years before.[41] While Fuller did some broadcasting over station KJS during the mid-1920s, he did not invest significant time and energy in radio until 1930. Three years later, convinced of his calling to be a broadcast preacher, Fuller resigned his Calvary pastorate and formed the nonprofit Gospel Broadcasting Association. Plans were made to expand the ministry through a network of California stations.[42] In October 1934, Fuller christened a new program, the "Radio Revival Hour," which originated from station KNX in Hollywood. Three years later the program was taken coast to coast over a skeleton network of 30 Mutual stations. Despite forbidding expenses, the renamed "Old-Fashioned Revival Hour" was soon carried over all of Mutual's 152 stations, and Fuller was preaching to a weekly audience of more than ten million people. By 1943 the "Revival Hour" was aired by 1000 stations at a cost of $35,000 per week. The program had become Mutual's largest commercial account, purchasing 50 percent more time than any other customer. When Mutual developed a more restrictive policy regarding religious broadcasts during the mid-forties, Fuller moved the program to an independent network of stations. In 1949, faced with increasing competition from television, the American Broadcasting Network welcomed the program into its weekly schedule.[43]

Fuller's broadcasts had a remarkable impact on the evangelical community. Like Maier, Fuller communicated in clear and convincing tones with little of the emotionalism that had become trademarks of some religious broadcasters. Fuller eventually left a nondenominational evangelical seminary as a legacy of his ministry. He also inspired a number of today's leading religious broadcasters, including Billy Graham and Jerry Falwell.

NETWORK BROADCASTING: MAINLINE MONOPOLY

As early as 1923 the Federal Council of Churches, an ecumenical agency representing twenty-five Protestant denominations, officially encouraged local church federations to develop cooperative radio ministries. The earliest and most significant joint radio venture occurred in New York City when Frank C. Goodman, on behalf of the Greater New York Federation of Churches, developed a schedule of three weekly programs on New York City radio stations. One of these programs, an interdenominational service from the Bedford Branch of the Brooklyn YMCA, was conducted by well-known preacher S. Parkes Cadman. First aired May 3, 1923, on station WEAF, the "National Radio Pulpit" became such a popular feature that, when the National Broadcasting Company was formed in 1926 with WEAF (now WNBC) as its flagship station, Cadman's program became network radio.[44]

NBC obviously expected the Federal Council to develop and sponsor religious programming, much as the New York Federation of Churches had done for station WEAF. Charles S. MacFarland, General Secretary of the Federal Council, was appointed to NBC's advisory council and chaired a subcommittee on religious affairs.[45] This cozy relationship between NBC and the Federal Council afforded the network a means for preempting programs produced by "sectarian" Protestant groups. All of this was made more plausible because the Federal Council was American Protestantism's only viable ecumenical agency. Similar arrangements were quickly made with representative Roman Catholic and Jewish groups, the National Council of Catholic Men and the Jewish Theological Seminary in America.[46] When NBC established a Committee on Religious Activities in 1928, MacFarland and his Roman Catholic and Jewish counterparts joined in an effort to bring religious broadcasting into harmony with the ecumenical philosophy of the network. The Committee formulated four general policies that shaped religious broadcasting for decades: (1) religious groups should receive free time but pay for production costs, (2) religious broadcasts should be nonsectarian and nondenominational, (3) network programs should employ one speaker for continuity, and (4) broadcasts should follow a preaching format "avoiding matters of doctrine and controversial subjects."[47]

A statement of principles issued by the Religious Activities Committee in March 1928 clarifies the second policy:

> The National Broadcasting Company will serve only the central or national agencies of great religious faiths, as for example, the Roman Catholics, the Protestants, and the Jews, as distinguished from individual churches or small group movements where the national membership is comparatively small.[48]

As long as NBC recognized the Federal Council as the representative agency of Protestantism, the vast majority of evangelicals were denied access to NBC; few evangelical churches belonged to the "liberal" Federal Council.

From its inception, NBC provided no commercial time for religious broadcasting and donated free time to Protestants only through the Federal Council (later the National Council of Churches). Thus, individual evangelical denominations or broadcasters were effectively barred from NBC. However, NBC's chief competitor, the Columbia Broadcasting System (CBS), immediately began selling time to religious groups upon its formation in 1927. Evangelicals who took advantage of this opening included Donald Grey Barnhouse of Tenth Presbyterian Church in Philadelphia and Walter Maier of "The Lutheran Hour."[49] However, CBS's liberal policy was short-lived. In 1931 the network decided to drop all paid religious programs. Unlike NBC, which still aired programs representing the major faiths, CBS produced its own "Church of the Air," inviting speakers from different denominations to its microphone. The Federal Council, already representing Protestantism for NBC, was invited to assist CBS's in-house advisory panel in the selection of the Protestant speakers for the new "Church of the Air."[50] In this manner CBS, like NBC, maintained tight control of its religious programming in order to avoid controversial sectarian broadcasts. The policy change at CBS left evangelicals without direct access to network broadcasting, though they still bought considerable air time from high-powered stations that could reach broad sections of the country. By the mid-1930s nearly all of the Protestant broadcasting over NBC and CBS was controlled by the liberal Federal Council.

Once again, the establishment in 1935 of a new national network, which was searching for revenues, provided a major opening for the evangelicals. In the face of the other networks' abhorrence of paid religious broadcasts, the Mutual Broadcasting System decided to accept *only* commercial religious broadcasting. Mutual quickly became "the bastion of numerous fundamentalist radio hours."[51] Among the notable broadcasts to be carried by Mutual were Maiers' "Lutheran Hour," back on the air after its abortive attempt with CBS, and Fuller's "Old-Fashioned Revival Hour," which started on Mutual in 1937. Within six years the "Revival Hour" and a second Fuller broadcast, "The Pilgrim's Hour," were heard over a thousand stations at an annual cost of $1,500,000. Mutual's policy was remarkably successful: Fuller was Mutual's most lucrative customer, and in the early 1940s more than a quarter of the nework's income came from the commercial accounts of religious broadcasters.[52]

Despite the popularity of its religious programs, Mutual nearly joined the other networks in refusing to sell time for all religious programs. After announcing a new restrictive policy in 1943, the network had second thoughts. In 1944 Mutual did restrict commercial religious programs to Sunday morning time-slots, established a one-half-hour time limitation, and ended on-air solicitation of funds. Mutual also added a few sustaining-time religious programs to its schedule, including evangelical and mainstream Protestant broadcasts. Not surprisingly, Mutual quickly lost many of its religious accounts and the related revenues. While some programs, most notably "The Lutheran Hour," bought Sunday morning broadcast time, others such as the "Old-Fashioned Revival Hour" and the "Haven of Rest" left Mutual.[53] For a while it appeared that evangelical broadcasters would move to yet another struggling new network, the Associated Broadcasting Corporation, established in 1944–45 by two Grand Rapids, Michigan, businessmen. This time, however, the new network was formed specifically to carry only non-profit religious broadcasts. Although the network signed up 189 stations, it folded a few years later, partly because it could not attract enough evangelical support.[54]

Mutual's decision to discontinue most paid religious programs was probably motivated by pressure from mainstream Protestant groups, which accused fundamentalist preachers of hucksterism and sectarianism. But it also appears that the network believed that it might make more money by selling the prime-time program periods to other commercial accounts.[55] One critic charged that Mutual had previously "tolerated" distasteful commercial religious programs because of the financial benefits and pointed out that the network would lose little money under its new policy of restricting religious programs to Sunday morning. Writing in the liberal *Christian Century*, the critic urged the network to take more drastic measures: "The network religious radio program racket, capitalized by independent superfundamentalist revivalists, will not be eliminated nationally until Mutual goes the whole way and bans paid religious programs altogether, as the other networks have done."[56]

In 1949, a change in religious broadcast policies at the American Broadcasting Company (ABC), formerly part of NBC, opened the network door once again. Partly because of a loss of advertising revenue to television, ABC began accepting commercial religious programs. It even invited Fuller to purchase time to air a transcription of the "Revival Hour" over 280 stations. "The Lutheran Hour" and the "Southern Baptist Hour" soon joined Fuller's popular program over ABC.[57] Largely because of the rise of television, evangelicals gained increasing access to the national radio networks during the 1950s. Able to purchase limited time from ABC and Mutual, evangelicals also gained some sustaining time for programming from all four of the major networks.[58]

NATIONAL RELIGIOUS BROADCASTERS

Their struggles to gain access to network radio, along with various internal theological disputes fueled by fundamentalist Carl McIntire, led a group of influential evangelicals to convene in St. Louis in 1942 to organize "The National Association of Evangelicals for United Action" (NAE). Unaware that network policies would soon change as a result of the growing prominence of television, the group seriously addressed the problem of network access for evangelical broadcasters. In his keynote address, evangelical Boston pastor Harold Ockenga said, "We are discriminated against, because of the folly of our divided condition."[59] A "Report of the Policy Committee" recommended that NAE establish a radio committee "to help in securing a fair and equal opportunty for the use of radio facilities by evangelical groups or individuals." According to one participant, the NAE sought to protect the rights of evangelical broadcasters: (1) the right to preach "doctrinal sermons" over the air, (2) the right to purchase time for "Gospel broadcasting" over national networks and local stations, and (3) the right of "representative evangelical interchurch organizations" to share the sustaining time allotted to Protestants.[60]

In 1944 some NAE members invited about 150 evangelical broadcasters to attend a conference at Columbus, Ohio, to form a separate organization, National Religious Broadcasters (NRB). With its executive council composed of members of the NAE,[61] NRB quickly attempted to dissociate itself from radio racketeers by adopting a code of ethics regarding program content, technical broadcast quality, and financial disclosure. Two years later the code was sent to every radio network and station along with copies of a resolution that sought to clarify alleged misconceptions about American Protestantism.

One misconception is that American Protestantism is one unified religious group, whereas in fact there are two distinct kinds of Protestants in America today. Each adheres to a particular form of teaching—the one the antithesis of the other.

One group believes the Bible to be the infallible rule for belief and conduct whereas the other does not.[62]

The NRB took credit for "saving" the network airwaves from the hands of liberal Protestants. Glenwood Blackmore, writing for *United Evangelical Action*, claimed in 1956 that "there would probably not be a single evangelical, biblical broadcast of the Gospel on the air in America today had the NRB not won that battle" for the airwaves during the 1940s.[63] Actually, the NRB had little to do with the network policies that eventually paved the way for more commercial evangelical broadcasts. During its early years the NRB was a relatively minor organization that even had some difficulty enlisting independent-minded evangelical broadcasters as members. Only three of the original members had broadcasts released on a national basis— Walter Maier ("Lutheran Hour"), M. R. DeHaan ("Radio Bible Class"), and Theodore Epp ("Back to the Bible"). Moreover, the NRB did not play a major role in helping evangelicals face the new challenges of FM radio and television.[64]

If the NRB did not save evangelical broadcasting, it played an important role in the rise of the electronic church by improving broadcast standards and isolating the most objectionable radio hucksters. It also served as a legitimate broadcast representative for millions of non–Federal Council Protestants. The networks recognized NRB claims and provided sustaining time to NRB-sponsored programs.[65] During the 1950s it became an increasingly effective lobbying group, developing cordial relations with representatives of the broadcasting industry, the FCC, and the United States Congress, which legislated broadcasting in America. In all of this the NRB served as a counterweight to the Broadcasting and Film Commission, an agency of the newly organized National Council of Churches (1950).

After Mutual eliminated nearly all religious broadcasts in 1944, evangelical broadcasters remained vigilant, lest liberal Protestants initiate any new measures to reduce or eliminate commercial religious broadcasting. Therefore, in 1956 when the National Council approved an "Advisory Policy Statement on

Religious Broadcasting," which advised against commercial religious time for radio and television, evangelicals were fully prepared to defend their broadcasting rights. The most pertinent section of the 1956 statement clearly stated the long-standing position of mainstream Protestant broadcasters.

> The Broadcasting and Film Commission advises against the sale or purchase of time for religious broadcasts. It holds this practice to be inconsistent with its own basis of operation and, by implication, with the position of the broadcasting industry as expressed in the Television Code. The Commission, therefore, requests its constituent communions, council of churches and councils of church women to exercise their influence in support of this position by discouraging the practice.[66]

Evangelicals issued a call to arms, and evangelical broadcasters took to the air and to the journals to protest the renewal of the liberal "conspiracy" to keep evangelical programs off the air. Peter Eldersveld of the "Back to God Hour" broadcast a sermon entitled "Freedom of Religion" in which he attacked NBC for interfering with "the freedom to purchase time on radio and television for the spread of the gospel of God's Holy Word!"[67] In his *United Evangelical Action* article, "Shall the NCC Control Religious Broadcasting?" Glenwood Blackmore insisted that the NCC policy was un-American and un-Christian—un-American because it violated constitutionally generated freedoms of speech and religion, and un-Christian because it would mean that the true Christian faith would no longer be broadcast over radio and television. Blackmore complained that NBC favored religious broadcasters who publicly denied the fundamental truths of the Christian faith—biblical inerrance, the virgin birth and deity of Christ, the atonement, the resurrection of Christ, and his second coming. It was the duty and responsibility of all evangelicals to counter "such apostasy with a positive declaration of Bible truth," he wrote.[68] An editorial in the evangelical *Christianity Today* surveyed the debate and concluded that liberals and evangelicals both had a right to be on the air, but insisted that it was "a sad commentary on both Americanism and the freedoms on which our land was founded" that liberals should insist on free time for themselves while "denying others the right to buy time."[69] Ironically, the whole issue was a political boon for the NRB and for evangelicals in general because it enhanced their status with broadcast executives and government officials. As NRB president Eugene Bertermann later pointed out, the BFC (Broadcasting and Film Commission) statement turned out to be a "colossal blunder" for mainstream Protestants.[70] Evangelicals were not alone in their condemnation of the BFC. Attacks came from the National Association of Broadcasters, *Broadcasting Magazine* (the major trade journal), and station owners. Harold Fellows, president of the National Association of Broadcasters, dismissed the BFC policy as "misguided" and chided the commission for suggesting that broadcasters were failing to provide enough free time.[71] *Broadcasting Magazine* defended the policy of selling religious air-time and blasted the BFC for attempting "to dictate how religion should be broadcast."[72]

Times had changed. With television and FM and AM radio stations vying for advertising revenue, commercial religious broadcasts were increasingly welcome. Furthermore, evangelicals were increasingly recognized as making up a significant proportion of America's Protestants. The BFC policy statement unified and strengthened evangelical opposition. Finally, willing to pay their own way, evangelicals had come to dominate religious broadcasting on the national and the local levels.

TELEVISION: RELIGIOUS RADIO'S PRECOCIOUS CHILD

Religious television was radio's offspring. Not only were most of the early stations and networks owned and operated by mainstays of the radio industry, but also many of the early religious television broadcasters started in radio. Moreover, the relationships between religious broadcasters, station and network owners, and government regulators followed patterns established in radio. Religious television began on Easter Sunday, 1940, when separate Roman Catholic and Protestant services were telecast in New York City. Following the precedent established during the early years of radio, the television networks initially sought to deal with "the respectable and mainline religious groups." In fact, television producers simply adopted those groups that had been advisers and sponsors of religious radio—the National Council of Catholic Men, the Jewish Theological Seminary of America, and the Federal Council of Churches. The networks generally provided production facilities, technical services, and even some financial resources to these groups. Programs were then fed to affiliate stations on a sustaining-time basis.[73]

The fifties have been described as "the heyday of network mainline programming," since a number of long-running and award-winning programs originated during this period: "Lamp Unto My Feet" (CBS), "Directions" (ABC), "Frontiers of Faith" (NBC), and "Look Up and Live" (CBS). The ecumenical programs were high-quality productions, expressing broad religious truths rather than pointed social or theological issues. Noting this deficiency, a few of the larger denominations, especially those not represented by the National Council, developed their own syndicated programs, some of which were granted free time by local stations. Despite high production costs, Southern Baptists syndicated "The Answer," Seventh-day Adventists produced "Faith for Today," and the Lutheran Church—Missouri Synod presented "This Is the Life."[74] In 1950 the first telecast of Billy Graham's "Hour of Decision" went out over the ABC network.[75] Three years later Rex Humbard launched a broadcast ministry from his Calvary Temple in Akron, Ohio. Humbard first used radio but quickly switched to television, which he later described as "a God-given miracle for reaching countless millions of unsaved persons with the saving message of Jesus Christ." After considerable struggle, Humbard was able to string together a network of stations that carried his "Cathedral of Tomorrow" across America. After the success of his "Healing Waters" radio broadcast, Oral Roberts began televising his healing crusades in 1954. This dramatic and emotional program became a lightning rod for controversy throughout the 1950s.[76]

During the 1950s paid evangelical programming shared time with the sustaining broadcasts sponsored by the National Council and a few denominations. By 1970 the paid independent evangelical broadcasts dominated the market, thanks largely to an FCC policy published in 1960 that stated "no public interest basis was to be served" by distinguishing between sustaining-time programs and commercially sponsored programs in evaluating a station's public interest performance.[77] In other words, the long-held assumption that stations had to serve "the public interest" by airing nonpaid educational and informational shows was largely defunct. Because sustaining religious programs had been one way for stations to meet that public-interest requirement, there was no incentive after 1960 for stations to air free religious broadcasts. The mainline church groups, especially those associated with the National Council, were largely left in the cold. As Hadden and Shupe have shown, the FCC ruling fueled the commitment of evangelicals to buy commercial time, resulting in fierce competition for existing time slots. Moreover, the rising evangelical demand for television time pushed up prices; stations that may have previously refused to sell time for religious broadcasts, soon decided to "cash in on the new demand."[78] Once again, the federal regulatory agencies had placed an expensive gift in the hands of evangelicals. In 1959, a year before the 1960 ruling, 53 percent of all religious television had been paid-time programming. In 1977, 92 percent of all programming was paid time.[79] America had moved into the era of the electronic church.

CONCLUSION

In spite of their frequent criticisms of modernity, evangelicals early and eagerly embraced electronic broadcasting as a means of spreading the gospel. To be sure, there were some evangelicals who initially considered radio a "tool of the devil,"[80] but most were enthusiastic advocates of religious broadcasting. In the twenties evangelicals lined up to purchase radio transmitters. Later they overcame numerous obstacles in efforts to reach national audiences over radio and television. Evangelism was certainly the principle motivation for the enthusiastic embrace of electronic broadcasting. Evangelicals believed that radio and television afforded them powerful tools to be used in the mission of reaching the world for Christ. As a result, new-age communications systems were used by proponents of the old-time gospel. As one evangelical associated with broadcasting put it, "Modern technology is here to be used."[81] In an arresting study, Quentin Schultze concludes that evangelical broadcasters too easily assumed that the gospel could be spread throughout the world like a consumer product. Infatuated with the latest communications technologies, they overlooked the complexity of human communication and were caught in the spell of American evangelical optimism.[82] Peter Horsfield, another student of religious broadcasting, contends that mission-minded evangelicals have reflected "a more utilitarian attitude toward technology" than have nonevangelicals.[83]

Religious broadcasting enhanced the status of American evangelicals. If, as some scholars seem to suggest, evangelicals (especially those known as fundamentalists) were affected with "status anxiety" following the fundamentalist-modernist battles of the first half of the twentieth century, some religious broadcasters helped to gain credibility for the movement. In spite of the antics of some radio hucksters and racketeers, broadcast preachers such as Walter Maier and Charles Fuller brought respectability to the entire evangelical movement. Today the wife of an American president would hardly label the speaker of "The Lutheran Hour" "a somewhat fanatic fundamentalist," as did Eleanor Roosevelt during the 1940s.[84] Like the evangelical movement itself, evangelical broadcasting has moved into the White House.

In addition, evangelical broadcasting contributed to the institutional growth and unity of the evangelical movement. In his studies of fundamentalism between the wars, Joel Carpenter has pointed out that radio ministries assisted in the development of a vast array of para-church organizations. WMBI, for instance, was a potent aid in the development of Moody Bible Institute.[85] Indeed, we have seen that evangelical concern for access to radio was one of the most important factors in the creation of the National Association of Evangelicals. Traditionally fractious, evangelicals have united around the common cause of religious broadcasting.

Although evangelicals sometimes wrongly accused the liberals of a conspiracy to keep them off the air, the battles between the two groups helped to unify and energize evangelicalism. The Federal and National Councils of Churches became the targets of evangelical wrath—villains against whom evangelicals could rally instead of simply fighting among themselves. Thus the mainline Protestants curiously aided evangelicals even though they were merely attempting to preserve their own special broadcast privileges. Evangelicals largely misread the motives of the Federal and National Councils, seldom blaming the stations or networks for discriminatory practices. After all, it was the broadcast industry that really controlled religious broadcasting in the United States. Networks and stations eventually supported paid religious broadcasting because it was in their own economic interests. The policies of the federal government and the actions of broadcast networks and stations reveal more about the history of religious programming than do the efforts of the mainline Protestants to hang on to their sustaining time. Broadcast policies that initially favored ecumenical Protestant groups turned out to be a blessing in disguise for the evangelicals. Forced to buy time, evangelicals learned to attract audiences and raise funds. As the networks and local stations drifted toward paid-time religious broadcasting, the evangelicals easily captured the market from the mainliners who had been nurtured on sustaining time. Evangelical broadcasting has played an important role in the evangelical resurgence of the late-twentieth century. Eager to use modern communications technologies, evangelicals became the broadcast professionals among American religious groups. Evangelicals hoped to spread their old-fashioned gospel and shape the surrounding culture. But the medium shaped their message as well. If evangelicals are the religious "insiders" in the United States today, it is because both evangelicals and American culture in general have been shaped by a powerful communications revolution.

NOTES

[1]R. Laurence Moore, *Religious Outsiders and the Making of Americans* (New York: Oxford University Press, 1986), 163.

[2]See J. Harold Ellens, *Models of Religious Broadcasting* (Grand Rapids: Eerdmans, 1974); Ben Armstrong, *The Electric Church* (Nashville: Thomas Nelson, 1975).

[3]See Quentin J. Schultze, "Evangelical Radio and the Rise of the Electronic Church, 1921–1948," *Journal of Broadcasting and Electronic Media* 32 (Summer 1988): 289–306.

[4]See Peter G. Horsfield, *Religious Television: The American Experience* (New York: Longman, 1984); Jeffrey K. Hadden and Charles E. Swann, *Prime Time Preachers: The Rising Power of Televangelism* (Reading, Mass.: Addison-Wesley, 1981); and Jeffrey K. Hadden and Anson Shupe, *Televangelism: Power and Politics on God's Frontier* (New York: Henry Holt, 1988).

[5]See William F. Fore, *Television and Religion: The Shaping of Faith, Values, and Culture* (Minneapolis: Augsburg, 1987); and Dennis N. Voskuil, "The Protestant Establishment and the Media," *Between the Times: The Travail of the Protestant Establishment in America, 1900–1960*, ed. William R. Hutchison (New York: Cambridge University Press, 1989): 72–92.

[6]See William Martin, "Mass Communications," *Encyclopedia of the American Religious Experience*, vol. 3, ed. Charles H. Lippy and Peter W. Williams (New York: Scribners, 1988), 1711–26.

[7]See Quentin J. Schultze,, "The Mythos of the Electronic Church," *Critical Studies in Mass Communication* 4 (1987): 245–61.

[8]J. Harold Ellens, *Models of Religious Broadcasting* (Grand Rapids: Eerdmans, 1974), 14–15; and Hadden and Swann, *Prime Time Preachers*, 8–9.

[9]Hadden and Swann, *Prime Time Preachers*, 72–73; Ben Armstrong, *The Electric Church*, 19–20; Eric Barnouw, *A Tower of Babel: A History of Broadcasting to 1933* (New York: Oxford University Press, 1966), 71; Spencer Miller, Jr., "Religion and Radio," *Annals of the American Academy of Political and Social*

Sciences 177 (January 1935): 135–40; idem, "Religious Radio 1921–1971," *Christianity Today* 15 (1 January 1971): 313–14; Vincent Edwards, "The First Church Broadcast," *The Christian Advocate* 12 (14 November 1968): 12; and Tamara N. Browning, "Christian Radio at 65," *Journal of Religious Broadcasting* 18 (June 1986): 14–16.

[10]Quoted in Hadden and Swann, *Prime Time Preachers*, 73.

[11]Hadden and Swann, *Prime Time Preachers*, 73; Edwards, "First Church Broadcast," 12; and Browning, "Christian Radio," 14–16.

[12]Herman S. Hettinger, "Broadcasting in the United States," *Annals of the American Academy of Political and Social Sciences* 177 (January 1935): 1–3; Miller, "Religion and Radio," 135–40; and Ellens, *Models of Religious Broadcasting*, 16.

[13]Hettinger, "Broadcasting," 1–3; Gleason L. Archer, *History of Radio to 1926* (New York: American Historical Society, 1938), 393–98; and Lowell S. Saunders, "The National Religious Broadcasters and the Availability of Commercial Radio Time" (Ph.D. diss., University of Illinois, Urbana, 1968), 31–32.

[14]Armstrong, *Electric Church*, 24.

[15]Quoted in Schultze, "Evangelical Radio," 292.

[16]Armstrong, *Electric Church*, 25.

[17]Charley Orbison, "Fighting Bob Shuler: Early Radio Crusader," *Journal of Broadcasting* 21 (Fall 1977): 459–72.

[18]Hadden and Shupe, *Televangelism*, 38–54, 86.

[19]Paul L. Maier, *A Man Spoke, A World Listened* (New York: McGraw-Hill, 1963), 69–136.

[20]Gene A. Getz, *MBI: The Story of Moody Bible Institute* (Chicago: Moody Press), 277–97.

[21]Ibid.

[22]Federal Radio Commission (1929), *Third Annual Report* (Washington, D.C.: U.S. Government Printing Office). Quoted in Schultze, "Evangelical Radio," 292–93.

[23]Schultze, "Evangelical Radio," 295.

[24]William Albig, *Public Opinion* (New York: McGraw-Hill, 1939), 447, cited in Christopher H. Sterling and John M Kittross, *Stay Tuned: A Concise History of American Broadcasting* (Belmont, Calif.: Wadsworth, 1978), 73.

[25]W. J. DuBordieu, "Religious Broadcasting in the United States" (Ph.D. diss., Northwestern University, Evanston, Ill., 1933). Cited in Schultze, "Evangelical Radio," 296.

[26]DuBordieu, "Religious Broadcasting," quoted in *Broadcasting and the Public* (New York: Abingdon, 1938), 132–33.

[27]Schultze, "Evangelical Radio," 295.

[28]*Broadcasting and the Public*, 32.

[29]Schultze, "Evangelical Radio," 295.

[30]"A Directory of Ecumenical Radio Broadcasts," *The Sunday School Times* 74 (23 January 1932): 44.

[31]Ibid., 44–45, 52.

[32]Armstrong, *Electric Church*, 20–21; and "Jazz Age Evangelism: Paul Rader and the Chicago Gospel Tabernacle 1922–1933," a pamphlet produced for an Exhibit of the Archives of the Billy Graham Center, March 16–October 27, 1984, 1–43.

[33]Clarence Jones, "Paul Rader—Pioneer of Gospel Broadcasting," included in a letter to Lyell Rader (July 23, 1960), located in the Archives of the Billy Graham Center, Wheaton, Illinois, 1–3.

[34]"Jazz Age Evangelism," 12.

[35]Paul Rader, "What About a Radio Church?" *World-Wide Christian Courier* (July 1926), 14–15.

[36]Quoted by Clarence Jones, in a letter to Lyell Rader (23 July 1960), 1–3.

[37]George H. Hill, *Airwaves to the Soul: The Influence and Growth of Religious Broadcasting in America* (Saratoga, Calif.: R & E Publishers, 1983), 7–8; and Armstrong, *Electric Church*, 23–24.

[38]Hill, *Airwaves to the Soul*, 10–11; and Armstrong, *Electric Church*, 59–60.

[39]Maier, "A Man Spoke," 110–25.

[40]Ibid.; "Maier v. Council," *Time*, 31 (11 April 1938), 47–48; and "Lutherans," *Time*, 42 (18 October 1943), 46, 48–49.

[41]Daniel P. Fuller, *Give the Winds a Mighty Voice* (Waco, Tex.: Word, 1972), 74–86.

[42]Ibid.

[43]Armstrong, *Electric Church*, 42–44; And Fuller, *Give the Winds*, 87–188.

[44]Ellens, *Models of Religious Broadcasting*, 16–18; and William F. Fore, "A Short History of Religious Broadcasting," in A. William Bluem, *Religious Television Programs: A Study of Relevance* (New York: Hastings, 1969), 203–11.

[45]Ralph M. Jennings, "Policies and Practices of Selected National Religious Bodies as Related to Broadcasting in the Public Interest, 1920–1950," (Ph.D. diss., New York University, 1968), 21–24.

[46]Hadden and Swann, *Prime Time Preachers*, 74–78; Ellens, *Models of Religious Broadcasting*, 18–20; and Horsfield, *Religious Television*, 12–15.

[47]Fore, "A Short History," 203–4; and Hadden and Swann, *Prime Time Preachers*, 27.

[48]Cited in Jennings, "Policies and Practices," 29.

[49]Jennings, "Policies and Practices," 489.

[50]Ibid., 489–90.

[51]Ibid., 490.

[52]William Martin, "Mass Communications," in Charles H. Lippy and Peter W. Williams, eds., *Encyclopedia of American Religious Experience*, vol. 3 (New York: Scribners, 1988), 1712–14; and Hadden and Swann, *Prime Time Preachers*, 78.

[53]Saunders, "National Religious Broadcasters," 105–6; Jennings, "Policies and Practices," 491; and Hadden and Swann, *Prime Time Preachers*, 78.

[54]Saunders, "National Religious Broadcasters," 106–8.

[55]Jennings, "Policies and Practices," 491; and Martin, "Mass Communications," 1714.

[56]Charles W. Crowe, "Religion on the Air," *Christian Century* 61 (23 August 1944), 973–74.

[57]Martin, "Mass Communications," 1714; and Jennings, "Policies and Practices," 492.

[58]Saunders, "National Religious Broadcasters," 113.

[59]Quoted in Hadden and Shupe, *Televangelism*, 48.

[60]James DeForest Murch, *Cooperation Without Compromise: A History of the National Association of Evangelicals* (Grand Rapids: Eerdmans. 1956): 75; and Saunders, "National Religious Broadcasters," 34.

[61]Saunders, "National Religious Broadcasters," 35–36; and Murch, *Cooperation Without Compromise*, 75.

[62]Quoted in Murch, *Cooperation Without Compromise*, 78–79. See also Saunders, "National Religious Broadcasters," 35.

[63]Glenwood Blackmore, "Shall the NCC Control Religious Broadcasting?" *United Evangelical Action* 15 (July 1956), 185.

[64]Saunders, "National Religious Broadcasters," 56–58, 218–19.

[65]Jennings, "Policies and Practices," 311.

[66]Broadcasting and Film Commission, Advisory Statement on Religious Broadcasting, 6 March 1956, quoted in Saunders, "National Religious Broadcasters," 150–51.

[67]Peter Eldersveld, sermon: "Freedom of Religion," quoted in Saunders, "National Religious Broadcasters," 153–54.

[68]Blackmore, "Shall the NCC Control Religious Broadcasting?" 185, 196.

[69]Editorial, "The Scramble for Radio-TV," *Christianity Today* 1 (18 February 1957): 23.

[70]Quoted in Saunders, "National Religious Broadcasters," 155.

[71]Ibid., 152.

[72]Editorial, *Broadcasting* (3 September 1956), 102. Quoted in Saunders, "National Religious Broadcasters," 152.

[73]Hadden and Swann, *Prime Time Preachers*, 81; and Horsfield, *Religious Television*, 1–3.

[74]Horsfield, *Religious Television*, 5–6.

[75]Armstrong, *Electric Church*, 93–97.

[76]Ellens, *Models of Religious Broadcasting*, 75; and David Edwin Harrell, *Oral Roberts: An American Life* (San Francisco: Harper & Row, 1985), 118–20.

[77]Horsfield, *Religious Television*, 13.

[78]Hadden and Shupe, *Televangelism*, 51.

[79]See Horsfield, *Religious Television*, 89; and Hadden and Shupe, *Television*, 51–52.

[80]See Wendell P. Loveless, *Manual of Gospel Broadcasting* (Chicago: Moody Press, 1946), 15.

[81]Barry Siedell, *Gospel Radio* (Lincoln, Neb.: Back to the Bible Broadcast, 1971), 14.

[82]Schultze, "Mythos of the Electronic Church," 247, 256–58.

[83]Horsfield, *Religious Television*, 18.

[84]See "Mrs. Roosevelt Attacks Lutheran Hour Preacher," *United Evangelical Action* 8 (1 October 1949): 12.

[85]See Joel A. Carpenter, "From Fundamentalism to the New Evangelical Coalition," in George Marsden, ed., *Evangelicalism and Modern America* (Grand Rapids: Eerdmans, 1984), 10–12; "The Fundamentalist Leaven and the Rise of an Evangelical United Front," in Leonard Sweet, ed., *The Evangelical Tradition in America* (Macon, Ga.: Mercer Press, 1984), 270–73; and "Fundamentalist Institutions and the Rise of Evangelical Protestantism, 1929–1942," *Church History* (March 1980), 67–73.

Part II

CONTEMPORARY EVANGELICAL MEDIA

4

SEARCHING FOR THE GREAT COMMISSION: EVANGELICAL BOOK PUBLISHING SINCE THE 1970S

JOHN P. FERRÉ

At the end of the nineteenth century, when formerly genteel American book publishers began using aggressive publicity and promotion techniques to carve out large middle-class markets, essayist Samuel Butler proclaimed the elusiveness of successful bookselling.

> There are some things which it is madness not to try to know but which it is almost as much madness to try to know. Sometimes publishers, hoping to buy the Holy Ghost with a price, fee a man to read for them and advise them. This is but as the vain tossing of insomnia. God will not have any human being know what will sell. . . .[1]

During the 1970s, evangelical publishers defied Butler's observation by issuing six books that each sold over two million copies, one of each to at least every one hundred Americans. Those remarkable best sellers were *Prison to Praise* and *Power in Praise* by Merlin Carothers, *The Late Great Planet Earth* and *Satan is Alive and Well on Planet Earth* by Hal Lindsey, *Angels: God's Secret Agents* by Billy Graham, and *Joni* by Joni Earekson. In fact, *The Late Great Planet Earth* sold over ten million copies, breaking the religious book sales record that Charles Sheldon's *In His Steps* had held for almost seventy-five years.

These best sellers signified a boom in evangelical book publishing that was part of the rise of popular evangelicalism, which followed a growing disillusionment with the social activism of the 1960s. While Harvard theologian Harvey Cox

demythologized the kingdom of God and prophesied its
realization in secular institutions, the endurance of the Vietnam
War into the second term of Richard Nixon's law-and-order
presidency, which ended in the shame of one too many
executive privileges, eroded faith in Cox's secular city.[2] Many
Americans, especially the so-called baby boomers, turned from
liberal politics, social ethics, and moral ambiguity to social
conservatism, individual piety, and biblical authority. And the
new evangelical best sellers reflected the changing American
culture. Like their secular counterparts, evangelicals acquired a
voracious appetite for answers to practical questions about
living successful lives. To help them make sense of the world,
they purchased millions of evangelical books, thrusting religious titles into the social mainstream and making the good
fortune of evangelical book publishing seem limitless.

But as *Joni*, the last of the 1970s blockbusters, was selling its
millions, Martin Marty of the University of Chicago Divinity
School foresaw the end of the era.

> It is unrealistic to picture the present prosperity continuing.
> Revivals usually breed reactions. Flows imply ebbs. The
> "free ride" the culture has given all religion is not apt to last
> too long. The public finds many religious promises un-
> fulfilled, and turns away.[3]

RELIGIOUS BOOK SALES IN UNITED STATES, 1967–1986

	Religious Book Sales (Million $)	1967 $	Average Annual Growth for Previous Decade (1967 $)
1967	108	108	
1977	304	168	5.5%
1986	685	209	2.7%

Based on John P. Dessauer, Paul D. Doebler, and Hendrik Edelman,
Christian Book Publishing & Distribution in the United States and Canada
(Tempe, Ariz.: CBA/ECPA/PCPA Joint Research Project, 1987), p. 127.

Since Marty's prediction, no religious book has sold to one
percent of the population. Moreover, as the accompanying
table illustrates, total religious book sales have slowed in the
1980s to half the annual growth rate of the 1970s. The

prosperity that evangelical publishers enjoyed in the 1970s, like the burgeoning of popular evangelicalism, has abated.

Logos International Fellowship exemplifies the recent rise and decline of evangelical publishing. A former jeweler without publishing experience, Dan Malachuk established Logos in 1967 as an Assemblies of God church, naming himself president, pastor, and elder. Logos' first book, *Run Baby Run* by Nicky Cruz, sold over eight million copies. Logos followed this blockbuster by selling more than four million copies of *Prison to Praise* by Merlin Carothers. Along with other popular titles by the likes of media revivalists Pat Robertson and Kathryn Kuhlman, Logos published a monthly magazine, *Logos Journal*, which gained more than fourteen hundred subscribers. Malachuk seemed to have the Midas touch.

But his reach eventually exceeded his grasp. In 1975, Logos bought a printing plant, hired 135 experienced Christian journalists at competitive wages, and began publishing the *National Courier*, a biweekly religious newspaper that gained a paid circulation of 110,000. In 1976, Malachuk directed the *National Courier* to drop its traditional news coverage and to focus exclusively on charismatic and other religious news. (Apparently Malachuk was concerned about the Internal Revenue Service's ongoing investigation of Assemblies of God churches.) With only a 25 percent renewal rate on subscriptions, the *National Courier* folded a year later. Logos continued publishing books and its magazine, but it never recovered the $5.5 million debt that the newspaper owed to eight hundred creditors. Eventually newspaper debts consumed book profits, and in 1981, Logos filed for bankruptcy. The publisher sold its copyrights to Bridge Publishing, a British and Canadian company, and its magazine subscription list to *Charisma* magazine.[4]

The rise and fall of Logos International Fellowship illustrates the shifting fortunes of evangelical publishing in the 1970s and 1980s. The absence of recent evangelical blockbusters, the decline in growth of religious book sales, and the failure of prominent publishers like Logos reflect an industry in recession. Although evangelical book publishing is still a significant American industry, many of its resources are now devoted to maintaining the market strength it won in the 1970s. The boom years are over. From the publishers to the wholesalers and the booksellers, evangelical book publishing is increasingly run like a business instead of a jubilant ministry. It has made great strides in the last decade toward more efficient operations and market research, but the quality of its products and its ability to penetrate the broader culture are less assured.

THE PUBLISHERS

In a sense, contemporary religious publishing is a schizophrenic industry. Its employees and trade magazines speak of the industry as a ministry, but the major publishers are now owned by public corporations whose primary "mission" is to generate profits for stockholders. This Janus-headed industry is unique in publishing history. In the early twentieth century, a tiny mail-order outfit like the Book Supply Company could sell religious blockbusters like Harold Bell Wright's *Shepherd of the Hills* and *The Calling of Dan Matthews*. Today, however, religious book publishing is dominated by denominational houses like Broadman Press (Southern Baptist) and Abingdon Press (United Methodist), and especially by Harper & Row and two publicly-owned corporations established by evangelicals: Thomas Nelson Publishers (Nashville) and Word, Inc. (Waco). In 1988 the Zondervan Corporation (Grand Rapids, Michigan), formerly one of the largest evangelical independents, became part of the Harper & Row empire.

Harper & Row is the only major trade company to maintain an aggressive religious division. General trade houses and university presses publish about one-fifth of all religious titles in the United States, and Harper & Row's annual production of some sixty-five titles comprises a significant portion of them.[5] Harper & Row is an ecumenical publisher—it produces Catholic, academic, mainline Protestant, evangelical Protestant, and new age books—so it sometimes encounters resistance by evangelical bookstores looking for doctrinally pure publishers and titles. However, the corporation's purchase of Zondervan gave it access to the largest chain (Family Bookstores) of religious bookstores in the world. Moreover, its access to other bookstores is enviable: B. Dalton, for instance, buys 90 percent of Harper & Row's religious titles.[6] A far cry from the mail-order ministries of the early 1900s, Harper & Row is part of a multinational media conglomeration, having been bought by Rupert Murdoch's News Corporation Limited in 1987.[7]

Like Harper & Row, Word and Thomas Nelson are public companies that began as small, private businesses. They grew steadily until they became predominant in the religious book industry. Despite their strength, though, each has faced financial trials common to companies in vicissitudinous industries.

Word, Inc. is a case in point. Word was founded in 1951 as a religious record company by twenty-two-year-old Jarrell McCracken, who recorded a song about a football scrimmage between good and evil called "The Game of Life." For thirty-five years, McCracken directed Word's remarkable program of recording profitable singers like Amy Grant and Evie and publishing successful writers such as psychologist James Dobson and evangelist Billy Graham. McCracken's success attracted the attention of media conglomerate ABC, which bought Word in 1974, keeping McCracken as president. However, in 1986, Capital Cities/ABC, facing its own financial crisis, pressured McCracken to resign. The changing of the corporate guard signified the plight of many evangelical entrepreneurs from an earlier era of independent publishing. According to the president of ABC publishing, the company had "to do a better job running [its] business from a profit standpoint." The house that McCracken built no longer had room for him.[8]

Thomas Nelson Publishers is another Horatio Alger story, but without the unhappy corporate ending. Although Nelson was established in the United States as a branch of its British parent in the mid-nineteenth century, its prominence in Bible publishing has more recent roots. Arriving in South Carolina from Lebanon in 1950 with only $600, Sam Moore paid for his education by selling Bibles door to door. In 1957, Moore borrowed $2000 to establish the National Book Company, a sales organization based in Nashville. In 1961, Moore founded the Royal Publishing Company, which went public the following year. Royal Publishing bought Nelson in 1969 for $2.6 million. Nelson had exclusive rights to publish the profitable Revised Standard Version of the Bible. The company also enlisted one hundred evangelical scholars, editors, and church leaders to produce the New King James Bible, an updated King James Version for which Nelson has exclusive publishing rights. Most of Nelson's income comes from five hundred varieties of Bibles in six translations.[9]

In the early 1980s, Nelson tried to expand its operations to Christian romance novels, archaeology books, academic books, teaching cassettes, and films. The company even bought Dodd-Mead in order to enhance its position in secular publishing. The expansion failed, however, and Nelson lost $5.3 million in 1985. It soon sold Dodd-Mead and other operations and laid off dozens of employees, including over half of the book division. Nelson found itself back in the business of selling its staples of Bibles and reference, trade, and children's books.[10]

Like Nelson, Harper & Row's evangelical subsidiary, the Zondervan Corporation, climbed the industry ladder through aggressive Bible publishing. Started by Patrick and Bernard Zondervan in the back bedroom of a farmhouse near Grand Rapids, the company acquired one of the most profitable Bible versions of all time—the New International Version (NIV). Because Zondervan provided the seed money, it secured a thirty-year exclusive publishing agreement with the New York International Bible Society to publish the NIV. Zondervan has sold one-third of the forty million NIV Bibles, New Testaments, and Parallels that have been published. Books like *Halley's Bible Handbook*, Cowman's *Streams in the Desert*, and Lindsey's *Late Great Planet Earth* gave Zondervan reason to call itself "The House of the Million Sellers."[11] Zondervan's status as a family-controlled but publicly owned corporation ended in 1988 when Harper & Row purchased it for $57 million. This purchase made Harper & Row the largest publisher of religious books in the United States, and perhaps the world.

Corporate success seems to have led evangelical publishers naturally into the world of public ownership, but not without an expensive price in limited editorial freedom. By selling stock on the open market, companies such as Word and Zondervan raised needed cash for expansion and acquisition. But public ownership also shifted the primary responsibility from the production of books to the enhancement of shareholders' investments. The shift was sometimes subtle, given that these publishers still produced evangelical books. Still, ministry gave way to marketing as management's goals changed. For a publicly owned evangelical publisher and bookseller, observance of the Sabbath might prove irresponsible, as would the publication of a book the editorial board believes is valuable but limited in appeal. In a growing number of situations, such a publisher would defy the interests of the shareholders only at great peril. Moreover, public ownership made evangelical publishers exceedingly vulnerable to takeovers by semi-friendly corporations hoping to gain a foothold in the evangelical market and to skim some of the financial cream from rights to Bible translations.

Harper & Row, Zondervan, Word, and Nelson may control a sizeable portion of the religious book market, but they face stiff competition from denominational presses, which enjoy the benefits of tax-exemption, as well as from a number of smaller publishers. The most notable newcomer is Multnomah Press of Portland, Oregon, established in 1969 under the auspices of Multnomah School of the Bible. Multnomah publishes thirty to forty new books a year and has 240 titles in its backlist, the bread and butter of religious book publishers. Multnomah signed such popular authors as Charles Swindoll and James Dobson. It has earned the respect of other evangelical publishers, winning several Gold Medallion awards from the Evangelical Christian Publishers Association[12] and being named in 1987 with Augsburg, Harper & Row, Zondervan, and Abingdon as one of the most highly regarded evangelical publishers in an industry survey.[13]

Regardless of the size or ownership of evangelical publishers, they are widely criticized within evangelicalism for their growing business mentality. To some observers of evangelical publishing, the decline in growth is just deserts for an industry long on the bottom line and short on literary and intellectual integrity. According to *Wittenburg Door* editor Mike Yaconelli, "the focus of Christian publishing has changed from providing resources for the church to making money." He contends that the phenomenal sales of *The Late Great Planet Earth*, in which a former riverboat captain linked contemporary world history to the imminent return of Christ, prompted Christian publishers and booksellers to focus on profits. "Why else would Zondervan publish the autobiography of former automobile industry executive John Delorean?" Yaconelli asks. "Surely not because of the great theological insights gained from over one year of being a Christian."[14] John H. Timmerman of Calvin College likewise decries the growth of commercialism, charging that religious publishers are usually more interested in whether a book will sell than in whether the book is worth selling in the first place. Publishers, he says, want books that are short and zippy, and they willingly sacrifice nuance and rhetorical flair to that end. "In the commercial approach to publishing," Timmerman says, "writing is not unlike commercial advertising, selling ideas in neat little packages."[15]

Many other writers who bemoan the poor quality of evangelical books blame the evangelical market more than the evangelical publishers. These writers indict contemporary evangelical books, first, for their parochialism. They question the books' evangelistic power given the fact that nearly all of them are written of, by, and for evangelicals. They say such books offer piety for the pious, and often in jargon or a dialect of Bible babble.[16] These critics indict evangelical books, second, for being simplistic. Floyd Thatcher, former editor-in-chief of Word Books, complains about what he calls the "hype of electronic Elmer-Gantry types" with their "ill-conceived razzle-dazzle, a series of sin-suffer-repent exposés, poured out passionately and hysterically, but failing to deal responsibly with the complexities and spiritual needs of life."[17] Similarly, Philip Yancey of *Christianity Today* argues that evangelical authors who gloss over ambiguous realities may find tolerance from true believers, but they will surely be rejected by the formerly curious.

> The Christian public will applaud books in which every prayer is answered and every disease is healed, but to the degree those books do not reflect reality, they will become meaningless to a skeptical audience. Too often our evangelical literature appears to a larger world as strange and unconvincing as a Moonie tract or *Daily Worker* newspaper.[18]

Critics like Yancey call for honesty and complexity, for books that discover instead of rationalize, for authors who understand doubt and disbelief before they dispense their faith. Critics argue, third, that evangelical books are mediocre. With the exception of classics from previous eras—books by G. K. Chesterton, C. S. Lewis, George MacDonald, J. R. R. Tolkien, and Dorothy Sayer—Christian fiction of the twentieth century is notorious for its heroes-and-villains plots and lobotomized characters. "Among the books produced by evangelical authors today, good fiction is as rare as a snowflake in Florida," Yancey says.[19] These critics view evangelical nonfiction with equal dismay. Thatcher complains of drabness and irrelevance; rare is the quality of *Pilgrim at Tinker Creek* by Annie Dillard or *Celebration of Discipline* by Richard J. Foster.[20]

BOOK DISTRIBUTORS

Until recently, the plethora of small evangelical bookstores bought their stock directly from a myriad of publishers. Book ordering and shipping was a clerical and logistical nightmare that rendered the industry almost inescapably inefficient and costly. Without the standard Bibles and celebrity authors, such a system would have died long ago. Even after publishers computerized shipping and billing in the 1970s and 1980s, the myriad of publishers made it inefficient for bookstores to maintain their inventory and to serve the growing number of customers placing special orders for unstocked titles. Perhaps the most revolutionary development in evangelical book distribution is the growing dominance of influential wholesalers.[21] Bookstores generally place their initial orders with publishers and restock their shelves with books from the wholesalers.[22] The first national wholesaler of religious books was short-lived. Ingram Book Company of Nashville launched Reedwood House in 1976, but by the end of the following year it had only three hundred subscribers. Unable to penetrate the religious bookstore market, Reedwood was phased into Ingram, whose microfiches now list both religious and secular titles. Today Ingram targets religious departments in secular stores, foregoing religious bookstores altogether.

A year after Reedwood House folded, Spring Arbor Distributors was founded in Belleville, Michigan. Unlike Reedwood House, which had difficulty deciding what to stock and which never penetrated the religious bookstore market, Spring Arbor succeeded on both counts almost immediately. Perhaps Spring Arbor's success was the result of the experience of James E. Carlson, its founder, who attended Gordon-Conwell Seminary near Boston, served for several years as a counselor with InterVarsity Christian Fellowship, and founded the Association of Logos Bookstores. Carlson understood the evangelical book world.

Spring Arbor serves three thousand trade stores, including the B. Dalton and Walden chains, and has captured the religious bookstore business. This wholesale supermarket of religious products stocks 50,000 different items including 20,000 book titles and 3700 types of the Bible. It ships orders within twenty-four hours from its warehouses located around the country. Publishers sell Spring Arbor books at a "long" discount (50–55 percent), which enables the distributor to sell them at up to a 40 percent discount to stores. Spring Arbor's twenty-item or $100 retail minimum drives away few stores because it can be met with products from some five hundred vendors. Besides offering numerous titles and quick shipping, Spring Arbor has two other services for bookstores. One is an inventory list with a semimonthly report on which books are selling and which authors are scheduled for television appearances so that stores can do promotional tie-ins. The other service is a model inventory, a report geared to an individual store's size that recommends what titles to stock and in what quantity, based on figures of current and perennial best sellers. Despite resistance from both publishers and booksellers who believe that wholesaling diminishes their profits and from authors who worry that wholesaling reduces their royalties, Spring Arbor's product sales for 1988–89 totaled $95 million, a twelvefold increase from 1980.[23]

Another growing area of evangelical wholesaling is remainders, unsold books that can sell briskly when marked down as much as 80 percent on bargain tables. The remainder market enables publishers to clear valuable warehouse space rapidly and recoup some of the costs of printing, promoting, and editing. Remainders also help bookstores attract bargain-hunters and they save buyers money on books, some of which are notable titles by known authors. Religious remainders will never be a large market, however, because the rate of return for religious books is only 11 percent. As Ted Andrews, former executive director of the Evangelical Christian Publishers Association, says, "Booksellers feel that if they can't sell a book today, they'll sell it tomorrow."[24]

The major wholesaler of evangelical remainders is Book Bargains of Westwood, New Jersey, which began in 1981 and regularly stocks over seven hundred titles. Book Bargains not only sells remainders to bookstores, but through its parent, Barbour and Company, Inc., it also republishes remaindered titles that have received a second life on the bargain table, some of which sell better as remainders than they did initially. Barbour and Company also issues inexpensive hardbound editions of such perennial titles as *Pilgrim's Progress* and *In His Steps*.[25] Other companies in the religious remainder business are Baker Book House of Grand Rapids and Cokesbury, the United Methodist chain, which sells remainders through mail order catalogs.[26] Zondervan operates one factory outlet in Grand Rapids, where its own titles returned by stores outside the Family Bookstore chain are sold at discount prices. Within the chain, slow-moving Zondervan titles are discounted in each individual store.[27]

EVANGELICAL BOOKSTORES AND MARKETS

Most of the sixty-five hundred religious bookstores in the United States are small, independent outlets that make much of their profit on knickknacks and cards. But like the family publishers that were transformed into public corporations, bookstores are slowly becoming bureaucratized and centralized. Southern Baptist Bookstores' sixty-two outlets constitute the largest denominational chain. The largest nondenominational chain is Family Bookstores, begun in 1932, one year after the Zondervan brothers went into business. With eighty-two outlets, including two in Great Britain, Family Bookstores is the fourth largest bookstore chain in the country, behind only Waldenbooks, B. Dalton Booksellers, and Crown. Zondervan sells more than just its own products; in fact, only 18 percent of its sales are Zondervan's own books and records.[28] Family Bookstores' sole independent religious rival is the Association of Logos Bookstores. Begun in Ann Arbor, Michigan, as part of InterVarsity Christian Fellowship, Logos also publishes its own titles. In the 1970s, Logos expanded into an association of over eighty member-owned stores in the United States and Canada; two decades later the Association included less than half as many. Most of the Logos stores are for-profit, some are not-for-profit.[29]

The increasing centralization of the industry is problematic because booksellers and publishers are idea brokers who decide which ideas can be presented to the public and in what form. Media researchers refer to this role as gatekeeping, harking back to a study of a Peoria newspaper editor in the 1950s who refused to publish information flattering to the Roman Catholic Church or the Soviet Union. Although a potentially endless variety of religious ideas may be conceived, they must pass muster with publishers and booksellers alike before the reading public can entertain them. Ideas can stop at the "in" box of an editor's desk or at the briefcase of a publisher's representative. For evangelical publishing, which has always been sensitive to the demands of what Nathan Hatch calls the "sovereign audience," this gatekeeping has been both a blessing and a curse.

A religious publisher's initial approval of a manuscript does not guarantee a book's availability to readers, however. Such was InterVarsity's recent experience with *Brave New People*, a book on biomedical ethics by D. Gareth Jones, an evangelical who teaches anatomy at Otago University in New Zealand. In *Brave New People*, Jones said that therapeutic abortion may sometimes be "the least tragic of a number of tragic options." His ambivalence concerning cases such as Lesch-Nyhan syndrome, a genetic disorder that leads to uncontrollable self-mutilation, vomiting, screaming, and childhood death, was enough to raise the ire of a few very vocal pro-life groups. The Christian Action Council claimed that *Brave New People* "lent Christian respectability to the 'pro-choice' position" and urged subscribers to write to InterVarsity Press. The Pro-Life Action League of Chicago picketed InterVarsity Press headquarters in Downers Grove, Illinois, with placards reading "IVP Revives Eugenics" and "Unborn Babies Feel Pain."[30] And fundamentalist author Franky Schaeffer circulated a letter at the Christian Booksellers Association convention in which he called *Brave New People* "coercive, leftist, and pro-abortion," and advocated a boycott of all InterVarsity Press books.[31] InterVarsity withdrew the book from sale, complaining that abortion was no longer a debatable issue among evangelicals. The author, too, complained of unfair treatment:

> Many evangelicals and fundamentalists complain bitterly about the humanist bias of the media in America and also of the difficulty of getting a fair hearing for the evangelical point-of-view. Unfortunately, these same people do not appear to be worried about stifling freedom of expression when it suits their own purposes. Neither do they worry about unfair bias when it works in favour of their cause. It should not surprise us then, that those outside evangelicalism look with suspicion on our claims to revere freedom of expression and opinion.[32]

Usually publishers avoid public offense by rejecting manuscripts; the above-mentioned case of gatekeeping is notable because it occurred after publication. Although Eerdmans Publishing Company subsequently published *Brave New People*, evangelical publishers may have learned to toe the evangelical hard line. As a letter to InterVarsity asked, "So where does it stop? Whose book is next? What effect does this decision have on the editors of the press in their attempts to secure relevant manuscripts? What are the new criteria by which writers for IVP are to be judged?"[33] Prudence is central to gatekeeping.

Bookstores can keep the gate of ideas closed just as effectively as can publishers. Nathan and An Keats founded Keats Publishing, Inc. in New Canaan, Connecticut, in 1971 as a publisher of religion and health books. "We're not a religious house," Nathan Keats says, "but we publish religious books." Among their first titles was *Prophet of Destiny* by Ellen G. White, a Seventh-day Adventist. They managed to sell sixty thousand copies, but Nathan Keats learned a lesson in the process: "I wanted to start a line of religious books—Jewish, Unitarian, evangelical, whatever. But I learned fast that your religious line has to be evangelical or related in order to gain acceptance in most Christian bookstores."[34] Keats eventually found its religious niche with the Shepherd Illustrated Classics and Large Type Christian Classics. By publishing acceptable books such as James Stalker's *The Example of Jesus Christ* and Thomas à Kempis's *Imitation of Christ*, Keats avoided the disfavor of evangelical bookstores.[35]

Evangelical publishers and bookstores have every right to select what they will sell and to refuse titles antithetical to their professed mission. A pluralistic democracy requires not that all publishers issue variety, but that there be other avenues for the circulation of ideas that any one group may reject. If the world of religious books becomes dominated by any particular faith or group, then what the public is allowed to choose from becomes narrow and safe because little that lacks an imprimatur can reach it. Evangelicals have repeatedly shown that despite their diversity, they are often suspicious of the ideas of other faiths.

Nevertheless, in recent years evangelicals have expressed far greater concern with secular gatekeepers than with gatekeepers within their own ranks. Besides complaining about the secular books used in public schools, they have groused frequently and provocatively about the news media's inattention to their own books. Even when sales of evangelical books are brisk and voluminous, the most popular titles rarely appear on the prestigious and influential best-seller lists of the *New York Times* and *Washington Post*. The exceptions to this rule are notable: Robert Schuller's *Tough Times Never Last, but Tough People Do!* and *Tough-Minded Faith for Tenderhearted People*, Billy Graham's *Approaching Hoofbeats: The Four Horsemen of the Apocalypse*, and Peter and Barbara Jenkins' *Walk West*. Usually, though, religious titles are conspicuously absent, which leads some evangelicals to complain that the press either ignores or censors them. And it leads religious bookstores to wonder about lost revenues, since best-seller lists undoubtedly affect sales.

According to the *Times*, however, the rarity of religious titles on its list has to do with their marketing, not their message. In an article on religious publishing, *Times* reporter Edwin McDowell explained.

Most of the 100 or so religious book publishers are private, denominational firms that sell their wares by direct mail, through religious book clubs, in discount stores and convenience markets and in some 5,000 religious bookstores, which tend to be small "mom-and-pop" operations. All these marketing techniques help religious books reach wider audiences than they would otherwise, but they also explain why even runaway religious best sellers rarely show up on the best-seller lists of the *New York Times Book Review* and other publications, which report only the sales of trade or "general interest" books.[36]

In other words, only when religious titles sell rapidly in general-interest bookstores like Waldenbooks or Kroch's and Brentano's, the types of stores that newspapers survey, will they appear on the best-seller lists in Sunday newspapers.

Evangelical best-seller lists are just as exclusive as their secular counterparts; they too survey sales at their own outlets, including stores and Spring Arbor Distributors, which publishes its own list. In fact, *Bookstore Journal*, the monthly publication of the Christian Booksellers Association, did not list Robert Schuller's *Tough Times Never Last, but Tough People Do!* as a best seller because most of the copies sold through general-interest, and not evangelical, stores. Of course, religious best-seller lists never include general-interest best sellers. No list reflects what books have sold the most in the United States during the past week; instead, there are religious lists and general-interest lists, a sacred-secular split.

Evangelical authors and book outlets have criticized this sacred-secular dichotomy. Millionaire businessman Jerry Nims invested substantially in the promotion of Francis Schaeffer's *Christian Manifesto*, which sold some 300,000 copies. Angered because it never appeared on the best-seller list of the *Washington Post*, Nims asked *Post* editor Ben Bradlee for an explanation. Predictably, Bradlee explained that the book was not selling in general-interest stores. Nims, however, says that it did not sell in general-interest stores because general-interest publications like the *Post* would not review the book, following a policy that keeps evangelical viewpoints off of the public agenda.[37] Cal Thomas, former vice-president for communications of the Moral Majority, put the point bluntly. "The *New York Times* list," he said, "is a phony best-seller list. It does not deal with total sales in all stores. It is a gerrymandered system that routinely excludes the Christian sales."[38]

Such arguments about best-seller lists seem curiously self-contradictory. On the one hand is the desire for general-interest stores to stock evangelical titles, for general-interest publications to review these books, and then for general-interest publications to acknowledge evangelical best-sellers. This desire makes perfect sense because its fulfillment would presumably boost sales and open new channels for evangelism. On the other hand, evangelical separatism is evidenced in publishers who produce only "Bible-based" books, bookstores that carry only narrowly defined "Christian" titles, and the Christian Booksellers Association, an organization for the advancement of evangelical publishers and bookstores. Although in a pluralistic society it is expected that subgroups will maintain a strong sense of self-identity, evangelicals who complain that the *New York Times* and *Time* magazine routinely ignore them are asking for something more. They are asking for recognition and legitimation by the very culture that they reject. To paraphrase H. Richard Niebuhr, they want their Christ against culture and Christ of culture, too.[39]

THE FUTURE OF EVANGELICAL BOOK PUBLISHING

Despite improvements in wholesaling and the expansion of bookstore chains, a $75,000 study commissioned jointly by the Christian Booksellers Association, the Evangelical Christian Publishers Association, and the Protestant Church-Owned Publishers Association criticized the industry for ignoring religious book readers. The report asks,

> What could be more beneficial than to learn more about book customers, their identities, similarities, differences, lifestyles, backgrounds, spiritual commitments, reading habits, buying habits, interests, likes and dislikes, reactions to books read in the past, requests for new titles, etc., etc.? What could be more logical than to use a panel of readers as a sounding board before deciding to publish a title, adopt a cover design, or choose an advertising approach?[40]

The report urged publishers to base their publication schedule on audience research and involvement rather than waiting for manuscripts to arrive over the transom. Likewise, the report encouraged booksellers to broaden their local markets with tailored direct-mail campaigns designed to increase store traffic. Finally, the report optimistically claimed that publishers and booksellers can revitalize sales with aggressive marketing, finding an additional fifteen million people to buy between two and four religious books every year throughout the 1990s.[41] Finding fifteen million buyers of evangelical books will be difficult, however, because a small percentage of people buy the majority of books. At the very most, only 15 percent of adults regularly read religious books. The typical reader is a married evangelical woman, twenty-five to forty-nine, who lives in the Sun Belt from California to Georgia. She earns a moderate income, is at least high school educated, and attends church regularly. Evangelical book buyers are a committed, but relatively small, group of people.[42]

According to the report, evangelical publishers needed a concerted "outreach program" to tide them over until the next period of prosperity, which will occur on schedule during the decade of 2000–2010. These years, predicted the report, will see "one or several religious revivals" that occur cyclically in American history. The first part of the cycle is what the report called "seeding," an era in which new religious groups and heavy immigration introduce a challenge to the religious establishment. The challenge becomes an "upheaval," a period usually noted by the growth of evangelicalism. As institutions absorb the challenges of evangelicalism, upheaval subsides, and the churches enter a period of "consolidation." The report concluded that the upheaval stage was ending and consolidation was beginning in the late 1980s. Because the momentum that spurred the growth of evangelical publishing during the 1970s had subsided, the industry needed shrewd marketing to maintain its strength.[43] The advice of the report resembled that of the rabbi in *Fiddler on the Roof* who is asked whether forced emigration is a signal of the Messiah's coming. "We'll have to wait someplace else," the rabbi says. "In the meantime, let's start packing." The report hedged, "We'll have to wait for another revival. In the meantime, let's start marketing."

The report itself was a remarkable testimony to the state of the American evangelical book-publishing industry. Optimistic in the face of obvious industry decline, the report reflected evangelicalism's long-standing optimism about its own future. And placing such hope in the hands of marketing and promotional techniques, the report echoed evangelicalism's close affinity to mass persuasion and free-enterprise capitalism. The report revealed an optimistic but worried industry in search of solutions, an industry, as Butler said, "hoping to buy the Holy Ghost with a price."

Although it comes as no consolation for publishers and booksellers who have budgets to meet, downturns in religious book sales do occur occasionally. There was no reason to believe that the boom of sales in the 1970s would continue. Indeed, only a few years before, religious publishers had been predicting their own demise! In 1970, Doubleday editor John J. Delaney said, "We are in the most critical situation religious publishing has ever experienced in the United States,"[44] and Werner M. Linz, executive vice-president of Herder and Herder concurred: "It seems to have been generally proven that no publisher can live by publishing religious books alone."[45] The circumstances, in retrospect, were no more dire than those of the late 1980s, but they were sufficient cause for caution. At least for the time being, the public has stopped buying evangelical books by the bushel even though marketing and distribution are better coordinated and more efficient than ever. Apparently, much of the audience has turned to other books or to new video technologies. Perhaps evangelicalism itself is experiencing a general decline.

Nevertheless, not all of the readers are gone. Christian book publishing is a billion-dollar industry, still selling a lot of books. Only now it is selling almost exclusively to the evangelical subculture, hardly penetrating the broader culture. The evangelical publishing industry—from writers and publishers to wholesalers and bookstores—defines its audience as the already devout; it rarely includes doubters and disbelievers. Perhaps the plethora of Christian bookstores and publishers has robbed writers of the incentive to produce works compelling to those outside the fold. Whatever the reason, evangelical book publishing serves more of a pastoral than an evangelistic role—an irony, clearly, but one with benefits, as Martin Marty noted: "Tribalism . . . can . . . be a creative deterrent to totalitarian Bigness in church as in world. It helps give value to group life in a day when super-individualism often drives people into do-it-yourself religion and utterly private world views."[46] Indeed, evangelical books do not have to reach beyond their devotees to perform a service.

Throughout the twentieth century, religious titles have accounted for about 5 percent of all books published in the United States. Despite the recent cooling of sales, this figure still holds true, indicating an enduring industry. Evangelicalism

116 I **John P. Ferré**

may have faded somewhat from the cultural limelight, but it remains a dominant force in religious book sales and a subcultural mainstay. Evangelical publishing, for all of its problems, is testimony to the endurance of that subculture.

NOTES

[1]Henry Festing Jones, ed., *The Note-Books of Samuel Butler* (New York: Dutton, 1912), 160.

[2]Harvey Cox, *The Secular City*, rev. ed. (New York: Macmillan, 1966).

[3]Martin E. Marty, "A Spiritual Revival, a Commercial Boom, and yet . . . ," *Publishers Weekly*, 13 February 1978, 84.

[4]Rodney Clapp and J. Alan Youngren, "Logos Publishing, High-Flier in the '70s, Files Bankruptcy," *Christianity Today*, 6 November 1981, 69, 88; "Publisher Bankrupt," *Christian Century*, 16 December 1981, 1305.

[5]Stella Dong, "Faith in the Trade Houses," *New York Times Book Review*, 11 April 1987, 12.

[6]Jerome P. Frank, "Harper's 'Bishop' Reflects on 50+ Years of Religious Bookselling," *Publishers Weekly*, 4 March 1983, 66.

[7]Lisa See, "Harper, San Francisco: Experienced at Weathering Change," *Publishers Weekly*, 31 July 1987, 49.

[8]"McCracken Leaves Word, Publishing House He Started," *Christianity Today*, 17 October 1986, 48.

[9]Madalynne Reuter, "Nelson, Bible Publisher, to Acquire Dodd, Mead," *Publishers Weekly*, 1 January 1982, 12; Edwin McDowell, "Publishers: A Matter of Faith," *New York Times Book Review*, 6 April 1980, 8.

[10]Dale D. Buss., "The Problems at the 'Big Three,'" *Christianity Today*, 17 October 1986, 60–61.

[11]LeRoy Koopman, "The Netherlands Quartet," *Publishers Weekly*, 26 September 1980, 63–64; Charles Storch, "Murdoch Faces Battle for Evangelical Publisher," *Chicago Tribune*, 19 July 1988, sec. 3, p. 4; telephone interview with Mark Rice, Supervisor of Market Research for Books and Bibles, Zondervan Publishing House, 12 September 1988.

[12]Roy Paul Nelson, "The Multnomah Formula," *Publishers Weekly*, 6 March 1987, 41–42.

[13]John P. Dessauer, Paul D. Doebler, and Hendrik Edelman, *Christian Book Publishing & Distribution in the United States and Canada* (Tempe, Ariz.: CBA/ECPA/PCPA Joint Research Project, 1987), 72.

[14]"Religious Flea Market," *Christian Century*, 30 October 1985, 967–68.

[15]John H. Timmerman, "Train of Robes, Plume of Feathers: Rhetoric in the Religious Publishing House," *The Cresset*, October 1986, 12.

[16]Philip Yancey, *Open Windows* (Westchester, Ill.: Crossway, 1982), 176–78.

[17]Floyd Thatcher, "Welcome to a New Breed of Religious Writers (And About Time, Too)," *Publishers Weekly*, 4 March 1986, 46.

[18]Yancey, "Open Windows," 182.

[19]Ibid., 204.

[20]Thatcher, "Welcome," 46.

[21]Dessauer, Doebler, and Edelman, *Christian Book Publishing*, 108–9.

[22]Judith S. Duke, *Religious Publishing and Communications* (White Plains, N.Y.: Knowledge Industry Publications, 1981), 104.

[23]Bill Dunn, "Spreading the Word by Discount and Computer," *Publishers Weekly*, 9 March 1984, 39–41. Telephone interview with David B. Dykhouse, vice-president for marketing development, Spring Arbor Distributors, 8 March 1990.

[24]Lisa See, "Speaking for the Evangelical Publishers," *Publishers Weekly*, 30 September 1983, 59.

[25]Hugh R. Barbour and Bruce R. Barbour, "Born Again Books," *Publishers Weekly*, 28 September 1984, 52–53.

[26]Gerald N. Battle, "The Unexploited Part of the Remainder Explosion," *Publishers Weekly*, 24 September 1979, 42–43.

[27]Chris Meehan, "Carrying the Christian Message: Zondervan's Mission and Marketing Goals Translate into Retail Expansion," *Publishers Weekly*, 9 March 1984, 90–93.

[28]Ibid., 90–93.

[29]Stanley P. Shank, "A Word about Logos," *Publishers Weekly*, 26 September 1980, 60–61.

[30]Randy Frame, "InterVarsity Withdraws a Book Opposed by Pro-lifers," *Christianity Today*, 21 September 1984, 63, 66.

[31]Franky Schaeffer, "An Open Letter to the Christian Booksellers Association and Christian Bookstore Owners and Buyers in America," 1984.

[32]D. Gareth Jones, "A View from a Censored Corner," *Journal of the American Scientific Affiliation* 37 (September 1985):175.

[33]James W. Sire, "Brave New Publishers: Should They be Censored?" in *Evangelicalism: Surviving Its Success*, ed. The Evangelical Round Table (St. Davids, Penn.: Eastern College and the Eastern Baptist Theological Seminary, 1987), 142.

[34]Judd P. Anderson, "Soul and Body Catered to at Keats," *Publishers Weekly*, 1 October 1982, 49.

[35]Anderson, "Soul and Body," 48–49.

[36]McDowell, "Publishers," 8.

[37]Randy Frame, "Jerry Nims: Backing Books from the Religious Right," *Christianity Today*, 26 November 1982, 38–40.

[38]Steve Rabey, "Despite Recent Breakthroughs, Most Christian Books Don't Make Best-Seller Lists," *Christianity Today*, 17 February 1984, 45.

[39]H. Richard Niebuhr, *Christ and Culture* (New York: Harper & Row, 1951).

[40]Dessauer, Doebler, and Edelman, *Christian Book Publishing*, 85–86. The College of Arts and Sciences at the University of Louisville provided funding for the purchase of this report.

[41]Ibid., 140–41.

[42]Duke, *Religious Publishing*, 13; Dessauer, Doebler, and Edelman, *Christian Book Publishing*, 102, 125.

[43]Dessauer, Doebler, and Edelman, *Christian Book Publishing*, 97–98.

[44]"Publishers Comment on Problems and Opportunities of Religious Publishing Today," *Religious Book Guide for Booksellers and Libraries*, (January–February 1970):13.

[45]Werner Linz, "Surviving: A Report on the Present and Future of Religious Publishing," *Religious Book Guide for Booksellers and Libraries*, (May–June 1970): 10, 12.

[46]Marty, "A Spiritual Revival," 84.

5

MOVING THE WORLD WITH MAGAZINES: A SURVEY OF EVANGELICAL PERIODICALS

STEPHEN BOARD

If magazines are "the interior dialogue of a society," as John F. Kennedy declared, the conversation is indeed rich and noisy. There are 111,000 periodicals around the world[1] and almost exactly one-tenth of these are in the United States.[2] While very few may be "storehouses," as the etymology of the word "magazine" implies, all promise reading of timely interest in accessible format for their audiences. Most of them benefit from preferential postage rates, a centuries-old bias in favor of keeping the interior dialogue going.

To factor by tenths once more, it appears about one-tenth of the magazines in the United States can be categorized as "religious."[3] From *Christian History*, a 1741 magazine that lasted two years, to *Christian Parenting*, which began in 1988 with higher hopes for longevity, the Protestant press has never lacked for publishing ideas.[4]

Since World War II, the evangelical scene has flourished with para-church organizations, missions, broadcasts, and schools. Periodicals have been a major part of the growth of this venture in Christian free enterprise, breaking down old denominational barriers, introducing new leaders and ideas, and providing access by mail to numerous homes for ideas that the pulpit alone would never broach. The 315 current members of the Evangelical Press Association, a professional society begun in 1949, range from little more than advertising pieces to journals of record.

A TYPOLOGY OF RELIGIOUS MAGAZINES

Only dates, paper, and ink are necessary to call reading-matter a magazine, and some taxonomy will be useful to classify the variety. If we arrange the variety of periodicals around two characteristics, we discover a matrix (see figure 1) into which, without too large a shoehorn, most of the periodicals seem to fit. The two principles are (1) the degree of sensitivity to the readership and (2) the degree of control by an establishment, such as a denomination.

From less official to more

Independence → Official Body

| | The agenda is that of the vision or cause of the owner or chief supporters.

I. | The agenda is that of the organization and its promotional program.

II. | |
| C a u s e D r i v e n M a r k e t | The agenda is regulated by the subscribers or target market.

IV. | The agenda is that of a constituency sharing a common membership.

III. | Increasing degree of control by readers |

Figure 1

A position left to right charts the publication's attachment to an established body, such as a denomination or para-church institution. An entrepreneur would be in the left corner; a church body in the right.

Up-and-down, the matrix illustrates a lesser or greater degree of deference to an audience. Toward the top are those fortunate publications that consult only their own owners, charters and passions; those toward the bottom attend more to the tastes and interests of readers. These may be consumers (left quadrant) or members (right quadrant).[5]

Now let us look at the Christian magazine world with this device, using examples from present and past, and see whence and whither the journalist comes. Moving clockwise (see figure 2) from the top left:

	Independence	Official Body	
C a u s e D r i v e n M a r k e t	The agenda is that of the vision or cause of the owner or chief supporters.	The agenda is that of the organization and its promotional program.	Increasing degree of control by readers
	Examples: *The Liberator, The Presbyterian Layman, Sojourners, The Other Side,* the early *Christianity Today, Good News, Christian Beacon*	Examples: Publications that go to donors such as mission magazines. *World Vision, Possibilities, Decision, ABS Record, Abundant Life*	
	The agenda is regulated by the subscribers or target market.	The agenda is that of a constituency sharing a common membership.	
	Examples: The later *Christianity Today, Charisma,* the later *His [U], Christian Life, Eternity, Christian Century, Moody Monthly, Christian Herald.*	Examples: Denominational organs, alumni or scholarly magazines. *The Banner, The Church Herald, The Evangelical Beacon, CMS Journal, Journal of the American Scientific Affiliation, United Evangelical Action*	

Figure 2

Tracts for the Times: Publishing for a Cause

The independently owned advocacy publishers promote and combat ideas. This is propaganda in the best and worst senses of the word. They face the world with a message, pay for its dissemination, and submit gladly to the abuse that has fallen on prophets throughout history. William Lloyd Garrison's *Public Liberator and Journal of the Times*, begun in 1831, announced the tradition:

> I will be as harsh as truth, and as uncompromising as justice. On this subject [of slavery] I do not wish to think, or speak, or write, with moderation . . . I am in earnest—I will not equivocate—I will not excuse—I will not retreat a single inch—**AND I WILL BE HEARD**.[6]

The "cause" may be antiabortion, antialcohol, anticommunism, antislavery. Less commonly has been a cause promoting a positive message, even evangelism.[7]

Among modern publications in evangelical circles, I would surely put here the now-defunct *Moral Majority Report* (Jerry Falwell) with eight hundred thousand free circulation at its peak, and *Focus on the Family* (James Dobson) with 1.1 million. Likewise the *Christian Beacon*, Carl McIntire's weekly, has crusaded for separatism and anticommunism.

A number of conservative protest publications within denominations have left their marks. *The Presbyterian Journal* (1941–1987) advocated conservative theology in the Southern Presbyterian Church and was finally instrumental in the founding of a secessionist body, the Presbyterian Church in America (1973). A similar Methodist voice, *Good News*, has given a monthly "forum for biblical Christianity" to the nation's second largest Protestant denomination. *The New Oxford Review* began as a voice for conservative Episcopalians, evolving later into a de facto Roman Catholic voice. The early *Christianity Today* was very much an advocacy publication.

Billy Graham was the organizing force behind *Christianity Today*, drawing in a number of evangelical leaders in the mid-fifties. And its first editor, as early as 1946, voiced the tones of the publisher-with-a-cause in a letter to Wilbur Smith.

> The hour is ripe for an evangelical magazine. My hope is that when such a magazine is launched, it will center attention on the great essentials that we may be hammering away at the main enemy fortresses and not at our own outposts which some extremists of conservative convictions themselves may be holding. Perhaps it could display enough editorial acumen to permit reprinting of certain articles each year in book form by appropriate assignment of contributions.[8]

The Presbyterian Layman, one of at least two efforts funded by J. Howard Pew, the chairman of Sun Oil, with a free circulation as high as four hundred thousand, has been a monthly for exposure and complaint in the United Presbyterian denomination (now Presbyterian Church, USA). The same benefactor contributed heavily to the early years of *Christianity Today*. Mr. Pew felt that a publication for the nation's clergy could persuade and restore them to a conservative view, theologically and socially, and that as the clergy went, so went the church. Consequently, the early years of this "fortnightly of evangelical conviction" (*C.T.*) were heavily subsidized to enable the publication to go to well over two hundred thousand Protestant clergyman free from 1956 to the early sixties.

Sojourners (1968) and *The Other Side* (1965) were born out of the sixties' peace and civil-rights movements, respectively. While never heavily funded or widely promoted, they enjoyed a de facto subsidy through very modestly compensated staff and some donations from sympathetic subscribers. In the seventies they turned more toward antinuclear and feminist messages.

In this category also are the periodicals that grow up around personalities. John R. Rice's *Sword of the Lord* and Donald Grey Barnhouse's *Revelation*[9] and his early *Eternity*[10] were personality cult products dealing with subjects in each man's range of interests. The cause was the man. Circulation was welcomed but the magazines ignored the ups and downs.[11]

Advocacy publications tend to have short life spans— usually related to their cause or their editor—but their public recognition and even secular acclaim are far beyond their paid circulations. "Hammering away at enemy fortresses," focusing on a common foe, these are magazines of noble effort, like Garrison's *Liberator*. They also can become publications of demagoguery, sectarianism, and character assassination. They represent the best and worst of the first amendment.

Official Promotion: From Hype to Ministry

Moving across the matrix, we come to officially sponsored publications that advocate an organization, a mission, or a charity. There is still a cause but it is more the growth and survival of a program than a set of ideas. Some of these publications are a species of advertising; others are almost consumer magazines. All have in common the absence of a clear marketplace test of their readers' loyalty, since they tend to be free, or virtually free, to the readers. They accept no advertising and are not available in normal subscription channels.

The most ready examples are the mission magazines, sent monthly to remind donors of the ongoing activity of the mission. Fund raisers have learned that voluntary support of a charity requires frequent reminders of that organization's continuing need and existence. The oldest mission magazine still published is surely the *American Bible Society Record*, begun in 1865. *World Vision*, with a million circulation, is a more recent example.

Closer to consumer magazines are *Decision*, the monthly magazine of evangelism and Christian living from the Billy Graham organization, with two million in circulation, and *Possibilities*, a bi-monthly of the Robert Schuller organization with a circulation of eight hundred thousand. Both are sent free to donors (*Decision* has a nominal five dollar subscription price) and both contain editorial content that supports the theology and ministry of the sponsors. Oral Roberts' *Abundant Life* is another example. Promotional of their organizations, all these magazines regard their role as an extension of a total ministry.

Non-profit organizations, including colleges, missions, and para-church agencies, have invariably felt they needed a regular vehicle of communication for their constituency. But such publications have rarely enjoyed a shared sense of dialogue and community like the paid-for magazines in the lower half of the matrix. They rarely permit letters to the editor critical of the institution or publication; consequently the readers feel little ownership in the publication and may treat it like any other promotional mailing.[12]

Members and Their Friends: House Organs

Moving down the chart, we arrive at official publications that give their readers more of a vote in the product. This is the lower right quadrant. An alumni or fraternity magazine would be the perfect example. In the religious field, denominational magazines usually function as official communication with a membership, even if they sell subscriptions and even if they propagandize for the home office. Glenn Arnold reports that before the Civil War each major Protestant denomination had at least twenty periodicals; the Congregationalists had twenty-five.[13]

Church house organs and denominational vehicles are

somewhat akin to officially sponsored donor magazines, but they demonstrate a greater deference to a reading audience. They usually require formal subscriptions, but sometimes those subscriptions are garnered in anonymous collectivities like "every home" programs for churches to give every family a subscription for a flat fee. This tends to diminish the quality of readership and discounts the size of circulation accordingly.[14] Advertising has never been a significant part of the income of this category of publication. None of the denominational magazines has existed without some subsidy from its sponsors.

Among the largest of the official denominational magazines in the Evangelical Press Association are *The Lutheran Standard*, the voice of the former American Lutheran Church (now a part of the Evangelical Lutheran Church), with a circulation of 550,000. The Assemblies of God's *Pentecostal Evangel*, with 287,000, and the Church of the Nazarene's *Herald of Holiness* (170,000) follow. Most in this category report circulation in the range of a few thousand (*Conservative Baptist*, 7,000) to well under a hundred thousand (*The Banner* of the Christian Reformed, 48,000).

This is a day of rather small, narrowly focused magazines. As recent as the 1950s, the denominational organs of the Methodists and Presbyterians boasted circulations in the one million vicinity. But the Methodist *Together* (1956–1975) went from 900,000 to 140,000 and ceased. *Presbyterian Life* has also gone through some evolution, first as A.D. and now as a much smaller *Presbyterian Survey*. The American Baptist *Crusader* went from 375,000 in the early 1970s to a new format, *The American Baptist*, with about 150,000 in circulation.

The nation's two largest Protestant denominations presently have no single periodical. Neither the Southern Baptist Convention nor the United Methodist Church, among their numerous periodicals from numerous church agencies, speaks in print with a single voice. The independent *United Methodist Reporter*, published from Dallas as a news weekly for the Methodist communion, functions for many congregations as their church paper; but it has maintained an uneasy independence toward the church agencies and takes no consistent theological stand.

A semi-independent periodical from the past was the *Watchman-Examiner* (1819–1964).[15] A professed Baptist weekly, it nonetheless was not the official voice for any one denomination and should be regarded as close to a consumer magazine.

Its most notable contribution was to coin the term "fundamentalist" in 1920, referring to those who sided with the ideas in *The Fundamentals*. In 1964, when the *Watchman-Examiner* folded, its remaining ten thousand subscribers merged with *Eternity*. (As for *Eternity*, not a denominational magazine, its own circulation in the 1980s declined from some fifty thousand to some twenty thousand, and it ceased publication in January 1989.)[16]

Church house organs are the magazines of obituaries, conventions, and anniversaries. They love nostalgia, old school ties, in-language, pillars of the church, sacred cows, and taboos. In earlier sectarian days, church organs were known for strident cross-denominational attacks. Today, in a more ecumenical age, many still engage in lively debate within the rules of the club. Their editorial quality varies with their editors and the support of their sponsors.[17]

Another kind of membership periodical deserves attention: the scholarly or professional journal. Although these have been few in the Christian field, several stand out as remarkably influential. *The Princeton Theological Review* during its history (1829–1931)[18] rendered profound leadership in the field of academic theology. Almost all of what we now esteem from the pen of B. B. Warfield appeared first in that journal. It never exceeded a few thousand in circulation,[19] but it interacted with the intellectual ferments of the day and was regarded by one contemporary as "the most powerful organ in America."[20] Its readership was chiefly among the educated clergy, first of whom were the alumni of "old Princeton."

Among modern evangelical periodicals of a scholarly nature, we could mention *The Journal of the American Scientific Affiliation*, a membership publication of Christians in science, *The Journal of The Evangelical Theological Society*, *The Christian Scholar's Review*, and the journals of seminaries—*Concordia*, *Westminster*, *Asbury Theological Journal*, and *Bibliotheca Sacra*. The last, published by Dallas Theological Seminary since 1934, traces its history to 1844. None of these has a circulation that exceeds ten thousand, but each serves a crucial role for its constituency.

Consumer Magazines

Most of us find the consumer magazines the most interesting of all, in part, perhaps, because they seem to be an instant readout of public opinion. Their subscribers are voluntary. To know the circulation of *Playboy, National Review,* or *Charisma* is to know something about the interest and values of our society. These readers have chosen and paid for a distinct periodic visitor to their homes, identifying themselves with social movements and styles of life.

When we identify a publication as "market driven" we do not mean it defers to all potential subscribers everywhere; rather, it attends to the interests of those subscribers within its chosen market. *Moody Monthly* is sensitive to the Moody market, The Wittenburg Door to *The Wittenburg Door* market, and so on. The editorial goals of a magazine thus link with a defined group of magazine readers. Those publications we are calling "consumer" are those that function in a commercial relationship with their defined market. And if their chosen market is not pleased with their product, the magazine is shortly out of business. This is not the case with the publications higher on the chart that are more promotional in purpose. The period following World War II has been especially rich with consumer magazines, including a variety of new religious ones. I begin, however, with three that trace their ancestry to the nineteenth century.

The Sunday School Times (1859–1967) carried the torch for popular evangelical piety throughout the Protestant denominations. It was a voice for both premillennial interpretation of the Bible and the "Keswick" or victorious life approach to sanctification.[21] A weekly, the Philadelphia-based *Times* offered teacher aids for the Uniform Lesson series used by many of the larger denominations. Its teaching aids created for it a certain necessity in the lives of its subscribers—an element rarely present in religious magazines. It also gave it an audience in church circles that would otherwise have been closed to its distinctive theology. Though the *Sunday School Times* began with the American Sunday School Union, it was purchased by John Wanamaker, the Philadelphia department store entrepreneur, in 1871. By 1876 it had a circulation of one hundred thousand.[22] By comparison, *The Atlantic* had a circulation during that era of no more than fifty thousand,[23] and even the *Saturday Evening Post*, the various *Harpers*, and other periodicals did not exceed the circulation of the *Times*.

The editors of the *Times* were widely esteemed: H. Clay Trumbull (editor from 1875–1903), his son Charles G. Trumbull,[24] Charles' nephew Philip Howard, Sr., and his successor, Philip Howard, Jr.[25]

A strategic blunder occurred in the history of the *Times* in the late 1940s. Under criticism from the fundamentalist right, chiefly Carl McIntire, the *Times* was pushed into dropping the uniform Sunday school lesson series, which was tainted by its Federal Council of Churches sponsorship. Following great subscriber protest, the magazine resumed these lessons a short time later. But the confidence in the uniform lessons among conservatives was shaken, while Scripture Press lessons and other alternatives were gaining ground in the curriculum field. The key selling point for this century-old weekly was thus mortally wounded. Its circulation, which had exceeded one hundred thousand, declined in the 1960s to fifty thousand. Advertising income had never been significant and after an abortive effort to merge with *Eternity*, the prestigious name of the *Sunday School Times* was sold to Union Gospel Press, where it lost its identity in a merger with their *Gospel Herald*, a Sunday school devotional magazine.

Another general audience weekly, the *Christian Herald*, began in 1878 as a branch of the English evangelical scene. Early leadership and articles were from Charles Spurgeon, A. J. Gordon, and A. T. Pierson. Among its distinctives at the turn of the century were its editorial commitment to progressive social legislation, such as labor and immigration laws, and its emphasis on world peace. Circulation exceeded 250,000[26] in 1910. The charities of the organization, including a rescue mission in the Bowery and an orphanage, early gave the magazine a humanitarian, trustworthy image.

The *Christian Herald* decreased its emphasis on prophetic themes and refused to side with the fundamentalists during the 1920s when Charles M. Sheldon, author of *In His Steps*, was the editor. Jesus, Sheldon declared, would not have participated in the fundamentalist debates.[27] The peak years for New York-based *Christian Herald* were during the editorship of Daniel Poling, in the 1930s through the 1950s. Circulation reportedly hit a half million[28] with a regularly claimed advertising base of four hundred thousand. Newsstand and "agency" services generated the vast subscription flow.[29] A weekly until 1930, the magazine was frequently mentioned in the same company with other mass audience general magazines like *Life*.

Dan Poling, who ran for mayor of Philadelphia in the early 1950s, was an institution in himself. He embodied a mainline, mildly conservative Protestantism, without a doctrinaire style. His magazine sometimes had a "Church in the Wildwood" generality to it; it honored few of the taboos of the fundamentalist movement (in the 1950s it carried movie reviews but always sided with the temperance movement) and was not regarded as a champion of the evangelical cause by the conservatives of post-World War II. Some called it liberal.

Today the magazine survives with a chastened circulation of under 150,000, considered its "natural level" by the present management, whose evangelical credentials cannot be doubted. It now considers its closest competitor to be Moody Monthly.

That magazine of Chicago's Moody Bible Institute dates from 1900, when it evolved from The Institute Tie, an alumni magazine. It grew to a circulation of 19,431 by 1921 in its search for a ministry among lay Christians in the Moody circle of influence. Advertising, including promotion of competing schools, aromatic toothpicks, and fountain pens, gave it the consumer magazine appearance.[30] The editorial emphasis of this periodical has always been Christian living for the laity, with the boundaries defined largely by the constituency of the Moody organization. As an announced "family" magazine, it has included some fare for children, youth, and homemakers.

The Moody Monthly of the 1970s became a formidable competitor for advertising and subscribers. With a heavy investment on the part of the school, plus the use of direct mail solicitations offering a subscription with a premium book, the circulation hit three hundred thousand. There was talk of possibly reaching five hundred thousand subscriptions. Today the magazine has a list of two hundred thousand subscribers and is considered one of the few profitable Christian periodicals.[31] Like Moody Press, it earns a profit for the school.

Though Moody is a consumer magazine, it carries its institutional sponsorship as a visible blessing and burden. Not strictly promotional of Moody Bible Institute, it nonetheless observes the school's taboos, cultivates its image, and attends to its market. On the matrix chart, Moody Monthly is close to the center—just inside the market-driven, consumer quadrant, but within sight of the publications that promote something official.

The most aggressive growth since World War II has been among the smaller publications that have brought journalism school expertise to the Christian press. In the period of the forties and fifties, a variety of magazine experiments were tried, such as the Christian Digest, the Christian Newsette, and the

Christian Life and Times. The last of these came under the control of a Northwestern journalism graduate named Robert Walker. A recent convert himself, he saw no reason why the Christian community could not have a commercially successful magazine, sold by subscription and supported up to 50 percent by advertising. In 1948 he turned a digest-sized Sunday school publication into a contemporary format and began promoting it in the para-church markets of the evangelicals. "We had no economic model for what we were doing," Walker recalls.[32] He aimed for a fifty-fifty split of advertising and circulation, settling for thirty-seventy. His entrepreneurial ambitions, if not business necessity, generated a family of related magazines such as the *Christian Bookseller* (1955) for retail bookstores, *Choice* (an advertising vehicle for bookstores, (1957–59), and a magazine for camps and conferences.

A number of organizational publications grew beyond their borders to become significant players in the larger picture. Chief among these was *Youth for Christ Magazine* (1944), which became *Campus Life* (1965). Originally a house organ for the organization, "YFC Magazine" was promoted in the Saturday night rallies of the teen evangelism movement. By the late sixties it had evolved into an influential independent product for youth and those concerned about them. Its role as a promoter of Christian colleges is unmeasurable. On a smaller scale, *His* (1941) grew from a house organ of InterVarsity Christian Fellowship to an independent monthly for college students and alumni. As a source of lay-level apologetics it filled a niche unfilled elsewhere. With never more than thirty or forty thousand subscribers, the magazine struggled to an end in 1988, after attempting a name change to *U* in a final marketing move.

The launch of *Christianity Today* in 1956 marked an audacious and remarkably successful experiment in religious magazines. As noted previously, it grew out of Billy Graham's vision for "nothing else but the finest journal in the Western world, comparable to what *Time* is in current events."[33] *Christianity Today's* founding editor, Fuller theologian Carl F. H. Henry, valued journalistic reporting, scholarly credentials, and, most of all, serious debate.[34]

However, we must observe several key turning points in the history of this periodical. In the late fifties and early sixties, the magazine converted from a free circulation to a paid circulation. This meant it had to make a transition from a "cause" publication to a market-driven one. Therefore it started down the road of aggressive promotion, including book premiums and direct-mail programs.[35] Carl Henry's departure in 1968, whether by his initiative or that of Harold Ockenga, the chairman of the board,[36] proved tumultuous. His successor, Harold Lindsell, brought a more parochial agenda to the magazine at a time when its economic fortunes were increasingly tenuous. In the early seventies, the magazine entered an ill-fated book publishing venture, Canon Press, and teetered on bankruptcy.[37] Harold Myra, whose successful tenure at *Campus Life* was highly regarded, joined the magazine in 1975 as president and chief executive. He supervised the magazine's move from Washington to Wheaton and weaned the magazine from subsidies. By 1978 the economic corner had been turned and black ink began to appear on the financial reports. Circulation is now in the 170,000s, which is considered by its management to be "optimum."

Myra was widely criticized for the evolution of the magazine from one that spoke for evangelicals to one that spoke to them, from one that published across the street from the White House to one that published across the street from the National Association of Evangelicals, and from one for intellectuals to one for a popular audience.[38] Yet the reader research for the magazine shows its clergy-laity proportions have not greatly changed—about half and half; and the percentage of professional scholars has always been in Myra's words, "around one or two percent."[39]

Two strategic moves in the late seventies have put the magazine on a firmer footing. One was Myra's view that a "family" of magazines, more than just one, was needed to disperse overheads. *Leadership*, a quarterly for clergy, was the first (1980) to join the family and has proved dramatically successful and profitable with a circulation of close to one hundred thousand. Shortly after, *Campus Life, Marriage Partnership*, and *Today's Christian Woman* joined the family. *Leadership 100* for lay church leaders and the earlier *Partnership* for clergy wives were not successful, however. A second strategic turn has been the use of readership surveys by Christianity Today, Inc., to determine reader interest for specific features. Since 1980, they have conducted a semiscientific survey to detect the extent of readership for various articles and features. For example, a survey might show that a column on the arts may attract only ten percent of the readers, and an article by Billy

Graham may garner well over half. "If we're going to get them to pay, we have to know what they think," says Myra. "The magazine's survival is at stake."[40] This is the nearest to an actual show of hands among the buyers for any publication we have discussed.

The seventies and eighties have proved quite fertile for new consumer magazines. Every year a significant new one hit the evangelical market. Among the best known are *Virtue, Today's Christian Woman, Charisma, The Fundamentalist Journal, The Wittenburg Door, Kindred Spirit, The Journal of Christian Nursing,* and *Discipleship Journal.* The fall of 1988 witnessed a new, aggressively capitalized publication, *Christian Parenting.*[41] Common elements among all these seem to be specialization and an issue frequency of less than monthly.[42] However, not all efforts have succeeded. An ambitious biweekly newspaper, the *National Courier,* went through several million dollars beginning in 1975, seeking a mass audience acceptance for news.[43] In 1978 two newsstand attempts by secular concerns attracted meteoric interest—*Inspiration* and *Faith and Inspiration.* Both hit the newsstands in large numbers with Billy Graham on their first covers.

Probably *Charisma* (1975) has been the most numerically successful of the newer magazines. Begun by a recent journalism graduate from the University of Florida, Stephen Strang, it was sponsored first by a Florida Assembly of God congregation. As it grew, *Logos,* an earlier charismatic bimonthly declined; Strang bought *Charisma* and proceeded to build a small conglomerate, Strang Communications, publishing *Christian Retailing, Ministry Today,* and Creation House books.

Charisma, by 1988, had tied or topped *Moody Monthly* as the largest subscription-based magazine in the evangelical marketplace, with over two hundred thousand subscriptions. It retains its old Pentecostal culture, adding the newer charismatic population and, since merging with Robert Walker's *Christian Life,* the traditional midwestern evangelicals. The Pentecostal movement now appears established and prosperous.

Before leaving this simple four-element typology, we might note that the history of magazines is marked by an effort of a publication to leave its box. House organs seek to move into market-oriented magazines; likewise, cause-oriented tracts become consumer products. And within the staff and management of a publication, most of the problems and conflicts arise over what kind of publication theirs actually is—"Are we representing an organization or meeting a market?" is a commonly heard question.

THE MEANS AND THE ENDS

Evangelical consumer publications survive as businesses and, like other periodicals, they must create a product that will be in demand by a particular market. This pragmatic necessity, combined with religious idealism and mission, imposes numerous paradoxes and constraints on the "business." Among these are economics, circulation, and cultural impact.

"It is so easy to fail with a magazine. Editorial, circulation, and advertising must hit like three pistons in an engine—perfectly—for success." That comment from Harold Myra, president of Christianity Today Incorporated, carries extra credibility because of the history of his flagship publication. *Christianity Today* began in 1956 and did not break-even until 1978. Initially it was entirely subsidized; later, subsidies from key donors covered the last half of its expenses—hundreds of thousands of dollars every year.

The three pistons, or the three-legged stool of editorial, circulation, and advertising, have baffled many an accountant and traditional business person. This is a business in which the customer pays in advance. At least two streams of income—circulation and advertising—seem independent yet they are interdependent, for the decline of circulation will jeopardize the sale of advertising. And is circulation an asset or a liability? The accountants will call it a liability, because it is an obligation incurred. The advertising manager will regard it as his chief asset. The bank will side with the accountants as they wince at the balance sheet: all that obligation with only intangible future editorial product to offset it!

To cast the magazine industry in traditional business terms, the key elements are quantity of units (circulation), price of the units (subscription price), ancillary income (mainly advertising, but also list rentals, books, and services), and repeat business (renewals). Blending these requires very delicate fine tuning. Indeed, the formula varies with each magazine; there are few industry-wide norms, either for religious or general magazines. Renewals, for example, must be sufficient for a stable circulation, especially for those magazines that have assured advertisers of a guaranteed circulation (rate base). If the renewal rate is poor, a promotion campaign for replacement subscriptions will prove so costly that red ink is inevitable. "We had to struggle to keep renewals above 50 percent," says Robert Walker of his *Christian Life* days. *Virtue* reported a renewal rate of 72 percent in 1987. *Guideposts* has claimed a renewal rate of 75 percent.[44] Most experts would say 70 percent is good; 50 percent is adequate if promotion is inexpensive. *The New Yorker* and *National Geographic* have long enjoyed renewal rates well above 80 percent, the envy of the industry. Most of the consumer Christian magazines will not disclose their renewal rates, but the consensus prevails that any periodical that must replace over half its list each year will find profitability elusive. Renewals are widely regarded as the single best evidence of reader satisfaction—not letters to the editor, citation in public, or praise from journalistic experts. Salability among those who know the product best, the current subscribers, defines editorial and (usually) economic success.

Smaller magazines, such as those with under thirty thousand in circulation, cannot win much space advertising except from highly specialized products targeted for their unique audience. Less than twenty thousand in circulation will mean advertising is negligible or even more trouble than it is worth.[45] A valuable mailing list, however, even for a tiny publication, can generate substantial income currently in the range of $50 to $100 per thousand names per rental.

In the religious media, advertising has evolved and shifted in this century. In the 1920s and 1930s, the mix of advertisers in the *Christian Herald* or *Moody Monthly* included a wide variety of consumer products. The *Herald* of the 1930s had ads from Ipana toothpaste, Olson Rugs, and Burpee seeds. Later, with specialization, these magazines found such "secular" advertising harder to get; commercial religious products became the chief category. Robert Walker, the *Christian Life* editor, recalls the 1940s: "We found mission organizations, para-church organizations, travel agencies, and Bible publishers would advertise. The book publishers were not dominant in the early days." By the 1960s, book publishers were the key category of advertisers in Christian media. And the period of the mid-seventies to early eighties was the golden age for the Christian book publishing industry. After those heyday years, however, the magazines that took advertising found they could not count on ever-increasing space sales. The book industry had turned flat, notable indeed among the three largest publishers.[46] *Christianity*

Today enjoyed a peak of $1.9 million in space advertising in 1983, but saw a drop the following year to $1.6 million. In 1989 it anticipated $1.8 million.[47] *The Christian Herald*, with somewhat less circulation, anticipated $500,000 to $700,000 in advertising per year.[48]

A final economic element foreign for outsiders to this industry is the art and science of subscription promotion. Circulation must be bought, like office supplies or any other purchase, and it can be bought cheaply or expensively. (Either way the risk is poor renewals.) Through the science of computerized direct mail, however, a vast number of people can be wooed to subscribe. A tiny portion, perhaps 1 or 2 percent, will agree to purchase, some on trial (a "soft" offer) and some with actual payment (a "hard" offer). These new subscribers thus become the growing edge for a consumer magazine.

The larger Christian magazines will commit hundreds of thousands—perhaps millions—of dollars to this quest for new subscribers. This is why a magazine start-up turns out to be capital intensive. The "up-front" money creates the audience, and the payback, several years away, will depend on renewals and advertising. Only a handful of Christian magazines are known to be profitable, for these very practical reasons.[49]

CIRCULATION

The 315 member publications of the Evangelical Press Association range in circulation from two hundred to two million. Approximately one out of ten has a circulation over one hundred thousand and of the thirty-four that go above one hundred thousand, twenty-two arrived in that coveted company by giving their product away.[50] The median circulation is only twelve thousand.[51] Why is this, in a nation where evangelicals number somewhere between fifteen and forty million? A 1980 study by researcher George Barna showed that only 12.7 percent of "Christians" subscribe to a Christian magazine (of that group 62.2 percent subscribe to any magazine). Even among a group in that survey called "committed Christians," only 18.8 percent take a Christian magazine.[52]

Granted, magazines lend themselves to small, tight definitions of special audience and special interest. None of the religious magazines—Catholic, Protestant, or Jewish—soar to vast numbers. The *Christian Century*, an influential weekly from the more liberal Protestant tradition, has a circulation of thirty-five thousand, of which 25 percent are libraries and institutions. Nevertheless it is clear that evangelicals do not read religious periodicals any more than they listen to religious radio stations. All of the rhetoric in recent years about the booming evangelical "business" has been overdrawn. Evangelicals, like the wider American society, consume a variety of media, only a few of which are specifically religious.

Given the advertising base and the subscription price ceilings open to Christian magazines, it requires great faith to see how any magazine will rise above the two hundred thousand to three hundred thousand subscription level in the present market. It could be done but the formula would have to be: (1) a subscription price high enough to compensate for a reduction in advertising revenue (an increase in circulation equals an increase in ad rates. An increase in ad rates usually causes a reduction in ad revenues, thus higher subscription rates) and (2) a product in such demand that renewal rates could remain high. (The replacement of expired subscriptions would then not be seen as being overly expensive.)

Some might hope that larger advertisers would be attracted to a Christian magazine of larger circulation. Might automobiles, appliances, cosmetics, or clothing turn up in *Charisma* or *Christianity Today*? The consensus among present publishers is that this will not happen. A number of attempts have been made, from the 1960s to the 1980s, but with no real progress.[53] Today the advertising community usually favors highly targeted media placement, for example, cat food in *Cat Fancy*, and for more general products the inexpensive general media. In addition, there are some nonrational considerations involved in advertising. Many advertisers are loathe to entangle themselves in anything religious, regardless of the audience size. It is therefore doubtful that secular advertisers would be attracted to large religious magazines, and it is certain that smaller religious advertisers could not afford them.

Equally daunting in larger circulation ventures is the quest for an audience. Out of a highly segmented, divided church scene, an audience would have to be drawn to some common interests or beliefs. They would have to feel an urgency or even a necessity about timely contact; yet even among militant fundamentalists and evangelicals, religion has typically not been propelled by day-to-day events but by timeless truths. Christian magazines that have proffered news, whether secular events or sacred, have not been successful. The evangelical periodicals now on the market are compelled to use premiums, reduced prices, and sweepstakes to keep their advertising base. Competition for readers, including that from free publications and secular media, is keen.

Do evangelical magazines make a difference, either within or without their boundaries? Looking outside evangelicalism's "interior dialogue," it appears that only two or three evangelical periodicals ever turn up in a typical public library. For serious research, only about 35 of the 425 periodicals of the American Theological Librarians' *Religion Index* are distinctly evangelical. Most telling of all, for a mass movement, there are no newsstand success stories. Potential readers are culled almost entirely from internal networking—chiefly direct mail. A Gallup study in the last decade found that among American clergy, *Christianity Today* was first of the ten most widely read magazines. Yet national, public impact cannot be claimed for even the largest evangelical magazines.

At the same time, the traditional newspapers and magazines in the general market have largely given up their own role as disseminators of religious ideas and events. The secular press in previous generations devoted much more space to Christian themes and exposition than they do today. For example, the Philadelphia newspapers published complete transcripts of Billy Sunday's sermons during his 1914 crusade. That was an age that did not feel religious themes were out-of-bounds. Today, secular media, though swift and usually accurate in their religious reporting, focus more on conflict and institutional change than on ideas.[54] Martin Marty puts the problem into the mouth of a fictional religion reporter.

> We cover other dimensions of life and interests in more ways than just to deal with conflict. Our paper talks about athletic games and not just about athletic scandals. We report on financial trends and not just on "insider trading" sleaze. . . . Will you [the secular editor] let me dig up and focus on analogues to these in religion?[55]

As a result, evangelical magazines contribute primarily to the internal dialogue of the religious community and to the economic health of some religious businesses. "Magazines become a part of the family, they take on a familiarity that people relate to, perhaps more even than books" (Harold Myra). Every magazine subscriber feels supported by a larger community and therefore less isolated, less provincial, more a part of the "great conversation," whatever it may be. "Magazines have supported the book industry, discovering authors and subjects that later became best sellers," adds William Carmichael. Numerous authors discovered they could write while working on an article for a magazine. Magazines respond swiftly to hot topics; books may take a year or two to develop. "An alert press can expose situations that, with public exposure, will be corrected," suggests William Petersen.[56] The para-church, independent religious enterprises will only be monitored by the Christian or secular media. They fear publicity and take it seriously;[57] they can be held accountable, in part, through responsible coverage in the media. The examples of this are few, however.

Investigative journalism within the Christian press has probed a number of allegations or problems for its readers. In the last twenty years, these include the organization Underground Evangelism, the Bill Gothard ministry and staff, Robert Schuller's theology, and the charges of heresy directed at Tony Campolo. It is fair to say, however, that numerous moral eyesores, the PTL and Swaggart scandals among them, have been left for the secular media to expose.

Less dramatic, but equally valid, is the published discovery of any previously obscure ministry or method that works well in the life of the church. But good news or bad requires a huge investment of time, money, and a measure of risk; most of the Christian press has not pursued it.

Magazines sometimes cast themselves in an admirable "prophetic" role.[58] But the ineluctable canons of marketing throw doubt on so noble a function. Voluntary subscribers have bought the publication because they essentially agree with it. If it differs radically from their opinions, they simply fail to renew.[59] It is arguable that Harriet Beecher Stowe's *Uncle Tom's Cabin* had more impact than Garrison's *Liberator*.

But might magazines change minds with new facts or daring leadership? They can at least inform. However, studies of crucial turning points in American life have not been reassuring about the magazines' role of leadership.[60] A survey of general Christian magazines in the 1950s would not inspire the word "prophetic" about the racial issue. Yet this turned out to be one of the key social changes from 1954 to 1964—and one with a clear ethical element.

We all can remember the experience of reading an analysis

that articulated and captured our own best instincts and values, as only language can do. We looked up from the page and knew what we thought on a given subject. We were emboldened then to follow our better, more mature judgment. This rhetorical mystery occurs rarely for it requires writers of depth and substance.[61] We magazine readers chiefly want publications with credibility. We want good writing, clever packaging, interesting layouts, titles, and graphics. But we first want credibility. Having that moral and intellectual credibility, we will find in magazines a measure of leadership. Where are these strong editors—not just journalistic craftsmen—who will bring such credibility? Or is an internal dialogue the best that can be achieved?

NOTES

[1]*Ulrich's Periodical Directory*, 1988

[2]The *1986 Ayer Directory of Publications* lists 11,328 periodicals in the United States.

[3]The *Magazine Industry Newsletter* estimated there were twelve hundred religious publications plus an unknown number for which no information was available, according to William H. Taft, *American Magazines for the 1980s* (New York: Hastings House, 1982), 216.

[4]Two recent historical studies are worth reading: Nathan O. Hatch, *The Democratization of American Christianity* (New Haven: Yale University Press, 1988), chapter 4. And Mark Noll, "Mainliners and Evangelicals," *The Reformed Journal* (June 1988): 14–19. Noll draws on Hatch's research in this speech to the Evangelical Press Association and the Associated Church Press.

[5]*Folio*, the magazine of the magazine industry, has divided periodicals into "special interest" and "special audience" publications (*Solving Publishing's Toughest Problems*, 1984). Using that division, the consumer magazines on the left tend to be special interest; they are oriented to a subject area. Those on the right are special audience; they are delimited by some demographic boundary. If this seems a bit pedantic, remember that journalism doesn't have many chances at it.

[6]Quoted in Sydney E. Ahlstrom, *A Religious History of the American People* (Yale University Press, 1972), 651.

[7]The only real magazine that I know currently to be evangelistic is *These Times*, a pre-evangelistic tool of Seventh-day Adventists. It is used to interest friends and neighbors in topics that can lead to serious questions about that faith.

During the Jesus movement of the late 1960s, a number of handout publications had an evangelistic purpose. The *Hollywood Free Paper* hit a circulation of 425,000 (free) and claimed over two thousand conversions. See Ronald Enroth et al., *The Jesus People* (Grand Rapids: Eerdmans, 1972), 74.

[8]Wilbur Smith, *Before I Forget* (Chicago: Moody Press, 1971), 177.

[9]This publication, begun by the Philadelphia Presbyterian in the 1920s, failed after a board of directors conflict with Dr. Barnhouse over control precipitated his resignation as editor (1949). Within the year he began a new one, *Eternity* (1950), and an ailing *Revelation* soon merged back into it.

[10]From 1950 until Barnhouse's death in 1960. The magazine repositioned as a general consumer magazine in 1961.

[11]"They dragged in the subscription cancellations in mailbags," was the description of older *Eternity* staff who recalled the month that magazine under Barnhouse dropped from thirty three thousand to twenty nine thousand. The protest was over a series of articles on Seventh-day Adventism, considered the "last straw" of a series of disquieting trends in the magazine. Personal conversation, William J. Petersen, July 1988.

[12]The readership studies introduced most notably by Professor James Engel at Wheaton College Graduate School of Communications have stimulated a healthy scrutiny and pragmatism on the part of the organizations that have used them.

[13]*Writing Award Winning Articles* (Nashville: Thomas Nelson, 1983), 19. The opening chapter is a helpful overview of the history of Christian magazines, drawing on the authoritative 1957 study by Frank Luther Mott, *A History of American Magazines*.

[14]Denominational periodicals, for example, have had difficulty selling advertising because the advertisers suspected the circulation numbers were artificially enlarged.

[15]With that life span it competes with The *Church Herald* of the Reformed Church in America (originating in 1826) as one of the longest continuously published church magazines.

[16]The circulation was taken over by *World*.

[17]"Denominational publications are, in fact, beholden to the church bodies and the constituencies they serve. No publication, of course, succeeds with an unwilling constituency, but a special factor is introduced in denominational publishing." Dennis Shoemaker, "The Ministry of the Church Journalist," *The Church Herald* (April 2, 1976): 12.

[18]It had a number of names, beginning with *Biblical Reportory and Princeton Review*.

[19]Princeton Seminary, with 110 students in 1905, was among the largest of the Protestant seminaries.

[20]The editor of the *Autobiography of Lyman Beecher*, cited in Mark Noll, *The Princeton Theology* (Grand Rapids: Baker, 1983), 22.

[21]For an explanation of these distinctives see Douglas Frank, *Less Than Conquerors* (Grand Rapids: Eerdmans, 1986), 22.

[22]The information here on the *Sunday School Times* has been secured from Herbert Fryling, the last surviving officer; James Reapsome, the concluding editor; and Russell T. Hitt.

[23]Roland Wolseley, *Understanding Magazines* 2d. ed. (Ames: Iowa State University Press, 1972), 32.

[24]"The greatest editor of any Christian journal in America," according to Wilbur Smith, *Before I Forget*, 77.

[25]Technically, Philip Sr. was "president" and Philip Jr. was both editor and president for part of the time.

[26]George Marsden, *Fundamentalism and American Culture* (New York: Oxford University Press, 1980), 84.

[27]Ibid., 270.

[28]Robert Metcalf, currently on the staff of the *Herald*.

[29]As with *Saturday Evening Post* and other mass audience magazines, agents or sales people in towns across the land took orders from friends and neighbors for subscriptions. A small commission was earned.

[30]Robert Flood, "Moody Monthly: Yesterday and Today," *Moody Monthly*, (February, 1986): 62.

[31]Much of the statistical data on *Moody Monthly* I secured from Robert Flood, currently on its staff. Flood was responsible for the program that gave *Moody* the circulation boost from about 110,000 to 250,000 in the early 1970s. For subscription premiums he used Moody Press books, such as the *Wycliffe Commentary* in a special edition. He credits "mass mailing, large premiums," and low postal rates as the components of his effort from 1972 to 1978.

[32]Private conversation, July 1988.

[33]Notes from Wilbur Smith, an early compatriot with Graham and L. Nelson Bell, in the founding of the magazine. *Before I Forget*, 178.

[34]Henry's autobiography, *Confessions of a Theologican* (Waco: Word Books, 1986), details his philosophy and experience with the magazine.

[35]The Iverson-Ford agency of New York introduced one of the first modern premiums among Christian magazines, the *Four Version New Testament*, in 1963. In later years, numerous other book premiums were tried, a venture that current president Harold Myra considers counterproductive. Myra tells of a parishioner in his church in the early seventies who told him she was returning two copies of *The Living Bible* to her bookstore. She had discovered she could buy two subscriptions to *Christianity Today* and get two free *Living Bibles* for less money than if she would purchase the books alone. Such premium offers thus created a subscriber base that lacked affinity for the magazine itself, and renewals suffered.

[36]The two men differed regarding what actually happened. Henry insists he was fired (see *Confessions*), but Ockenga insisted the editor resigned.

[37]Heavy subsidies from J. Howard Pew, industrialist Maxey Jarman, and the Billy Graham organization enabled the publication to survive.

[38]See Henry, *Confessions*, especially the final chapter.

[39]Conversation, August 11, 1988. A Gallup poll has shown *Christianity Today* to be the magazine subscribed to by more of America's clergy than any other, a fulfillment of the original dream of Billy Graham, J. Howard Pew, and Carl Henry.

[40]Myra notes that the Carl Henry column was dropped after reader research showed it was the least read of any of their features.

[41]The sponsors are the David C. Cook Company and William Carmichael, publisher of *Virtue*.

[42]Higher subscription prices plus reduced number of issues per subscription term have become commonplace. The fortnightly *Christianity Today* now serves only 18 issues per year. The conventional wisdom among their publishers (my paraphrase): "People don't really notice if you come every month. But they do notice the gross price."

[43]William J. Petersen, formerly with *Eternity*, recalls an initial ambiguity in the editorial purpose of the *Courier*. He notes that a presentation at the May 1975, EPA convention by the publication's first editor and sponsor implied two different editorial philosophies. Robert Slosser, formerly with the *New York Times*, hoped the future periodical would be an evangelical version of the *Christian Science Monitor*. Dan Malachuk, owner of Logos International, a book publishing firm that funded the venture, seemed to imply that it would be more like a Christian *National Enquirer*, sold in supermarkets. As it progressed, Malachuk prevailed, and the publication emphasized charismatic reporting.

[44]Taft, *American Magazines*, 219.

[45]The conventional wisdom has been that only half the revenue from a page of advertising is kept as profit. About 25 percent is consumed in selling expenses and an equal amount in extra printing costs.

[46]Word, Zondervan, and Thomas Nelson.

[47]I am indebted to Roy Coffman, CTi executive, for disclosure of these and other statistics on the magazine.

[48]Robert Metcalf, advertising manager, August 1988 conversation.

[49]Many of these observations about the business side of magazines I owe to Russell T. Hitt, a veteran editor and publisher, who managed *Eternity* through a number of difficult transitions.

[50]Although a price is put on many of these that are given away, and money will be accepted, the product is basically free to all who contribute to an organization or who support a ministry.

[51]Based on the reported circulation figures of the 1987–88 *Membership Directory*. This does not include publications that did not report circulation, almost all of which are Sunday school curriculum products.

[52]The study was called The *Christian Marketplace* and was carried out by Barna's organization, then called the American Research Bureau. A private project of supporting corporations, it was not made available to the general public.

[53]The most recent was by CTi in the mid 1980s, an effort to secure "secular" advertising for *Today's Christian Woman*, under the direction of Kenneth Johnson and Dale Hanson Bourke. In the 1960s, an effort was made to form a consortium of large-circulation denominational magazines, led by A. D. In the 1950s Daniel Poling sought large general advertising and met with nominal success.

[54]See Roderick P. Hart et al., "Religion and the Rhetoric of the Mass Media," *Review of Religious Research* (Summer 1980), 256–75. This is a study of the religion coverage in *Time* magazine from 1947 to 1976. They argue that the magazine depicts religion as a "conflict-ridden human enterprise."

[55]*Context*, 1 June 1987, 1.

[56]William J. Petersen and Stephen Board, "Our Non Prophet Press," *Eternity* (March 1977), 43–46.

[57]An illustration shared with me by a former editor of *Christianity Today*: During a series of news articles exposing a scandal in the Bill Gothard Basic Youth Conflicts organization, Gothard called the magazine and asked them not to publish an article. When told the magazine had gone to press and was about to be mailed, Gothard offered to pay for the entire printing and fund the reprinting of the magazine without the embarrassing news story. *Christianity Today* did not accept Gothard's offer.

[58]For a nuanced statement of purpose for *Christianity Today*, see "The Difference CT Means to Make," *Christianity Today*, 2 January 1981, 12.

[59]I have argued in "Jeremiah Monthly: That's no prophet, it's a magazine" (*Spectrum*, 1979) that *Sojourners* is no more prophetic, to its own audience, than *Moody Monthly*. All have their own stable of sacred cows. The apparent difference may be in the tolerance that various magazines have for criticism.

[60]One study can be mentioned: Robert W. Ross' *So It Was True: The American Protestant Press and the Nazi Persecution of the Jews* (Minneapolis: University of Minnesota Press, 1980).

[61]This was part of Joseph Bayly's appeal in *Eternity*'s "Out of My Mind" column, which appeared from 1961 to 1986.

6

CONTEMPORARY CHRISTIAN MUSIC: THE BUSINESS OF MUSIC MINISTRY

WILLIAM D. ROMANOWSKI

In 1968 Larry Norman left the rock group "People" when Capitol executives changed the title of the band's LP from *We Need a Whole Lot More Jesus and a Lot Less Rock and Roll* to simply *I Love You*. The following year, Norman produced a solo album with Capitol, *Upon This Rock*, which is considered the first Jesus rock album in America. He and other "Jesus musicians" began a musical trend among young Christians of the post–World War II generation, popularly known as the "baby boom." Nearly twenty years later, Amy Grant became the first contemporary Christian artist to sell over a million copies of an album—*Age to Age*. She became the most popular artist in contemporary Christian music (CCM), the most commercially successful category of gospel music.

CCM encompasses most of the currently popular musical styles, including folk, rock, MOR (middle-of-the-road), heavy metal, punk, new wave, synth pop, etc. CCM resists clear definition, but it is essentially a mixture of popular musical styles and religious lyrics. Songs are usually autobiographical, expressing the need for personal salvation or praising God; songwriters often use scriptural texts for lyrics. Grant's successful career became a symbol of the growing Christian music industry in the United States, which evolved from a fledgling adventure among a small group of long-haired Jesus musicians into a multimillion dollar business.

The Christian music industry is a dramatic illustration of

143

144 I William D. Romanowski

how diverse American cultural traditions are combined to establish identity, achievement, and purpose for a subculture within a broader pluralistic society. Its evolution was a continual interplay of Christian allegiances and beliefs with other social and cultural forces in America, particularly those that propelled the secular entertainment industries. The CCM industry grew out of the tumultuous soil of American culture in the late 1960s, when the country was torn apart by the agony of the Vietnam War, the failure of Great Society programs, and the political and cultural rebellion of the postwar baby-boom generation. Christian rock was pioneered by members of the Jesus Movement as a modernization of church music—evangelism in the musical language of the Woodstock generation. Synthesizing the fundamentalist church tradition with the liberal cultural trends in American culture, these musicians created a persistent tension in their worldview between sacred and secular ideals and sensibilities. Soon a Christian music industry formed around this common vision of using rock music as a vehicle for ministry and evangelism in the youth culture, and as an alternative to the secular entertainment system. By 1985, gospel music was outselling jazz and classical records. Meanwhile, tensions between sacred and secular concerns reached a peak in the 1980s; the growing Christian music industry increasingly adopted the capitalistic values and marketing ethos of the secular entertainment industry. Ministry was subjugated to financial profits. Evangelism was the rhetoric, business the reality. When contemporary Christian artists captured large enough sales in the gospel market to attract the attention of the mainstream recording industry, Christian separatists protested. The CCM community was in disarray over the means, the motives, and the outcome of Christian music.

Although still a small piece of the $6.5 billion annual sales for the record industry, the over $300 million Christian music business has attracted considerable attention as a seemingly strange and often confusing synthesis of Christian values and the trappings of secular culture. One writer called Christian rock "the most peculiar hybrid of all in Christian culture."[1]

Few scholars have studied the contemporary Christian music industry. Carol Flake discussed contemporary Christian music as a hybrid of Christian and secular views of culture. In a survey of CCM artists, Bill Young concluded that the broadened appeal of Christian music in the mainstream market and on video channels resulted from the increased commercialization of the music. Several biographies of CCM artists provided only peripheral information about the Christian music business and, oriented to CCM fans, the biographies lacked critical evaluation. The only historical survey was Paul Baker's *Contemporary Christian Music: Where It Came From, What It Is, Where It's Going*, a revised and expanded sequel to *Why Should the Devil Have All the Good Music?* It was a collage of short essays and interviews loosely arranged historically to trace the development of contemporary Christian music. A disc jockey who pioneered Jesus music on the airwaves in the early 1970s, Baker offered first-hand experience and personal interviews. However, he provided little critical analysis of the trends in popular music and the recording industry.[2] Like much of the research of and by evangelicals, it was rather Pollyannish and evangelistic.

GIVE ME A J-E-S-U-S: THE ULTIMATE TRIP

The Christian music industry exists as an identifiable American subculture with members sharing common beliefs and values. The CCM "family," as members sometimes refer to it, includes everyone involved in production and consumption: record executives, advertising people, management, artists, agents, promoters, retailers, journalists, youth leaders, and fans.[3] Their worldview is a complex web of religious and industrial values. Its roots, like the music, can be traced back to the Jesus Movement in the late 1960s.

Born-again Jesus People were members of the largest generation in American history—the postwar baby boom. The baby boom was something unique in American history and the media covered it with labels: Pepsi Generation, Rock Generation, Woodstock Generation, Protest Generation, and Me Generation. Reared in a period of unprecedented affluence and prolonged peace, baby boomers had great expectations for their own lives as well as for the impact their generation would have on improving the quality of life and social and political conditions in the world. Like Beatle John Lennon, they "imagined" a future world of peace, harmony, and love. However, the spirited idealism of the early sixties, when America stood on the threshold of President Kennedy's New Frontier, came spiraling down in the second half of the decade. American society reeled under the stress of rapid technological change, political assassinations, and especially the growing unpopularity of the war in Vietnam. The modern civil rights movement prompted dramatic strides toward legal equality but witnessed little progress toward improved living conditions. The gap between expectations and reality widened; frustration led to riots in many American cities and to demonstrations on most college campuses.

The baby boomers, now university students, decried the plight of the nation's poor and minorities as well as the United States' involvement in Southeast Asia. To many of them, these problems were manifestations of racism, sexism, and oppression inherent in the American socio-economic system. The countercultural rebellion that emerged took shape in a variety of ways—rural communal living, inner-city political activism, experiments with mind-expanding drugs, and various nontraditional religious experiences—but all shared a common enemy in the reigning liberal consensus concerning American social, economic, and political life.

The Jesus Movement was a synthesis of opposing cultural forces at work in the late sixties—a mixture of the liberal social and political ideas of the countercultural rebellion with a conservative evangelical revival in the church. "Jesus freaks" were not systematic philosophers; however, there were three main tenets of the faith held by those in the movement. First, the Jesus Movement shared the countercultural rejection of the industrial/technological society. It was partly a reaction against poverty and racism, environmental pollution, militarism, the threat of nuclear annihilation, and middle-class materialistic values. But that was as far as the countercultural influence went—an identification of the problems. Although Jesus People shared the countercultural distrust of established institutions, they never wholly embraced "new left" politics or mind-expanding drugs. Jesus was their drug. The countercultural influence was easily retired in the late 1970s when the gospel music audience was identified as conservative evangelicals.

Second, the Jesus Movement was a rejection of modern theology and the role of mainline Protestantism as "chaplain of the status quo."[4] Young people found it difficult to reconcile American Christianity with the injustices and violence that surrounded them during the sixties. Feeding the poor and freeing the oppressed seemed more consistent with the teaching of Jesus than fund-raising and building programs. Like their secular counterparts, the hippies, Jesus People largely rejected the social institutions to which their parents belonged. They accepted the liberal social agenda of mainline Protestantism, but rejected modern theology in favor of the personal religion of traditional evangelicalism. Their piety was not primarily ideological, but religious.

Finally, like evangelicalism, the Movement was Bible-based and centered on the person of Jesus, who was represented somewhat as the original hippie. Members emphasized a personal relationship with Jesus Christ and the working of the Holy Spirit. They practiced evangelism and discipleship. Attempting to make God "relevant," Jesus People created new forms of ministry in tune with the social and cultural winds of the times: street preaching, Christian communes, drug hotlines, shelters for runaways, and inner-city groups working to change urban conditions.

In spite of the apparent social concerns of the Jesus Movement, many of its members saw Jesus as what Os Guiness called "the ultimate trip, beyond marijuana and LSD, safe, satisfying and spiritual."[5] Jesus People viewed American society in the late sixties as truly on the "eve of destruction," as one popular song put it. While stressing the authority of the Bible and criticizing the values of the wider culture, they turned the Christian message almost entirely inward. Instead of transforming the structures of American society, the Movement emphasized personal piety and evangelism as the solution to social and political problems. Everything would be all right when people "put Jesus on the throne of their heart."

WE'RE GONNA ROCK AND ROLL FOR JESUS

Rock music was a major dialect in the language of the youth culture in the 1950s and 1960s. It was a central means of communication for the postwar generation, reflecting new ideas and values. Sociologist Landon Y. Jones described the music as "a language that taught the baby boom about themselves."[6] Amidst cries of "relevance," the Jesus Movement began producing its own music as a means of propagating the Christian message of salvation on their own side of the generation gap. Christian DJ and author Paul Baker said, "For the first time in that generation of wars, riots, and tumultuous unrest, the young people were being offered the love and peace of Jesus on recordings which could be played over and over, ministering in their own language."[7]

Jesus musicians envisioned themselves as the high priests of a new age in church music when they spearheaded a contemporary style of music with traditional Christian themes in the current vernacular. Early influences came from both the church and the secular rock scene. Youth musicals were early attempts at "modernizing" church music. Following the popularity of *Up With People*, Kurt Kaiser, a composer at Word Records in Waco, Texas, and Ralph Carmichael, who scored soundtracks for Billy Graham films, collaborated on the music for several Christian youth musicals in the late 1960s and early 1970s. *Tell It Like It Is, Natural High*, and *I'm Here, God's Here, Now We Can Get Started* used a mild quasi-rock score and spawned a flood of imitations.

More vital inspirations were songs like Barry McGuire's popular protest song—"Eve of Destruction": "And you tell over and over and over again, my friend / That you don't believe we're on the eve of destruction." The song's straightforward lyrics, simple melody, and moralistic tone were examples of what became the chief characteristics of the highly individualistic and evangelistic messages of the Jesus music in the late sixties and early seventies. "When you ask somebody what our songs are about there's no ambiguity," said Jesus musician Chuck Girard. "It's right there in plain simple language with no deep intellectual vibes. What we're saying is Jesus, one way. If you want the answer follow it."[8] The simple assurance of the message was appealing partly because of the great social upheaval and uncertainty of the time. "In this desperately critical and chaotic hour when the entire world is engulfed with a spirit of revolution," wrote Campus Crusade for Christ leader Bill Bright, Jesus was "History's Greatest Revolutionary."[9] Thus, uncertainty itself became a basis for faith, and revolution a springboard for evangelism.

Initially Jesus rock was frowned upon by members of established churches, evangelical and mainline Protestant alike. However, gradually it was seen by some church leaders and Christians working in the entertainment fields as a potential vehicle for evangelism among the young. Here too, revolution would serve to keep old institutions alive. Sparrow Records' founder Billy Ray Hearn, a former church minister of music, recalled: "I saw in contemporary music the best vessel to reach young people with the gospel. . . . They listen to the music that is current. That's their language."[10] This was the great justification for new musical styles—evangelization of lost youth, and there were plenty of them in the 1970s.

CHRISTIAN LYRICS FOR THE DEVIL'S MUSIC?

American popular music has always been a fusion and popularization of diverse traditions. The vitality and appeal of American popular and folk music traditions resulted from a synthesis of musical and thematic elements from the songs of various racial and ethnic groups. Even conventional performance and instrumentation were borrowed by popular musicians from earlier traditions. This was true of early gospel music as well. Although gospel and secular music traditions were virtually inseparable musically, they were kept distinct by lyrics, purpose, and physical location—the church as opposed to the juke joint, for instance. Some of the most expressive forms of popular music have emerged from the interaction of sacred and secular culture. Rockabilly was forged by artists like Elvis Presley and Jerry Lee Lewis, whose Southern Pentecostal roots seemed to conflict with what Jerry Lee called "worldly music, rock'n'roll."[11] When Ray Charles performed beloved gospel songs in a rhythm-and-blues style, it was considered apostasy. But the soul music he created infused secular concerns of blacks during the years of the civil-rights struggle in the 1950s and 1960s with the jubilation and triumph of the gospel. Both rock and roll and soul brought musical and cultural elements together to make something new; the élan and driving immediacy of these musical hybrids embodied the tension in American culture between religious ideals and secular realities. They became symbolic expressions of shared feelings, sentiments, and hopes.

Jesus rock, however, was less a musical hybrid than a co-optation of existing rock music for evangelistic purposes. The Jesus Movement's combination of Christian lyrics and rock music was not motivated by artistic concerns; baptizing rock music with Christian lyrics was a way of legitimizing the music for born-again hippies and making it viable in the youth market. Jesus musicians treated rock music as a neutral form of communication merged with the sacred gospel message. In *Contemporary Christian Music* (CCM), the *Rolling Stone* of the Christian music industry, one writer asked, "Should We Take Jesus Out of Christian Music?": "Sorry folks, but that's like taking the steel guitar out of country music, the drums out of rock and roll and the bass out of disco."[12] From this perspective, Christian music was identified by the words, not the musical style. Gospel Music Association executive director Don Butler said: "There is no such thing as gospel "music"—the lyrics are what make songs religious or secular."[13] To qualify as a Christian song, *CCM* editor John Styll argued, "the song should offer praise to God or contain some aspect of the gospel."[14] Considered neutral, musical style was left to secular innovation and Christian imitation; Christian popular music was literally "not of this world," but a parasite on secular industrial and artistic achievements.[15]

This pragmatic concept of popular music as a tool for evangelism drove the Jesus Movement headlong into industrial co-optation. Contrary to the beliefs of the Jesus Movement, musical style is not neutral. Rock music was organically wed to the socio-cultural setting in which the music was created and developed. Early rock music fused American folk music: blues, country, ethnic folk music, and traditional gospel. Rock was cultivated by artists in the soil of racial strife, disillusioned youth, experimental lifestyles, and the divisive Vietnam War. Jesus music captured the spirit of those times in spite of its religious lyrics. "Rock and roll is more than just music," *Rolling Stone* rightly proclaimed. "It is the energy center of the new culture and youth revolution."[16] Jesus music plunged evangelical youth into that new culture—or at least into an evangelical version of it.

Some evangelicals sensed this tension, though often misguidedly. A host of antirock crusaders blasted rock music in publications and pulpits as devil worship, a Communist plot, and destroyer of the minds and morals of youth. In 1981, *CCM* magazine ran a series of articles in an attempt to provide "a comprehensive apologetic for Christian rock music."[17] The three-part series outlined the controversy among Christians over the fusion of secular rock with gospel lyrics and demonstrated different views of culture espoused by Christians. But the series also became a forum for Pentecostals and other evangelicals to criticize the cultural basis of the music. Writer David Noebel and televangelist Jimmy Swaggart flailed the music as inherently evil and called Christian rock "spiritual fornication." Contemporary Christian music "unites the holy and the unholy," argued Lowell Hart, author of *Satan's Music Exposed*. On the other hand, apologists for Christian rock said the message of music was contained only in the lyrical content.

Christian rock stars and the industry have argued repeatedly for the neutrality of music as a defense against contentions that the beat of rock is inherently evil. At the same time, they welcomed criticism that portrayed the evils of secular rock music. They had much to gain by encouraging Christian record buyers to shun secular recordings and purchase their evangelical versions.

In addition, the Christian music industry naïvely assumed rock music was effective evangelistically. The audience for contemporary Christian entertainment rapidly became twelve to thirty-five-year-old evangelicals, not the "unsaved youth" for whom the music was allegedly written. In an evaluation of popular music as political propaganda, sociologist R. Serge Denisoff demonstrated that Top Forty songs are potentially an excellent vehicle for publishing protest/topical songs, especially among listeners under thirty. The commercialization required to make a Top Forty hit, however, transforms propaganda into rather bland entertainment.[18] Also, most popular culture theorists agree that popularity, though certainly unpredictable, is determined at least partly by how well the popular artifact affirms people's existing beliefs.[19] It is difficult to imagine song after song produced by Christian artists—"In God we trust / His Son we must receive"—dominating the popularity charts in the United States. The general public simply does not wish to hear such religious lyrics. As a result, the most popular music must capture broader beliefs than those of a particular religious group. Popular music propagandizes religious subcultures in the United States—not the other way around.

Nevertheless, the evangelistic model matched the marketing strategy of the mainstream entertainment industry. The success of evangelism is calculated by the number of souls that are saved; reaching as many people as possible easily translates into increased record sales, extensive airplay, and sold-out concert halls. Evangelism is the industrial rhetoric, not the spiritual reality, of Christian popular music. This rhetoric justifies the industry to the Christian community and to the Christians within the industry who want to believe in the propaganda value of their work. Also, the rhetoric linguistically transforms money-making into ministry, easing the consciences of those few who earn healthy incomes off the music.

Since the 1970s, the Christian music industry has been a peculiar combination of evangelistic impulses and business savvy. The artists, executives, and fans alike consider it a ministry; for them, music is a medium for evangelization. They approach concerts as if they were worship services or evangelistic meetings. "Christian musicians," asserted one writer, "should be ministers singing mini-sermons or lessons."[20] They see themselves as musical troubadors for the Lord, and their ecclesiastical model for music turns churches into concert networks. As para-church workers, they usurp the role and many of the functions of the institutional church, including worship and evangelism. One CCM spokesperson even referred to the Christian music industry, from musicians to deejays, as the body of Christ.[21]

THE BUSINESS OF MUSIC MINISTRY

Throughout the 1970s, the Christian music industry organized around several common difficulties: (1) a lack of audience acceptance for contemporary Christian music, (2) technically inferior record production, (3) severely limited radio exposure for artists, and (4) a small and inefficient network for distribution, which was limited mainly to Christian bookstores. With these problems identified, the industry created an alternative entertainment system geared toward the growing youth market. The industry scaffolding began to go up as concert halls replaced coffeehouses and church fellowship halls, as record labels replaced custom recordings, and as contemporary music radio formats replaced tapes of preachers.

In the beginning, Jesus musicians traveled in vans, played for free-will offerings at near-empty auditoriums, and were at the mercy of nonprofessional sponsors for food and lodging. Albums were custom projects made on shoestring budgets that sold a few thousand copies largely through distribution at concerts. The Christian music industry was primarily a localized business organized around the talents of regional performers. It thrived in particular areas where symbiotic relationships could be developed between concert promoters, radio personnel, retailers, and especially the local churches. While the mainstream record business had national radio (and later cable channels like MTV), CCM artists had to rely on personal touring and the limited distribution network of religious bookstores. Consequently, a CCM artist could be popular in one market and almost unknown in another. Record sales remained significantly below those in the mainstream music business in spite of the local success and popularity of some performers.

In the absence of radio airplay and national record distribution in the mid-1970s, Christian musicians looked for alternative avenues for exposure and publicity. The revitalized coffeehouse circuit and the Jesus festivals, patterned after the large rock festivals, became important showcases for Christian groups and artists. In the summer of 1975, the First Annual Christian Artists' Seminar was held at Estes Park, Colorado; it has since become an important showcase for new talent. The Fellowship of Contemporary Christian Ministries (FCCM) was formed that year to organize performers and management and to create a national avenue for exposure through enlarged personal contacts and by publishing a directory of artists for Christian programmers. *Contemporary Christian Music* began as a monthly publication in July 1978; issues were given free to twelve thousand people in the Christian music industry, including retailers and radio station personnel. Founded by former disc jockey John Styll, *CCM* included trade information as well as fan-oriented interviews and artist profiles. By 1988, *CCM* had forty-two thousand subscribers.

Christian record executives saw the potential of bringing Christian artists and audiences together and began establishing production and distribution companies. Word Records remains the largest, representing the major sales and business growth in the Christian music industry over the last two decades. Originally recording mostly traditional white gospel music, Word was founded by Jarrell McCracken in 1950 with one record and $70 for distribution. Billy Ray Hearn, who was hired to promote the Carmichael/Kaiser youth musicals, started Myrrh Records to record artists performing the new "Jesus Music." Myrrh quickly became a major part of Word's sales. Contemporary music grew from 10 to 12 percent of Word's total business in 1974, two years after the premiere of the Myrrh label, to 50 percent in 1981. Word's total volume that year was five times what it was in 1974. In 1977 Myrrh inaugurated an unprecedented $75,000 promotion campaign with the slogan "The music is today, the message if forever." Average budgets for album production grew throughout the decade from $8,000 to $35,000, and a successful record sold from twenty to fifty thousand copies. These figures paled in light of the larger record industry, but reflected growth in the CCM field. In 1986, Word's share of the $86.5 million Christian music industry was estimated at 60 percent.[22] The success of Word soon spawned rival companies. Billy Ray Hearn left Word in 1976 to found Sparrow Records. Meanwhile, the Benson Publishing Company in Nashville organized Greentree Records in 1976 to cash in on the growth in Christian music. These three companies remain the largest producers of Christian music.

During the same period, religious radio stations slowly increased airplay for contemporary Christian music. Some stations even changed to a new musical format called "Contemporary Christian Music," although they carefully maintained nonoffensive playlists that included much of the milder, middle-of-the-road music. One deejay described the standard format as "not too rocky and not too hokey."[23] As Schultze shows in chapter seven, evangelical radio had become a religious ghetto in the 1970s, alienating potential listeners with widely diverse formats.[24] The difficulty in getting contemporary music on the religious-radio airwaves was a result of what one Christian radio executive felicitously called the "donor pool syndrome." The majority of Christian radio stations depended on a group of middle-age to elderly donors for their financial survival. Unlike nonreligious stations, which simply matched their programming to the audience for their advertisers, these religious stations depended upon a rather small audience of direct financial contributors. Advertising was merely the financial cream for religious stations, whose economic future was tied to the goodwill of the local Christian community. Radio programmers were reluctant to hazard losing that audience; contemporary music formats were risky. "Economic concern is the number one factor," explained Chip Lasko, sales representative for KPRZ in Los Angeles. "We call it a ministry, but the decision makers know it's business."[25] Much to the chagrin of the recording industry, Christian radio never attracted large audiences.

Probably two major problems blocked commercially successful religious-music programming. First, too many religious stations were trying to please the entire Christian audience. The history of secular commercial radio shows how important market segmentation has been to the industry's survival in the post-television age. Religious stations, given their small potential audience, were hesitant to lose any listeners. Second, many Christian stations had programming techniques that were inferior to those of nonreligious stations; they lacked the typical professional sound of nonreligious stations. Like much of the music they played, Christian stations offered second-rate talent and operated with second-class production facilities.

In spite of these problems, in 1979 industry researchers optimistically predicted a bonanza for stations that adopted a professional contemporary music format geared toward a younger audience. Perhaps more than anything else, these findings launched CCM into the musical mainstream.[26] For the first time, both the Christian recording industry and the religious radio stations saw that musical compromises had to be made in order for both organizations to cash in on the religious market. Although stations feared alienating traditional contributors, they also saw that younger audiences could attract significantly greater advertising revenues. The solution was a highly conservative music playlist that would supposedly attract young listeners without offending older contributors. That excluded any hard rock. CCM was the ideal music for the birth of a new gospel market. Christian artists had no choice but to follow the lead; without air time their album sales were doomed. CCM became the musical mainstream of the reformulated gospel market.

Gradually the Christian music industry improved the quality of record production and increased product exposure and distribution. The result was a steady increase in record sales. In 1977, a Warner Communications poll put gospel in the "All Others" category that accounted for 3 percent of total record sales. By 1980, gospel had increased its share to 5 percent of the industry and warranted its own category.[27] Christian entrepreneurs were building a Christian entertainment industry that paralleled its secular counterpart not just in musical styles and trends, but in marketing techniques, management, concert production, publicity, and glamorization.

The commercialization of music ministry highlighted the difference between missionary goals and marketing requirements. As demand for Christian music increased, so did retail prices for records. A few artists tried to buck the trend. Songwriter Keith Green announced in 1980 that he would no longer sell his albums and tapes for a set price, a move that CCM rightly called "a withdrawal from the commercial side of Christian music."[28] In a similar vein, Christian artist Dallas Holm opted for love offerings instead of tickets at concerts. "The bottom line is souls," he said, "and there's no question in my mind that more people will come for free, especially the type we want to reach."[29] But these were minor plays in an increasingly important game of high finance, where artists jockeyed for a good public image and promoters moved for the best market position. Evangelical concert promoters, tired of meager profits from Christian productions, sought the apparent financial security and predictability of the secular recording industry. This meant enormous increases in marketing budgets, which would have to create relatively stable record demand and guarantee distribution. However, it was increasingly clear that the CCM industry could not keep Christian record buyers from purchasing secular recordings. The biggest untapped market was the young person who listened to non-Christian radio and bought secular records and tapes.

MOVING INTO THE MAINSTREAM

With the Christian music industry groundwork laid, several things happened in the early 1980s to put contemporary Christian music in a position to claim a share of the national recording industry. By this time, contemporary Christian music had replaced Jesus Music as the dominant term for popular, youth-oriented music. The Jesus Movement gradually faded away, forcing the industry to look for musical styles that neither protested the establishment nor reflected the taste of that movement. Following changes in American culture, the intimate folk music of James Taylor and Carole King, the soft rock of Fleetwood Mac, and the ballads of Barry Manilow seemed more appropriate for the unsaved of the seventies than the raucous sound of "Wowie, zowie, He saved my soul!" Christian recording mirrored the shifting tastes of its nascent consuming public. The Christian industry was finally tuned to a popular consumer culture, not simply to the church or religious music traditions. But the concept of a Christian popular music distinguished by the lyrics overlooked the reality of musical taste groups within the evangelical market. During the 1970s, the emergence of Christian artists using diverse musical styles subdivided the Christian subculture along the lines of taste groups. This reduced the size of the potential audience and limited record sales, keeping CCM artists out of the limelight of the recording industry. What was needed was a musical style that would consolidate the array of taste groups that made up the gospel market, and an artist who could appeal to different groups.

While CCM artists represented a myriad of popular musical

styles, for the most part they all worked within the Christian music industry based primarily in Nashville and Los Angeles. Gospel artists and executives rubbed shoulders in recording studios, conference rooms, and restaurants throughout the seventies. As a result, there was considerable crossover between gospel categories with songs, artists, and styles. Gospel record and publishing companies hired staff writers who wrote songs for artists working in different subgenres of gospel music. Increasingly the lines between different types of music within the broader "gospel" category began to disappear.

The music that emerged from this continual interaction within the gospel music industry was forged primarily in Nashville recording studios. A Nashville country flavor and neoclassical twist were added to current popular musical styles and fused with praise-oriented lyrics characteristic of much traditional gospel music. This "contemporary praise" was popularized most notably by Amy Grant on her *Age to Age* LP. Demonstrating the strength of its broad gospel market appeal, the album debuted at the top of *CCM*'s album sales chart as well as at the top of all three airplay charts—Contemporary, Adult Contemporary, and Inspirational. *Age to Age* rode the top of the *CCM* chart for twenty-two months and stepped down only to make room for Grant's next album, *Straight Ahead*, which also debuted at number one.

Gospel record executives happily recognized that overlapping styles could increase the marketing potential of an album. Thus greater profits would be reaped from increased sales for a single album project. Buddy Huey, then Word A & R (Artist and Repertoire) vice president, recognized a "melting pot effect" in Christian music. "The markets are overlapping," Huey said. "The various styles cross-fertilize each other, and there's no telling where a particular song or group may end up."[30] Stan Moser, then senior vice president and chief of operations of Word's Record and Music division, explained the marketing rationale in terms of ministry.

> Actually, the way that you count your success, in my opinion, is how far you're able to take the ministry of any one artist and develop it to a larger audience rather than having a whole bunch of artists and trying to reach the same number of sales with a bunch of different titles. . . . It's our concept of doing more with less; doing more volume and covering more people with fewer artists and fewer investments."[31]

Moser recognized the confluence of evangelical ministry and commercial marketing.

The growing Christian music industry in the United States reflected the popularization of contemporary praise; a few gospel artists were finally able to capture a wide demographic market. Gospel music sales began increasing, while overall annual record sales in the United States remained constant during the early 1980s. Christian booksellers saw a 250 percent increase in music sales, from 9 percent of total sales in 1976 to 25 percent in 1984. One industry report gave gospel a 7.5 percent share ($315 million) in 1985, an increase in sales from $180 million in 1980.[32] *Billboard* observed that "if those sales aren't in Michael Jackson's league yet, then that's true of every other artist in every other musical category these days."[33] Some observers credited CCM's durability to the spiritual value of the music, increased availability, and the growing spendable income for teens.[34] But the popularization of contemporary praise, which solidified the fragmented and leery gospel market, was probably the most significant factor. There was finally one religious mass market to be pursued by all the major Christian recording companies. At the Gospel Music Association in 1983, executive director Don Butler identified gospel music's market as the born-again Christian under thirty-five with an annual income over $20,000. A Gallup poll found that from fifty to sixty million Americans were in that category.[35]

Demographics had replaced religious traditions and music styles. The most significant issue now was marketing: how to reach the popular audience. Previously the Christian Booksellers Association, which included over three thousand stores, was the prime distribution system. But that system could not support the dreams of the industry. While two-thirds of Word's sales came through Christian book and record stores, research statistics revealed that fewer than 10 percent of all Christians frequented these outlets.[36] Also, a 1983 survey by National Religious Broadcasters found that the number of U.S. radio stations with religious formats had increased 13 percent in the previous year, but Christian stations had a meager 1.6 percent share of the listening audience in the U.S.[37] That put Christian programming ahead of Spanish-language, jazz, and classical stations, but it was not in the big leagues of popular music. A controversial survey report from Word Records that year "painted a vivid picture of an infant industry still struggling for a significant share of the marketplace—often using antiquated (if any) marketing research."[38]

These dreams and frustrations of the Christian music industry in the early 1980s coincided with a dismal financial period in the broader recording industry. The list of woes seemed endless: an economic recession, a drop in record and tape sales in the U.S., an increase in production and marketing costs, competition for leisure dollars from cable television, and the aging baby boomers moving past the prime record-buying years. Record executives were making dramatic changes, trying to reverse the trend. In a series of cutbacks, Warner Brothers Records dropped over thirty artists from its roster, including Van Morrison, Bonnie Raitt, and Arlo Guthrie. During this same time the ailing company signed Juluka, a popular and controversial biracial group from South Africa. While the mainstream recording industry saw a turnabout in 1983, the revitalization was almost exclusively because of the phenomenal sales of Michael Jackson's *Thriller* LP. Eager to be the first to catch the wave of a new musical megatrend, secular labels had reason for a new interest in gospel music.

Several past ventures had demonstrated that the successful merging of music markets could prove to be a financial bonanza, especially during an uncreative period in the recording industry. Just prior to the birth of rock and roll, rhythm-and-blues songs appeared on both the pop and rhythm-and-blues charts in the early 1950s, as did soul music in the sixties. In the early 1970s, CBS distributed the soul music of Philadelphia International Records in the white popular market, while Philly International executives handled the black audience. Country artists began placing songs on the popular music charts in the late seventies, a crossover trend that continues today. The few superstars in popular music, most of whom introduced musical hybrids, achieved their status by transcending musical genres. They demonstrated an ability to capture more than one market by scoring on different charts.

For some time gospel music seemed poised on the brink of a breakthrough into the mainstream popular market. However, several attempts made by mainline record companies to include the gospel market in their established production and distribution systems had been unsuccessful. As early as 1974, ABC attempted to distribute recordings from Word's Myrrh label but "barely survived the debacle."[39] Word, an independent subsidiary of ABC at that time, handled production and distribution in the gospel market. In 1981, MCA Records reestablished its Songbird label, which had previously carried black gospel acts, and signed several contemporary artists: B. J. Thomas, Dan Peek, and Mylon LeFevre and Broken Heart, among others. Late in 1981 CBS executive Dick Asher said,

> I'll not pretend that we're here because of some new burst of religious faith. We're here because of the potential to sell records in the gospel market. We want to put gospel records in stores that don't currently carry them. We want to transform gospel from a specialty market to a mass-appeal market.[40]

The CBS venture lasted only a year and a half before closing in July 1983. A CBS Records Group press release said it was "a matter of sheer economics . . . we just weren't selling enough records."[41] Distribution contracts were signed with Billy Ray Hearn's Sparrow Records and MCA, and also with Ralph Carmichael's Light Records and Elektra/Asylum. Both distribution programs failed because of poor record productions and poor record sales and seemed to signal an end to any sacred-secular collaboration in the record industry.

Nevertheless, the commercial success of Amy Grant's *Age to Age* album in 1983 kept secular recording companies interested in the growing Christian popular music market. Grant's album was a milestone in contemporary Christian music. In the past, sales of a meager 100,000 to 150,000 albums were a hit for a contemporary Christian album—a minuscule figure in the mainstream recording industry. Grant's music, by contrast, showed that there was an enormous audience for the right kind of recordings even in the face of poor distribution and promotion. *Age to Age* remained at the top of *Billboard's* inspirational chart for 158 weeks, and her next album, *Straight Ahead*, was number one for more than a year. In comparison, Michael Jackson's *Thriller*, the best-selling album of all time (forty million copies), lasted a record thirty-seven weeks at number one on the *Billboard* pop chart. The phenomenal success and longevity of *Thriller* was facilitated by exposure on the newly formed MTV video network and by an unprecedented seven singles in the Top Ten, two of which reached number one. Without the benefit of national video exposure or a singles market, Amy Grant became the first gospel artist to reach the platinum sales mark for an album.[42] Estimates were that Grant accounted for as much as 20 percent of Word

Records' $35 million in annual sales.[43] How much more business could the "Michael Jackson of gospel music" account for if she had similar access to secular channels of publicity, including secular radio and MTV? Other record companies wanted their own gospel queen.

Executives at mainstream A & M Records quickly identified gospel music with the conservative political agenda and social issues of Jerry Falwell's Moral Majority in the Reagan era. "Contemporary gospel falls right in line with the conservative state of the union," said Don Bozzi, director of promotion and marketing for A & M distributed labels. "A window's open in this country for this kind of music, and it's open because of Amy [Grant]."[44] Believing that gospel music was a potentially lucrative market, A & M manufactured and marketed Word products to conventional retailers, while Word continued to handle Christian book and record stores. Word Records' president Stan Moser explained the marketing rationale behind the A & M/Word arrangement.

> Our statistics show that about 50 percent of the U.S. population is active in some way in church. Roughly about 100 million people. Only 10 percent of that figure ever frequents Christian bookstores or shops, which is where the bulk of our albums are sold. So our market universe to this point has only been 10 million people.
>
> That means when someone like Amy Grant nears a million units sold, she's penetrating the universe that encompasses the other 90 million Christians who are "secular" in terms of their buying habits.
>
> That means we still have a huge untapped market in that 90 million. It is for all intents and purposes a secular market that's not going to be offended by our message. That's where our next thrust is going to be.[45]

Amy Grant's A & M/Word production *Unguarded* was certified gold in two months. By comparison, her previous LP, *Straight Ahead*, took one year to reach that sales mark. It was reported that some 60 percent of sales of *Unguarded* were made through A & M's twenty thousand record outlets. "Find A Way," the first single released from *Unguarded*, appeared on both the pop and adult contemporary charts, and the video was in the rotation on the VH-1 channel.[46] The album went platinum (over one million copies) in 1986, less than half the time it took *Age to Age*. The following year, "The Next Time I Fall," a duet with former Chicago member Peter Cetera, reached the top of the

Billboard Hot 100. A 1988 Amy Grant release, *Lead Me On,* sold six hundred thousand copies to record dealers in advance of its release. The album was an attempt to establish Grant as a mainstream artist, not merely as a CCM crossover star. The project did not live up to executives' expectations, however. Singles released from the LP failed to generate much airplay on secular radio stations. Despite a poor showing on the *Billboard* airplay charts, the album received platinum certification. Accepting her award for Artist of the Year at the GMA's annual Dove Awards in 1989, Grant said, "If you're in this field you're in a field with a family . . . I wouldn't want to be any place else." It was difficult to determine if gospel's most successful artist was renewing her commitment to the CCM audience or just expressing the limitations of contemporary Christian music.

Grant's limited success in the mainstream market still paved the way for an increasing number of gospel artists who were selling several hundred thousand copies of their albums and mounting financially profitable tours. In 1989 major record companies were establishing distribution deals with various independent labels, trying to find the next Led Zeppelin, U2, or R.E.M. in the underground rock scene. The Word/A & M pact and a similar arrangement between Sparrow and Capitol confirmed this development among the gospel labels. The majors were also creating specialized departments to develop and market alternative artists through nontraditional channels. The CCM industry was ecstatic when Warner Brothers/Reprise Records formed a contemporary gospel label that began operation in 1990. Neal Joseph resigned his position as vice president of A & R for Word, Inc. to become vice president and general manager of the new label. The first three acts signed were in black gospel, but Warner executives intended to add artists that represented a variety of styles in the Christian market. Sparrow/Star Song distributed the new label in the Christian market. Two decades after its birth, CCM was clearly beginning to move into the mainstream popular music market. It was finally achieving full commercial status and broad popular appeal, but there was a price to pay for such extraordinary success on the part of several artists and record companies.

ROCK'N'RELIGION: AN ETERNAL SEESAW?

The establishment of the multi-million dollar Christian music business and the initial success of the crossover trend fueled long-standing debates within the CCM community. In 1986, a group of Christian artists sent an open letter to *Contemporary Christian Magazine* complaining that the remarkable growth of the Christian music industry was now hampering their ministries.[47] "We who feel called as ministers of the gospel of Jesus Christ," the letter read, "feel that this label ["the industry"] is reflecting an unfortunate trend in Christian music brought on in part by the proliferation of airplay and sales charts and album reviews." Amy Grant, dubbed by some critics, the "Madonna of Christian Rock," was blasted by fundamentalists. One *CCM* reader wrote: "*Unguarded* isn't Christian music; it's moral and ethical humanism with a very slight religious perspective." A note attached to a bouquet of flowers presented to Grant at a concert read: "Turn back. You can still be saved if you renounce what you've done." Some CCM fans claimed that Grant had abandoned Christian ministry for secular entertainment. *CCM* editor John Styll defended the magazine's most popular artist, calling Amy's music "sanctified entertainment."[48] Even other gospel executives criticized the distribution agreement between Word Records and A & M. "When Christians go to a concert they don't want boogie for boogie's sake," said Billy Ray Hearn, whose Sparrow Records' distribution deal with MCA was short-lived. "They want to see a definite ministry with a clear opportunity to make a life-changing decision."[49]

A conservative backlash was felt throughout the Christian music industry. A slump in retail sales and the televangelism scandals in 1987 and 1988 made the crossover music trend more suspect as an avenue for music ministry. The CCM audience had accepted the utilitarian view of music as evangelism, striving for popularity and religious impact. But popularity required religiously shallow lyrics; songs not dealing overtly with the Christian life elicited harsh criticism from conservative evangelicals and especially from fundamentalists. Many Christian artists and executives realized they had to play it safe by protecting the vestiges of sacred symbolism in their recordings or they might alienate the evangelical market. To them, ministry was indeed good business; they simply could not compete with the mainstream recording industry on its own terms.

In the strangest twist of all, the publicity surrounding the initial success of the A & M/Word distribution deal led mainstream artists to a discovery of the evangelical market. Things had come full circle from the days when evangelical performers were trying to break into the secular market. Now secular artists were cashing in on the Christian market; they were the new evangelists. During a 1985 U.S. tour, the English band Foreigner hired local black gospel choirs in every major city as backups for their chart-topping "I Want to Know What Love Is." The "positive pop" trend reflected the popularity of Christian themes in music. For example, the rock group "Mr. Mister" had a chart hit with "Kyrie," which translated from the Greek means, "Lord have mercy." Band members said they were not Christians, let alone evangelicals, but they certainly had their eye on the Christian rock audience. We "can't help but find those little ties that draw people into our music," said a member of the group. " 'Kyrie' obviously has a Christian text."[50] In a *Rolling Stone* interview he said: "I think religion is probably the most positive thing in the world. But we don't want to preach or tell anybody to be a Christian."[51] Mr. Mister clearly was capitalizing on the evangelical market, blurring traditional record-industry distinctions between Christian and secular music. Even salacious Madonna had hits with religious, if sacrilegious, overtones. In 1989 the video "Like a Prayer" exploded in controversy, forcing Pepsi to drop the sexy superstar from a multi-million dollar advertising campaign.

The uniqueness of CCM was also confounded by successful Christian artists like Bruce Cockburn and U2, whose music explored new styles on secular labels. Instead of writing and performing songs that imitated current musical fashions with redundant Christian themes for the musically sterile Christian marketplace, they forged distinctive sounds and messages. Although Cockburn had only limited success in the U.S. market, he attracted a strong following in Canada, demonstrating that a Christian popular musician could succeed artistically and financially in the secular recording industry. Similarly, U2's *Joshua Tree* LP topped the U.S. national charts in 1987, while the Irish rock group swept the *Rolling Stone* Reader's Poll Awards that year, capturing Artist of the Year, Best Album, Best Single, Best Songwriter, Best Band, Best Live Performance, Sexiest Male, and Best Album Cover. A *CCM* review of a U2 concert concluded: "In a world where pop music is dominated by themes of sex, violence, and rebellion, U2 actively sells their product of hope—and many of today's hopeless generation are buying."[52]

In the late 1980s, the Christian music industry lost its direction. Some CCM artists and executives resigned themselves to the limited but safe gospel market. Others were still trying to penetrate the mainstream popular music market in the hopes of finding another Amy Grant. Word Records established a new label called What? Records to accommodate Christian artists who had commercial appeal with both Christian and secular audiences. Albums were distributed to Christian and conventional retailers. "This is material that is not for the most part about religious topics, but it's made by Christians—and I would hazard that that's 'Christian music,' if you must define it," explained What? Records' head Tom Willett. "Christians need to be writing songs about all areas of the human experience, not just sin, salvation, and the Second Coming."[53] What? artists were backed by relatively large production budgets and extensive A & M distribution through secular outlets. Higher production and marketing costs, however, sliced profits; Word could run three lower-quality productions down the CCM assembly line for the cost of one LP on the What? label. Also, executives were nervous about the conservative trend at the time. The standard CCM fare seemed safer and more profitable than attempts at innovation. Although Word made an initial three-year commitment to establishing the label, the company began cutting back before the completion of the first year and effectively dismantled What? Records in the second. This type of Christian music seemed, like the others, to lead nowhere.

The Christian music industry generally imitated commercially successful styles. Other musical subcultures, including punk and reggae, enlivened mainstream music with new ideas and musical innovations. CCM had little impact on other music. CCM undoubtedly appealed to more evangelicals than the relatively small number who bought most of the records and tapes. But the music was a popularization of so many disparate motives and musical traditions that it lacked a religious or even cultural home. It was no longer purely the lyrics of evangelicals, and its rock sound still elicited criticisms from many fundamentalists and Pentecostals. Marketing and demographics had become powerful impersonal forces that largely defined the music. At the 1989 GMA Convention in Nashville, Dan Harrell, co-manager of Amy Grant, argued that the goals of ministry and business are "exactly the same— market share."[54] Occasionally the altruistic dreams of the Jesus Movement echo in the words of CCM executives and especially artists. One reporter called this tension "the eternal seesawing between scriptural and commercial demands that sets the gospel industry apart from all others."[55] But that tension increasingly disappeared as profits and losses told the real story. Evangelism and Christian discipleship became lingering but distant ideals largely eclipsed by the drive for business success. After all, without adequate record sales, there would be no CCM industry. Depending on which evangelicals one asks, that could be a blessing or a curse.

NOTES

[1]Carol Flake, *Redemptorama: Culture, Politics, and the New Evangelicalism* (New York: Anchor Press, Doubleday & Company, Inc., 1984), 22.

[2]Carol Flake, *Redemptorama*; Bill Young, "Contemporary Christian Music: Rock the Flock," in *The God Pumpers: Religion in the Electronic Age*, ed. Marshall Fishwick and Ray B. Browne (Bowling Green, Ohio: Bowling Green State University Popular Press, 1987); Don Cusic, *Sandi Patti: The Voice of Gospel* (New York: Dolphin, Doubleday, 1988); Carol Leggett, *Amy Grant* (New York: Pocket Books, 1987); Bob Millard, *Amy Grant: A Biography* (New York: Doubleday, 1986); Sheila Walsh, *Never Give It Up* (New Jersey: Revell, 1986); Melody Greed and David Hazard, *No Compromise: The Life Story of Keith Green* (Chatsworth, Calif.: Sparrow Press, 1989); Paul Baker, *Contemporary Christian Music: Where It Came From, What It Is, Where It's Going* (Westchester, Ill.: Crossway Books, 1985).

[3]For example, Amy Grant said: "The Christian music realm is a family, and you can say things freely and openly with your family that you wouldn't say to a total stranger on the street." See Michael Goldberg, "Amy Grant wants to put God on the charts," *Rolling Stone* 6 June 1985, 10.

[4]Edward E. Plowman, *The Underground Church* (Elgin, Ill.: David C. Cook, 1971), 4.

[5]Os Guiness, *Dust of Death: A Critique of the Establishment and the Counter Culture and a Proposal for a Third Way* (Downers Grove, Ill.: InterVarsity, 1973), 327.

[6]Landon Y. Jones, *Great Expectations: America and the Baby Boom Generation* (New York: Ballantine, 1980), 72.

[7]Baker, *Contemporary Christian Music*, 35.

[8]Quoted in Patrick Corman, "Freaking Out on Jesus," *Rolling Stone* 24 June 1971, 25.

[9]Bill Bright, *Revolution Now!* (San Bernardino, Calif.: Campus Crusade for Christ, 1969), 10, 27.

[10]Quoted in Steve Rabey, "Fast-growing Gospel Music Now Outsells Jazz and Classical," *Christianity Today* 16 March 1984, 42.

[11]Quoted in Nick Tosches, *Hellfire: The Jerry Lewis Story* (New York: Delacorte, 1982). Also quoted in Ed Ward, Geoffrey Stokes and Ken Tucker, *Rock of Ages: The Rolling Stone History of Rock & Roll* (New York: Rolling Stone Press/Summit Books, 1986), 147. For a fuller discussion of this see Stephen R. Tucker, "Pentecostalism and Popular Culture in the South: A Study of Four Musicians," *Journal of Popular Culture* 16 (Winter 1982):68–80; Davin Seay with Mary Neely, *Stairway to Heaven: The Spiritual Roots of Rock'n'Roll—From the King and Little Richard to Prince and Amy Grant* (New York: Ballantine, 1986).

[12]Don Cusic, "Should We Take Jesus Out of Christian Music?" *Contemporary Christian Music*, August 1978, 6.

[13]Quoted in Millard, *Amy Grant: A Biography*, 152.

[14]John W. Styll, "What Makes Music Christian?" *Contemporary Christian Music* April 1987, 36. The struggle to keep the music relevant opened the potential for Christian musicians to explore certain social issues, especially those with a strong moral thrust—relationships, world hunger, abortion, prayer in the public schools. In the Christian music industry vocabulary, songs dealing with these themes were labeled "horizontal" (earthly) and remained on the fringe of what was generally considered Christian music. Songs focusing on the character of God and salvation were termed "vertical" (heavenly).

[15]Paul Baker's "Music Comparison Chart" dramatized this, listing contemporary Christian musicians and their secular music parallel. It was a Christian consumer guide. If a Christian enjoyed a certain "secular" artist, there was a Christian counterpart who sounded the same, but sang about the Lord. Of course, this was a comparison of musical style and not lifestyle. Baker pointed out that "a reference to Culture Club does not infer [sic] that the Christian counterpart dresses in women's clothes or wears lipstick and eye shadow." Baker's chart first appeared in *Group* magazine in September 1982. This quotation is from *Contemporary Christian Music*, 240.

[16]Quoted in Jones, *Great Expectations*, 125.

[17]This series began with "Does Rock'n'Roll Lead to Rack'n'Ruin?" *Contemporary Christian Music*, August/September 1981, 15–17. The series continued in "Can Religion Rock?" *Contemporary Christian Music*, October 1981, 20–23; "Our God, the Star, or Electric Guitar: Who Does Christian Rock Glorify?" *Contemporary Christian Music*, November 1981, 18–20.

[18]See R. Serge Denisoff, "Protest Songs: Those on AM Radio and Those of the Streets," in *Sing a Song of Social Significance*, 2d ed. (Bowling Green, Ohio: Bowling Green State University Popular Press, 1983), 149–67.

[19]See Christopher D. Geist and Jack Nachbar, eds. "Introduction: What Is Popular Culture?" in *The Popular Culture Reader*, 3rd ed. (Bowling Green, Ohio: Bowling Green University Popular Press, 1983); John Wiley Nelson, *Your God Is Alive and Well in Popular Culture* (Philadelphia: Westminster, 1976).

[20]Al Menconi, "What's Wrong with Christian Music?" *Contemporary Christian Music*, June 1987, 19.

[21]See Baker, *Contemporary Christian Music*, 162.

[22]See Bob Darden, "Word Inc. Chief Quits with Slap at Management," *Billboard* 4 October 1986, 85. Founder and president Jarrell McCracken sold Word to ABC in 1974 for stock valued at that time at $12.6 million. Word operated as an independent subsidiary of ABC. In 1984, Capital Cities Communications acquired ABC. Word Inc. became a subsidiary of Capital Cities Communications with an estimated value of $70 million.

[23]Quoted in Baker, *Contemporary Christian Music*, 91.

[24]See Schultze's essay, chapter 7 in this volume, "The Invisible Medium: Evangelical Radio."

[25]Quoted in Jim Palosaari, "The Christian Radio-Record Connection," *Contemporary Christian Music*, May 1981, 42.

[26]See "Christian Radio in Focus" series by broadcast consultant David Benware in *Contemporary Christian Music* December 1978–May 1979.

[27]Moira McCormick, "The A & M/Word Impact: Next Six Months Are 'Critical' for Gospel's Mainstream Voyage," *Billboard* 19 October 1985, G-20.

[28]John W. Styll and Paul Baker, "Pursuit of the Dream: A History of Contemporary Christian Music," *Contemporary Christian Music*, June 1988, 22.

[29]Baker, *Contemporary Christian Music*, 136.

[30]Quoted in Harold Straughn, "Word A & R: Setting the Example of Commitment," *Contemporary Christian Music* January 1981, W-10.

[31]"Stan Moser: Direction for the 80s," *Contemporary Christian Music*, January 1981, W-5.

[32]See Baker, *Contemporary Christian Music*, 143; McCormick, *Billboard*, G-20.

[33]Bob Darden, "Major Labels: Poised on the Brink of Breakthrough with Pop Music's Fastest Growing Genre," *Billboard*, 23 September 1984, G-5.

[34]Paul Baker, "Gospel Industry Braces for Recession," *Contemporary Christian Music* November 1979, 9.

[35]See Bob Millard, "Gospel Music Meet Buoyed by Rising Sales: Execs See Bright Future in New, Upscale Market," *Variety*, 20 April 1983, 179.

[36]Bob Darden, "Word's 30 Years Net 70% of Christian Record Sales," *Contemporary Christian Music* January 1981, W-18.

[37]See "Religious B'casting Study Finds Growth in 1983," *Billboard*, 21 January 1984, 46.

[38]Quoted in Bob Darden, "Christian Radio: Reach and Impact Grow As Struggle Continues for Greater Share," *Billboard*, 27 August 1983, G-12.

[39]Quoted in Bob Darden, "Word Records: A 30-Year Success Story," *Contemporary Christian Music* January 1981, W-5.

[40]Quoted in Flake, *Redemptorama*, 177.

[41]Quoted in Baker, *Contemporary Christian Music*, 154.

[42]Word Records did release a single, "Ageless Medley," a seven-inch, 33⅓ LP in 1983 to boost sales of *Age to Age*.

[43]See Steve Rabey, "Christian Singer Appeals to Fans of Secular Pop Music," *Christianity Today* 8 November 1985, 62.

[44]Quoted in McCormick, *Billboard*, G-33.

[45]Quoted in Bob Darden, "Major Labels: Poised on the Brink of Breakthrough with Pop Music's Fastest Growing Genre," *Billboard* 29 September 1984, G-5.

[46]McCormick, *Billboard*, G-20.

[47]"An Open Letter," Editorial, *Contemporary Christian Magazine* February 1986, 5. (*Contemporary Christian Magazine* changed its name to *Contemporary Christian Music* in October 1986.)

[48]John Styll, "Amy Grant's Sanctified Entertainment," Editorial, *Contemporary Christian Magazine* July/August 1986, 4.

[49]Quoted in Steve Rabey, "Hard Times Rock the Christian Music Industry," *Christianity Today* 2 October 1987, 59.

[50]Quoted in Chris Willman, "Mr. Mister: Have They Found What They're Looking For?" *Contemporary Christian Music* December 1987, 14.

[51]Quoted in Steve Pond, "Mr. Mister: Big Hits, Little Respect," *Rolling Stone* 24 April 1986, 27.

[52]Mike Atkinson and Dave Hart, "The New Idealists," *Contemporary Christian Music* June 1987, 26.

[53]Quoted in Chris Willman, "What?'s New: This Label Has a Real Point of View," *Contemporary Christian Music* June 1986, 10.

[54]Quoted in Quentin J. Schultze and William D. Romanowski, "Praising God in Opryland," *Reformed Journal* November 1989, 13.

[55]Edward Morris, "Meet Eyes Gospel's Problems," *Billboard*, 23 April 1983, 3.

7

THE INVISIBLE MEDIUM: EVANGELICAL RADIO

QUENTIN J. SCHULTZE

In sheer numbers, evangelical radio was the success story of the 1970s and 1980s. Evangelical magazine and book publishing were healthy but flat industries, while radio broadcasting continued to expand. Without the publicity accompanying evangelicals' entry into national television, evangelical radio seemingly took off on a quiet but steady course toward success. In 1973 there were 111 radio stations in the United States that devoted at least twenty hours per week to religious programming, from music to talk shows and Bible instruction. Three years later there were 341 such stations. By 1979 there were 449 of these religious stations representing nearly every state in the country.[1] The vast majority of them were intended for evangelical audiences; in fact, there were few nonevangelical religious stations. One decade later, in 1989, there were one thousand fifty two and the number continued to climb.[2] The average top one-hundred market in 1988 had three or more noncommercial religious stations.[3] If those data were not indicators of success, there was also a national sprinkling of noncommercial evangelical stations on the FM band.

A few audience studies also suggested that religious radio was quite popular. Already in 1970 nearly half of the adult population in the United States reportedly listened to religious programs at least occasionally.[4] One decade later, the percentage had not changed even though the population continued expanding.[5] But who were the *occasional* listeners? How popular were particular religious stations? And, perhaps most importantly of all, what was the impact of evangelical radio on American society? Was the plethora of evangelical stations merely serving the evangelical community or reaching out to a broader audience?

Statistically, evangelical radio seemed to be a booming industry. Behind the scenes, however, things were not nearly so encouraging. As the medium grew, it also settled into established patterns that virtually guaranteed it would reach few nonevangelicals and only a small percentage of evangelicals. By the early 1980s it was clear that evangelical radio largely served a small religious subculture. In short, evangelical radio won the battle to become a viable business while simultaneously losing the war against American secularization. Indeed, in the early 1990s it looked as if evangelical radio might become part of the wider consumer culture that it hoped to convert to the evangelical faith.

The fact was that few evangelicals, let alone all Americans, listened regularly to religious radio programs. The most optimistic surveys concluded in 1980 that about 17 million adults regularly tuned in religious radio programs—about one-tenth of the population.[6] However, there was considerable evidence that many of those listeners did not hear religious broadcasts on religious stations. One survey found in 1982 that only about 2.5 million Americans listened specifically to gospel music programs.[7] In the mid-1980s the typical religious station generally attracted the smallest audiences of any local stations. Most religious stations were not even included in local audience measurements by the major research companies.[8]

Audience surveys documented that from 1977 to 1984 the national audience share for religious stations (the percentage of radio listeners who tune in to religious stations) increased from .89 percent to 1.76 percent, but much of that growth could be explained purely by the increase in the number of stations, not the overall increase in audiences for each evangelical station.[9] The handful of high-rated religious stations in the country in 1988 attracted a mere 8 percent of the local radio audience. And they were atypical. Evangelical radio audiences were growing, but they were still remarkably small. Evangelicals seemed not to know how to attract even their own kind to the medium.

RADIO PREACHING AND TEACHING

The story of evangelical radio is a tale of ironies and paradoxes. In the 1960s conditions seemed especially ripe for the development of evangelical radio. First, the growth of FM radio provided evangelicals with an enormous opportunity to expand their radio efforts throughout the United States. Virtually all of the powerful AM radio licenses had already been granted to various broadcasters, some of whom had been in radio since the 1920s. Because of the proliferation of FM receivers in the 1960s, the potential FM audience increased rapidly. Within fifteen years most automobiles had FM radios, and the number of home stereo systems exploded. A once "inferior" FM license was quickly one of the best investments in American broadcasting. Many evangelicals saw the opportunity to get into radio via the FM band and established their own broadcasting operations. Instead of having to purchase an expensive AM license from an established broadcaster, they started relatively inexpensive stations on vacant FM frequencies.[10]

Second, during the same period the fledgling gospel music business became a significant industry. Gospel music had always had its fans who bought records and tapes from performers after church concerts. In the early 1970s, however, Nashville saw potential dollars in new forms of religious music. An evangelical recording business—called the "gospel music industry"—grew out of the established evangelical publishing business, using religious bookstores for retail outlets. Gospel music became much more than traditional gospel recordings. As Romanowski documented in the previous chapter, it soon included religious versions of practically every style of nonreligious music.[11] Among the most successful styles were Southern gospel, Jesus rock, religious MOR (middle-of-the-road music), and eventually a wide array of even more specialized styles of religious music. Suddenly the expanding evangelical radio business had plenty of recordings to play.

Third, the new FM stations, along with most of their older AM counterparts, discovered an easier way to generate revenues than with musical programming: prerecorded programs. From one coast to the other, religious radio stations opened their microphones to tapes from preachers and teachers of virtually every evangelical stripe, and even to some broadcasters who were at best marginally evangelical. Broadcast "pastors" realized that religious stations best reached their target market—evangelicals. More than that, they figured out that time on religious stations was much cheaper than equivalent time, if they could get it, on nonreligious stations.[12] From the 1970s on, most religious stations became public pulpits for Bible teachers and pastors, who bought fifteen- and thirty-minute program periods to reach their radio flocks. In the late 1980s about 37 percent of all programming on religious stations was preaching or teaching.[13] Some of these ministers were local pastors, but far more of them were national or international broadcasters who syndicated their programs to religious stations. These broadcasters also preferred religious stations because the audiences were more responsive and the program costs were significantly less expensive.[14]

Evangelical stations liked more than the revenues they received from daily and weekly program time sales. Whereas musical formats sometimes generated complaints from offended listeners, taped preaching and teaching shows elicited few objections; unhappy listeners simply tuned to other stations. Contemporary Christian music elicited objections especially from conservative listeners who believed that such music was more secular than Christian. They complained vigorously about the music's beat, but even the overall sound of contemporary Christian recordings was too similar to secular equivalents to suit some evangelical listeners.[15] Old-fashioned hymns were edifying to these critics, while popular tunes symbolized cultural and social liberalism. Even in the late 1980s many evangelical stations refused to broadcast popular religious recordings, fearing that they would lose their small but loyal audience for Bible programs.

There were two major kinds of syndicated religious broadcasts. Daily programs sought regular listeners and a small but loyal constituency. By far the most widely syndicated daily show was James Dobson's "Focus on the Family." Broadcast on well over seven hundred religious stations nationally, Dobson's practical advice about family life was enormously popular with several hundred thousand regular listeners. Most importantly, Dobson's "talk" show was intently followed by these listeners, who both heard and responded to Dobson's advice. The show was known by most evangelical publicists as the only truly influential religious radio program. It could easily generate thousands of book sales for authors who were interviewed on the show. And many listeners would respond to Dobson's request that they send letters to Congress or the President about legislation that might affect the American family. Most of the other daily programs were Bible instruction. (See chart 1.) Interesting enough, only one of the ten most widely syndicated religious programs had a successful counterpart in national television: Baptist preacher Charles Stanley's "In Touch" program. By and large, religious radio was independent of religious television; unlike televangelists, evangelical radio celebrities were largely unknown by most Americans.

Top Ten Daily Religious Programs

Title	Personality	# NRB Stations*
1. Focus on the Family	James Dobson	744
2. Thru the Bible	J. Vernon McGee (deceased)	496
3. Insight for Living	Chuck Swindoll	481
4. Back to the Bible	Warren Wiersbe	421
5. In Touch	Charles Stanley	398
6. Point of View	Marlin Maddoux	345
7. Haven of Rest	Paul Evans	275
8. Radio Bible Class	Darrow Parker	232
9. Minirth-Meier Clinic	Don Hawkins	216
10. Faith Seminar of the Air	Kenneth Hagin	207

(Source: "Top NRB Daily Religious Programs," *Religious Broadcasting*, April 1988, pp. 8, 14.)
*Stations belonging to National Religious Boradcasters

Chart 1

The other major kind of syndicated religious radio program, the weekly broadcast, was slightly more visible because many of these programs were also carried on nonreligious stations. Aired primarily on the weekends, especially Sunday, they generally attracted more listeners than the daily programs. Nevertheless, they, too had relatively small but loyal audiences. Most listeners did not support these programs financially. Given the low cost of program time on most religious stations, however, it did not take many supporters to keep most weekly broadcasts on the air. The Lutheran Church—Missouri Synod's

" 'Lutheran Hour" and Billy Graham's "Hour of Decision" were aired on over six hundred religious stations in the United States. (See chart 2.) The tenth most-widely syndicated show, deceased J. Vernon McGee's "Questions and Answers," delivered Bible instruction to fewer than four hundred stations. Overall, the weekly broadcasts, like their daily counterparts, were various forms of Bible instruction and preaching. They edified a rather small national flock of committed evangelical radio station listeners while largely escaping public notice.

Top Ten Weekly Syndicated Radio Programs

	Title	Personality/Sponsor	# NRB Stations
1.	Lutheran Hour	Oswald Hoffman/Wallace Schultz	645
2.	Hour of Decision	Billy Graham	620
3.	Children's Bible Hour	"Uncle Charlie" Vander Meer	592
4.	Revivaltime	Dan Betzer (Assemblies of God)	550
5.	Baptist Hour	Southern Baptist Convention	530
6.	Focus Weekend	James Dobson (Focus on the Family	510
7.	Unshackled!	Pacific Garden Mission	450
8.	Radio Bible Class	Richard DeHaan	439
9.	Moody Presents	Moody Broadcasting	410
10.	Questions and Answers	J. Vernon McGee (deceased)	380

(Source: "Top NRB Daily Religious Programs," *Religious Broadcasting*, May 1988, pp. 20, 35.)

Chart 2

THE RELIGIOUS RADIO GHETTO

These three factors—FM radio, religious recordings, and program time sales—conspired to turn evangelical radio into a religious ghetto. Like other specialized stations, religious stations were increasingly aimed at an identifiable American subculture. Evangelical radio joined the heavy-metal rock music stations, jazz stations, classical music stations, and all of the other distinct formats. Instead of reaching out to the general public for viewers, or even expanding their evangelical audiences significantly, most religious stations found in the 1970s and 1980s rather small but comfortable places in the broad mosaic of American broadcasting. They offered listeners edification and education instead of evangelism. They told the more conservative wing of evangelicalism what it wanted to hear about the world and about its own faith. They offered largely nonoffensive and noncontroversial musical recordings—except perhaps late in the evening or on Saturdays, when some stations bravely aired Christian rock programs. In summary, evangelical stations spoke overwhelmingly to the established evangelical community in its own language. As one observer put it after listening to one of these stations, "This was a clear display of in-group language on an in-group audience. It probably reached none of those it was intended for. It never left the ghetto."[16]

Compared with some of the nationally syndicated evangelical radio broadcasts of the 1940s and 1950s, programs on the new religious ghetto were invisible to the public. Charles E. Fuller's "Old-Fashioned Revival Hour," for example, established an enormous national audience in the 1940s by purchasing time on major nonreligious stations as well as on religious ones across the country. One estimate put Fuller's audience at twenty million—certainly more than the total national audience for all religious radio stations in the late 1980s, and even larger than the audiences for syndicated religious television programs during the same period.[17] By contrast, the new evangelical ghetto served essentially its own subculture. Unlike nationally syndicated television programs, few of the new radio shows were familiar to the general public. Most American radio listeners were too loyal to their own stations to tune across the dial. More than that, few syndicated religious programs attracted many listeners—evangelicals or nonevangelicals. After all, such syndicated programs required only a small but loyal following that would regularly send contributions to keep the program on the air. As long as these programs pleased their supporters, they were "successful" in the eyes of both local religious stations and the preachers themselves. As one critic put it, these syndicated evangelical broadcasters did not have to "understand the medium well enough to really use it wisely."[18]

The barrage of "successful" preaching and teaching programs deepened the roots of the evangelical radio ghetto. By pleasing the very small audience attracted to these kinds of broadcasts, stations virtually guaranteed that they would never attract a wider group of listeners. All evidence indicated that few evangelicals would listen for long to large blocks of syndicated programming. In 1980 only abut 20 percent of the religious radio audience tuned in for three or more hours weekly.[19] Few people listened extensively to most evangelical radio—not even most evangelicals.

Entering the 1980s, then, evangelical radio was limited by its own success. As an educational and inspirational medium it was rather solidly entrenched in an evangelical subculture. Few nonevangelicals tuned in evangelical stations; most evangelicals, like the population overall, were loyal listeners of nonreligious stations. The *raison d'etre* of evangelical communication, evangelism, was little more than empty rhetoric for most syndicated broadcasters. Preaching and teaching programs normally created small audiences for particular programs rather than larger audiences for the station overall.[20] The easy route to financial liquidity for evangelical stations, program time sales, dug such stations ever deeper into the religious ghetto.

Of course evangelical radio was successful in its own way as a national medium for delivering supporters to broadcast ministries. It was also successful at giving such supporters the feeling that their money was being used to spread the Christian gospel. As Hoover found with religious television (see chapter 10), the supporters of evangelical radio programs were not necessarily the listeners.[21] For supporters, evangelical radio was an important presence in American society, lending legitimacy to the evangelical cause even if not attracting many unconverted souls. However, the vast majority of religious stations had so few listeners that evangelistic rhetoric was at best a dream. Some of these stations survived primarily on the belief among members of the local evangelical community that someone must be listening even if they were not. When rumors were circulated among evangelicals in the 1970s and 1980s that well-known atheist Madalyn Murray O'Hair had petitioned the Federal Communications Commission (FCC) to eliminate religious radio stations, the federal agency received millions of letters of protest from evangelicals.[22] In fact, the FCC was eventually forced to hire a public relations agency to try to quell the outlandish rumors—to no avail. Evangelicals did not listen to much religious radio, but they would support it. To many evangelicals, religious radio was a rather sacred symbol of the evangelical presence in America.

THE PROMISE OF CHRISTIAN MUSIC

A growing number of evangelical broadcasters believed in the 1980s that musical formats were the answer to poor audience ratings. Popular Christian music, they thought, might pull evangelical radio out of the religious ghetto. In a nation where about one-third of all adults identified themselves as born-again or evangelicals, audience ratings suggested that no more than three or four million regularly listened to evangelical radio.[23] Virtually everyone in evangelical radio agreed that part of the audience problem was the dull programming offered by most stations, especially all of the chattering on syndicated preaching and teaching programs.

If nothing else, the optimists felt, music might attract more listeners to evangelical stations. Indeed, only a few major AM stations in the United States could survive on talk formats. Since the advent of network television, American radio was increasingly dominated by musical recordings. Americans turned largely to television for talk and to radio for music. Music-oriented evangelical stations certainly attracted larger audiences than those that emphasized preaching and teaching programs. On average, the audiences of religious music stations were 70 percent larger than their preaching-teaching counterparts. In addition, music audiences generally listened longer without tuning to different stations.[24]

It was increasingly obvious to religious station management that Christian music might help them carve out a larger niche in the radio marketplace. The fragmentation of American radio audiences made it increasingly necessary for each evangelical station to identify its own audience in the midst of competition from a growing number of stations, including other religious stations. Even in the religious radio ghetto, certainly a more exclusive audience than most, stations faced difficult times attracting audiences. As the number of evangelical stations increased dramatically during the late 1970s and early 1980s, they competed not only with secular stations but with other religious broadcasters. Evangelical stations became part of the growing herd of radio stations hoping to create their own viable audiences in the face of stiff competition.

In major cities there were dozens of stations vying for a small segment of the radio audience market, let alone for a small piece of the potential evangelical listenership. Virtually all radio stations, including evangelical ones, survived by finding a niche in the local market. Paid, syndicated religious talk shows were an increasingly tenuous niche, especially after the televangelism scandals of the late 1980s, which made it even more difficult to raise funds to support religious broadcasts. Music looked to growing numbers of evangelical broadcasters as a far more viable form of programming. Most important of all, contemporary music formats held out the hope that evangelical stations might capture a larger share of the younger evangelical audience, which was broadly dispersed over the secular radio spectrum.

One of the first stations to experiment seriously with a new format was KBRT, an AM station in Southern California. Already in 1978 it boldly challenged the invisible status of most religious stations by adopting a musical format that mixed contemporary Christian music with some of the more popular and upbeat nonreligious recordings. KBRT banned all of the recorded programs of preachers and teachers and established its own on-air personalities—the evangelical equivalent of the radio DJ. In an area where about one-quarter of the nine million residents claimed to be born again, station management hoped to lure hundreds of thousands of evangelical listeners from nonreligious stations.[25] It worked remarkably well for KBRT, which attracted a far broader audience than most evangelical stations. With the larger audience came greater advertising revenues and more funds for station promotion.

Few stations were willing to emulate the successful strategies of KBRT, however. By and large, evangelical stations simply mixed contemporary music with existing syndicated preaching-teaching programs. In 1985 about 42 percent of the programming on religious stations was music, while about 37 percent was preaching and teaching.[26] More importantly, religious stations wanted more music than any other kinds of programming, and they were looking most closely at contemporary styles of Christian music as the vehicles to expand their audiences.[27] The typical pattern was for religious stations to offer contemporary Christian music during the early morning and late afternoon periods when audiences were the largest. During the day and in the evening the stations usually continued to sell time to syndicated preachers and teachers. Hard-rock programs were generally run at night or during low-rated periods over the weekends.

This type of diverse programming was supposed to combine the best of both worlds—the highest-rated "drive time" and the solid financial base of syndicated time sales. In fact, such a mixture of contemporary evangelical music and old-fashioned preachers generally doomed stations to the same religious ghetto. American radio listeners were loyal to specific stations, not just to particular programs and formats. Listeners wanted consistency in their favorite stations. Few young evangelicals would listen persistently to radio preachers and teachers while waiting for a station to broadcast contemporary music. By combining widely different programming, from an 80-year-old Bible teacher to Christian rock music, most evangelical stations failed to win the loyalty of many evangelicals, let alone to attract many nonevangelicals. Most listeners to these kinds of stations simply tuned in for particular shows and then switched stations—if they tuned in at all. Simply put, by trying to become everyone's evangelical station most religious stations became no one's station, except for a few hard-core listeners. During the late 1980s evangelical stations in several large cities, including Dallas and Chicago, were sold and their formats secularized when it became obvious that they could not compete for listeners.

EVANGELICAL STATIONS VS. THE GOSPEL MUSIC INDUSTRY

The unwillingness of most religious radio stations to commit themselves strongly to musical formats frustrated the gospel music industry. Few industry executives believed that evangelical radio was a significant economic force in their business. They generally spent far more money and effort helping Christian bookstores market their recordings than they did trying to promote them through evangelical radio stations. In their view, except for a handful of exceptions, the vast majority of religious stations could not significantly influence record sales. Partly because their audiences were so small, and partly because their audiences preferred nonreligious music, evangelical stations indeed had a difficult time convincing the gospel music industry to take them seriously. The industry hoped that stations would duplicate the successful marketing and promotional techniques of nonreligious music stations, but they did not believe it would happen. They felt instead that poor station management and narrow-minded Christian audiences would lead to nothing more than piecemeal formats and lower audience ratings.[28]

Diverse evangelical radio formats, then, were attempts by station management to avoid offending existing listeners and to maintain established sources of revenue while expanding their audiences. Older listeners, who historically were the financial backbone of religious stations, tuned in primarily to hear their favorite Bible teachers. They were easily offended by the contemporary music segments, often agreeing with well-known fundamentalist leaders such as televangelist Jimmy Swaggart, evangelist David Wilkerson, and Bible teacher Bill Gothard that contemporary Christian music was evil.[29] Young listeners, on the other hand, were put off by old-fashioned hymns and especially by syndicated preachers and teachers. They wanted radio stations that served as a juke box for their favorite recordings. Although they might tune in to an evangelical station specifically for a popular-music program, they were generally far too loyal to other stations and much too committed to the secular recording industry to seek out Christian music shows. In trying to be all things to all radio listeners, the mixed-format religious stations frequently alienated nearly all potential listeners with one or the other part of their programming. Listeners sought more consistency, while station management attempted to hang on to both the syndicated program revenues and local advertising revenues.

This situation led some people in the gospel music industry to openly criticize the evangelical radio business. Realizing how beholden most religious stations were to their conservative constituencies, gospel-music industry executives in the late 1980s sometimes told stations that they were rather unprofessional compared with their secular counterparts. Artist manager Dan Harrell, whose successes included Amy Grant, expressed this openly to a group of religious radio station managers and employees at the Gospel Music Association convention in Nashville in 1989. Christian radio had yet to prove whether it was a trend or merely a fad, he said. Lamenting the lack of vision and creativity among stations, he said that stations' desire to "please God" had become a "crutch and an excuse for mediocrity."[30]

The gospel music industry was loaded with quiet critics who shared Harrell's view of religious stations. They felt that religious stations had done an incredibly poor job of attracting young record buyers, the most important potential market for their products. Although the average age of the typical religious radio listener was slowly decreasing, it was a long way from what the recording companies wanted—and needed. Only 2 to 6 percent of the average religious station's audience was under eighteen years of age.[31] Young evangelicals simply were not listening to Christian radio stations. In 1988 only one-fifth of the subscribers of *Campus Life* magazine, the major publication for evangelical young people, had become aware of new Christian music the previous year through Christian radio. Moreover, these young evangelicals listened to twice as much "secular" as Christian radio each day. In fact, half of them did not listen to any Christian music.[32]

Unlike secular radio, then, evangelical radio never established strong ties to the recording industry. While such links were forged between popular music stations and the nonreligious radio industry beginning in the 1950s, even in the early 1990s it was not clear whether evangelical stations would ever seriously follow suit. A few creative broadcasters such as KBRT were moderately successful. In addition, in the 1980s there were two contemporary Christian music "charts" that supposedly reflected the most popular recordings on evangelical stations. Also, there was a growing number of evangelical consultants who would help stations establish potentially successful musical formats. Nevertheless, evangelical radio largely remained in the religious ghetto. Until the recording and radio industries were able to work together to the benefit of both, there was little likelihood that stations could climb out of that ghetto. The prospects were not rosy.

TECHNOLOGY VS. PROGRAMMING

As evangelical radio waltzed with a relatively small and conservative evangelical subculture, it also began spreading its energies across a wide spectrum of opportunities. For one thing, not all evangelical broadcasters were satisfied with making programs for small, homogeneous audiences of born-again Christians. Some broadcasters genuinely sought to win the nation and even the world to Christ via the radio. For another thing, not all evangelical stations were contented members of the religious ghetto. Some of them still looked hopefully for alternative models of radio broadcasting that would both attract more listeners and broaden the evangelistic impact of their programs. All in all, by the early 1990s evangelical radio was an odd but changing collection of different stations with a growing desire to pull itself out of the religious ghetto.

However, most of their resources and energy was channeled into market-driven technological advancements rather than into major programming changes. Among the most significant technological developments in evangelical radio in the late 1980s was the growth of various networks. Few evangelical stations became part of established nonreligious news and entertainment networks. Instead, evangelical broadcasters began establishing their own networks of stations across the country.

Among the most successful was Chicago's Moody Bible Institute, which had been broadcasting since the 1920s. One of the most experienced religious broadcasters in the nation, Moody had developed a successful twenty-four-hour format that combined talk and "safe" music for a relatively conservative constituency. First Moody established its own eleven-station network in Illinois, Ohio, Tennessee, Washington, and Florida. In 1981 it inaugurated the Moody Broadcasting Network, which combined translators, satellators, local cable TV audio transmission, and affiliate stations.

By late 1989, forty-one translators picked up Moody's signal from one station and rebroadcast it on a different frequency about fifty or sixty miles away, effectively doubling the area covered by a station. Each translator was like a new station that simply rebroadcast the signal of the original station. Translators increased the number of transmitters without adding many new staff—only technicians to keep the translator on the air. At the same time, eight satellators in Alaska received Moody's signal from a satellite and rebroadcast it on a local radio transmitter for local listeners. Satellators were like translators in the way they increased the number of stations (actually, only the number of transmitters) while keeping down the costs of personnel. In both cases, the new technologies merely rebroadcast signals from other Moody stations. Fifty-one cable TV systems enabled subscribers to receive Moody's audio signals from their local cable television system. Finally, 229 affiliate stations around the nation supplemented their own programming with shows from the Moody network.[33]

While Moody's programming was a rather traditional combination of music and talk, other networks were not quite as technologically sophisticated but were more adventurous in their programming. Moody's listenership was heavily fundamentalist, but other networks tried to reach a more broadly evangelical audience. The CBN Radio Network, started in 1987, included hourly news updates and a talk show, as well as musical programs. M. G. "Pat" Robertson, founder of CBN and former candidate for the Republican presidential nomination, began hosting a half-hour news show on the network for its 230 affiliate stations in the fall of 1989.[34] The USA Radio Network, which included about 300, aired news, sports, talk shows, various kinds of music and other features. In 1985, before the CBN Radio Network began, 20 percent of religious stations used the Satellite Radio Network, 8 percent used Moody's network, and about 3 percent subscribed to the International Broadcasting Network, a news and information network in Washington, D.C.[35] If nothing else, these networks helped stations sound more like professional radio stations and less like church pulpits. They also delivered national advertising to affiliate stations across the country.

Some of the programming on these networks was remarkably innovative. News and feature programming sometimes rivaled the nonreligious networks. But evangelical radio, like nonreligious radio, was not particularly interested in becoming primarily a network medium. Most successful stations, religious and secular, found it necessary to have a significant local presence in their communities. From the early days of television, radio stations had survived by emphasizing local advertisers and local radio personalities. In short, radio depended heavily for its financial health on community ties. Networks often provided news and some national texture in the programming, but it was nearly always the local programming emphasis that attracted local audiences and advertisers. Stations could air national programs and especially popular music, but they had better emphasize local news, weather, sports, and especially local personalities. Thus, the lure of the satellite network technology could easily hinder evangelical radio's long-desired success.

By and large, evangelical stations never learned how to successfully promote themselves as community-oriented broadcasters. Instead of emphasizing news and weather, along with locally recognized programs' hosts, they often tried to yoke themselves to the churches through worship announcements and congregational advertisements. Evangelical stations had to be careful, because if they appeared to be favoring one church or denomination over another they could be in serious audience trouble. Local churches did not work well together in most communities; their rivalry translated into potential audience problems for evangelical stations. The irony was clear: evangelical stations had to gingerly cultivate their most important local constituency. As a result, most stations restricted their local involvement to broadcasting church services and sponsoring the performances of various national Christian recording artists. Even then, they worried about the appearance of church favoritism.

The technologically sophisticated evangelical radio networks, then, would not alone pull stations out of the religious ghetto. Professionally produced, locally oriented programming was very important. The networks helped stations sound more professional, but the immediacy of extensive local news and weather, along with the attractiveness of local personalities, was lost when stations relied too extensively on network programming. Generally speaking, evangelical radio had the poorest local news coverage in each community. In 1985 30 percent of religious stations relied entirely on syndicated news.[36] Evangelical radio similarly had the most obscure on-air personalities—poorly paid announcers and DJs who jumped at the opportunity to get on the air, but who often ended up frustrated with management. Evangelical radio also had some of the most tenuous links to the local merchants—links founded more on a sense of obligation induced by guilt than on anything else. Christian merchants were sometimes persuaded to advertise on evangelical stations as a means of expressing their religious faith, not as a means of really increasing their store traffic or boosting their sales.

Moreover, the technologically sophisticated networks merely created the illusion that some of the local stations were up-to-date. A few evangelical radio stations had some of the most advanced equipment for taping, editing, and airing programs. The vast majority, however, were simply trying to keep the old equipment working and to stay on the air. Instead of investing in new equipment, they generally maintained out-of-date equipment as long as they could. To most evangelical station management, technology was merely an expense, not an investment. Their approach to making money was based on the short-term strategy of minimizing investment and ongoing expenses while maximizing income. Technology itself seemed to most evangelical stations to have little or no relationship to future revenues—unless it was cheap. For that reason more than a few evangelical stations aired poor-quality signals. Similarly, religious radio would not invest significantly in on-air personalities. If technology seemed necessary only to get the signal out, employees were important only to keep the station on the air. At many of the most popular nonreligious stations the highest salaries were paid to on-air personalities, not to management. Personalities were often viewed as the hooks that attracted local listeners from one station to another. Music could be essentially the same across stations, but the personalities were necessarily different. In evangelical radio, on the other hand, nearly all of the large salaries were paid to management, especially the owners. All employees, even those on the air, were usually poorly compensated—as if they were the recipients of "free-will" offerings from the owners. Although commercial evangelical radio was unquestionably a business, management implicitly defined it as a "ministry" on payday. If any major checks were to be written, they would have to be for necessary technological replacements rather than for human resources. In most cases the only exception was the boss's check.

THE FUTURE OF EVANGELICAL RADIO

The ironies and paradoxes of evangelical radio slide smoothly into the future. Evangelical radio is so poorly researched, compared with nonreligious broadcasting, that no one knows for certain where the industry has been, let alone where it is headed. Religious stations have survived in spite of a lack of market research and careful market planning. Popular journalists who portray evangelical broadcasting as a well-organized movement are sadly and rather humorously mistaken. In the late 1970s and early 1980s religious radio was one of the few general formats to show steady growth, but that was probably largely because of the growth in the number of stations more than in the increase of audiences. During that period formats such as easy-listening music and classical music declined while religious radio increased about 84 percent.[37] By 1990, however, evangelical radio was still largely invisible to all but a small group of dedicated listeners. Whether or not it would remain invisible depended primarily on three problems that the industry faced.

**Evangelical radio has to clear up a lot of confusion over
its goals and purposes.**

Contrary to some perceptions both within and outside of
evangelical radio, the industry was enormously confused about
why it existed, who it was supposed to serve, and how it was
supposed to do that. Part of the confusion was institutionalized
in the gap between noncommercial and commercial stations.
Probably several hundred religious radio stations were legally
nonprofit endeavors licensed to broadcast on the educational
end of the FM frequency spectrum. They could not sell regular
advertising, although they could mention program "under-
writers" as did similarly licensed National Public Radio stations. Behind such institutional differences, however, was the
more serious identity problem among religious radio stations as
a whole. The extent to which evangelical stations were supposed to be businesses or ministries was never really settled.
Although individual stations might solve that dilemma in their
own ways, they also needed to solve it as an industry, for their
futures were clearly bound together.

More than anything else, the business-ministry dilemma
usually came down to how to define "Christian radio." Some
people in evangelical radio still clung to the idea that the
medium was supposed to be primarily evangelistic. The fact
was, however, that even the "ministry" stations with back-to-
back preachers and Bible teachers were not evangelistic. For
one thing, few nonevangelicals tuned in the stations. For
another, the programs themselves were designed to attract
evangelicals and to solicit contributions from them, not to lure
unconverted radio listeners. Undoubtedly some listeners happened upon evangelical stations and were converted by the
broadcasts. But that was hardly the result of the plans of the
industry to save souls.

The multifarious uses of the term "Christian music"
similarly caused the industry problems. The most generally
accepted use seemed to mean "Christian lyrics." However,
even then there were major differences of opinion. As Romanowski documented (see chapter 6), concepts of Christian
music have varied from scriptural lyrics to traditional musical
styles.[38] These differences of opinion are not merely semantic.
They reflect fundamentally disparate ways of looking at the
relationship between North American culture and the evangelical faith. At the same time, they match the various social and

economic differences within American evangelicalism. Every definition comes out of the assumptions held by a particular group that supports and/or criticizes evangelical radio. Not only is evangelical radio management unclear about these definitions; so are the many constituencies that produce the syndicated programs and listen to the stations.

Until evangelical radio decides on its purpose it will continue to spend more time figuring out what to do than doing it. The intimate relationship between the recording industry and the nonreligious radio business suggests that evangelical radio will not be able to satisfactorily solve its problems without assistance from its program suppliers, including networks and especially the gospel music industry. Evangelical radio might depend somewhat on the evangelical church for its future, but it more likely depends upon other businesses, especially the recording companies. American radio is more oriented toward music now than it ever has been. Most listeners want and expect music from their home and car radios, more and more of which are high-fidelity stereos. For this reason evangelical radio will likely have to define its mission at least partly in terms of musical entertainment. Certainly some listeners will always want "ministry" from their evangelical stations, and that desire, too, can be met partly through music. In the end, however, the ways most Americans use radio will likely determine how evangelicals will use it as well.

In short, evangelical radio has never been completely comfortable with the goal of entertaining listeners. Instead, it has repeatedly opted to "edify," "uplift," or "educate" them. As long as the industry's goals are defined in those kinds of religious terms, it will not be able to compete significantly with secular radio. American radio listeners largely expect radio to be entertaining, and evangelical stations will not easily be able to buck that clear and powerful trend. The safety of the religious ghetto will continue to make it difficult for stations to evangelize the outside culture.

The evangelical radio industry suffers from poor national organization.

As I indicate in the introductory essay to this volume, American evangelicalism has always been animated by the energy and will of individuals. Evangelical radio is no exception. It is possible to describe evangelical radio as hundreds of broadcasters in search not only of a common purpose but of shared ways of doing things as well. If there is no agreed-upon definition of evangelical radio there is similarly no organization of evangelical radio. By and large, each station is constantly reinventing the proverbial broadcast wheel. Compared to nonreligious radio, where new programming ideas and techniques fly through the industry, evangelical stations are remarkably isolated from each other. Given how small the industry is compared with its nonreligious version, there is an incredible amount of disorganization and disarray in evangelical radio.

There are some national and even international evangelical broadcasting organizations, but stations remain heavily independent in their thinking and action unless threatened from the outside, particularly by government regulation. National Religious Broadcasters (NRB), the largest organization, was formed in the 1940s, as Voskuil shows (see chapter 3), partly to keep the airways open to evangelical broadcasters.[39] The Gospel Music Association has its National Christian Radio (NCR) group, but it too has not had a major impact on the programming standards and professional practices of its members. NRB and NCR meetings invariably become celebrations of what the industry has supposedly accomplished and lamentations about what it has not accomplished. The need for national organization generally gets lost in the shuffle between those contradictory perceptions that the industry has of itself.

Perhaps more than anything else, the industry desperately needs common programming practices. Each station plays pretty much what it wants and calls it just about anything it desires. Musical formats have meaning in nonreligious radio, where stations largely follow established practices. In evangelical radio programming is nearly up for grabs. A growing number of stations agree that it needs to air more music, but the same stations can't agree on what kinds of music to play. Worse than that, they sometimes agree on the kinds of music to play and end up, because of confusion over musical terms, playing very different music. In the early 1970s, however, evangelical recording was an incredible smorgasbord of different styles, substyles, and hybrids. Black gospel music was on average the most popular religious music format, but even the substance of that format was unclear by 1990.

In nonreligious radio the lack of format standards was not nearly so crucial because there were so many competing stations that had to find their own niches in the local market. For secular stations, nationally defined formats remained a guide to establishing their own versions. By contrast, evangelical radio audiences are so small, and the number of stations so few, that the industry would eventually have to define its formats more carefully if it ever expected to climb out of the religious ghetto. Without better organization, it would simply be impossible for stations, consultants, the recording industry, and the audience measurement companies to work together.

The same problem is obvious in station policies—or lack of policies—regarding syndicated programming. There is no doubt that some of the paid preaching and teaching programs are both theologically and technically at odds with what some stations profess. It appears that instead of making hard decisions about who they should sell air time to, at least some stations open the airwaves to the highest bidders. Virtually anyone who has the money is sold program time. All they have to do is call themselves Christians and the microphones are theirs. Because television is considerably more expensive— both in air time and production costs—fewer religious TV stations are riddled with so many idiosyncratic broadcasters. As long as evangelical radio stations will let any small, supporting audience have its own religious broadcast, the vast majority of listeners will not make the station their listening home. American evangelicalism itself is diverse, but evangelical radio amplifies and distorts that diversity in the name of practically anyone who can generate enough cash or credit to keep the show on the air.

While Americans celebrate freedom and individualism, these characteristics have become a Janus-headed curse on the evangelical radio industry. There are very few common practices in the business. The result is less creativity than it is chaos and uncertainty. That is why the recording industry lacks faith in evangelical radio and why stations sometimes lack faith in each other. If evangelical radio is to become a considerably more visible and influential force in American society, it will have to turn the chaos into some form of shared purposes and practices. In short, it needs organization.

The evangelical radio industry faces cultural co-optation.

Ironically, the success of the evangelical radio business might come as a result of the industry's co-optation by the

American consumer culture. To put it starkly, evangelical radio might become so commercial that it loses its religious distinctiveness and its evangelical faith. Herein lies the greatest hope and the greatest potential despair of the industry. The greatest success could conceivably result in the greatest loss. Like the biblical parable about the man who got everything on earth and nothing in heaven, evangelical stations face their greatest challenge in defining the terms of their own success. At issue here is really whether evangelical radio in the United States will remain evangelical or be transformed into solid-gold commerce.

As the industry moves toward greater organization and clearer self-definition, it will be encouraged from within and without to model itself after nonreligious American broadcasting. This is already evident in the rise of various market research specialists and consulting agencies who are increasingly setting the direction of the business. Consider only the quest for accurate audience ratings, the drive for demographic audience profiles, the emergence of several recording "charts," and especially the trend toward spot advertising as opposed to program time sales. None of these developments will necessarily drive the evangelical faith out of radio. However, each of them could be signs that the marketplace is beginning to set the agenda and determine the course of evangelical radio.

By 1990 it was especially clear that evangelical radio might be able to shed its invisible clothing by gathering and selling affluent American audiences to advertisers. Research showed that religious radio audiences were higher educated, more affluent, and more likely to be employed as professionals. They were, as the market researchers would say, more "upscale" than the average radio listeners.[40] Or, to put it more crassly, religious radio listeners were a more lucrative market than some others. They were even more likely to own a car than was the reader of *Car and Driver* or *Road and Track*. As faithful consumers, they bought more cassette recorders/players and turntables than viewers of MTV, the rock video channel on cable television. If that were not enough to attract advertisers, they enjoyed spending their way through leisure time, participating more than viewers of ESPN (a sports-oriented cable TV channel) in sports such as downhill skiing, hunting, ice-skating and motorcycling. If advertisers still needed evidence for the "power" of this market, they could learn that religious radio listeners bought more groceries, household products, appliances, term life insurance, and personal-care products than listeners of other radio formats.[41] Once the evangelical market was in place on the radio, it would not be long before the advertisers ran the stations. As one radio market specialist put it, radio salespeople "today are now concentrating less on the missionary activities of the programmers and specializing more heavily on the science of selling."[42] Such "science" was nothing short of managing and marketing the upscale evangelical demographics—those elusive audience characteristics that interest advertising agencies and local retailers. By the early 1980s about half of the average religious station's income came from spot advertising sales, and the percentage was increasing slowly but steadily. Even some of the noncommercial religious stations established a sales staff to sell short "promotional" spots to local businesses.[43] Religiously oriented sales techniques, which played on the faith of the sponsor, were giving way to demographic-based marketing. More than some other radio stations, the evangelical ones were ripe for the new methods. As one person put it, the religious audience was composed of "Guppies"—God-fearing urban professionals.[44]

Most frightening of all to some evangelical station employees, management was increasingly interested in profits rather than in the nature of programming. In fact, a number of evangelical stations were not even owned by evangelicals, but by savvy businessmen who realized the profitability of the preacher-teacher programming formulas. Some evangelicals within the industry wondered if it were not only a matter of time before religious radio was simply another profit-making format rather than a real ministry. One profitable station regularly aired an anti-Catholic program in the morning and a recitation of the rosary in the evening. Both programs were merely part of the program "mix" that attracted viewers and elicited contributions. They were part of the "business" of giving listeners whatever they wanted. As American society became more affluent, perhaps even those kinds of programs would give way to new kinds of radio entertainment designed specifically to attract Guppies for waiting advertisers. As long as the market was going to determine programming, such a scenario was indeed possible.

Nevertheless, it was still a long way from evangelical preachers and teachers to Guppies. Evangelical station management increasingly realized the marketing potential of its stations, but it also saw how rapidly audience competition could gobble up adventurous stations. There was safety in small numbers and even in invisibility. Evangelical stations were not taking the nation by storm—neither a commercial nor an evangelistic storm—but they were successfully treading water and staying afloat. And for their management, at least, these stations generally made money. In a world where radio stations changed formats with the winds of competition, that was hardly something to be taken lightly. It was better to be invisible and to remain profitable than to gamble away the safety of the past.

NOTES

[1]Carl Douglas Windsor, "Religious Radio in the 1970s: A Uses and Gratifications Analysis" (Ph.D. diss., Ohio State University, 1981), 69.

[2]*Broadcasting Cablecasting Yearbook* (Washington, D.C.: Broadcasting Publications, 1989), F88, F93–95.

[3]Gary Crossland, "The Changing Face of Christian Radio," *Religious Broadcasting*, September 1988, 13.

[4]Ronald L. Johnstone, "Who Listens to Religious Radio Broadcasts Anymore?" *Journal of Broadcasting* 16 (Winter 1971–72): 92.

[5]Ben Armstrong, "How Big Is the Religious Radio-TV Audience?" *Religious Broadcasting*, May 1981, 33.

[6]Ibid., 34.

[7]Robyn Wells, "Listener Habits Are Outlined by Survey," *Billboard*, 30 January 1982, 57.

[8]Crossland, "The Changing Face," 35.

[9]Gary Crossland, "Vital Signs Improve for Christian Radio" *Religious Broadcasting*, February 1986, 45.

[10]Peter Fornatale and Joshua E. Mills, *Radio in the Television Age* (Woodstock, NY: Overlook Press, 1980), 90.

[11]Romanowski's essay in this book (see chapter 6).

[12]Windsor, "Religious Radio," 134.

[13]Paul H. Virts, "Surprising Findings in Christian Radio," *Religious Broadcasting*, February 1986, 42.

[14]Stuart Philip Johnson, "Contemporary Communication Theory and the Distribution Patterns of Evangelical Radio Programs" (Ph.D. diss., Northwestern University, 1978), 213.

[15]Quentin J. Schultze and William D. Romanowski, "Praising God in Opryland," *Reformed Journal*, November 1989, 13.

[16]Jim Pennington, "Christian Radio: Breaking Out of the Gospel Ghetto," *Christianity Today*, 29 June 1979, 32.

[17]Quentin J. Schultze, "Evangelical Radio and the Rise of the Electronic Church, 1921–1948," *Journal of Broadcasting and the Electronic Media* 32 (Summer 1988): 301.

[18]Johnson, "Contemporary Communication Theory," 124.

[19]J. Thomas Bisset, "Religious Broadcasting: Assessing the State of the Art," *Christianity Today*, 12 December 1980, 28.

[20]Gary Crossland, "How Do Various Christian Formats Compare?" *Religious Broadcasting*, December 1988, 16.

[21]Hoover's essay in this book (see chapter 10).

[22]"The Petition Against God," *Channels*, September/October 1984, 10–14.

[23]Kenneth A. Briggs, "Evangelicals in America," *The Gallup Report*, April 1987, 3.

[24]Crossland, "How Do Various," 16.

[25]Ray Herbeck, " 'Born Again' AM Format Hits L.A.," *Billboard*, 6 May 1978, 6, 33.

[26]Virts, "Surprising Findings," 42.

[27]Ibid,, 44.

[28]Schultze and Romanowski, "Praising God in Opryland," 11.

[29]Ibid., 13.

[30]Ibid., 11.

[31]Rupert R. Ridgeway, "Reflecting on Radio, Ratings and Religion," *Religious Broadcasting*, April 1982, 37; Crossland, "Vital Signs," 43.

[32]Research Department of Christianity Today, "Christian and Secular Radio and Music Listening Habits Among Leading Christian Music Buyers," unpublished research report, 1988.

[33]Moody Broadcasting Network, telephone call by the author, November 3, 1989.

[34]"CBN Radio News Adds Pat Robertson as Anchorman," *Religious Broadcasting*, October 1989, 36.

[35]Virts, "Surprising Findings," 44.

[36]Ibid.

[37]Gary Crossland, "Where Christian Radio Excels," *Religious Broadcasting*, June 1986, 17.

[38]Romanowski's essay in this book (see chapter 6).

[39]Voskuil's essay in this book (see chapter 3).

[40]Gary Crossland, "Religious Audiences: More Upscale?" *Religious Broadcasting*, March 1985, 28, 30.

[41]Gary Crossland, "Advertising Opportunities on Christian Radio," *Religious Broadcasting*, April 1985, 20, 25.

[42]Crossland, "The Changing Face," 12.

[43]Ibid. Also see Bob Augsburg, "Alternative Fundraising for Non-Commercial Stations," *Religious Broadcasting*, May 1989, 36–37.

[44]Crossland, "The Changing Face," 35.

Part III

TELEVANGELISM

8

RELIGION AND TELEVISION: THE PUBLIC AND THE PRIVATE

ROBERT WUTHNOW

Religion is a way of coping with the pathos and paradox of our lives. But when religion is beamed into our living rooms from sleek, high-technology studios via satellite and cable television hook-ups, it creates its own pathos and becomes the source of paradox itself. The pathos is obvious enough. The paradox, as paradoxes always do, requires closer attention.

Let us consider a typical—but hypothetical—example: the case of Mrs. Miller, or Mabel, as her hypothetical friends call her. Mabel has tuned in the popular televangelist Jimmy Swaggart on more than one occasion—at least she did before Jimmy confessed his sinfulness on the tube. She also watched Jim Bakker's "PTL Club"—that is, before Jim and Tammy fell from grace. And from time to time she picked up the "700 Club" on one of her cable channels, although she regretted Pat Robertson's absence during his bid for political office.

On the whole, things haven't been going so well for Mabel's religious television heroes. But still, she has no trouble finding preachers with a flair for the fiery pulpit rhetoric she loves and the reassuring devotional messages that warm her heart. There are, after all, Jerry Falwell and Robert Schuller and Rex Humbard and others.

This particular day happens to be a Sunday, and as she has done on Sunday mornings for nearly sixty-five years, Mabel rises early. As a child growing up in Iowa, she used to be awakened promptly at seven o'clock on Sunday mornings so her mother could braid her hair and make sure everyone had a hearty breakfast in time to get to Sunday school by 9:45. That was always the appointed hour at the little Baptist church seven miles down the road. Later on, it was Mabel's turn to rise in time to get her own children dressed for Sunday school, and in time to get the pot roast in the oven and the table set for the Sunday feast. In recent years, Mabel has been alone, but the habit of early rising persists. And so, as she sits down to breakfast, she flips on the television and automatically passes by the morning cartoons, the old movies, the local version of Oprah Winfrey, and the weather channel, and settles into an hour of inspiration and revival.

Mabel, as I said, is a typical viewer. She does not watch television preaching every afternoon and evening, and she sometimes does not even feel like watching on Sunday mornings. But she has—like about a third of the U.S. population—watched at least one religious program on television in the past month.[1] Were the omnipresent Gallup pollster to come to her door this morning, there would also be no surprises. She fits all the stereotypes of the average religious television viewer; she is a woman in her 60s, she has never attended college, she lives in the Midwest, and has identified all of her life with a fairly conservative brand of Protestant theology.

If a Gallup pollster were to quiz Mabel more closely about her viewing, some interesting—and again typical—responses would come forth. She likes to watch Jimmy Swaggart and the others, she says, because of the music and the preaching. She feels close to God when she does. The music lifts her spirits. The preaching challenges her to be a better Christian. She simply feels good about watching. In fact, she sometimes feels more inspired at home in front of the set than she does at the Baptist church down the road. She even sent in a check once when Jimmy seemed to be in really desperate straits.

There we have it: Mabel alone in her living room getting God via satellite. She epitomizes what sociologists have been calling "privatized religion"—the scourge of modern society.[2] Here is Mabel, no longer active in the Ladies' Missionary Society, a thousand miles from her nearest kin, cut off from the real world except for the few friends she plays canasta with on Thursday afternoons. And now she does not even need to venture down the road to the Baptist church to fulfill her religious needs. Next thing, she will have abandoned her religious community entirely and will have developed her own unique version of personalized religiosity—"Mabelism," she will probably call it.

Sociologists would tell us that Mabel is caught up in the powerful vortex of a downward social spiral. It is not exactly her fault that her faith has become privatized. Even when her mother was rousting her out of bed as a little girl, the Baptist church was becoming more privatized simply by virtue of having to compete with two hundred other denominations, no one of which could speak authoritatively about the Word of God. In the intervening decades, privatization was also reinforced by the growth of anonymous urban places, by the shattering of local kin networks as college training required children to move away and then as professional occupations required them to stay away. There was, in all of this, a kind of rugged frontier spirit that animated everyone's sense of their individual uniqueness. Too, one could not help having been shaped by all those commercials that said you could have your hamburgers done "your way," by all those car salesmen that encouraged you to have your Chevrolet customized to your own specifications, and by all those *Readers' Digest* articles about brave soldiers and eccentric millionaires who succeeded by bucking the system.

But televised preaching seemed to be the final stroke. If anything should draw people out of the secret recesses of their homes and force them to live (as clergy liked to say) "in community," it was the church. The Bible itself commanded believers not to forsake the assembly. It was in the midst of the assembled faithful that the miracle of *kerygma* happened. Now television was replacing this community with a miracle of its own—the miracle of sitting motionless and alone before a preacher who was thousands of miles away and who could not listen nor love—only speak.

Of course, this depiction of religious television is—in the hypothetical way I have presented it—a caricature. It is, nevertheless, a very familiar and disturbing image of the fruits of religious television. It lies behind the anxious questions one hears from clergy about religious television; it reinforces the cynicism that college students always express toward television preaching; and it has funneled hundreds of thousands of dollars into the hands of television preachers (and into the budgets of research institutes and polling agencies). It is a caricature that contains a great deal of truth, and yet one that neglects an extremely important dimension of religious television.

Let us return momentarily to our hypothetical case. Mabel sits alone in her living room watching her favorite television preachers. But the spectacle she views is also very much a part of our public religion—for good or for bad. The Bakker and Swaggart sex scandals in 1987 and 1988 prompted widely publicized discussions of the nature of morality and its relation to public religious figures. Pat Robertson's abortive campaign for the Republican presidential nomination generated hopes and fears about the mixing of religion and politics. Falwell has used the money his viewers send in to launch a vast movement to restore morality to American public life. Robert Schuller routinely gives his pulpit to guest speakers from Washington who tell how important their faith is to their work as public officials.

And where is Mabel in all of this? Simply a passive spectator like one of the nameless faces in the crowd who looked on as Hitler rose to power? She might be. But let us pursue her interview with our imaginary Gallup pollster a bit further. Why does she watch? Her concerns, it turns out, are not so strictly private as we thought. She tells us of her deep interest in the country's declining moral standards in recent years. She watches, she says, to gain information about important social and political issues of the day, from abortion to foreign policy. She routinely receives letters from Falwell, sometimes sent by certified mail, which keep her abreast of the latest developments at the Supreme Court and in the White House. Once, shortly after she had mailed her second check to Lynchburg, she even received a phone call asking if she couldn't sign a petition and send another check to help fight a worthy cause. In recent weeks she received newsletters from Senator Jesse Helms, the National Rifle Association, and from a former Air Force general who is running an organization called "High Frontier." Mabel feels more connected than ever to national politics.

What should we infer? Certainly the development of televised religion has done more than simply contribute to the privatization of faith. Much of it has also reinforced the role of religion in the public sphere. Some of the programs have generated huge sums of money from which political candidacies could be launched. Religious television provides new ways for private citizens like Mabel to express their sentiments and see them mobilized along with the sentiments of millions of others. She can return petitions about abortion and see Falwell carry them to the White House. He is a public figure no less than Ronald Reagan or Citizen Kane. His acts and his rhetoric place religion on the national agenda. He has done for our generation what Theodore Weld or Billy Sunday or Aimee Semple McPherson did for previous generations: he has made religion something people talk about, an item of public debate. The secularists may well have the final say, but they find themselves having to confront religion all over again—and long after they thought they had simply pushed religion into the dark crevices of our private lives.

So the paradox of televised religion is this: at the same time it privatizes, it also makes public. And at one level this conclusion should not surprise us. Only the theoretical blinders that have guided the social scientist in probing this issue have prevented us from recognizing, as Mabel Miller herself probably would, that religious television is both consumed in private and acted upon in public. But having made this simple observation, we are now in a position to press the matter onto somewhat less-charted terrain. I would like to focus on four aspects of the private and the public dimensions of religious television.

To what degree does religious television encourage active, spontaneous involvement on the part of the individual in the construction of his or her religious expressions, as opposed to a more passive and externally guided form of religious expression?

If we think for a moment about devotional religion in general, we immediately recognize wide variation in the extent to which active and spontaneous involvement is encouraged. In many liturgical traditions, for example, the individual believer is encouraged to participate actively in personal and group prayer or in the sacraments, but only to the extent of mouthing what is recommended in a standard guide, such as a book of common prayer or a printed order of service in the weekly church leaflet. In contrast, many other traditions encourage the individual believer to create his or her own prayers, to use new words, and to tailor them to his or her immediate situation. Some traditions go further still, encouraging the believer to study the Bible, keep a daily diary of his or her thoughts about

God, or seek out ways to witness or give testimony to his or her faith.

It is often difficult to know whether the individual is genuinely acting from spontaneous internal impulses or conforming to some external set of expectations generated by other individuals or by institutions. The motivation behind such religious practices is not the issue; it does not necessarily run counter to active, spontaneous forms of religious expression to follow various role models or scripts. Nevertheless, there are important differences between the two extremes.

At one extreme, the individual sits passively and does little else but listen: someone reads the Scriptures to him, prays for him, and plays or performs music for him; his attention is guided from one activity to another; he therefore has little opportunity to make choices about when and how to respond or participate; even his opportunities to respond may be highly structured. He sings on cue and confesses his sins by reading a prescribed prayer. At the other extreme, the individual moves and speaks somewhat spontaneously: he may go on a religious pilgrimage or at least go to a specially designated place of worship; he reads for himself and sings for himself; he is suddenly so flooded with ecstasy that he can no longer read or sing and has to pause momentarily to soak up the moment and give thanks for it; or he finds himself utterly bored and emotionless so he decides to abandon the devotional book he was reading and do something else instead.

Religious television viewing clearly falls on the passive end of the scale. The viewer sits quietly and listens to the words of the talk show host or televangelist. He has only to listen as the Scripture verses for the day are read to him. Rather than picking up his own Bible and finding the passage for himself, he watches as a teleprompter shows him the words on the screen. He listens as the choir sings instead of rising to his feet and singing along. Even his responses are modeled for him: after the televangelist says something humorous, the camera zooms in on the face of someone in the crowd who especially enjoyed the joke; when the choir raises its voice in a crescendo of praise for the beauties of nature, the camera focuses on the bouquet before the altar or takes the viewer on a quick, visually uplifting tour of beautifully landscaped grounds. And when it is time to receive the offering, an 800-number flashes on the screen and the quiet voice, not of the viewer's conscience, but of the announcer, suggests that a pledge of $100 would be appropriate for today. The couch-potato image of the habitual television viewer comes inescapably to mind. A viewer could spontaneously register her boredom with the screen by switching channels or even by turning off the set. She could even become actively involved in the devotional reflections stimulated by the program by writing to the televangelist for his latest book, by reading carefully the direct mail solicitations he sends to her house, or by putting the VCR on hold and spending a few moments in private prayer. The religious television programmers do not encourage most of these spontaneous actions, however. Like the commercial networks, they hope to program millions of viewers to watch at the same time every week, to sit passively and listen uncritically, and to send in dutifully a check for the amount prescribed.

In this sense, religious television privatizes faith less than it renders it passive. Perhaps the individual who actively and spontaneously works out his own way of responding to God has a more privatized faith than the person who simply responds like millions of other viewers. A passive faith is private only in the additional sense that if one never speaks, never behaves, and never ventures beyond the confines of one's living room, then nobody else is ever likely to know of one's faith commitments. Prayer has truly remained in the closet, and one's light has stayed hidden beneath a bushel basket.

It is not only religious television that turns people to a passive faith. The institutional church has always had a stake in promoting passivity. Preachers who fill live pulpits generally find their burdens easier if their parishioners sit quietly and listen, responding only when the choirmaster directs or when the plate is passed. Any orderly worship service, at least by white middle-class standards, requires it, although the anomaly between such passivity and a genuine spirit of worship is often striking. Annie Dillard has captured well this ironic sense of anomaly. "Does anyone," she writes, "have the foggiest idea what sort of power we so blithely invoke?"

> The churches are children playing on the floor with their chemistry sets, mixing up a batch of TNT to kill a Sunday morning. It is madness to wear ladies' straw hats and velvet hats to church; we should all be wearing crash helmets.

Ushers should issue life preservers and signal flares; they should lash us to our pews. For the sleeping god may wake someday and take offense, or the waking god may draw us out to where we can never return.[3]

But even more private expressions of religious devotion, where greater variation might be tolerated, confront a constant tension between activity and passivity, spontaneity and conformity. Daily prayer books and meditation guides encourage routine in order to make sure the believer does something: rise at the same hour each day, pray at the same time, read a one-page devotional from the guide provided for that month. But they encourage active responses as well: think through one's own religious needs, keep a journal of one's faith journey, and if one feels an urge to burst forth in praise, let it rip! As with most aspects of the religious life, the tension between passivity and activity is resolved by finding an appropriate balance. Religious television appears to tip the scale far in the direction of passivity and thus gives rise to concerns about what kinds of more active devotional expressions should be encouraged. But an element of passive, externally guided behavior is inescapable.

To what degree does religious television encourage imagi-
nation in the expression of faith, as opposed to a more
conformist or doctrinaire style of faith?

This question is closely associated with the previous one: passive religious expression should result in a more conformist or doctrinaire style of faith. However, the media of communication themselves may promote or inhibit the religious imagination. Consider the effects of televised media compared with live productions and the printed word.

Two historic episodes in the transition from live productions to the printed word shed light on the contemporary situation. One occurred in the sixteenth century in conjunction with the Reformation's emphasis on the printed word in opposition to the iconography and festivals of the medieval church. The other came in the eighteenth century during the transition in elite culture from the stage to the novel. In both cases it was argued—by contemporaries and historians—that the printed word was superior to the live productions that it superseded. In the sixteenth-century case, the arguments focused on the tendency for believers to concretize iconography and festivals, thereby confusing the images for the divine truths they represented. The Reformers railed against the idolatry of graphic images and live productions of all kinds, preferring to limit the believer's sensory stimuli to that of the read and spoken Bible. In the eighteenth-century case, the arguments focused more squarely on the limitations of drama compared with the novel. Stage productions were limited in the overall number of scenes they could depict, in the number and types of relations among characters that audiences could be expected to follow, and in the voice and sense of time that characters could adopt. The novel was said to be more adaptable to the complex plots, situations, and relationships of modern urban life.

Interestingly enough, both arguments bear directly on the relation between the printed word and the imagination. And the relation suggested curiously challenges contemporary theories that suggest that the printed word, by virtue of codifying and formalizing discourse, tends to limit meaning. Printed discourse supposedly specifies and elaborates meaning; in contrast, icons, festivals, and stage plays leave more to the ambiguity of imagination.[4] But the arguments used in these two historic episodes suggest the opposite: the printed word leaves more to the imagination.

In the Reformation case, the printed word required the believer to develop his or her own abstract sense of the divine, rather than having the divine concretized in a visual image. In the Enlightenment case, the printed word required the reader of, say, *Moll Flanders* to imagine what Moll must have looked like, how her various lovers may have been dressed, and how houses, rooms, and streets all may have met the eye. People apparently found the printed word more appealing precisely because it did not serve everything up on a prearranged platter.

These arguments suggest an interesting parallel for assessing the implications of religious television. Conventional wisdom might again suggest that television enriches the imagination. How much more vivid it is to see the movie rather than read the book! Similarly, how much more effective it is to be able to see Robert Schuller on the screen and to have the camera pan the splendors of the Crystal Cathedral than to spend a dry half hour reading the book of Romans.

If the historic arguments apply, religious television stifles the imagination, rather than facilitates it. By framing the visual stimulus, religious television circumscribes the viewer's imagination. The Crystal Cathedral becomes an icon as the camera prompts the viewer to focus for ten seconds here and ten seconds there. The viewer's attention necessarily follows the images selected by the director and depicted on the set. Compared with sitting in the pews at Anaheim, where the individual congregant decides what to observe, the television program limits the picture frame and eclipses peripheral vision.

Similarly, on television the face of Jerry Falwell becomes an icon that directs our attention to the minister more than in a local congregation. The camera zooms in on Falwell's face; we see every feature; and we see only those expressions the film editors want us to see; whereas our own minister's face on Sunday morning, seen from fifty or one hundred feet back, constitutes a much smaller proportion of our overall vision, and we see him or her in unguarded moments that may convey some humanness, rather than the carefully edited incarnation we see on our television screens.

Such iconization on television is tempered by the spoken word. Much of religious television is like listening to the tapes or even reading the books of televangelists. Religious television has largely avoided featuring graphic images, such as pictures of Jesus, and it has relied little (probably because of financial costs) on televised drama, situation comedies, and documentaries. When Jerry Falwell describes the scourge of immorality that is marching at this very hour on our nation's capitol, the viewer's imagination is stimulated.

Nevertheless, religious television stifles the religious imagination. Even if the spoken word dominates films of church services and talk show formats, the camera offers much visual imagery. The meanings of Falwell's words are limited by the way he says them, by the images of his audience, by shots of the choir behind him, and by the candid conversational close-ups in his office. Similarly, Pat Robertson's words on the "700 Club" are inextricably interwoven with images of the famous Robertson grin, the carefully groomed co-hosts, and the polished stage settings.

The contrast between the religious devotion that comes from these highly structured settings and the lonely prophet in the wilderness contemplating the mysteries of the Great Commandment is profound. So is the contrast between the person whose vision is filled with images of Falwell's Thomas Road Baptist Church and the child who hears the 23d Psalm read during family devotions and imagines vividly what the "valley of the shadow of death" must be like.

Which of these examples is really the purer form of a

privatized religion? Certainly the person who imagines the meaning of the Shepherd's Psalm has a more privatized religion than does the person who sees it enacted in a Cecil B. deMille panorama, or the person who lets Schuller paint the imagery of what it means. At this level, one would scarcely be inclined to criticize the believer for practicing a privatized form of faith.

To what degree does religious television encourage a style of faith that emerges from and is reinforced by social interaction, as opposed to a style of faith that remains more purely the unspoken attribute of the individual?

There is some evidence to indicate that many viewers of religious television discuss these programs with their families, friends, and fellow churchgoers. In that sense, religious television is not strictly a private matter. One can say to a friend, "What did you think of Jerry Falwell yesterday?" just as easily as one can ask their reaction to yesterday's sermon at the local church. Indeed, the odds of any two people having watched the same religious television program are much higher than any two people having attended the same church, given the diversity of our society and the demise of the neighborhood church.

Such interaction probably reinforces certain beliefs. When one's friend responds, "I thought he really said some important things," your own conviction about Falwell's credibility may rise. Or when you show someone a direct-mail solicitation containing alarming news about how the Soviets are planning to poison our drinking water, and that person registers an appropriate level of concern, your own alarm may well increase. This kind of reinforcement may not be terribly different from that gained at the local church, where mutual sharing simply confirms your commitment to the common faith.

In another way, though, the social interaction associated with religious television is likely to be quite different from that occurring in a local Bible study or Sunday-evening discussion group. The reinforcement one receives about Jerry Falwell's latest sermon is still reinforcement about an authoritative figure. He remains the voice of wisdom, and even if one disagrees, those disagreements never feed back into a genuine dialogue. Falwell may castigate his villainous detractors, but the camera seldom shows him in a roundtable discussion involving genuine give and take. The best small Bible study or discussion group is dialogic, enabling a participant to express a tentative view and have it disputed by another member of the group. One can share a personal anecdote and have it reinforced, but given a slightly different twist, by someone else relating a similar experience. No authority figure dominates. The learning that takes place occurs dialogically and the group itself provides a model of the mutual respect that lies at the heart of the religious worldview.

However, the dialogic experience in which genuine learning takes place may well be absent in primary religious communities, just as it is on religious television. Rather than consensus arising out of the group's deliberations, consensus may be so highly valued that no one feels free to share his or her honest opinions. Churches can become models of a tacit consensus that no one dares question. Consequently, serious disagreements never surface; the disgruntled move on to another parish rather than risk unsettling the waters. Polite conversation prevails; sermons focus on "unity" and "brotherhood"; and collective pronouns predominate.

In a pluralistic society fraught with deeply individualistic values the virtue of public discussion is to temper purely private sentiments and let consensus emerge through open dialogue. Religious television may promote some public dialogue, but its focus on single authoritative leaders runs counter to the more reciprocal kinds of interchange that can take place at more intimate levels.

To what degree does religious television integrate concerns from the private realm into public discourse, as opposed to keeping these two spheres separate?

The example of Mabel Miller suggested that religious television is a force in the public sphere, whether or not it also encourages a certain kind of private religion. Robertson's presidential candidacy and Falwell's role in organizing the New Christian Right are examples of purely public behavior. To what extent do they infuse the private into the public realm?

Some of the religious sentiments, concerns, and activities that have long been pushed out of the public square have now reemerged as items of public display. The most vivid example was Swaggart's public confession of his sinfulness.

So unusual was his public display of emotion—tears streaming down his face, voice trembling, begging God's forgiveness—that the mass media were pained to make sense of it all. Some interpreted it in a theatrical frame: Swaggart proved once again what a good actor he is; he really felt nothing but made us think he did. Others placed a medical frame around the episode: Swaggart was simply distraught and recovered quite quickly; or, Swaggart had a mental problem that caused him to do schizophrenic things (he does need rehabilitation). And still others, failing in any way to make sense of it at all, poked fun: "The beaches were wild today—beer parties, sex orgies, strip shows," television comedian Johnny Carson quipped, "It's time we got those televangelists back to work."

There were perhaps many reasons why the media were unable (or unwilling) to make sense of the Swaggart confession. One is the fact that biblical repentance and forgiveness are themes that have virtually disappeared from public life. Americans are far more comfortable with retribution, punishment, paying for one's mistakes, lawsuits, vendettas, keeping the record straight, establishing guilt, and fixing the blame than they are with repentance and forgiveness.

Yet repentance and forgiveness are clearly essential parts of the Christian message. Preachers talk about them all the time. Swaggart made it a public spectacle. Confess one's sins; claim God's forgiveness; go forward from there. Surely God was good enough to forgive Swaggart. (And so, by implication, others might be expected to forgive him, too.) Questions about the public propriety of maintaining a high leadership position were, of course, put aside. But on the surface, the Swaggart scandal functioned as a kind of morality play. Indeed, the Swaggart team was quick to recognize this role. As Swaggart's son Donny articulated it, appealing for viewers' financial support shortly after the episode became public, "If there's no forgiveness for Jimmy Swaggart, there's no forgiveness for you either."

Religious television has brought a number of other previously private issues into the public realm in less exceptional ways. Arguments about abortion and homosexuality have made these issues public and placed them on the national agenda. Religious television has contributed to this development. The televangelists have argued that such matters really cannot be left purely to individual discretion; instead, morality bears on the collective strength of a nation, and thus must become an item of political policy and legislation. These examples suggest that religious television has actually reversed some of the tendency toward privatization in American culture. If Americans have increasingly withdrawn into their own private lives, then turning private concerns into public issues is surely a step toward redressing the balance. Critics have suggested that televangelists have merely contributed to the further privatization of the public sphere. They charge that society has become so obsessed with things like a presidential candidate's sex life that the public cannot consider his potential on the basis of the issues themselves. And they wonder if media responses emphasizing the president's hernias more than the negotiations for an arms agreement are not a great disservice to the American people.

Those criticisms, however, have more to do with personality politics than with the publicizing of private concerns. They glamorize politics and give us unrealistic role models in the same way that Hollywood does. But if religion does have an intensely private dimension—if it is concerned with repentance and forgiveness, with redemption and sorrow, with morality and devotion—then it may not be an altogether negative development to see some of these private issues modeled and made the subject of public discussion.

To conclude, I have argued that religious television has both a private and a public dimension. In evaluating its cultural impact, we must consider the *quality* of its impact in both these realms. We want some aspects of religious devotion to be intensely private. We expect individuals to use their religious imaginations and to personalize their faith by tailoring it to their own experiences. Sitting alone in one's living room before the television, one may be able to do that, but we must also consider the consequences of religious television promoting a purely passive, unspontaneous, and unimaginative style of faith.

We may also discover that religious television gives people something to talk about with their friends and makes them feel part of some broader religious or political movement. In that sense, religious television viewing cannot be considered a strictly private affair. Nevertheless, it is the quality of this interaction with which we must concern ourselves. We must consider the kind of faith that results from listening to a single authoritative voice, as opposed to engaging in open dialogue with fellow believers who may represent a wide variety of views and experiences.

It is, finally, important to consider the pluses and minuses associated with bringing public personalities such as Falwell into our living rooms and with taking private issues such as sexuality or forgiveness into the public realm. Some way to bridge the two realms is of course vital to the functioning of any society. We must, however, be careful about the ways in which the two are interrelated. Too much privatization of the public realm contributes to the narcissism that already plays a prominent role in our culture. And too much infusing of the public into our private lives constitutes a potential violation of our personal rights and our sense of personal integrity. Indeed, it is perhaps this sense of violation—the intrusion of such public faces as Jerry Falwell and Pat Robertson into our private lives—that has been behind much of the annoyance that the public has begun to register toward the televangelists.[5]

These lines, penned by W. H. Auden, provide a fitting commentary on the delicate balance between the public and the private—the balance that religious television influences in so many ways:

> *Private faces in public places*
> *Are wiser and nicer*
> *Than public faces in private places.*[6]

NOTES

[1]This figure and the social characteristics of viewers discussed in the following paragraphs are based on findings from a national survey conducted by the Gallup Organization in 1984 as part of a major study of religious television; see G. L. Gerbner et al., *Religion and Television: A Research Report by the Annenberg School of Communications, University of Pennsylvania, and the Gallup Organization, Inc.* (Philadelphia: The Annenberg School of Communications, 1984); for additional analyses of these data and commentary, see the articles in *Review of Religious Research* 29 (December 1987): 97–210.

[2]See especially Thomas Luckmann, *The Invisible Religion* (New York: Macmillan, 1967); on the relevance of the privatization thesis to religious television, see Robert Wuthnow, "The Social Significance of Religious Television," *Review of Religious Research* 29 (December 1987): 125–34.

[3]Annie Dillard, *Teaching a Stone to Talk* (New York: Harper & Row, 1982), 40–41.

[4]Relevant arguments can be found in Jerome S. Bruner, Rose R. Oliver, and Patricia M. Greenfield, *Studies in Cognitive Growth* (New York: Wiley, 1966); Basil Berstein, *Class, Codes and Control* (New York: Schocken, 1975); and Robert N. Bellah, *Beyond Belief: Essays on Religion in a Post-Traditional World* (New York: Harper & Row, 1970).

[5]As one indication of the negative sentiment, a 1987 Harris poll showed

that 77 percent of the American public agreed with the statement, "The TV evangelical movement has been harmful to the conservative cause, has made a mockery of what religion should be, and has taken advantage of millions of followers by urging them to give their money"; reported in *Index to International Public Opinion, 1986–1987* (Westport, Conn.: Greenwood Press, 1988), 477.

[6]Quoted in Anthony Arblaster, *The Rise and Decline of Western Liberalism* (Oxford: Basil Blackwell, 1984), 45.

9

TELEVANGELISM AND POLITICAL MOBILIZATION

JEFFREY K. HADDEN

Scholars agree that religious broadcasters, especially the televangelists, have been instrumental in the emergence and development of the New Christian Right (NCR) during the 1980s.[1] Several politically conservative groups emerged in the late 1970s, e.g., Moral Majority, Christian Voice, Religious Roundtable, Christian Freedom Foundation, and National Christian Action Coalition. The press, and hence the general public, became aware of the NCR during the 1980 presidential campaign. Ronald Reagan's meeting with NCR leaders during the Republican National Convention in Detroit and then later addressing two NCR-sponsored meetings during the campaign played an important role in giving the movement visibility.

The importance of this social and political movement, however, remains controversial. Historian Erling Jorstad argues that "the resurgence and intertwined growth of religious fundamentalism and political conservatism in the United States in the 1980s stands as the dominant theme in American religious history of this decade."[2] Most of the support for this perspective comes from countermovement organizations, such as People for the American Way and Americans for Common Sense, which have as their *raison d'etre* the mission of persuading Americans that these "right-wing extremists" represent a grave threat to civil liberties and to the separation of church and state.

At the other end of the continuum are scholars and

journalists who would assign little, if any, importance to the New Christian Right. A few see the phenomenon almost purely as media hype. As National Public Radio Reporter Tina Rosenberg wrote in *Washington Monthly:* "Falwell wants attention, liberals want an ogre, the press wants a good story. Whenever all parties want the same thing, they tend to get it whether they deserve it or not."[3] Still other observers believe that President Ronald Reagan's public support of the religious broadcasters has created the *perception* that the televangelists are significant players in the conservative politics of the 1980s. These observers are certain that the *poli-preachers* will vanish in the post-Reagan era.

Most serious scholars of contemporary religion stand somewhere in the middle. They acknowledge the potential for the emergence of a significant social movement but most are not convinced that the empirical indicators point to the formation of an epoch-altering movement.[4] In fact, there has been little empirical research about the movement, primarily because funds are not easily available. Hence, scholars have tended to study only limited aspects of the movement.

After eight years of high media visibility, and a presidential primary season in 1988 that openly addressed religion in both parties, the New Christian Right appeared to have vanished in the general election. The skeptics were again telling us that the religious right was dead. On the face of it, they appeared to have a case. Defeated presidential candidate Pat Robertson returned to the "700 Club." Jerry Falwell, founder of the conservative Moral Majority, appeared to leave politics in order to concentrate on building Liberty University. Jimmy Swaggart was preoccupied with attempting to halt the free fall in his audience ratings and revenues. Even Jim Bakker, whose "People That Love" centers were celebrated in a speech by President Reagan, went to federal prison for his mismanagement of Heritage USA.

All of this did not seem to bode well for the argument that televangelism remains an important force in America, much less the proposition that televangelists will yet lead a significant social and political movement. But as Peter Berger has reminded us, and we need to keep reminding ourselves periodically, "the first wisdom of sociology is this—things are not what they seem."[5] In 1979 Jeremy Rifkin published *The Emerging Order* in which he concluded: "Of one thing there is little doubt, the evangelical community is amassing a base of potential power that dwarfs every other competing interest in American society today. A close look at the evangelical communications network . . . should convince even the skeptic that it is now the single most important cultural force in American life."[6] I found Rifkin's argument compelling in the late 1970s. A decade later, I still do, in spite of the pronouncements of various scholars and media pundits.

While most political commentators ignored the Robertson campaign in 1988, or saw it as a failure, I believe his candidacy provided abundant evidence that a movement was afoot. Major social movements do not unfold on schedules to accommodate mass media deadlines; their surges are seldom predictable. Like major advances in the stock market, analysis of fundamentals can anticipate advances, but the timing of market thrusts is seldom precisely forecast. Rifkin's assessment rightly focused on *potential*, not actualized power. I too believe that we are looking at political potential rather than established political power.

But after nearly a decade of nascent political potential, what can we say has happened? Has the movement stalled? If not, why is it not more visible and why do we not see more evidence of the movement's success? Is the assessment of movement potential wrong? It is altogether appropriate that skeptics ask why, if there is so much potential, the leaders have not taken the movement on a swifter trajectory toward the realization of political clout. This chapter explores these issues by examining the role of the televangelists in the mobilization of the New Christian Right movement. I shall identify some fundamental elements of social movement analysis and then apply them to the development of the movement and the role of the televangelists.

RESOURCE MOBILIZATION THEORY

The conceptual model I have used to organize and focus my thinking about the growing political consciousness of conservative Christians is known in sociological literature as the *resource mobilization theory* of social movements.[7] Mayer Zald, of the University of Michigan, and John McCarthy, of Catholic University, have popularized the term, pioneered research utilizing the orientation, and recently published a volume of essays of their research that gives considerable structure to an emerging theoretical orientation.[8]

In my own development of this theoretical orientation, there is a close connection between social problems and social movements.[9] *Social problems* are social conditions that have been collectively identified as intolerable. *Social movements* are collective activities aimed at mobilizing resources for the purpose of changing intolerable conditions. A social movement is the action that follows the identification of a social problem.

Not all intolerable social conditions lead to social movements. Many groups stage protest demonstrations without necessarily being committed to the arduous task of mobilizing to affect change. Similarly, many groups take initial steps toward mobilization only to discover that the commitment and resources required are greater than they have or are prepared to commit. This is the fate of most movements. Protest demonstrations differ from symbolic crusades, which tend to be ad hoc, resulting directly from a particular happening or development that was unpopular with the demonstrators. Symbolic crusades usually start out as social movements. They become symbolic crusades when the leadership recognizes that the movement is not going to succeed in achieving the change it desires but values the activities that publicly affirm the moral perspective of the group. Some scholars have defined movements emanating from the radical right as mere symbolic crusades because they assume that these movements cannot succeed. This unsupported assumption renders leadership quixotic and removes any serious need of assessing the resources a group may be able to bring to a movement.

In contrast to the theory of symbolic crusades, resource mobilization theory is not anchored in any ideological posture. Instead, resource mobilization theory focuses upon the resources groups are able to muster in the struggle to achieve change. It is conceptually useful to separately examine (1) the *grievance claims* made by a social movement and (2) the *goals* they seek to achieve. Claims and goals establish the credibility and plausibility of a movement. Claims that are vaguely stated, inadequately focused, or demonstrably false are less likely to be judged credible than are reasonable claims.[10] Obviously, the credibility and plausibility of grievances and goals will vary, depending upon the audience. It is most important for leaders to establish credibility and plausibility with those persons and groups the movement hopes to enlist as adherents. Establishments, i.e., political and corporate elites, almost always see movements at the onset as lacking credibility and plausibility.

Establishments can be expected to shift toward support or adamant opposition, depending upon their value preferences, as the movement gains momentum. Social movements can be analyzed in terms of six broad types of resources: (1) leadership, (2) legitimating symbols, (3) organization, (4) money, (5) adherents, and (6) media access. Leadership is critical at the onset of any movement, for it is responsible for framing the grievances, establishing goals, and developing the legitimating symbols. Grievance claims and goals are for public consumption, whereas legitimating symbols are for participant consumption. Legitimating symbols motivate movement workers and, when effectively framed, help transform latent adherents into active adherents. Legitimating symbols include (a) symbols of evil, (b) symbols of good, (c) a utopian or millenarian vision, (d) textual legitimacy, (e) symbols of group solidarity, and (f) leadership symbols.

THE BIRTH OF THE NEW CHRISTIAN RIGHT

The emergence of the New Christian Right near the end of the 1970s has been reasonably well documented.[11] Several key leaders of the New Right, including Howard Phillips, Paul Weyrich, and Richard Viguerie, saw the possibility and strategic advantage of forging coalitions with conservative Christian groups. Ed McAteer and Robert Billings were key figures in linking the secular right and the religious right together. McAteer, a retired salesman, was working with Howard Phillips' Conservative Caucus when he created the Religious Roundtable. And Robert Billings, who had been a Christian college president before getting turned on to politics at a New Right workshop, formed the National Christian Action Coalition in 1977. Both played significant roles in encouraging Jerry Falwell to become more actively involved in politics. When Falwell made the commitment in 1979 to create the Moral Majority, Billings served as the organization's executive director until joining the Reagan presidential campaign as liaison to the religious community. McAteer, in the meantime, recruited televangelist James Robison to be the vice president and media spokesman for the Religious Roundtable. The Roundtable Board of Directors included two other television preachers, D. James Kennedy and Charles Stanley, and the larger "Council of 56" included the National Religious Broadcaster's Executive Director Ben Armstrong, Jerry Falwell, E. V. Hill, Richard

Hogue, Tim LaHaye, and Pat Robertson.[12] With several significant televangelists on board, the movement was well positioned to gain national visibility. That visibility came first at the Republican National Convention in July 1980 and then in Dallas at the National Affairs Briefing sponsored by the Roundtable. On both occasions, Ronald Reagan's embracing of the televangelists and their agenda helped give the movement front-page visibility.[13]

At the onset, New Right operatives saw the mobilization of conservative Christians as a way of bolstering their movement. The recruiting of television preachers was a means to that end. Ronald Reagan saw the televangelists as a means of reaching conservative Christians in support of his candidacy. But the emergence of the politically oriented television preachers produced something more than either the New Right operatives or candidate Reagan expected. It enhanced the movement's resources on almost every front. First, televangelists enriched the movement by providing energetic new leadership. Second, they brought proven skills in fund raising on a major scale. Third, they provided media access through their regular religious programming, When it became evident to the secular media that the televangelists were regularly reaching significant audiences, and that this communications access was being used to encourage audiences to mobilize new political activists, the credibility of the movement increased significantly.

Taken together, the new resources supplied by televangelists were an enormous boost to the New Right movement. Moreover, the televangelists soon created a separate movement that emphasized moral issues such as abortion, pornography, school prayer, and the evils of secular humanism. Jerry Falwell and the Moral Majority came to be seen as symbols and the core of the new movement. In early 1986, Falwell surprisingly abandoned the Moral Majority, though it was not immediately clear whether Falwell intended merely to change the name of the widely criticized organization to the Liberty Federation. The answer became evident in 1989 when the Moral Majority was formally dissolved. In any case, Falwell remained highly visible.

Oddly enough, Falwell's disestablishment of the Moral Majority corresponded closely with the first national news about the presidential aspirations of Pat Robertson. Robertson's candidacy elicited a few public fears that he might have an invisible army staged to make a serious bid for the Republican nomination. It was soon clear, however, that Robertson's campaign and the social movement it represented were overshadowed by the sex scandals of two of the most prominent televangelists—Jim Bakker and Jimmy Swaggart. Because Robertson's bid for the Republican nomination netted him only a handful of delegates, the media created the impression of a failed campaign.

ASSESSING THE REAL POTENTIAL OF THE NEW CHRISTIAN RIGHT

There is a wide spectrum of views about the New Christian Right as a viable and dynamic political movement in America. Assessing the organizational strength of social movements is virtually impossible. Leaders typically make exaggerated claims, and since they are not obligated to make public information about their organizations, scholars can only estimate organizational strength. Typically this takes the form of developing rationales for why the leadership claims are exaggerated.[14] But most scholars of social movements would readily acknowledge that the size of an organization's paid-up membership is not as important as the potential of a movement to arouse public sympathy for the movement's cause.

First, it is difficult to determine the potential size of the public that might, given the right conditions, become adherents to the movement. Few scholars agree on how to define and measure membership in the evangelical community. But viewed through the macroscopic lens of resource mobilization theory, it really doesn't matter. White evangelical Christians, by any definition, constitute a very large minority in America. By conservative estimate, white evangelical Christians are a group about twice as large as black America.

The fact is that social movements normally require very few working adherents. Only financial support and organizational "membership" involve a larger base. The evangelical community in America constitutes an enormously large pool of potential recruits for social activism and financial support, although they are greatly divided over many political issues. When it comes to expanding the core of participation in a movement, churches represent the single largest organizational base for recruiting social movement participants in society. No other organization has such a vast infrastructure in place.

Movement leaders do not have to build organizations; they merely have to tap into existing organizational infrastructures. Second, the televangelists have represented a key resource in the initiation and promotion of the movement to date, although it is unclear if they are really able to reach and persuade large numbers of citizens to become politically involved. There are very large discrepancies in the various estimates of audience size.[15] Some critics of religious broadcasters have sought to build a case for extremely small audiences. William Fore, for example, argues that no more than 7.2 million Americans watched fifteen minutes or more of religious broadcasting in an average week in 1983.[16] But Gallup polls have consistently placed viewership much higher. During roughly the same time period, Gallup found almost one out of every three adults (more than seventy million) watch some religious programming during the course of a month.[17] Nielsen's cumulative audience data also reveal similarly high numbers.[18]

Regardless of the audience size, the syndicated and satellite television programs represent only one segment of a much larger communications structure. The 1,393 commercial Christian radio stations and over 259 Christian TV stations could not be sustained without some market share.[19] In addition, the evangelical marketplace also includes a very large publication and recording industry. Much of this communications structure is involved in the production of inspiration and entertainment. But running through much of it is a moral message that evangelical Christians understand in increasingly political terms. This is the growing communications network that impressed Jeremy Rifkin.

Such leadership and audience potential do not make a movement. However, there is evidence that most evangelicals support the agenda of the New Christian Right even if they do not identify themselves with specific organizations and leaders.[20] The task of movement leaders is to transform *latent adherents*, i.e., people who express value preferences consistent with movement goals, into *adherents*, or supporters of movement goals. In *Televangelism, Power and Politics*, Anson Shupe and I assembled a wide array of public opinion poll data that indicate that support for many of the New Christian Right positions extends substantially beyond the evangelical community. This suggests that latent adherents could become supporters of specific goals of the movement if these goals are packaged in the right language and symbols. However, the movement has had little success at drawing people into active participation. The Moral Majority, for example, saw little change in the proportion of Americans who claimed to be members or supporters of the group. There are other measures that also call into question the organizational strength and effectiveness of the Moral Majority.[21]

On the other hand, one of the important goals of Falwell, and every other New Christian Right leader, was the election and support of Ronald Reagan. In 1980, 62 percent of white evangelicals voted for Reagan, up from 55 percent voting Republican in 1976. The 1984 election saw Reagan's support among evangelicals increase to 80 percent. In 1988, the New Christian Right leadership supported George Bush. Bush, of course, won handily with 54 percent of the popular vote and 426 of the 538 electoral votes. A *Times Mirror* poll conducted two weeks before the election indicated that Bush would receive 93 percent of the votes of people they classified as "moralists."[22] Furthermore, while representing 12 percent of the registered voters, they were expected to constitute 14 percent of the voting population. The *Times Mirror* classification of "moralists" is not synonymous with evangelicals, but it is a good surrogate.

Evangelical support for Reagan and Bush is not necessarily evidence for the existence of a social movement. But it is clear that evangelical Christians are moving toward a consensus as to which individuals and political party best represent their values. This growing consensus may eventually evaporate, but in 1988 it still constituted a political identity and alliance that approached the strength of blacks' allegiance to the democratic party. No other interest group even approaches such a solid alignment. More remarkable, it is a transformation that has taken place in less than two decades. Perhaps the New Christian Right and the televangelists have not been instrumental in the shift of evangelical allegiance from the Democratic to the Republican party. Clearly, direct effects can't be quantified. But it is clear that (1) the moral content of religious broadcasters on television and radio is highly similar, and (2) the media visibility of some of the politically engaged broadcasters has served to heighten evangelical consciousness about politics as well as specific issues. Thus, the case for the televangelists affecting the shift of evangelicals to the Republican party seems more plausible than the argument against this proposition. Critics of the New Christian Right are quick to point out that none of the major stated goals of the movement have been achieved. Abortion is still legal. Pornography is widely available. Prayer in public schools is still unconstitutional. There has been little change in the moral content of public school curricula. Many of the major public issues were long on the Christian right's agenda, but only in 1988 did the country and the secular media became preoccupied with the agenda.

Rather than pursuing evidence for a burgeoning social movement, an alternative proposition may be explored, namely that the movement never really got off the ground because it was quickly co-opted by Ronald Reagan. There is substantial evidence to support this proposition. Reagan's annual address to the National Religious Broadcasters was the highlight of their convention. Reagan's addresses served both to legitimize the New Christian Right's social agenda and to assure him of evangelical support of much of his own agenda. Since August 22, 1980, when Ronald Reagan rose to address fifteen thousand evangelical leaders at the National Affairs Briefing in Dallas, beginning with the magic words "I endorse you, and what you are doing," the New Christian Right leadership has never doubted his support.[23]

As a legitimizing symbol of good leadership, Reagan has certainly been a sterling champion for the New Christian Right. Ironically, his legitimizing of the social-issues agenda may also have had the effect of blunting the movement. Reagan's position as president may have dissipated some of the movement's steam by creating the impression that the battles were being won; the sense of urgency to organize for the purpose of pressing claims was not as evident as it might have been with someone unsympathetic in the White House.

From this perspective, it would appear that evangelical Christians have become an interest group that has found a home in the Republican party. This proposition is more problematic. The Robertson candidacy made it abundantly clear that evangelical Christians were more welcome in the White House than they are in the Republican National Committee (RNC). Many RNC regulars are uncomfortable with the personal morality agenda of conservative Christians. Equally important, the infusion of new blood into the party in significant quantity could represent a threat to established party leaders. Local party politics is especially vulnerable to takeovers by newcomers.

Pat Robertson understood this vulnerability and planned a campaign strategy based on blitzing local precincts. But the long-convoluted delegate-selection process in Michigan served as a bellwether. Bush's supporters, using the vice president's control of the RNC, succeeded in blocking the Robertson forces, but not before Robertson gained or nearly gained control of the party in several states.

A serious assessment of the New Christian Right as a social movement and the role of the televangelists have played in forging this movement, must take seriously the presidential campaign of Pat Robertson. Contrary to the impression created by the media, Robertson achieved some remarkable successes. Foremost was the fact that Robertson's organization was the first to cultivate grass-roots support in the national political process. Previously the New Christian Right had relied primarily on direct-mail, mass-media organization, and ad hoc piggybacking on existing organizations, primarily churches.

The 1980s may have been the stage for the movement. Evangelical Christians became much more comfortable with political involvement. Carl Henry's message from the 1940s that evangelicals should become involved in the world, was finally falling on receptive ears.[24] There was in the 1980s a growing sense that civic duty is a religious duty. The progressive movement in this direction could be symbolized by presidential candidate Jimmy Carter telling evangelical Christians that it was proper to be involved in politics, Jerry Falwell telling them it was their duty, and eventually Pat Robertson showing them how to do it.

As the same time, however, theological fissures within evangelicalism cast a long shadow over the potential movement. Televangelists have been important in raising political consciousness, but it is less clear that they have successfully forged ecumenical coalitions. From the beginning, Jerry Falwell made much about the Moral Majority being a broad-based organization. Pat Robertson similarly claimed that his campaign drew upon a wide spectrum of religious traditions. But these kinds of claims have always been made by organizations who wished to legitimize their goals and methods. On the surface, such claims appeared to be credible. Leaders appeared together at rallies, meet annually at the National Religious Broadcasters' convention in Washington, served on the boards of some of the same organizations, and were often seen powwowing with their pal at 1600 Pennsylvania Avenue. But these surface indicators were misleading. The truth is that Jerry Falwell is still more welcome at a businessmen's luncheon in Salt Lake City or a gathering of conservative Roman Catholic bishops than he is at the podium of a Southern Baptist Convention. Not until 1988, after his aborted attempt to bail out the faltering PTL ministry, was he invited to address the annual meeting of the National Association of Evangelicals. And the core of Robertson's support was from the charismatic community.[25]

The future of the New Christian Right as a discernible social movement may hinge on whether Republicans accommodate evangelical Christians mobilized by the Robertson campaign or attempt to roust them out of the party. Accommodation will keep the movement concentrated in normal party politics. Hostility toward evangelical Christians will likely trigger renewed efforts to take over local, district, and state political machinery. But hostility will also leave many alienated from party politics and turn the movement toward its own organizational activity.

People who worked in the Robertson campaign learned grass-roots organizational skills far more sophisticated than those of the other sectors of the New Christian Right movement. If these skills are used to broaden the base of grass-roots support in the evangelical community, the New Christian Right could eventually become a very formidable political force. However, the New Christian Right needs political leadership soon. Televangelists will remain important figures in stimulating involvements, but they are also easy targets for vigorous countermobilization. The movement needs leaders who are not so easily stereotyped by political rivals. Robertson may eventually tell his constituency that God's intent, in instructing him to run for the presidency, was to mobilize evangelical Christians. But in 1988, after the termination of his candidacy, Robertson was working to hold onto his constituency for his own future political ambitions.

In the meantime, Carl Henry's assessment in *Confessions of a Theologian* of the evangelical phenomenon seems to fit well the phenomenon of evangelicals in the political arena. The New Christian Right of the 1980s ". . . is broadening but not significantly deepening. It lacks cohesion. No intellectually articulate spokesman has both acknowledged authority and universal acceptance to speak for the entire enterprise."[26]

NOTES

[1]Robert C. Liebman and Robert Wuthnow, eds., *The New Christian Right* (New York: Aldine, 1983).

[2]Erling Jorstad, *The New Christian Right 1981–1988* (Lewiston, N.Y.: Edwin Mellen, 1987).

[3]Tina Rosenberg. "How the Media Made the Moral Majority," *Washington Monthly* (May 1982), 26–34.

[4]Stuart Rothenberg and Frank Newport, *The Evangelical Voter: Religion and Politics in America* (Washington D.C.: Institute for Government and Politics of the Free Congress Research and Educational Foundation, 1984); Joseph B. Tamney and Stephen D. Johnson, "The Moral Majority in Middletown," *Journal for the Scientific Study of Religion*, 22 (1983): 145–57; Lee Sigelman and Stanley Presser, "Measuring Public Support for the New Christian Right," *Public Opinion Quarterly*, 52 (1988): 325–37.

[5]Peter L. Berger, *Invitation to Sociology* (Garden City, N.Y.: Doubleday, 1963).

[6]Jeremy Rifkin, *The Emerging Order* (New York: Ballantine, 1979), 98.

[7]John D. McCarthy and Mayer N. Zald, "Resource Mobilization and Social Movements: A Partial Theory," *American Journal of Sociology*, 83 (1977): 1212–41.

[8]Mayer N. Zald and John D. McCarthy, *Social Movements in an Organizational Society* (New Brunswick, N.J.: Transaction Books, 1987).

[9]Jeffrey K. Hadden, "Religion and the Construction of Social Problems," *Sociological Analysis*, 41 (1980): 99–108.

[10]Rodney Stark, *Social Problems* (New York: Random House, 1975), 6.

[11]Jeffrey K. Hadden and Charles E. Swann, *Prime Time Preachers* (Reading, Mass.: Addison-Wesley, 1981); Samuel S. Hill and Dennis E. Owen, *The New Religious Political Right in America* (Nashville: Abingdon, 1982); Jorstad, *New Christian Right*.

[12]Hadden, *Prime Time Preachers*.

[13]Ibid.

[14]Ibid., 164–65; Seymour M. Lipset and Earl Raab, "The Election and the Evangelicals, *Commentary* 71 (March 1981): 25–32.

[15]Jeffrey K. Hadden, "The Great Audience Size Debate," *Religious Broadcasting* (January 1986); idem, "Getting to the Bottom of the Audience Size Debate," *Religious Broadcasting* (February 1986).

[16]William F. Fore, *Television and Religion* (Minneapolis, Minn.: Augsburg, 1987).

[17]Gallup Organization, Inc. Appendix V in George Gerbner, et al. *Religion and Television* (Unpublished research report of Annenberg School of Communication, University of Pennsylvania, 1984), 7.

[18]David W. Clark and Paul H. Virts, "Religious Television Audience: A New Development in Measuring Audience Size" (Paper presented at the Annual Meeting of the Society for the Scientific Study of Religion, Savannah, Georgia, October 1985).

[19]National Religious Broadcasters, *The 1988 Directory of Religious Broadcasting* (Morristown, N.J.: National Religious Broadcasters, 1988).

[20]John H. Simpson, "Moral Issues and Status Politics," in *The New Christian Right*, ed. Robert Liebman and Robert Wuthnow (New York: Aldine, 1983); Anson Shupe and William A. Stacey, *Born Again Politics and the Moral Majority: What Social Surveys Really Show* (Lewistown, N.Y.: Mellen, 1982).

[21]Robert C. Liebman, "Mobilizing the Moral Majority," in *The New*

Christian Right, ed. Walter C. Libman and Robert Wuthnow, (New York: Aldine, 1983).

²²"Mirror Poll," *New York Times,* 6 November 1988.

²³Ronald Reagan, "Address to National Affairs Briefing," Speech given to the Annual National Affairs Briefing sponsored by the Roundtable at Reunion Arena, Dallas, Texas, 22 August 1980.

²⁴Carl F. H. Henry, *The Uneasy Conscience of Modern Fundamentalism* (Grand Rapids: Eerdmans, 1947).

²⁵Jeffrey K. Hadden, "Washington for Jesus II" (Unpublished manuscript, 1988).

²⁶Henry, *Uneasy Conscience,* 387.

REFERENCES

Berger, Peter L. *Invitation to Sociology.* Garden City, N.Y.: Doubleday, 1963.

Clark, David W., and Paul H. Virts. "Religious Television Audience: A New Development in Measuring Audience Size." Paper presented at the Annual Meeting of the Society for the Scientific Study of Religion, Savannah, Georgia, October 1985.

Fore, William F. *Television and Religion.* Minneapolis, Minn.: Augsburg, 1987.

Gallup Organization, Inc. Appendix V in *Religion and Television,* George Gerbner, et al. Unpublished research report, Annenberg School of Communications, University of Pennsylvania, 1984.

Hadden, Jeffrey K. "Religion and the Construction of Social Problems." *Sociological Analysis* 41 (1980): 99–108.

_____. "The Great Audience Size Debate." *Religious Broadcasting,* January 1986, 20–22.

_____. "Getting to the Bottom of the Audience Size Debate." *Religious Broadcasting,* February 1986, 88, passim.

_____. "Religious Broadcasting and the New Christian Right." *Journal for the Scientific Study of Religion* 26 (1987): 1–24.

_____. "Washington for Jesus II." Unpublished manuscript.

Hadden, Jeffrey K., and Charles E. Swann. *Prime Time Preachers.* Reading, Mass.: Addison-Wesley, 1981.

Hadden, Jeffrey K., et al. "Why Jerry Falwell Killed the Moral Majority." In *The God Pumpers: Religion in the Electronic Age.* Edited by Marshall W. Fishwick and Ray B. Browne. Bowling Green, Ohio: Bowling Green State University Popular Press, 1987, 101–5.

Henry, Carl F. H. *The Uneasy Conscience of Modern Fundamentalism.* Grand Rapids, Eerdmans, 1947.

_____. *Confessions of a Theologian.* Waco, Tex.: Word, 1986.

Hill, Samuel S., and Dennis E. Owen. *The New Religious Political Right in America.* Nashville, Abingdon, 1982.

Jorstad, Erling. *The New Christian Right 1981–1988*. Lewiston, N.Y.: Edwin Mellen, 1987.

Liebman, Robert C. "Mobilizing the Moral Majority." In *The New Christian Right*. Edited by Robert Liebman and Robert Wuthnow, 50–74. N.Y.: Aldine, 1983.

Liebman, Robert C., and Robert Wuthnow, eds. *The New Christian Right*. N.Y.: Aldine, 1983.

Lipset, Seymour M., and Earl Raab. "The Election and the Evangelicals." *Commentary* 71 (March 1981): 25–32.

McCarthy, John D., and Mayer N. Zald. "Resource Mobilization and Social Movements: A Partial Theory." *American Journal of Sociology* 83 (1977): 1212–41.

National Religious Broadcasters. *The 1988 Directory of Religious Broadcasting*. Morristown, N.J.: National Religious Broadcasters, 1988.

Reagan, Ronald. "Address to National Affairs Briefing." Speech given to the Annual National Affairs Briefing sponsored by the Roundtable, Reunion Arena, Dallas, Texas, 22 August 1980.

Rifkin, Jeremy. *The Emerging Order*. N.Y.: Ballantine Books, 1979.

Rosenberg, Tina. "How the Media Made the Moral Majority." *Washington Monthly*, May 1982, 26–34.

Rothenberg, Stuart, and Frank Newport. *The Evangelical Voter: Religion and Politics in America*. Washington, D.C.: Institute for Government and Politics of the Free Congress Research and Educational Foundation, 1984.

Simpson, John H. "Moral Issues and Status Politics." In *The New Christian Right*. Edited by Robert Liebman and Robert Wuthnow, 188–207. New York: Aldine, 1983.

Shupe, Anson, and William A. Stacey. *Born Again Politics and the Moral Majority: What Social Surveys Really Show*. Lewistown, N.Y.: Edwin Mellen, 1982.

Sigelman, Lee, and Stanley Presser. "Measuring Public Support for the New Christian Right." *Public Opinion Quarterly* 52 (1988): 325–37.

Stark, Rodney. *Social Problems*. New York: Random House, 1975.

Tamney, Joseph B., and Stephen D. Johnson. "The Moral Majority in Middletown. *Journal for the Scientific Study of Religion* 22 (1983).

Zald, Mayer N., and Jon D. McCarthy. *Social Movements in an Organizational Society*. New Brunswick, N.J.: Transaction Books, 1987.

10

THE MEANING OF RELIGIOUS TELEVISION: THE "700 CLUB" IN THE LIVES OF ITS VIEWERS

STEWART M. HOOVER

The phenomenon of the electronic church has led to a good deal of theoretical and methodological soul-searching among researchers who normally assume that religion is peripheral to contemporary social and cultural change. Recently, Jeffrey Hadden has argued that this "secularization thesis" must now be discarded.[1] The rise of worldwide fundamentalism and the tenacity of personal religiosity suggest that secularization may not explain many contemporary social and political movements and events. In addition, the electronic church and the wider evolution of the religio-political "New Right" have arisen while the field of communication research is undergoing theoretical and methodological change. Dominated since the 1950s by positivist empiricism, communication research now often focuses on meaning, not just the quantifiable behaviors. Sociologist Peter Berger has rightly suggested that researchers should not focus on the easily measurable "functions" of religiosity, at the expense of religion's "substantive" reality.[2]

Unfortunately, most religious broadcasting research has been dominated by the quantitative and functional approaches. Survey research[3] has repeatedly established the demographic characteristics of the audience: viewers are typically female, less educated, of lower incomes, and lower social class, and much more conventionally "religious" than are nonviewers or nonlisteners. Traditional audience research[4] has shown that the audiences of even the best known of these programs are rather small. Finally, quantitative content analyses[5] have shown that most contemporary religious broadcasts have politicized their messages.

Ironically, one of the first studies of religious broadcasting, published in 1955,[6] included in-depth interviews with viewing and listening families. More recently, Bourgault[7] has conducted an exhaustive ethnographic study of the audience for the "PTL Club" in a small town in Ohio. Historians have also done some interesting and illuminating work. Harrell's study of Oral Roberts,[8] Joel Carpenter's work on the origins of evangelical radio,[9] books by Frankl[10] and Fore,[11] and a forthcoming work on Billy Graham by Martin all provide additional insights into the phenomenon. Hadden and Shupe[12] have recently published a social and political account of the rise of religious broadcasting as part of the rise of the New Right. Schultze has also written a critique of the Annenberg-Gallup study of religious broadcasting[13] and a more recent cultural analysis of the mythology that guides evangelical involvement in the electronic church.[14] Taken as a whole, these studies have proven the value of qualitative research in the study of religion and especially in the electronic church.

The large-scale study released in 1984 by the Annenberg School of Communications and the Gallup Organization, *Religion and Television*,[15] provided an opportunity to conduct in-depth interviews with twenty families who were members of the "700 Club." I call the methodology used in the interviews and analysis "elaboration." It enabled me to evaluate quantitative questions by elaborating from semistructured interviews with respondents. The survey form gave structure to interviews while teasing out meanings behind the questions and answers. The interviews were conducted simply. I first reviewed the questionnaire used in the Annenberg-Gallup study, discussing each question and answer in an unstructured, conversational format. This revealed much about what viewers intended their responses to mean, confirming some of the conclusions traditionally drawn from surveys and undermining others.[16] Next, I asked each respondent, couple, or family, to recount their "faith history," taking extensive notes and tape-recording every interview. This technique revealed *where* the "700 Club" and other religious television programs fit into the development of viewers' religious consciousness. These "faith trajectories" gave insight into whether, for these viewers, religious broadcasting had been a "first cause" of their current faith (it had not been).

THE ELECTRONIC CHURCH

The study also attempted to place the electronic church in a larger historical, institutional, and cultural context; it located the phenomenon in the neoevangelical revival of recent decades, including the religio-political New Right movement of the late 1970s and early 1980s. The electronic church supports one side of what Martin Marty has called the "two party system of American Protestantism." It is oriented toward conservatism rather than modernism, evangelism rather than social action, and independence rather than ecumenism. It conveys the evangelical and Pentecostal critique of modernist and secularized denominational Christianity. Perhaps most importantly, the electronic church is also embedded in the long-standing American Protestant Voluntary Association movement. Often the institutional church has not fully satisfied the religious hunger that is so pervasive in the United States. For at least a century, Americans have established para-church institutions and agencies that are intended to supplement the evangelical and social work of conventional churches. The neoevangelical movement is in many ways defined by this "para-church religiosity," and the electronic church is both one of the agencies of the para-church and also an important tool of enlistment for the rest of them.

SUBSTANCE VERSUS PERCEPTION

The study also distinguished the *substance* of the electronic church from its *perception*. This distinction is most clear when we consider the role the electronic church has played in setting forth certain leaders as symbols of contemporary American religion. Jimmy Swaggart, Jim and Tammy Bakker, and (more importantly) Jerry Falwell, have been taken to be important religious figures, at least by the media and political establishments. No one, apparently, was regularly looking at their viewership figures, though. While Falwell was for many years a regular spokesman, based on his media profile (and the audience claims he could make, based on the number of stations on which he could afford to syndicate his program), anyone who could read a ratings book would have known that Falwell's audience was not even the largest of the electronic church audiences, *and* that, as a whole, the electronic church was pulling audiences so small as to be not reliably measurable.

This issue of audience size is a major field on which we might begin to separate substance from perception. Simply put, the audience for the electronic church is small compared with the television audience as a whole. Moreover, in spite of all of the public rhetoric, the religious television audience is not growing significantly. Instead, the electronic-church audience is growing only when new television stations or cable systems are brought on-line. However, the key claim of the electronic church (and, as we will see, its major justification) is that both the *size* and *composition* of its audience are expanding. If the basic demographics of the audience are stable, the only way to significantly increase the reach and effect of religious television is to alter those demographics. Adding new markets (and there are very few of them left that do not already have religious programs on the air) will only add more typical viewers. In other words, the audience must become more heterogeneous if it is to increase significantly. Commercial broadcasters know that the most dependable and effective way to alter audience size and composition is through scheduling. A great program at a bad time does poorly. A poor program "hammocked" between *The Cosby Show* and *Moonlighting*, for example, does very well. Satellite-fed religious cable channels had this scheduling flexibility as their goal because religious broadcasting had always been confined to the "religious ghetto" of late-nights and weekend mornings. A purely religious channel, so the argument went, would lower access costs to better times for broadcasts.

It is not clear that the electronic church has failed to live up to these expectations of audience size and composition. However, the justifications for such claims are questionable. Audiences are not as large as many interested observers and the media have claimed. Most large audience estimates, such as the one-hundred-million figure, are based on the results of opinion surveys (predominantly those by Gallup) that have found as many as 40 percent of respondents claiming to regularly view religious television.[17] Other claims are based on the practice of reporting duplicate audience figures; they wrongly combine the total audience of all of the nationally syndicated programs. Each viewer is counted more than once. Other inflated audience estimates are based on the practice of including all viewers who tune in for only a short time—a major problem in the cable TV, remote-control age. Clark and Virts, for example, estimated in 1985 that 40 percent of American households are regular viewers of religious television based on all people who viewed as little as six minutes *per month* of religious television.[18] The audience-size debate raises the important issue of what it means to view religious television. How much is significant viewing? Six minutes a month, or fifteen minutes a week (the standard for commercial broadcasting)? More than that, what is a religious program? In the Annenberg-Gallup study we found that some survey respondents included such "religious" programs as *The Ten Commandments* or *The Thorn Birds*. And who is a religious viewer: one who watches a program occasionally, or a lot of them regularly? It also appears unclear that the audience has become appreciably more heterogeneous in the electronic-church era. Even Clark and Virts, who have made much of shifting demographics, have failed to document statistically significant changes. Cable-television households do not view any more religious television than those without it.[19] While some may have initially subscribed to cable in order to watch religious shows, they are attracted to nonreligious programming once they have it. These are important issues not adequately addressed by traditional communication research.

The fact that the electronic church has few major, measurable effects supports much social-scientific research about the impact of the mass media in general. The media have rarely been found to have important direct effects. At best, mass media have indirect and conditional effects. Even where mass media have been shown to be effective in changing minds (in political communication, for instance) they function *through* other channels of communication, especially through interpersonal interaction with neighbors, family, and friends. However, a study of the "700 Club" suggests that the substance of the electronic church may be something different from (though it is based in) these perceptions.

It is helpful to make a distinction between the constituents and the audience of a ministry. Constituents are people who constitute the group. In a local congregation, they are the members who contribute time, energy, and money to making the church work. They are also the audience on Sunday morning and during other preaching services. Congregational evangelism identifies another audience, however: friends, neighbors, strangers, and many others who can and should be the objects of the church's witness. During evangelism, the constituents join the leaders in witnessing to this larger community—those *out there* who need to hear the word of salvation. Researchers of the electronic church mistakenly assumed that TV ministries exist entirely to serve a more or less passive audience. When I began to interview *members* of the "700 Club" it became clear to me that I was talking not to audience members, but to *constituents*. They saw themselves to be "on the same side of the camera as (program host) Pat Robertson." More importantly, for many of these viewers, the program was important not for what it did for *them*, but what it did for other people, for "those people out there who *really* need it." They saw the show *not* as a servant of *their* needs, but as a ministry to *others*. In fact, the families who contributed the most financially were the most infrequent viewers.

In addition, all of the contributors were convinced that by supporting this ministry on the important, national, cosmopolitan medium of television, they were ensuring the ultimate triumph of their worldview. Carpenter has identified such a perception as being important to fundamentalist broadcasting in an earlier era.

> The evangelical coalition's mastery of mass communication, claims one observer, has been the matrix of its survival and success. I don't see it exactly that way. Rather, in an age of sight and sound, evangelicals have used the reality-establishing force of mass communications to convince themselves— and many others, apparently—that they are a real presence in American public life. They have transmitted their images into the "show windows of modern publicity."[20]

This view of the constituency of the electronic church partly explains why so many religious broadcasters claim exaggerated audiences: the ministries' financial life requires them to promote the myth that religious television is serving increasingly large audiences. It is important for television evangelists and their supporters to be able to claim a large and growing (in real numbers and in composition) community of viewers.

Some people view who are just "audience," to use my formulation. The testimonies of such viewers—particularly striking conversion experiences as a result of viewing the electronic church—justify these ministries to their constituents. Such anecdotal conversions are shared with the local religious community and repeatedly recounted by the programs and their supporters. It is unclear if these conversion stories are "typical," although it appears that the most striking experiences and anecdotes of the "direct ministry" of programs like the "700 Club" may be relatively rare compared with the experiences of the total audience. This is not to say that the ministries of the electronic church are not significant, important, or meaningful. Nevertheless, some of the most widely held assumptions about the programs do not withstand ethnographic scrutiny.

A TYPOLOGY OF VIEWERS

The complexity of the viewing experience, and of the interaction between viewing and other religious beliefs and behaviors, becomes clear when we hear from the viewers I interviewed. These interviewees were *members* of (and contributors to) the "700 Club" and were selected out of the entire mailing list of members in one metropolitan area. While the total sample was small (twenty families), it was representative of important demographic categories. However, such contributors are probably the most committed and involved segment of the audience. The Annenberg-Gallup study found, for instance, that contributors to television ministries are more likely to be heavily and regularly involved in conventional churches. Analysis of the faith trajectories of these viewers revealed three major themes that describe a rough typology of involvement. Some viewers fit into more than one of them. Each describes the various broad motivations and saliencies of involvement with the "700 Club."

THE EVANGELICALS

The vast majority of these were evangelicals, and had been for most of their lives. The evangelical message of the "700 Club" was nothing new to them. They were familiar with the ideas and language of evangelicalism, fundamentalism, and Pentecostalism before they began watching religious television. Some of them had also always been involved in churches that they considered to be theologically consistent with their evangelical beliefs. More of them, however, had once experienced some dissonance between their faith communities and their beliefs. "We were members of a Presbyterian church," one of them said, "but that church moved more and more away from fundamentalist principles." For this latter group of "stranded evangelicals," the "700 Club" and the broader evangelical para-church proved to be an important source of support for their beliefs. The show had even led some of them to find a congregation that more closely fit their own worldview. For others, the program gave them moral support to "stay and fight" in their churches for what they believed was more authentic faith and practice.

EXPERIENCES OF CRISIS

For some of these evangelical viewers and for most of the others, the viewing of the "700 Club" was associated with a *personal crisis*. There was an unbelievable range of such crises among these twenty families: two suicides by children, one by a spouse; a marriage that was annulled after the wife found out her husband was both a gangster and a bigamist; the death of a child due to medical malpractice (after the parents thought the child had been cured of leukemia through prayer); two personal bankruptcies; a woman who was widowed by a car accident in which she was the driver; alcoholism; various sexual and marital crises and problems. Among this "crisis" group of viewers were two Catholics, a Jew, a backsliding drinker and smoker, two black Baptists, and a woman who disagrees with Pat Robertson's entire political and social agenda. In only one case was a viewer's spiritual crisis directly ministered to by the Club. His testimony was striking, however.

> I was watching it on Christmas Eve and I had an experience, and then I just started watching it all the time. . . . I had seen it before, but I had never really followed it. My hand had just hit the [remote control] button and they were there saying the "sinner's prayer." It was a mistake, really. I hadn't planned on watching it, and suddenly I was on my knees, praying along with it. I must have passed out or something, because suddenly I was crying. I just sat there and cried for fifteen minutes, and then I found myself sitting there talking to them on the telephone. . . . I didn't even know what had happened. The lady on the phone explained to me that I had given my life to Christ and that I was now a new person. I was healed of everything, in an instant. I was healed of smoking cigarettes, alcohol, drinking, in a matter of seconds, it went away, just like that.

As moving as this story is, this viewer was quick to point out that he was not new to Christianity. He had been raised in a home where religion was important but had slid away from it as he entered adulthood.

This image of a lonely, depressed individual reached, almost accidentally, by the ministry of the electronic church confirms for those who hear it the unique role and power of television ministries. These broadcasts can reach people in their living rooms. They can convey a powerful message of salvation simply and directly. They have almost a mystical power to convince. Moreover, because the new formats of the electronic church mimic conventional television, these programs can almost sneak up on people who would not otherwise watch a religious program.

Other viewers offered different personal crises. For most of them, the spiritual faith generated by viewing the show helped them through such crises. June Mason had been a Southern Baptist all her life, and became a "dedicated Christian" as a result of her interest in the "700 Club." Her crisis came later.

> God must have known I needed to be prepared [by viewing the Club] because a few months later our son died . . . committed suicide. . . . It makes me cry to talk about it even now. So in those six months around the time of his death I needed a strong faith badly. . . . If I hadn't had God, I wouldn't be here today. He pulls you through, and you just melt, you just can't get away from God.

Most of the viewers I spoke with, for whom a personal or faith crisis was important in explaining their involvement in the Club, saw their viewing merely in conjunction with the crisis. It was helpful to them, but its immediacy and its direct impact were less important than were other things. Most notably, *all* of the viewers who had experienced crisis found their involvement in local church communities, Bible studies, and prayer groups to be far more important to them than the "700 Club" was.

LOCALISM AND TRANSLOCALISM

By far the most interesting viewer theme was the dynamic of localism and translocalism. Carpenter has observed that in the early days of fundamentalist radio, the *fact* that a fundamentalist voice was present in this important, public context, was as important as were its substantive *effects*. The broadcast media are important and prominent institutions in American life. They are its "show windows"—to use the language of the time. Viewers were comforted that the fundamentalist—and now the neoevangelical—worldview was and is present there. The sheer existence of the program was a source of great hope and satisfaction for these viewers. The sophisticated format of the "700 Club," its smooth delivery, and its commercial-television-like production values were important to these viewers. One of them, a military chaplain, felt that the presumed power of the Club was a major justification for his support of it.

> Obviously, Pat Robertson can reach more people, because [he uses a] satellite and he's worldwide. But I think that the quality is better, too, because in my denomination—which [consists of] small churches, and mostly farmers, and workaday people, and not doctor-lawyer-Indian chief, college professor types, you know—small churches are always struggling, and they don't have the wherewithal to do big things. The "700 Club" can do a lot of things a small church can't do, and it can do them well. . . . Robertson is a "high vis" person in America. He's well-educated, his father was a senator, his wife is a nurse, he has a law degree from Yale. It's just that echelon he travels in, his exposure to the things that come back to the local church through the people who watch, and I think that that's the kind of quality you just don't get when you're pastoring a local church. . . . It all translates into *power*. They're able to feed many more people, because, here again, he got hooked up with these big supply houses of food and he was able to start these big warehouses of food. The little local church, what's he going to do? He's going to go to the local supermarket and get dented cans. . . . And I think that's quality as well as quantity.

The majority of viewers saw the program's apparent sophistication and power against the backdrop of the traditional working-class roots of fundamentalism and evangelicalism. They said that until recently most people thought of them as being representative of rural, backwater, "fringe," sectors of American society. That is what makes a sophisticated, public, national program like the "700 Club" so exciting to them. They see it as transcending the local and the particular, introducing their worldview into the public stage where it can receive the respect and the hearing it deserves. The program enhances the credibility of their beliefs and affirmations, which were previously marginal in American social and intellectual life. For this reason it is important to them for the Club to break the stereotype of religious broadcasting and have a *universal* appeal. It does not always appear to be religious. It has feature stories and news. That is fine, because it affirms that the program can play a more direct and central role in American polity. In fact, CBN intentionally waters down the most unique and particular claims of its theological roots so as ". . . not to turn the audience off too quickly." Everyone—producers, phone counselors, and these viewers—is aware that television is a public medium intended to reach beyond local and particular communities to a national community of viewers.

The contrast between traditional and contemporary evangelical and fundamentalist culture was well illustrated by a retired American Baptist minister. Joe seemed inordinately concerned with education and with the contrast between the received stereotype of his fundamentalist roots and this new, more sophisticated television version of the faith. Joe and his wife, Doris, described with great satisfaction a trip they took to a seminar at CBN headquarters in Virginia.

> The whole trip was fantastic, from the time we arrived at the hotel, the best there is, and they paid for it, and they called us over and gave us name tags, and they gave us a schedule, and we were busy every minute. What impressed me was the whole thing was so organized. . . . Everything was done top-notch. Nothing was left to chance, from the entertainment, the food, the service, you stayed in the best hotel, you really felt like you were "king's kin.". . . And it's not that they [the people they met there] were fanatical, these were people who had college degrees and had been in manufacturing. As you got into conversation, they were people who could express themselves, and for the first time, I said to myself "this is a taste of heaven."

Joe believed that CBN leaders and members were typical of a new class of intellectually and socially sophisticated evangelicals prepared for "a new age."

> At CBN you're getting *leaders*. There's a difference. Humility is important, but here you could tell by the people and by the way they talked, the vocabulary and everything else, the things they expressed, and their spirituality. . . . I get a blessing from people with degrees, top people, who are servants. I love people with degrees, consecrated. And the other brothers and sisters, too, of course, but there's something special about these top people.

242 I Stewart M. Hoover

The "700 Club" is important to Joe both because of what it says and what it *represents*; the show symbolizes for him the resurrection of evangelicalism out of the social ghetto and into a more central place in American intellectual and spiritual life. This salience of the program was shared by nearly all of the viewers I interviewed. For many of these viewers, the electronic church is central to both a spiritual and a political re-birth in America.

DYNAMICS AND SALIENCIES

First, it is clear that nearly all of these viewers operated within an understanding of what I have called the two-party system. They were well aware of the existing tensions between the worldview of modernist, mainline Protestantism and that of their faith. Many of them were tired of such controversies, however, and expressed a desire (satisfied in some ways by the electronic church) for a new Protestantism where denominational and sectarian boundaries would no longer be relevant.

Second, they believed that Christianity, and Protestantism in particular, faces a virulent challenge from secularism. "Secular humanism" was mentioned repeatedly, as were criticisms of contemporary American materialism, hedonism, and general moral decay. The social institutions that used to be the front line of defense—the schools, the family, and even the churches—have given up the fight. For most of these viewers, this is a critical time to support a powerful, influential ministry like the "700 Club" because it represents a broad-based coalition of people and institutions who are prepared to hold back this secular tide.

Third, the viewers make it clear that the so-called establishment era of American Christianity has now ended. The nation is well past the time when a Will Herberg could write that Catholicism, Protestantism, and Judaism pretty much describe the alternate worldviews of America.[21] These institutional faith groups have lost their hold and their meaning for many people. The Protestant establishment has been replaced by an anti-establishment or nonestablishment bias (both in the mainline and nonmainline churches and faith groups), which is much more typical of everyday faith and practice. Christian faith and practice now take place, perhaps to a greater extent than ever, in contexts other than the formally sanctioned ones. The electronic church and a myriad of other agencies are increasingly significant as contexts of faith expression. The end of the establishment and the rise of a new movement where such labels are irrelevant have become important for viewers. The electronic church is held by its viewers to be an embodiment of an authentic faith consistent with their most basic beliefs. This faith need not be celebrated in all of its detail. They know and trust Pat Robertson and the others who represent the voice of conservative Christianity at this point in American history. The show is important to them because of the dislocations of modernity, the social change and dislocation of recent decades. For them the electronic church is a community of like-minded people, whose values enter the public sphere via television. It symbolizes what Richard Quebedeaux has called the new "worldly evangelical," who is assumed to be better equipped to speak to a modern world.[22] These viewers accept the fact that the "700 Club" and other religious programs will have to make certain programming concessions in order to gain access to the public sphere. They generally believe that some of the particularist affirmations of the past must be replaced with a universal, evangelical appeal. For viewers such as Joe, the more such programs and ministries contrast with the past, the better. Sophisticated and influential programs affirm that his faith can encompass more than his local community and faith group.

ANTHROPOLOGICAL PERSPECTIVES

I suggested earlier that the impact and meaning of mass communication could be enhanced by qualitative research of audience experiences. The field of anthropology provides many such tools for such investigations of culture. Geertz has provided many insights into the process of studying meaning, ritual, faith, and practice in the context of daily living.[23] Turner's work is even more useful. Turner was centrally concerned with what Van Gennep called "rites of passage," those points in life journeys where transformations of consciousness take place.[24] Turner saw these points of transformation as taking place within the context of a tension between the profane, hidebound structures of social life and social practice, and the ebullient, voluntary, emotive urges of the self. Rites of passage are more integrative at each step, bringing the individual to an ever-greater level of mastery of, and fealty to, authentic communities of belief, and to a true, ideal community as the ultimate goal of cultural and transcendent belief.

Turner found that this occurs in traditional societies through the ritual suspension of worldly structures, enabling the individual to rise above them and attain an awareness of the existence of a more universal and motivational community of belief. He called this context "liminality" from a Latin word for threshold. He saw this threshold experience as being a place from which individuals could look back on their former selves, and forward to a more-integrative, more-conscious self driven by the consciousness that he or she is involved in cultural realities much larger than the local, home culture. In traditional societies, liminality is brought about through intentional, communitywide rituals and social dramaturgy. In more advanced societies, this process is taken over by other processes and other contexts, including the rite of pilgrimage. According to Turner, pilgrims experience liminality through travel.[25] They leave home on an arduous journey, placing themselves in a position of risk. As they travel, their traditional relationships and loyalties are in suspension. They encounter other pilgrims, and mix with pilgrims from other cultures and other classes and backgrounds, thus suspending those important structures. As they near the pilgrimage center, they encounter more and more people who are on the same quest as they are. Finally, at the pilgrimage site, nearly everyone they meet is there for the same reason. Eventually, pilgrims return home with a renewed sense of the universal appeal, power, and relevance of the faith that took them on the pilgrimage in the first place—if their faith is large enough to encompass all they have experienced, then its power is reemphasized. Further, they come away with the sense that a universalized community of belief is both possible and desirable.

Religious television probably cannot support "armchair pilgrimage," as some have claimed.[26] However, some of the central dynamics of Turner's vision of pilgrimage are present in the viewing experience of the "700 Club." The earlier account of a visit to the CBN center certainly conveys this sense of pilgrimage. Joe and Doris went from their local, particularist community to CBN, where they experienced a new kind of evangelicalism that encompassed classes, cultures, and ideas of great diversity. The result for them was a powerful reaffirmation that their faith was important and broad enough to explain and contain everything they experienced. Their faith

thus transcended many of the social and ecclesiastical structures and barriers that have divided Christians. The universalism of the "700 Club" is vital to such a vision. So is the idea that
it has power and importance in the national, public sphere. By
appearing on the national, secular, public medium of television,
the show affirms the ultimate power and ascendancy of the
evangelical worldview.

TRANSFORMATION

The meaning and importance of the electronic church are
best characterized as *transformation*. Such religious broadcasting
has transformed the traditions of evangelical programming
while simultaneously transforming the meaning and importance of the particularist visions of the faith of its viewers. The
electronic church has made evangelical broadcasting more
sophisticated by borrowing the visual sensibilities and programming conventions of secular broadcasting. The most
prominent and seemingly most powerful religious broadcasts
effectively mimic the style of commercial television, especially
network programs. For instance, the "700 Club" is described as
a Christian talk show by observers, producers, and viewers.
The new religious shows have also introduced sophisticated
nonbroadcasting elements, practices, and technologies from
computerized direct-mail solicitation to banks of trained telephone counselors to minister to their audience and take
financial pledges. Even printed materials and mission outreach
are examples of the sophisticated leadership spoken of by one
of the interviewees. The universalism of the electronic church
has allowed viewers to contend with one of the greatest
challenges they face—the problem of cultural diversity. This
synthesis of modernity and traditionalism, professionalism and
emotionalism, speaks to the modern, secularized, cosmopolitan
world, with a message of authentic belief, faith, and culture.

The cultural meaning of the electronic church for the
viewers apparently operates on three contextual levels. On the
individual level, the electronic church has helped to create a
new self-identity for its viewers. They are part of a reality larger
than themselves. On a community level, the electronic church
cooperates with other para-church institutions to affirm that the
traditional social, religious, and cultural structures are no
longer adequate to meet the demands of the age. It has given
this community of common purpose a new status in public

discourse—some would say it has actually captured that discourse. On a societal level, the electronic church proposes to transform society. In Nebuhr's classic *Christ and Culture*,[27] it has helped to capture the transformational position away from modernist, denominational, mainline Christianity.

Is the electronic church actually capable of the universal appeal and transformation sought by these viewers? There are reasons to doubt that the contemporary audiences are larger or more diverse than was the case in the pre-electronic church era. It further seems that the most ardent viewers are, in fact, constituents and not just viewers, and that the belief in the power of the electronic church is as important as any real power it exerts.

Perhaps Robertson's unsuccessful bid for the Republican presidential nomination in 1988 suggests the discrepancy between the real and perceived power of the electronic church. It was touted—and feared—that Robertson's viewers were an invisible army. But the army never materialized. Robertson did well only in those states where a few very committed workers could make a great difference by appearing at precinct caucuses, for instance. In states where he had to rely on a popular referendum, where a larger army of pure viewers might be more important, he did poorly. Robertson's appeal has always been rather politically diffuse. The universalist intentions of his program and his public persona have enforced on him a least-common-denominator social agenda held together by little more than a hackneyed conservative rhetoric and presumed roots in the evangelical movement. His general social critique, his social agenda, plays well with a wide variety of viewers and nonviewers alike, including some Catholics and Jews. Certainly the program's generalism and lack of virulent particularism allow many such people to feel involved. The triumphalism of the program, as well as Robertson's actual candidacy, reinforced the myth of real participation among the more committed viewers. But at the same time, Robertson's rhetoric spoke to everyone in general and no one in particular. Ironically, he failed to attract a large enough following partly because no one could be sure about what he would do as president. This calls into question the substance of his triumph as well as the future exhortations of politically minded television evangelists. The new evangelism of the electronic church cannot easily speak with power to contemporary society.

In the nineteenth century, American religious culture was evangelical, and Protestant, and Christian, to a far greater extent than it is today. The traditionalist and nativist appeals of the Great Awakenings had broad potential for support in the society as a whole. When the preachers of the Great Awakenings spoke of reform and return to authenticity there were clear, commonly understood implications to their words.[28]

Pat Robertson may return to politics—perhaps even as a political candidate. He may ultimately have more success than he did in 1988. However, a very diverse America is no longer the society that Robertson describes when he talks about returning to the values of the founding fathers. Many Americans agree that the society needs transformation. Post-industrial life places stresses and strains on people from all cultural and faith backgrounds, and most of them would support a general (but perhaps not a *specific*) call for a return to "traditional values." The electronic church can issue such a call, and it seems to derive a good deal of its importance from the fact that it appears to speak for a cultural critique and cultural reality that is large enough to reform society. It may not, however, be capable of realizing the substantive coalition—political or religious—necessary to carry out that reform.

NOTES

[1]Jeffrey Hadden (Remarks to the Annual Meeting, the Society for the Scientific Study of Religion, Washington, D.C., November 16, 1986).

[2]Peter Berger, "Some Second Thoughts on Substantive Versus Functional Definitions of Religion," *Journal for the Scientific Study of Religion* 13, no. 2 (June 1974): 125–33.

[3]For example, see Fred Casmir, "A Telephone Survey of Religious Program Preferences Among Listeners and Viewers in Los Angeles" *Central States Speech Journal* 10 (Spring 1959): 31–38; Ronald L. Johnstone, "Who Listens to Religious Radio Broadcasts Anymore?" *Journal of Broadcasting* 16 (Spring 1972): 90–102; Judith Buddenbaum, "Characteristics and Media-Related Needs of the Audience for Religious TV," *Journalism Quarterly* 58 (Summer 1981): 296–72; George Gerbner et al. *Religion and Television*, The technical report of the Annenberg-Gallup Study of Religious Broadcasting (Philadelphia: The Annenberg School of Communications, University of Pennsylvania, 1984); Gary Gaddy and David Pritchard, "When Watching Religious TV Is Like Attending Church," *Journal of Communication* 35 No. 1 (Winter 1985): 123–31.

[4]For example, see Jeffrey Hadden and Charles Swann, *Prime-Time Preachers* (Reading, Mass.: Addison-Wesley, 1981); William Martin, "The Birth

248 | Stewart M. Hoover

of a Media Myth," *The New Yorker* (June 1981); Peter Horsfield, *Religious Television: The American Experience* (London: Longman Press, 1984); David Clark and Paul Virts, "The Religious Television Audience: A New Development in Measuring Audience Size" (Paper presented at the Society for the Scientific Study of Religion, Savannah, 1985); Stewart M. Hoover, "The Religious Television Audience: A Matter of Significance, or Size?" *Review of Religious Research* 29 no. 2 (December 1987): 135–51.

[5]For example, see Gerbner, George et al., *Religion and Television*; Robert Abelman and Kimberly Neuendorf, "How Religious Is Religious Television Programming?" *Journal of Communication* 35, no. 1 (Winter 1985): 98–110; Robert Abelman and Kimberly Neuendorf, "Themes and Topics in Religious Television Programming," *Review of Religious Research* 29, no. 2 (Winter 1987): 152–74.

[6]Everett Parker, David Barry, and Dallas Smythe, *The Television-Radio Audience and Religion* (New York: Harper & Row, 1955).

[7]Louise Bourgault, "The 'PTL Club' and Protestant Viewers: An Ethnographic Study," *Journal of Communication* 35, no. 1 (Winter 1985): 132–48.

[8]David E. Harrell, *Oral Roberts: An American Life* (Bloomington: Indiana University Press, 1985).

[9]Joel Carpenter, "Tuning in the Gospel: Fundamentalist Radio Broadcasting and the Revival of Mass Evangelism, 1930–1945" (Paper delivered to the Mid-American Studies Association, University of Illinois, Urbana, 13 April 1985).

[10]Razelle Frankl, *Televangelism: The Marketing of Popular Religion* (Carbondale: Southern Illinois University Press, 1987).

[11]William F. Fore, *Television and Religion* (Minneapolis: Augsburg, 1988).

[12]Jeffrey Hadden and Anson Shupe, *Televangelism: Power and Politics on God's Frontier* (New York: Holt, 1988).

[13]Quentin Schultze, "Vindicating the Electronic Church? An Assessment of the Annenberg-Gallup Study," *Critical Studies in Mass Communication* (Fall, 1985).

[14]Quentin Schultze, "The Mythos of the Electronic Church," *Critical Studies in Mass Communication* 2, no. 3 (Fall 1987): 283–89.

[15]Gerbner, et. al., *Religion and Television*.

[16]For a complete discussion, see Stewart Hoover, *Mass Media Religion: The Social Sources of the Electronic Church* (Beverly Hills: Sage, 1988).

[17]Gerbner, et al., *Religion and Television*.

[18]David Clark and Paul Virts, "The Religious Television Audience."

[19]Stewart M. Hoover et al., "The Religious Audience: The Contribution of Cable Television," *Religious Television: Controversies and Conclusions*, ed., Robert Abelman and Stewart Hoover (Norwood, N.J.: Ablex, 1990).

[20]Carpenter, "Tuning in the Gospel."

[21]See R. Laurence Moore, *Religious Outsiders* (New York: Oxford).

[22]Richard Quebedeaux, *The Worldly Evangelicals* (San Francisco: Harper & Row, 1978).

[23]Clifford Geertz, *The Interpretation of Cultures* (New York: Basic Books, 1973).

[24]Victor Turner, *The Ritual Process: Structure and Antistructure* (Ithaca: Cornell University Press, 1969).

[25]Victor Turner, "The Center Out There: Pilgrim's Goal," *History of Religions* 12, no. 4 (1972): 191–238.

[26]Daniel Dayan, Elihu Katz, and Paul Kerns, "Armchair Pilgrimages: The

Trips of Pope John Paul II and Their Television Public" (Paper presented at the American Sociological Association, San Antonio, August, 1984).

[27]H. Richard Niebuhr, *Christ and Culture* (New York: Harper & Row, 1951).

[28]Hoover, *Mass Media Religion*.

Part IV

EVANGELICALS
AND THE NEWS

11

BELIEVERS AS BEHAVERS: NEWS COVERAGE OF EVANGELICALS BY THE SECULAR MEDIA

MIKE MAUS

Evangelicals seem to have a love-hate relationship with the secular media. They love to use the technology to spread the Good News, but hate what is said—or not said—about them in print or on the air. And some feel persecuted, left out, ignored. David Aikman claims the media have been "blind" to "religious faith."[1] Robert Fowler says one reason people do not know more about evangelicals is the media's *decision* "to ignore" them, "to push the concept of a large, grassroots American evangelical community out of sight and mind."[2] Actually, while secular journalists may have professional "cataracts" that blur their view of religion stories, there is no conspiracy against news of religion. Journalists and news organizations do not make conscious efforts to push the evangelical community "out of sight and mind."

Being out of sight and mind, though, may have been just what earlier evangelicals wanted. R. Laurence Moore writes that "in the period around World War I, theologically conservative Protestants began to step self-consciously into outsider roles," even though such a move may have been unwarranted. "Whatever aspects of minority consciousness they assumed and whatever divisions they maintained among themselves," he argues, "their point of view represented the majority of American Protestants who held strong religious commitments." Moore claims this history "is vigorously suppressed in some quarters and simply forgotten in others."[3] Timothy Smith brings this into more modern times, saying fundamentalists typically act like a "beleaguered minority fighting with their backs to the wall."[4] Sociologically speaking, the evangelicals' persecution complex strengthens their unity. As Lewis Coser argues, "Conflict with other groups (i.e., the secular media) contributes to the establishment and reaffirmation of the identity of the group and maintains its boundaries against the surrounding social world." The conflict has a group-binding function, he adds, mobilizing a group's energies and increasing its cohesion.[5] By emphasizing the enemy without, in this case the news media, a group develops greater togetherness.

The real issue is, what is news? In Luke 15, Jesus says the point of the parable of the lost sheep is the shepherd's search for the one who was lost. While he was gone, the rest of the sheep stayed in the fold. The *news* was not that ninety-nine sheep were in their usual spot, but that a single lost sheep was sought and found. Similarly, reporters are not interested primarily in what is supposed to happen that does happen. Instead, a reporter's first interest is that which is supposed to happen and does *not*, or that which is *not* supposed to happen and *does*. There are legitimate questions to ask in connection with this definition. For example, who does the supposing? On what basis is the supposing being done? What is normative in society, do the norms change, and who decides? And is it a "faith statement" when a journalist decides a norm has been breached and an event is newsworthy?

Millions worship each week. Many of them answer God's call in Christ to proclaim the Gospel and to serve humanity by feeding the hungry, building homes for the homeless, and working for justice and peace. Pastors and lay persons minister to each other and to the needs of their communities. These are not the kinds of events journalists normally define as news. It *is* news, though, when partisan politics enters the picture, or when a popular minister gets caught in greed or lust. The secular media report the unusual; they seldom deal with the usual, and the more usual something is, the less attention it gets.

The newspapers I read have special sections for business news, sports, science, the home, lifestyle, opinion, and even the upcoming weekend. There *never* is a special section on religion, though one paper has a weekly "religion page" and another recently began to report "Notes on Religion." This may say something about regional differences in newspapers, since some papers in the Midwest and South have regular *sections* devoted to religion and religious news. It may also say something about regional differences in journalists, or at least about an eastern definition of news. But this minimal news coverage of religion, especially in comparison to the coverage of other subjects, does not seem to hurt organized religion a great deal. More people probably attend religious services and give more money to religious causes than attend sporting events or invest in the stock market.

American journalists could do a much better job of reporting on religion. Trends sometimes go unnoticed. Trustworthy sources largely remain untapped. The church has people everywhere, literally, and they often tell stories much different from those we get from government officials who must put the proper political "spin" on developments in order to defend certain policies or actions. And the church as institution gets scant notice. This bothers Wesley Pippert (see his essay in the next chapter), a former White House correspondent for United Press International, who says, "The process of a religious institution ought to be covered as thoroughly as a political campaign or yesterday's game."[6]

The truth is, the news media seldom hire journalists who specialize in religion reporting. While the Associated Press and UPI each have at least one full-time person on the beat and major newspapers and weekly news magazines have staff members covering religion, broadcasters do not. CBS News, for example, has no staff religion correspondent. The Religion Newswriters Association has only 225 members, not one of whom is a broadcaster.

However, the coverage of religion is not the same as religious news. News reports are stories about something, including religious personalities, institutions, and events. Such news stories should be factual, straightforward accounts. Good journalism may point to relationships or offer historical perspective, but a reporter's task is not to draw moral lessons from the news of the day or to give the news a particular religious "slant." Yet evangelical and fundamentalist critics sometimes claim that this dimension is missing from the secular media's coverage. They are right, and their observation is a clear sign that reporters are doing their jobs properly. It is the job of specialized religious media, not the general news media, to provide religious perspective for particular audiences in a pluralist society. Although they are correct in claiming that journalists could give religion better coverage, evangelicals wrongly and self-interestedly want the news to reflect their own views of the world.

"The role religion plays in America and the world has been a well-kept secret in most of the nation's newsrooms," observed one journalist.[7] Martin Marty writes, "To look at American religion and to overlook Evangelicalism and Fundamentalism would be comparable to scanning the American physical landscape and missing the Rocky Mountains."[8] Yet overlooking these important parts of the religious landscape is what most American journalists have done for decades.

Evangelicals as evangelicals are not newsworthy to the secular media, nor have they been in the past seventy years, except as they misbehave, act politically, or stand against cultural change. Since the end of World War I, the secular news media have extensively covered evangelicals only three times: (1) during the fundamentalist-modernist controversy of the twenties, which culminated in the Scopes trial; (2) from 1976 through 1982, when evangelicals openly entered the public arena; and (3) starting in 1987, when some of the well-known television evangelists were caught with their pants down. In each case, the coverage focused on evangelicals as behavers rather than believers, worshipers, or inheritors of a tradition. The news has indeed not been kind to evangelicals.

"The evangelical Protestant denominations," writes historian Robert T. Handy, "made up the dominant religious subculture of nineteenth-century America."[9] This dominance slowly waned as the nation grew and as Roman Catholic and non-Christian immigrants arrived from overseas. Nevertheless, evangelical Protestantism remained an important and positive force in society even though it received little attention in the general press.

This important feature of the American religious landscape has been ill-reported partly because of a general lack of understanding among journalists of what it means to be evangelical. A good starting place for understanding may be Romans 12:2, "Do not be conformed to this world, but be transformed by the renewal of your mind" (RSV). At least from the days of revivalists such as Charles G. Finney, Dwight L. Moody, and Billy Sunday, transformation through a personal experience of rebirth in Christ has been central to the evangelical life. So has the authority of Scripture. Many—if not most—evangelicals believe the Bible to be inerrant, that is, without historical or factual error in the original autographs. In addition, evangelicals usually believe that they are called by God to preach the gospel to those they see as unsaved. More than most other Protestants and Roman Catholics, Schultze argued in chapter 1, evangelicals are serious about "spreading the Word," about telling the story of Jesus Christ and the power of God's redeeming love. Theologian Donald Bloesch said an evangelical would list as key elements of the Christian faith "biblical fidelity, apostolic doctrine, the experience of salvation, the imperative of discipleship, and the urgency of mission."[10]

Most journalists are unfamiliar with such biblical and theological concepts. One study found that reporters generally are less interested in and less involved with religion than the general public. Half of the journalists and media executives surveyed by Lichter and Rothman said they had no religious affiliation. "Another 14 percent are Jewish, and almost one in four (23 percent) was raised in a Jewish household. Only one in five identify themselves as Protestant, and one in eight as Catholic. Very few are regular churchgoers. Only 8 percent go to church or synagogue weekly, and 86 percent seldom or never attend religious services."[11] Probably as a result of their own disinterest in religion, most journalists missed the evangelical mountain rising on the American religious landscape. As Mattingly said, "The leaders of American media are not typical of the culture they are in charge of reporting."[12] However, Ernest Hynds found newspaper religion editors were older, better educated, and less secular than the average journalist. Slightly more than three out of four were members of a church, synagogue, or other religious body, but he noted there still was "some reluctance to give religion news trends their due."[13] Apparently, religion editors, unlike most other reporters, understand from personal experience aspects of the stories they cover.

Dan Ranly surveyed religion editors at large newspapers and found them to fall into three types. In the largest group were "humanists or relativists" who found it hard to believe that some people take the Bible literally. Next were the "neutralists," who believed religion news was important but had less confidence in the competence of the people assigned to cover it. In the smallest group were the "believers or traditionalists." Ranly says they were the only ones active in religious organizations and believed more strongly than the others that religion should compete with other news for position in the paper rather than have its own special page.[14] Clearly, journalists' own religious involvement—or the lack of it—influences their views of the significance and nature of religion in American life.

THE SCOPES TRIAL REVISITED

In the early part of the 1920s, a controversy raged between fundamentalists and the more liberal modernists. Modernism had begun toward the end of the preceding century. Its adherents were described by one speaker at the World Parliament of Religions held in Chicago in 1893 as those who would "reconcile reason and faith, science and religion, . . . the teachings of sacred scripture and the results of modern research."[15] This controversy received considerable notice in the press and seemingly peaked in 1925 at the trial of John T. Scopes in Dayton, Tennessee. Scopes was accused of violating a state law prohibiting the classroom teaching of Darwin's theory of evolution. He was convicted and fined $100.

Famed newspaperman H. L. Mencken may have given the trial the most biased and influential coverage. His biographer, Carl Bode, says Mencken saw it as an opportunity to describe the clash between the "fundamentalist, parochial, mean . . . majority" and the "enlightened, open, liberal . . . minority" which, of course, Mencken believed he represented.[16] The images Mencken created were indelibly etched on the public's imagination. Mencken linked fundamentalism to the unsophisticated backwardness of rural life. Historian George Marsden gives Mencken credit for expanding the meaning of fundamentalism to apply "to almost every aspect of American rural or small-town Protestantism."[17] In this way, Mencken served as a model for later generations of journalists, who similarly depicted fundamentalists as anti-intellectual bumpkins from a bygone era.

The *New York Times*, on the other hand, gave the Scopes trial fairly balanced coverage. The story ran on page one *every day* of the trial, and the coverage concluded with a summary article on Scopes' conviction. In all, there were more than thirty trial-related stories on page one throughout the trial. An editorial shortly after Scopes was indicted said most newspapers were choosing correspondents from their "sporting, scientific, and religious staffs," and offered the *Times'* perspective on the case.

Behind narrow creeds, religious intolerance, manifestations of Ku Kluxism, and fears of a moral order endangered by new ideas and reflected in a "wild" young generation, is the pathetic faith in which most of us share that the way to safeguard the True and the Good is to put something into the statute books or to strike something from the textbooks. . . . To a certain extent the whole American people will be on trial at Dayton on the charge of monkeying around with the laws and the textbooks for the satisfaction of a local pride.[18]

In the weeks before the trial, the *Times* ran at least seven front-page stories and filled out the coverage with interpretive or feature articles. In late June, the *Times* asked J. Gresham Machen of Princeton Theological Seminary and Vernon Kellogg of the Natural Research Council to write separate explanations of the fundamentalist and evolutionist positions. They were comprehensive and readable, and were given all of the front page of Section IX, along with space on an interior page.[19] On July 5, "The Evolution Arena at Dayton" was the cover story in the Sunday Magazine. It described the scene and the principals, and said, "The strain of this trial probably will fall hardest on the dishwasher at the Hotel Aqua" who was likely "to handle 18,000 dishes a day. Feature writers are advised to watch this dignitary for signs of collapse."[20] The *Times* coverage included little of the Menckenesque caricatures of fundamentalists that influenced future generations.

Coverage of the trial was important to the public's perception of evangelicals. Among other things, it helped blur the line between evangelical and fundamentalist, a distinction that even now is difficult for most people, journalists included, to make. Historian Lawrence Levine said, "It is doubtful if [William Jennings] Bryan ever realized just how much harm" was done by the barrage of bad publicity during and after the Scopes trial.[21] This was the first time, but not the last, that the fundamentalist movement was "done in" by the mass media. Martin Marty called the Scopes trial "the best-remembered Protestant event of the decade," but added that it was an "irrelevancy" that came "fifty years late" and "was hardly representative of the main Protestant parties."[22] In contrast, Marsden concluded, "It would be difficult to overestimate the impact of the 'Monkey Trial' . . . in transforming fundamentalism." It gave the public an "indelible image" and reinforced stereotypes, making it "increasingly difficult" after 1925 "to take fundamentalism seriously."[23]

Frances FitzGerald wrote that since the Scopes trial, "American historians have tended to neglect the fundamentalist constituency as vestigial, the last cry of the still backwaters of the South against the modern world."[24] Journalists gave it the same treatment, allowing fundamentalists and most other evangelicals to slide into the journalistic equivalent of a black hole of neglect where they remained nearly unnoticed for decades. But while they "backed off from politics and hunkered down in their own cultural preserves," they did not die. Wilentz has suggested that they were "outside the gaze of the tone-setting press," building churches, Bible schools, colleges, and radio ministries across America.[25] But with the exception of a few brief bursts of attention, evangelicals were not covered by the secular media for a quarter of a century. Even the October 1941 meeting that led to the formation of the National Association of Evangelicals went unreported by the nation's major media. The first mention of the organization was in *Time* magazine nearly two years later.[26]

Evangelicalism's "big break" in media coverage probably came in 1949, when newspaper publisher William Randolph Hearst sent his editors and reporters a cryptic memo: "Puff Graham." From then on, said Graham, "the two (Hearst) papers gave me great publicity. The others soon followed."[27] But the puffing of Graham had little impact on religion coverage overall. Evangelicals had to make their own news. In the fifties evangelicals and fundamentalists were ready for television. Among the pioneers were Graham, Rex Humbard, and Oral Roberts, who all shared a heritage in revivalism and a vision of the growing power of the new medium.[28] But while they and others, including Pat Robertson, Jim Bakker, and Jimmy Swaggart, were buying time, establishing their own syndicates and even networks, the secular media were paying closer attention to other matters.

In the mid-sixties, the "God is dead" controversy erupted, getting far more media play than did evangelicals. It continued, with diminishing interest, until 1969. Buchstein concluded that the media's most important roles in the controversy were "watcher," observing it as it developed, and "forum," making it public. He asserted that the coverage was "balanced," but said the media found "God is dead" an attractive "catch phrase." He concluded that without media coverage, "there probably would have been no widespread controversy," but adds that "the media did not substantially affect the ideas or thinking of the theologians or their critics."[29]

EVANGELICAL POLITICS

Evangelicals, in 1976, again became news. *Newsweek* dubbed it "the year of the evangelical" in a cover story that admitted that journalists had missed the "emergence of evangelical Christianity into a position of respect and power . . . the most significant—and overlooked—religious phenomenon of the seventies." Both presidential candidates, Gerald Ford and Jimmy Carter, were evangelicals. Many presidential campaign reporters saw the importance of faith to the candidates, but few reported much about it. Even Carter's active church life was largely ignored.

During the same period, a Gallup poll found that half of all Protestants, and a third of all Americans, claimed to have been born again . . . and nearly half of all Protestants believed in taking the Bible "literally, word for word."[30] Some of those people were "stepping out of cultural isolation and assuming the burdens of political responsibility once exercised largely by mainline Protestants in consort with Jewish and Catholic leaders."[31] The *Newsweek* report indicated that the political activism of evangelicals surprised the secular media.

The entry of evangelicals into the political arena focused the news media on their activities and, occasionally, even on their faith. From 1976 until the mid-eighties, the secular media's treatment of evangelicals concentrated on their political efforts and on the "electric church,"[32] which also was highly political. During the 1976 presidential campaign, the secular media began to sense there was a new political current in America. Even before its cover story, *Newsweek* said, "Religion seems likely to be a significant factor in this year's election. . . ."[33] Garry Wills wrote, "Religious love is sweeping the country," and said evangelicalism had "made a stunning comeback. It has, in fact, become the major religious force in America, both in numbers and in political impact."[34] Like other journalists, Wills failed to note that evangelical Protestantism had been "the major religious force" from the nation's earliest days until the start of this century.

Nevertheless, evangelicals suddenly merited close media attention, and a few of the reports provided historical perspective. *Time*, for example, explained evangelical beliefs and indicated how their version of Protestantism, dominant for decades in the South, had spread nationwide.[35]

In 1977, the NBC Radio Network reported, "Christianity is being born again in America. The rebirth is shaking the organized church, challenging the religious establishment and awakening it to new life. It's a revolution and millions are part of it."[36] Marty explained that the evangelical and Pentecostal movements were filling a vacuum left by the mainline churches. "People are hungry for authority," Marty told NBC. "When a religious leader in Catholicism or the Episcopal Church says 'I'm not sure' or 'I don't know,' people are going to look for somebody who says 'the Bible says. . . .' People are starved for (a personal) experience and I think that's the void these two movements are filling."[37]

A *Time* cover story reported, "U.S. Evangelicalism is booming," quoting Rice University sociologist William Martin: "The Evangelicals have become the most active and vital aspect of American religion today."[38] But *Time* noted "there is little Evangelical leverage in the great universities or communications outlets," quoting theologian Carl Henry's lament that another year has passed "in which the movement has registered no notable influence on the formative ideas and ideals of American culture."[39] The article was generally sympathetic, even noting that "a certain radiance, kindness and integrity do seem to flow from many born-again Christians."[40] That was a far cry from the caricature of intolerance and backwardness spun by Mencken five decades earlier.

Notwithstanding these scattered examples, it was not until the 1980 presidential campaign that the secular media really *found* religion. This time the political context was the so-called New Christian Right. Television preacher Jerry Falwell was the most important factor in the discovery. A fundamentalist pastor from Lynchburg, Virginia, Falwell started Moral Majority, a national organization that took advantage of evangelicalism's rapid growth, encouraging believers to be active in politics by supporting various conservative causes and politicians. The news media carried stories during the campaign about this new force in American politics. But the *Wall Street Journal* said that, unlike the Great Awakening of the eighteenth century, the new "spirit of religious awakening" was having little impact. "Even though evangelicalism has been attracting growing numbers of adherents, Americans in parts of the country where it hasn't caught on remain largely unaware of the movement's scope."[41]

Tens of thousands of evangelicals gathered in the nation's capital in late April 1980 for a "Washington for Jesus" rally. A preview article in the *Washington Post* quoted organizers as saying they hoped several hundred thousand theologically conservative Christians would join in prayers "to combat the nation's drift from God."[42] The following day, the story was page one in both the *Post* and the *New York Times*. Each noted it had been the largest religious gathering in Washington in years, the crowd larger than drawn by the Pope a year earlier. The articles emphasized the calls from various preachers "to save America from sin."[43] The *Post* also ran an excellent feature piece on the rally, complete with pictures that caught its size and spirit.[44] For the *Washington Post*, however, this was a local story that merited the page-one treatment it received. While the "Washington for Jesus" rally probably did not get the kind of dramatic attention its organizers had hoped, the coverage it did receive was accurate.

Sometimes it takes an outsider, someone other than the shepherd, to notice a problem in the flock. The weekend after the rally, a British journalist, Tony Thomas of *The Economist*, noted there had been "radical shifts in the behavior of the American Protestant majority" that had gone largely unreported by the secular media. Thomas said journalists and academics were astonished by the changes, but argued this was hardly surprising, since the "great American newspapers rarely give religious news prominence. . . ."[45] It was one of the few articles in the secular press to criticize the news media for the paucity of its coverage of religion. Network television began to notice the convergence of evangelicalism and Republican politics at about the time the 1980 national conventions ended. ABC News offered the most extensive coverage, over seventeen minutes in four long reports. CBS had three reports totalling less than eight minutes, and there were three reports on NBC Nightly News totalling over six minutes.

Newsweek's 1976 cover story on evangelicals (October 25) had brought them into the public's eye, and a 1980 cover showing Falwell in a cross at the center of the word "voTe" pictorially prefaced a long story on "Born-Again Politics." It said, "There is no mistaking the enormous potential of evangelical politics," but warned that the potential could be diminished quickly by divisions among evangelicals. *Newsweek* quoted televangelist Pat Robertson as saying "active partisan politics" is the wrong way for true evangelicals to follow, a lesson he would toss on the scrap heap of expediency a few years later in order to seek the Republican presidential nomination.

For the most part, the secular media's reports during 1980 saw evangelicals as more political than religious. The focus almost exclusively was on the political actions of the emerging New Christian Right and its colorful leaders. One writer noted "the current clamor over a new Christian right continues a long tradition of misunderstanding" that often was made more confusing by the interchangeable use of "fundamentalist," "evangelical," and "born-again" to describe some Christians.[46] The secular media's stories fit the standard definition of news. Journalists did not expect conservative Christians to come out of their churches and into the political arena. But when that happened, it was newsworthy and the media covered it.

The emergence of evangelicals from the political closet produced a lot of post-election analysis. Jerry Falwell bragged that Moral Majority had made the difference in defeating Jimmy Carter and electing Ronald Reagan, and in defeating several liberal senators who had been judged un-Christian. Evangelist James Robison of Fort Worth, Texas, one of the founders of the conservative Religious Roundtable, bluntly said, "The people that put Jimmy [Carter] in, put Jimmy out."[47] But political scientists Lipset and Raab said the evangelical message to vote for Ronald Reagan apparently had a *smaller* impact on the election than trumpeted by people like Robison and Falwell. They cited the *New York Times*/CBS News Election Day poll's finding that "a slightly smaller percentage of born-again white Protestants (61%) than of other white Protestants (63%) actually voted for Reagan. A comparison of the 1976 and 1980 votes indicated as well that Carter lost less support among his fellow born-again Protestants than among others."[48] Lipset and Raab also noted that even though there had been a recent increase, membership in orthodox churches was considerably less than it had been in the 1920s and 1930s, partly because of "structural changes in society which have weakened the base of the fundamentalist-traditionalist forces."[49] This broader perspective was largely forgotten by analysts examining Pat Robertson's presidential potential in 1988. It also was missed by Robertson, who won only a handful of convention delegates. As political scientist Michael Lienesch concluded, "The Christian right is in large part an elite phenomenon, a relatively small group of preachers and politicians allied to the right-wing of the

Republican party." It is "interest-group conservatism."[50] If anything, the media over-reported the Robertson campaign potential, possibly because they did not want to miss the evangelical part of the story as they had in 1980.

RELIGION AND SCANDAL

Evangelicals next surfaced in the secular media in 1987, when scandal struck. Editors like religious scandals, especially when a popular preacher gets caught with his hands in the collection plate or somewhere else they don't belong. Jim Bakker was the first major televangelist to provide a good scandal, but he was not to be the last. Even as he was excoriating Bakker and demanding swift evangelical punishment, fellow televangelist Jimmy Swaggart was involved in sins he later admitted without any details. A New Orleans prostitute, for an unspecified price, revealed the details later.[51] *Penthouse*, a "sextarian" journal, described Swaggart as the "commanding general in an army of right-wing fundamentalists (who) ralied against fornication, adultery, pornography, homosexuality, sin—deviance in all its satanic forms. . . ." Swaggart's confession, said *Penthouse*, followed leaks that he "was in trouble for sexual misconduct. . . . It was the most bizarre, damaging twist in a year that sorely tested the bedrock faith of America's 70-million born-agains, and shattered the glitz, glory, and fund-raising magic of televangelists."[52]

The differences between fundamentalists and other evangelicals were highlighted in the intramural fighting that followed Bakker's fall. Stories with such headlines as "Heaven Can Wait" and "War in the TV Pulpits" reported Swaggart's angry denunciations of Bakker, and focused on the fight between Bakker, a neo-Pentecostalist, and the fundamentalist Jerry Falwell for control of the PTL television ministry and Christian theme park in North Carolina.[53] The *Washington Post* did a long page-one story that put Swaggart and Falwell on one side of the fight, and Bakker and faith-healer Oral Roberts on the other. Although the story was rather detailed and dull, it offered the best summary of the situation to appear in any major national newspaper in part because it helped to explain the differences in doctrine and religious practice among the popular television preachers.[54]

Some features on the " holy war" were either trivial or cynical. One story focused on Tammy Faye Bakker's use of industrial-strength makeup and her worldly addiction to shopping, calling the whole affair "a heavenly mess." *Mademoiselle* said, "Everybody needs God. What with home shopping, you can buy anything else simply by activating the remote; why not Him?"[55] In addition to the Bakker/PTL case, there was speculation that Roberts had lost his marbles. He implied God was an extortionist when he said God would call him "home" if he didn't raise eight million dollars for medical missionary work. *U.S. News and World Report* asked, "Where does religious broadcasting go from here?"[56]

The *Los Angeles Times* had looked into the future even before *U.S. News* asked. A nationwide survey conducted just after news of the Bakker scandal broke found agreement among "fundamentalists, Pentacostals and other Christians . . . that they will watch television evangelists less, believe them less and contribute less money to their ministries." As people came to know more about television preachers, unfavorable opinions about them increased.[57]

The following months were hardly good times for televangelism, and the secular news media watched closely. Pat Robertson, founder of the Christian Broadcasting Network, resigned his ordination and ran for president of the United States. Dan Wasserman, an editorial cartoonist for the *Boston Globe*, pictured him as an embarrassment to the Republicans.[58] And Robertson denied his past. Tom Brokaw of NBC News, in an interview during the early primaries of 1988, referred to him as a former televangelist, a reference Robertson angrily branded as a "bigoted slur." A cartoon in the *Atlanta Constitution* pictured Robertson as a hypocrite. A woman holding out a telephone said, "Mr. Robertson, it's God!" Robertson jumped on an elephant and said, "Later!"[59] Not surprisingly, Robertson won little support. His failure, coupled with those of Jack Kemp and Pete duPont, seemed to be a sign that the New Christian Right had run out of steam. Wilentz wrote, "Rarely in modern times has a movement of such reputed magnitude and political potential self-destructed so suddenly."[60]

But there was more. Jimmy Swaggart, who played a key role in the stern punishment of Jim Bakker, was pictured on the cover of *Penthouse*, his tearful face in a mock television screen over the headline "Swaggart: the Lady, the Story, the Pictures." Newspapers, news wires, and news magazines pounced on Swaggart's problems, proving again Mattingly's contention that religious scandal is the one religion story that every editor will pursue.[61] Russell Chandler of the *Los Angeles Times* told Mattingly, "I don't personally relish doing such stories . . . but it's part of the job of the secular press to work on some of these things, because . . . it's the only way some people will be made to be accountable."[62] But Chandler insisted the secular media should not let the sideshow interfere with the coverage of ideas and trends in religion, even though critics say it often seems to do just that.

The Swaggart story immediately grabbed the headlines. *Time* said, "Now It's Jimmy's Turn. The sins of Swaggart send another shock through the world of TV evangelism." In hyperbolic fashion, *Time* called Swaggart's unspecific confession "the most dramatic sermon ever aired on television."[63] *Newsweek's* first article, "A Sex Scandal Breaks Over Jimmy Swaggart," talked of the confession of immorality and quoted sociologist Jeffrey Hadden as saying the revelation could be "shattering," prompting the public to wonder whether any televangelist was honest.[64] *Newsweek's* followup a week later, "The Wages of Sin," called Swaggart "televangelism's latest fallen angel" and said he had "lost the moral swagger that made him the televangelism industry's avenging spirit."[65]

Two weeklies made Swaggart's troubles their cover story. *U.S. News and World Report's* banner read, "The Devil and Jimmy Swaggart." The magazine said it was surprising that Swaggart's "nationally televised confession . . . rated little more than a ho-hum on the outrage meter of a nation numbed by a year of similar sordid revelations."[66] *People's* cover showed Swaggart, his Bible open, with the quote, "I HAVE SINNED AGAINST YOU" in one-inch type. The story was headlined, "The Fall of Jimmy Swaggart: Having cast the first stone more than once, the self-appointed judge of America's televangelists finds himself the penitent."[67]

Major newspapers also focused considerable attention on Swaggart's problems. The *Washington Post* carried twenty-four articles, two on the front page. The *New York Times* carried thirty-four stories, three on page one. The *Christian Science Monitor* featured a long front-page article analyzing public attitudes toward televangelists in the wake of Swaggart's fall. Even the *Wall Street Journal* took brief page one note of Swaggart's televised confession.

In the wake of the Bakker's excesses, Oral Roberts' portrayal of God as an extortionist, and Jimmy Swaggart's publicized sinfulness, "donor paralysis" hit many of the TV ministries during 1988. *Business Week* said televangelists had two "saving graces:" the PTL cable network and "the unshakable faith of (televangelism's) core of believers."[68] Still, many of the operations were trimmed because audience size and weekly donations plunged dramatically. Swaggart lost more than half of his audience, Roberts more than two-thirds, Robertson's "700 Club" was down by nearly half, and PTL's donations were only one-third of what it needed just to survive.[69] Hadden and Shupe contended the "system is working. . . . When raw ambition and greed turned preachers of the Gospel into hucksters, their motives were discovered and their clients sought another product."[70]

William Martin said that the audience wasn't nearly so large as some believed. While the electronic preachers had "more undisputed access to the airwaves than any other social movement in American society,"[71] Martin contended audience claims of 1.3 million were a "media myth." Martin said the audience was "predominantly female, over fifty, working- and lower-class, and, true to stereotype, likely to live in rural areas, towns, and small cities in the South and Midwest. [The audience] is composed almost entirely of believers, most of whom are members of conservative Protestant churches."[72] Martin's findings indicated little change from an earlier study that found the religious *radio* audience was primarily made up of older, less-well-educated Protestants in the South or Southeast who were regular church attenders and believed religion was very important in their lives.[73] Martin concluded these believers were noticing that "virtually all the religion on radio and television is their kind of religion, that the secular media are fascinated by it, and . . . that they are no longer a beleaguered, backwater minority but a significant and thriving part of mainstream American Christianity."[74]

TV and radio religion is worth at least one billion dollars annually to the broadcasting industry and yet, said Stephen Winzenburg, it is "rarely taken seriously." He noted television evangelism is "an industry oddity, paying stations large amounts of money for undesirable time slots to reach small audiences." Winzenburg concluded the recent scandals, rather than killing off the ministries, had "increased national curiosity in religious television."[75]

Believers as behavers have been the focus of the secular media's coverage of evangelicals since the story of the Bakker scandal broke in 1987. Martz said the collapse of PTL in 1987 provoked "a sort of morbid fascination" with the electronic church and its leaders.[76] Religion again became an issue discussed in newsrooms. Journalists, whose understanding of the subject was limited, began to seek out knowledgeable sources, but thoughtful stories about evangelicals and their beliefs remained, for the most part, unwritten. Most coverage of evangelicals was limited to areas that previously had received attention. Evangelicals still were oddities, obstructionists, political extremists, or people led by misbehaving preachers. The sincerity of their religious faith, except perhaps among the televangelists, largely went unquestioned. And regardless of the news reports, that faith was put into political action, something that Hunter indicated would continue. He said, "A substantial portion of Evangelicals are conservative or very conservative with a specific political agenda; they are almost uniformly committed to their rights as religious people to engage in political action to realize their plan. . . ."[77]

The political and the religious intersected in the media's coverage of the conflict among Southern Baptists, the largest evangelical denomination. Secular reporters tended to describe the fight in much the same terms as a political campaign, indicating the conservatives were ahead but, because of a change in sentiment, the moderates might be on the upswing. Stories often mentioned doctrinal differences. As in the past, though, those differences were seen as less important than the more-political fight to control the Southern Baptist power structure and seminaries. The winning side, the media presumed, probably would control the denomination's theology *and* political stance for decades.

CONCLUSION

Evangelicals are an important part of the American religious landscape, but now as in the past, the secular media notice them more for what they do than for who they are. The public actions of evangelicals always have drawn media attention, but their vigorous entry into politics has solidified their newsworthiness. In general, early coverage included brief discussions of the faith of evangelicals, although hardly enough to generate much understanding among readers, listeners, or viewers, or among reporters and editors. More recent coverage of evangelical faith is better, but hardly comprehensive. As mere behavers, evangelicals were interesting news. It is as believers, however, that they probably have had the most significant impact on American culture, even though that impact has gone largely unreported.

We can conclude several things from this exploration: that evangelicals are news to the secular media when they do something to get the attention of journalists, that the political involvement of evangelicals and the conflicts it creates will continue to be a media focal point, and that misbehavior by highly visible televangelists will be considered big news by secular journalists.

One final observation comes out of this work: evangelicals and the secular media need to understand each other better. Stereotyping by journalists *and* evangelicals has been counter-productive, leading most reporters to miss important trends and most evangelicals to fail to communicate their stories as effectively as possible to reporters and the general public. Informed evangelical action in this area could produce news coverage that evangelicals might consider more balanced, informed, and fair, and that in the end would benefit the wider audience served by the American media.

NOTES

[1]David Aikman, "The Press is Missing the Scoop of the Century," *Christianity Today*, March 4, 1988, 12.

[2]Robert Booth Fowler, *A New Engagement: Evangelical Political Thought, 1966–1976 (Grand Rapids: Eerdmans, 1982)*, 1.

[3]R. Laurence Moore, *Religious Outsiders and the Making of Americans* (New York: Oxford, 1986), 163–65.

[4]"Interview with Timothy Smith," *Christianity Today*, November 19, 1976, 24, quoted in Moore, *Religious Outsiders*, 163.

[5]Lewis Coser, *The Functions of Social Conflict* (New York: The Free Press, 1964), 33–38, 87–95.

[6]Wesley Pippert, (Remarks at Wheaton College Conference on Evangelicals, the Mass Media and American Culture, September 30, 1988).

[7]Terry Mattingly, "The Religion Beat," *The Quill*, January, 1983, 14.

[8]Martin E. Marty, *A Nation of Behavers* (Chicago: The University of Chicago Press, 1976), 80.

[9]Robert T. Handy, *A Christian America: Protestant Hopes and Historical Realities* (New York: Oxford University Press, 1984), ix.

[10]Donald G. Bloesch, *The Future of Evangelical Christianity: A Call for Unity Amid Diversity* (Colorado Springs: Helmers & Howard, 1988), 17.

[11]S. Robert Lichter, Stanley Rothman, and Linda S. Lichter, *The Media Elite: America's New Powerbrokers* (Bethesda, Md.: Adler & Adler, 1986), 22.

[12]Mattingly, "The Religion Beat," 15.

[13]Ernest C. Hynds, "Large Daily Newspapers Have Improved Coverage of Religion," *Journalism Quarterly* (Summer-Autumn, 1987): 444–47.

[14]Dan Ranly, "How Religion Editors of Newspapers View Their Jobs and Religion," *Journalism Quarterly* (Winter, 1979): 844–49.

[15]Martin E. Marty, *Modern American Religion: The Irony of It All: 1893–1919* (Chicago: University of Chicago Press, 1986), 20–21.

[16]Carl Bode, *Mencken* (Carbondale, Ill.: Southern Illinois University Press, 1969), 265.

[17]George Marsden, *Fundamentalism and American Culture: The Shaping of Twentieth-Century Evangelicalism: 1870–1925* (New York: Oxford University Press, 1980), 187–88.

[18]*New York Times*, 27 May 1925.

[19]Ibid., 21 June 1925, Sec. I, and Sec. IX.

[20]*New York Times* Sunday Magazine, 5 July 1925.

[21]Lawrence E. Levine, *Defender of the Faith: William Jennings Bryan: The Last Decade, 1915–1925* (1965; reprint Cambridge, Mass.: Harvard University Press, 1987), 352.

[22]Martin E. Marty, *Protestantism in the United States: Righteous Empire*, 2d. ed. (New York: Scribner, 1986), 215–16.

[23]Marsden, *Fundamentalism*, 184–91.

[24]Frances FitzGerald, "A Disciplined, Charging Army," *The New Yorker*, May 18, 1981, 63.

[25]Sean Wilentz, "God and Man at Lynchburg," *The New Republic*, April 25, 1988, 31.

[26]*Time*, May 17, 1943, 46.

[27]*Time*, March 20, 1950, 72–73.

[28]See Razelle Frankl, *Televangelism: The Marketing of Popular Religion* (Carbondale: Southern Illinois University Press, 1987).

[29]Frederick D. Buchstein, "The Role of the News Media in the 'Death of God' Controversy," *Journalism Quarterly* (Spring, 1982): 79–85.

[30]*Newsweek*, October 25, 1976, 68.

[31]Ibid., p. 70.

[32]Ben Armstrong, *The Electric Church* (Nashville: Thomas Nelson, 1979). Armstrong coined the phrase "Electric Church," which has been altered slightly over the years to "Electronic Church." It often is used pejoratively, something Armstrong never intended.

[33]Kenneth L. Woodward, "Politics from the Pulpit," *Newsweek*, September 6, 1976, 49–51.

[34]Garry Wills, " 'Born again' politics," *New York Times* Magazine, August 1, 1976, 9.

[35]"A Born-Again Faith," *Time*, September 27, 1976, 86–87.

[36]Mike Maus, "Second Sunday: The New Old-Time Religion" (Broadcast on the NBC Radio Network, October 9, 1977).

[37]Ibid.

[38]"Back to that Oldtime Religion," *Time*, December 26, 1977, 53.

[39]Ibid., 57.

[40]Ibid., 55.

[41]"Old-Time Religion: An Evangelical Revival Is Sweeping the Nation But with Little Effect," *The Wall Street Journal*, July 11, 1980.

[42]Marjorie Hyer and Athelia Knight, "Christians Rally," *The Washington Post*, April 29, 1980.

[43]Ben A. Franklin, "200,000 March and Pray at Christian Rally in Capital,"

New York Times, April 30, 1980; Paul W. Valentine and Marjorie Hyer, "Vast and Joyous Crowd," *The Washington Post*, April 30, 1980, 1.

[44]Neil Henry, " 'Holy Roller' Resounds With Joy, Wrath," *The Washington Post*, April 30, 1980.

[45]Tony Thomas, "Behind That New Time Religion," *Washington Post*, May 4, 1980.

[46]Leo P. Ribuffo, "Liberals and That Old-Time Religion," *The Nation*, November 29, 1980, 571.

[47]"Religious Right Goes for Bigger Game," *U.S. News and World Report*, November 17, 1980, 42.

[48]Seymour Martin Lipset and Earl Raab, "The Election and the Evangelicals," *Commentary*, March, 1981, 29.

[49]Ibid., 31.

[50]Michael Lienesch, "Right-Wing Religion: Christian Conservatism as a Political Movement," *Political Science Quarterly*, Fall, 1982, 407.

[51]Art Harris and Jason Berry, "Jimmy Swaggart's Secret Sex Life," *Penthouse*, July 1988, 104.

[52]Ibid., 106.

[53]Russell Watson, "Holy War: Heaven Can Wait," *Newsweek*, June 8, 1987, 58–65; Lewis J. Lord, "An Unholy War in the TV Pulpits," *U.S. News and World Report*, April 6, 1987, 58.

[54]Jeffrey A. Frank and Lloyd Grove, "The Raging Battles of the Evangelicals," *Washington Post*, March 25, 1987.

[55]Barbara Grizzuti Harrison, "TV Evangelists: What a Heavenly Mess," *Mademoiselle*, November, 1987, 208.

[56]Gordon Witkin and Jeannye Thornton, "Stones Fly in the TV Temple," *U.S. News and World Report*, June 8, 1987.

[57]Russell Chandler, "Bakker Scandal Damages Standing of TV Preachers," *Los Angeles Times*, March 31, 1987.

[58]*Boston Globe*, October 6, 1987, 18.

[59]*Atlanta Constitution*, October 19, 1987.

[60]Wilentz, "God and Man," 30.

[61]Mattingly, "The Religion Beat," 17.

[62]Ibid.

[63]*Time*, March 7, 1988, 46.

[64]*Newsweek*, February 29, 1988, 30–31.

[65]*Newsweek*, March 7, 1988, 51.

[66]"Of Rolexes and Repentance," *U.S. News and World Report*, March 7, 1988, 62.

[67]*People*, March 7, 1988, 35–39.

[68]"TV Evangelists Are Looking for a Few Miracles," *Business Week*, February 1, 1988, 32.

[69]"TV Preachers on the Rocks," *Newsweek*, July 11, 1988, 26–28.

[70]Jeffrey K. Hadden and Anson Shupe, *Televangelism: Power and Politics on God's Frontier* (New York: Henry Holt and Company, 1988), 134.

[71]Jeffrey K. Hadden and Charles E. Swann, *Prime Time Preachers: The Rising Power of Televangelism* (Reading, Mass.: Addison-Wesley, 1981), 16.

[72]William Martin, "The Birth of a Media Myth," *The Atlantic*, June, 1981, 7–11.

[73]Ronald L. Johnstone, "Who Listens to Religious Radio Broadcasts Anymore?" *Journal of Broadcasting* 16, no. 1 (Winter 1971–72): 91–102.

[74]Martin, "Birth," 16.

[75]Stephen Winzenburg, "Monday Memo: On Understanding TV Evangelists," *Broadcasting*, July 18, 1988, 25.

[76]Larry Martz, *Ministry of Greed: The Inside Story of the Televangelists and Their Holy Wars* (New York: Weidenfeld & Nicholson, 1988), 137.

[77]James Davison Hunter, *Evangelicalism: The Coming Generation* (Chicago: University of Chicago Press, 1987), 148–49.

12

WORLDLY REPORTERS AND BORN-AGAIN BELIEVERS: HOW EACH PERCEIVES THE OTHER

WESLEY G. PIPPERT

There is a harsh reciprocity in how the world and born-again Christians see each other. This mutual misunderstanding and mistrust is the key to assessing the difficult relationship of *worldly* reporters and *born-again* believers.

HOW THE WORLDLY REPORTER VIEWS EVANGELICAL RELIGION

In short, the worldly reporter these days is newly aware of religion as a significant news story but still views it with cynicism and a lack of understanding. (By secular or worldly reporter, I mean the reporter who is employed by a secular publication.)

The mass media's coverage of religion as hard news, and especially of evangelicals, is a relatively recent phenomenon. To examine this, we need a brief review of recent history in describing how journalists assess religion in current affairs.

In general, for a long time there had been silence in the mass media about what was happening in the field of the evangelicals, or fundamentalists, as they were known when I was growing up. Parenthetically, this general inattention by the world at large also was true when applied to the work of evangelical scholars in most disciplines. They simply did not get wide attention in the literature of their field, no matter how deserving and meritorious they were.

In the 1950s the silence persisted in the mass media despite the reality that at least half of all Americans regularly went to church or to synagogue, and many of those congregations were theologically conservative. Few avowed fundamentalists or evangelicals were public personalities. Aside from pedestrian coverage of denominational meetings and the National and World Councils of Churches, about the only thing to make news was the dramatic conversion of a celebrity (generally a Hollywood actor or a crook!). There were stories about Dwight D. Eisenhower's personal prayer at the start of his 1953 inaugural address, Hearst covered Billy Graham's first crusades and there were the occasional conversion stories—of Jim Vaus, the criminal; of Stuart Hamblen, the singer; of actress Dolores Hart's decision to enter a convent; of Pat Boone, who wouldn't kiss a woman in his films.

This fit my own experience during my first few years as a reporter in the late 1950s and 1960s. There was little awareness of what was going on in religion aside from the weekly column written by UPI's religion editor, Louis Cassels, although it was the most widely read column we distributed. As a fledgling but eager reporter in Minneapolis, I did a feature on the St. Paul Bible Institute's rather impressive—or so I thought—World Missions Night. My bureau chief took me aside and said that what really made a good story was the kind of thing that would make one man in a bar say to another, "Say, did you see that story about——?" Occasionally a religion story would get page-one attention—Karl Barth's visit to the University of Chicago and Billy Graham's crusade at Chicago's McCormick Place in the early 1960s. But these were the exceptions.

One vivid example happened at Wheaton College while I was covering the 1972 presidential campaign. George McGovern, the Democratic nominee, gave during the regular morning service in Edman Chapel what one of his top aides told me was the definitive speech of his campaign. As we were filing out of Edman after McGovern's talk, my competitor remarked to me, "I think I'll skip that—that's religion." The candidate and the press bus went on to Chicago for a meeting with Cook County labor leaders. That night, on TV, all three networks reported on McGovern's long-since forgotten meeting with the labor leaders and skipped Wheaton. To further my belief in evil, my story about Wheaton was lost in a computer crash. So that meant one of McGovern's most important speeches of the campaign went unreported. And given the fact that the press did not really start to cover Nixon's role in the Watergate break-in and cover-up until after the election, most of the American people that autumn voted without the truth—a word to which I shall return—about either candidate. Later, Michael McIntyre wrote in *Christian Century.*

> Many in the working press were unable to deal with the moral categories being used by candidate McGovern. Time after time, he lapsed into the language of morality, judgment and justice, only to see reporters close notebooks, glance at each other in embarrassment or grin indulgently, or look at their watches. It was as though all the refugees from countless Sunday schools had suddenly been trapped back in a lesson from Chronicles and were waiting for the bell to ring. . . . What is most significant about McGovern's "moralizing" is that he uses the language which is understood in Midwest and southern Bible belt—and he uses it without manipulation and without cynicism. It is as valid indigenous language as any we possess in this country. . . . At Wheaton it was authentic and it said precisely what he meant—if you could understand the nuances. My judgment is, again, that many in the working press could not; and in that respect we had an uninterpreted campaign.[1]

However, things began to change. Not all at once, but in spurts and retreats. I leave it to sociologists to determine whether there was any relationship in America between this increasing media attention to religion in the 1960s and 1970s and the convulsions manifested in the political assassinations, the riots in the inner cities, and the Vietnam War.

Unfortunately, the media's increased attention was not necessarily accompanied by an increase in understanding. I recall writing a story in 1970 about the conversion experience of Windsor Elliott, a model with several magazine covers to her credit. Bruce Manning, managing editor of the *Florida Times-Union*, wrote us to say: "I can't hardly think of anything we've done in years and years that so touched a nerve as did this UPI yarn. Perhaps there is a gnawing hunger abroad for a taste of the wholesome, a touch of cleanliness and good will. But whatever it is, we are grateful for the response. . . ."[2] Windsor Elliott now is the wife of Dr. Os Guinness, the acute British observer of American religion and culture.

Two things, both of them dealing with being born again, market the real start of the mass media's attention to evangelicals. Charles W. Colson revealed that he had been born again while he was a target of the Watergate investigation. Just before Christmas 1973, I interviewed him in his posh law offices—the Teamsters were his chief client. And my story on his conversion and his terse but insightful analysis of the cause of the scandal—"arrogance was the great sin of Watergate," he said—moved on a "spot," or immediate, basis on the prime UPI-AAA wire, one of the longest stories ever to run spot. *Born Again* became the title of Colson's post-Watergate book, a title he says his wife found in a Catholic hymnal, not in the gospel of John.[3]

Two and a half years later, former Georgia Governor Jimmy Carter was campaigning for the presidency in the Carolina primary. It came to someone's attention that he professed to be born again. Reporters asked him about it, and he acknowledged that he was born again. NBC anchorman John Chancellor showed the clip, and then added, in what he obviously intended as a bit of in-depth coverage, "By the way, we've checked this out. Being 'born again' is not a bizarre, mountain-top experience. It's something common to many millions of Americans—particularly if you're Baptist." The anchorman's attempt to add depth to his reporting was admirable; his understanding of religion was abysmal. Later on during the campaign, I asked Jody Powell, who was Carter's press secretary, how he felt the press had handled that aspect of Carter's life. He replied,

> The American people, as a whole, are probably better equipped to understand that aspect of Jimmy Carter's life than are the people who are trying to explain it to them. There have been stories that have been superficial and slipshod and biased to the extreme, not necessarily against him, but based on what I take to be a general distaste for religious faith.[4]

Whether we believe Carter was an effective president or not, I think we can agree that his faith was essential to understanding him. Yet, the White House press corps, of which I was one, never wrestled with the ramifications of this. As president, Carter continued his practice of teaching Sunday school frequently. Almost from the start, the only reporters to cover those classes were the White House "pool," made up of correspondents from the two wire services and one network. They treated it more as a death watch than as a place to get insight. On one typical occasion, the network reporter noted in his pool report, which is distributed to all other White House reporters, that Carter taught and "nothing else of substance occurred during Sunday School." Even if a journalist has no interest whatsoever in faith and religion, he or she ought to be concerned about how those factors affect a president. The big flaw in press coverage of Carter's faith was not in misunderstanding his born-again experience (by now everyone had a rough idea of what that meant) but in failing to see the ramifications of that experience in shaping major decisions of his presidency. My own systematic study of Carter's faith[5] uncovered a great deal about the way he viewed the world and his own responsibilities. One area, that of his understanding of power, proved to be highly significant in his presidency.

Early in his term of office, Carter remarked to employees at the old Department of Health, Education and Welfare that he came to them not as "First Boss" but "First Servant."[6] About that same time, he remarked to the elite religious and political audience at the National Prayer Breakfast,

> When the disciples struggled among themselves for superiority in God's eyes, Jesus said (paraphrasing Matt. 20:27), 'Whoever would be chief among you, let him be servant.' Although we use the phrase—sometimes glibly—'public servant,' it's hard for us to translate the concept of a president of the United States into genuine servant.[7]

Carter's concept of power suggested that he would use force with restraint and moderation, an interpretation confirmed by one of Carter's key aides. In my view, this explained Carter's restraint and caution in dealing with the Iranian hostage situation and the Soviet invasion of Afghanistan. During his final campaign, he frequently remarked: "I have always tried to use America's strength with great caution and care and tolerance and thoughtfulness and prayer," and "Once we inject our military forces into combat, as happened in Vietnam, it's hard to control it from then on, because your country loses prestige if you don't ultimately go ahead and win." But those comments, growing, I believe, out of his religious experience, never saw air time or news print.

During Harvard's 350th anniversary celebration in 1986, one of the panels dealt with politics, television, and religion. Cal Thomas, a columnist and a fundamentalist Christian, was one of the panelists as was John Chancellor, the NBC news commentator. Thomas told the story about Chancellor's remark in the 1976 campaign, and everyone, including Chancellor, laughed appreciatively. Later during the panel, Harvey Cox, a Harvard theologian, used the term "liberation theology." Chancellor leaned over and asked in an audacious whisper, "What's 'liberation theology'??"

This somewhat sketchy history, culminated by Harvard's panel, demonstrates my general conclusion: The mass media are aware that we need to pay attention to religion as real news occasionally deserving page-one treatment, not something saved for the weekend religion section. But the history also indicates that most of the mass media do not grasp the nuances and subtleties of covering institutional religion and the religious experience.

The mass media still treat religious matters with cynicism, some justified, some not. For instance, since Charles Colson and Jimmy Carter made the biblical term "born again" famous, meaningful religious terms have been bandied about. Born again has become a cliche that is used in ads, in political campaigns, and other things that have no relationship whatsoever to the original meaning. "And what about the incorrect, and often pejorative, use of the word 'fundamentalist,' which has come to mean anyone behaving in a fanatical manner?" asks Cal Thomas, a syndicated columnist and a fundamentalist Christian.[8]

In any story about fundamentalists or charismatics, the mass media still treat them as caricatures, the men typically in polyester suits and the women usually overweight and wearing bouffant hair-dos. Pat Robertson was treated primarily as a TV evangelist who healed tumors and headed off hurricanes, so much so that James M. Wall, editor of the theologically liberal *Christian Century*, finally condemned the snide coverage of this so-called "wacko factor."[9] Malcolm Muggeridge makes an even more basic criticism of the mass media. He said,

> The prevailing impression I have come to have of the contemporary scene is of an ever-widening chasm between the fantasy in terms of which the media induce us to live, and the reality of our existence as made in the image of God. . . . The media have created, and belong to a world of fantasy, the more dangerous because it purports to be, and is largely taken as being, the real world.[10]

Why do the mass media lack understanding about religious matters? A reporter does not need to *experience* a story in order to write about it. Someone once remarked to me that since I was not a Jew, it must have been difficult for me to write insightfully about Israel while I was a foreign correspondent there. I obviously reject that. One does not need to be a communist to write about the Soviet Union. A sports announcer does not need to be an ex-professional athlete—it only seems that way! There is something arguably preferable for the layman, not the professional, to describe things to the public. Yet, there is something about the religious experience that unless it *is* experienced it cannot be fully understood. Jesus asked, "Can the blind lead the blind?" (Luke 6:39 KJV). As Russ Pulliam has written about the media and coverage of Christians doing newsworthy things, "They just can't write the story because they can't believe it." Or, he adds, "what a lot of reporters know about Christianity they learned from a small-town, anti-intellectual fundamentalism."[11] When Fred Barnes of the *New Republic* asked Ronald Reagan and Walter Mondale about their faith during the 1984 presidential debate, it was reported in a gossip column in the *Washington Post* that Barnes had become a born-again Christian. Barnes said he expected to get a number of sympathetic calls from reporters who were "closet believers." He said he got not one. The 1982 study by the Lichters and Rothman indicate that more than 80 per cent of the members of the media seldom or never attend religious services.[12] I simply raise the question: If members of the mass media have not had a religious experience, can they truly understand a religious experience, and if they can't, can they really report about it insightfully, even accurately?

Many in the mass media are cynical about religion. Sometimes the so-called religious leaders, and many of the political leaders who profess religion, often turn out to be, frankly, frauds. It used to be a rarity for a politician to profess to be born again. Now, with only slight hyperbole, I must say I don't know of any politicians who don't profess to being born again! The media know this, so much so, that when they hear a profession of faith, they instinctively get suspicious. The biggest monument to the genuineness of Carter's faith is that although many White House reporters doubted it at first, not one that I know of doubted it by the end of his term.

In short, the religious world can do little about the journalists' lack of religious understanding but a great deal about reporters' cynicism. The religious world could produce qualified, insightful, and *knowledgeable* journalists who *do* believe and understand religious faith. But I doubt whether religious people will ever dominate the mass media or even be a dominant force in the media. In regard to the media's cynicism about religion, evangelicals must demonstrate integrity. In recent years this has certainly not been the case.

HOW EVANGELICALS VIEW THE WORLDLY MEDIA

If the world cynically sees evangelicals as a bit quaint and naïve, evangelicals often view the world with hostility and suspicion.

As a result few evangelicals have entered the worldly media professions. When I came to Washington in 1966, the evangelicals in the Washington press corps were so few they could caucus in a phone booth. Over the years, I tried to keep track of how many journalists in the media throughout the country were identified as evangelicals. After years of careful notes, I came up with a list of only forty or fifty. Perhaps there were many more closet believers. It was as if Christians thought of secular journalism as being intrinsically evil and avoided it. There probably were fewer evangelicals in secular journalism than in almost any other profession, including politics and professional sports. Now there is a sizeable number. The evangelicals in the Washington press corps had a retreat in February 1988, and about forty turned out, including reporters from the *New York Times*, the *Baltimore Sun*, *Time*, the *New Republic*, Cable News Network, National Public Radio, and local television.

Consider some of the headliners in 1987 and 1988: Gary Hart, Oliver North, Jim Bakker, Jimmy Swaggart—evangelicals or former evangelicals, all. Hart, a presidential candidate, was born and raised a Nazarene, went to a Nazarene college, and married a daughter of one of the six general superintendents of the Church of the Nazarene. It was ironic that the woman with whom he allegedly had an extramarital affair, Donna Rice, had a similar background. The media covered the sins and lifestyles of Jim and Tammy Bakker and Jimmy Swaggart and their brethren in embarrassing detail. The saturation coverage was entirely appropriate, as I have suggested earlier. The trust of many of the faithful was invested in these evangelists, and it was a trust that was broken.

The world of religion suffers from its own version of the mass media's failure to cover religious stories even when these stories are significant. Often religious publications have seen their audience and/or editorial content far too narrowly, often focusing too much attention on pastoral and para-church organizations. The activities and influence of huge blocs of evangelicals in secular fields have been left out or ignored in the religious press as well as in the secular press, thereby greatly contributing to the lack of appreciation and attention for what evangelicals have achieved in the various fields of endeavor. The evangelical media have done an exceedingly poor job of reporting their own warts. It's ironic—and a glaring fact that ought to lead the so-called religious press to some rigorous self-examination—that the secular press and not the evangelical press was the prophet in calling them to account for their sins. It was a reporter from the *Washington Post*, not *Christianity Today* or *Eternity*, who asked presidential candidate Gary Hart if he had ever committed adultery. One might have assumed just the opposite. The evangelical press should have known the televangelists better than their secular brethren in the press; after all, the evangelicals had watched and listened to them for years. Yet, it was the secular press who pointed out the weaknesses of these public men.

In fact, the religious press often seemed to be more understanding and tolerant of the sins of the fallen than was the secular press. Often the evangelicals tended to blame the worldly reporters for Pat Robertson's problems, when, in fact, his political problems by and large had nothing to do with his religious beliefs. He proved to be a testy campaigner who often spoke without careful thought, and *these* things, not his prayers that averted a hurricane or that led to physical healings, spelled the doom of his candidacy.

Perhaps more serious, religious institutions go merrily on their way without being subjected to the vigilance of a watchdog press. Many denominations and para-church organizations are subjected to much less scrutiny than are many secular institutions. Hence, the financial practices, the personnel policies, the decision-making process in religious institutions go unchecked. Many in the religious press impose more censorship than the worldly press ever encounters. Many evangelical denominational or collegiate publications are prohibited from printing a negative story under ultimate threat of censorship, "We are doing the work of the Lord. This story would hurt the kingdom. It must not be printed." The process of decision-making in religious institutions ought to be covered as thoroughly as the process of a political campaign or yesterday's NFL game.

During the Watergate scandal, an evangelical magazine asked me to write an article on Billy Graham and his relationship to Richard Nixon. I suspected that Graham was too close to Nixon to confront him, so, following a mind-set I am now criticizing, I refused for one year to write an article, saying, "I don't want to do anything that would hurt Billy Graham's ministry." The culprit, however, is generally not the evangelical reporter, who in my experience has proved to be as hard-driving and able as his or her counterparts in the secular media. Rather, the religious institutions control the budget and the personnel of these publications. Roy Howard Beck, a prize-winning reporter, spent six wrenching years at the *United Methodist Reporter* and what he has endured at the hands of denominational officials since publication of *On Thin Ice* hasn't been any easier.[13] His struggles are common for evangelical reporters who seek to cover their own denominations and para-church ministries. One evangelical editor told me the problem also lay with the readership. "They don't want to read anything negative or critical of their church," he said. So the magazines don't print anything that is negative or critical of the religious community.

Why are evangelical media often unwilling to report carefully and critically the weaknesses and immoralities of the abuse of sex and, especially, the abuse of power within evangelical institutions? There are reasons that, ironically, go to the heart of evangelicals' belief—or lack of it—in their own doctrines.

1. As we have noted, the evangelical media often have defined their audience and their editorial content too narrowly because they saw the Gospel too narrowly. If religious experience affects the whole spectrum of human thought and activity, then the religious press ought to cover any human endeavor where the spirit is at work.

2. The evangelical media may suffer a lack of faith, and more specifically, a lack of faith in the efficacy of truth. Truth is at the heart of the task of the journalist. Truth is also at the core of the Christian message. In the Hebrew Bible, the word for truth, אמת, *ᵉmet* implies trustworthiness and faithfulness. In fact, the English translations occasionally translate the Hebrew word for truth as "faithfulness." To fear the publication of the truth as being anything other than emancipating is, quite

literally, a lack of faith. Therefore, evangelical institutions that impose censorship or strict guidelines on their publications are guilty of a lack of faith in truth. Often secular reporters, the so-called worldly reporters, are much more committed to the pursuit of truth, wherever the chips may fall, than some evangelical publications are.

3. Evangelical journalists must model journalism at its best, both professionally and personally. Evangelical journalists must cover the truth-centered issues of justice, mercy, and peace even if their secular colleagues do not. Evangelical journalists ought to model the same kind of courage that has sent secular brothers and sisters to jail for flouting censorship. Evangelical journalists must demonstrate utmost integrity in getting the story, in not resorting to dishonesty or the bending of principles to get the information. There is a certain self-righteousness among evangelicals operating as activists in the social arena that is distasteful to the point of being appalling. Often, particularly in dealing with the so-called social issues of abortion and pornography, the evangelicals engage in words and actions that are violent in and of themselves. One kind of violence does not justify another kind of violence. Evangelical journalists need to demonstrate that the ways and means are as important as the objectives.

In many ways, although we have seen some small breakthroughs in how the mass media view religion, I have seen few breakthroughs in how the world of religion views the mass media.

In conclusion, is there any hope for a common ground between the secular reporter and the evangelical? I think there is. It falls in our common pursuit of truth. By truth I simply mean the heart or core of the story. And in this pursuit we are partners not antagonists.

NOTES

[1]Michael McIntyre, "Religionists on the Campaign Trail," *The Christian Century*, 27 December 1972, 1319–20.

[2]"Response." *UPI Log*, New York, 25 July 1970.

[3]Charles W. Colson, *Born Again* (Old Tappan: Chosen, 1976).

[4]Interview aboard press plane, sometime during the 1976 presidential campaign.

[5]Wesley G. Pippert, *The Spiritual Journey of Jimmy Carter* (New York: Macmillan, 1978).

[6]Speech to employees of the Department of Health, Education and Welfare, February 16, 1977. See *Public Papers of the President, Jimmy Carter, 1977* (Washington: Government Printing Office, 1977), 167.

[7]National Prayer Breakfast, January 27, 1977. See *Public Papers of the President, Jimmy Carter, 1977* (Washington: Government Printing Office, 1977), 25.

[8]Cal Thomas, "Not Ready for Prime-Time Prayers," *The Quill*, October 1986, 19.

[9]James M. Wall, "The Wacko Factor," *The Christian Century* 103 (June 1986): 635–63.

[10]Malcolm Muggeridge, *Christ and the Media* (London: Hodder and Stoughton, 1977), 30, 107.

[11]Personal correspondence. Pulliam is an editorial writer and columnist for the *Indianapolis News*.

[12]Results of the study have been published by Linda Lichter, S. Robert Lichter and Stanley Rothman, "Media and Business Elites," *Public Opinion*, October-November 1981: "The Media and Business: A Conflict of Classes," *Public Interest*, Fall 1982, 118–125, and "The Once and Future Journalists," *Washington Journalism Review*, December 1982, 26–27.

[13]Roy Howard Beck, *On Thin Ice: A Religion Reporter's Memoir* (Wilmore: Bristol, 1988).

Part V

THE INTERNATIONAL CONTEXT

13

THE GOSPEL ACCORDING TO THE UNITED STATES: EVANGELICAL BROADCASTING IN CENTRAL AMERICA

DENNIS A. SMITH

We all believe that we are not subject to the vagaries of ideology. We are normal. We know the truth. Ideology is responsible for confusing those who differ with us, especially foreigners. Ideology contaminates or distorts other peoples' ways of looking at the world. So goes the popular canard, especially among those of us raised in the United States.

Although United States citizens are world-famous for such ingenuousness, they are hardly alone when it comes to living life within a closed ideological circle. In reality, ideology enables people to achieve a sense of belonging and place in society, easing the burden imposed by the dominant political and economic system. Contrary to the narrow and self-justifying view of ideology accepted by most North Americans, ideology perpetuates and legitimates the dominant social system more than it offers an *objective* view of reality.[1] Educational systems, religious institutions, historical interpretations, and even popular news reports all bear ideology. François Chatelet argues,

> An ideology is a cultural formation (implicit) or a cultural production (explicit) that expresses the point of view of a social class or caste; such a point of view concerns a person's relations with nature, imagination, others, and with himself. Ideology presents itself as having a universal validity; but in reality it not only expresses a particular point of view, but it

also tends to mask its particularity by proposing compensations and imaginary or fleeting solutions.[2]

Ideology's function, then, is to paper over the essential contradictions of a political and economic system: divisions such as those based on class, sex, race, or age, or the system's skewed distribution of opportunity, resources, and power. Ideology can create in us a false consciousness, giving us the illusion of understanding that which we do not understand and of explaining that which is beyond our grasp. The media, in particular, create the public belief that a nation's own particular approach to politics, economics, or religion is the norm and that nations holding other views are misguided or even dangerous rivals.

Under the spell of popular and pervasive ideology, evangelicals in the United States are frequently nurtured on the following over-simplifications and distortions: (1) Spiritual matters are distinct from and more important than material matters, such as health care or food distribution, unless the latter are used to lead people to Christ. (2) Communists are cruel, opportunistic, violent atheists. (3) All social and political problems can be solved through individual initiative and ingenuity, free enterprise, scientific research, and technological invention. (4) The only sure cure for such deep-seated social ills as violence, injustice, poverty, and oppression is for individuals to experience a saving, personal encounter with Jesus Christ. (5) God chose and blessed the United States to be a "light unto the nations." (6) The United States, therefore, has a special responsibility to share its culture, technology, religion, and political and economic system with the entire world. (7) White Christian citizens of the United States are peaceful, whereas Moslems, Communists, and Third World peoples are violent. (8) Poverty results from the laziness of poor people who squander their resources on vice. Most Protestant missionaries who have worked in Central America in recent decades, especially those in the broadcast media, came out of this type of ideological background. As we shall see, this has shaped the impact of religious broadcasting in Central America.

CENTRAL AMERICAN EVANGELICALS

In Central America, the most commonly used term for Protestant is *evangélico*, indicating their historic affinity with the evangelical and fundamentalist communities in the United States. The first five Protestant groups to establish mission efforts in Guatemala, the first Central American country to be targeted by U.S. Protestant missions, were the Presbyterians, the Central American Mission, the California Meeting of Friends, the Nazarenes, and the Primitive Methodists. None of them were theological liberals or social activists. These denominations form the nucleus of Guatemala's historic Protestantism. None of these denominations have advocated social justice and progressive political causes in Guatemalan society frequently associated with mainline Protestantism in the United States.

Especially influential throughout the region has been the dispensational theology developed at Dallas Theological Seminary in Texas. The influential Central American Mission is a product of Dallas Seminary, and dispensationalism has been its special contribution to theological reflection in Central America. These dispensationalists divide history into seven time periods, or dispensations, during each of which "man is tested in respect to his obedience to some specific revelation of the will of God."[3] Humankind is now in the dispensation of the Church, also known as the dispensation of Grace, when the church's task is the Great Commission (Mark 16:15, Acts 1:8). According to this scenario, Christians must quickly present the gospel to all the individuals on the planet because Christ's second coming is imminent. When Jesus returns, those who have not accepted the free gift of salvation will be condemned for eternity.

Moreover, the dispensationalists often hold that it is useless or even heretical for the church to engage in other labors such as a prophetic witness against social injustice. After all, Jesus will bring in perfect justice and lasting peace when he inaugurates the dispensation of the Kingdom with his second coming. In any case, human efforts to establish justice and well-being are but a pale reflection of the real thing, which only God can manage. One of the more well-known dispensationalists in Central America is North American television preacher Jimmy Swaggart, who has led numerous revivals in the area and has funded various missions and Christian schools. Dispensationalism is far more influential in Central American evangelicalism than is Calvinism or Reformed theology, even in the region's Presbyterian and Reformed churches.

Another formative element of the Protestant experience in Central America is its informal alliance with a school of politics and economics known as liberalism, a nineteenth-century precursor of modern capitalism built upon positivism and social Darwinism. Liberals saw themselves as the enlightened and progressive alternative to the more traditional conservatives. Under conservative regimes, the Roman Catholic church was entrusted with overseeing the cultural, educational, and moral well-being of society. In the process, the Catholic church had become one of the region's largest landholders and was highly influential in regional politics. The liberals, while not anti-Catholic per se, were decidedly anticlerical. Guatemalan history provides a graphic illustration. After taking power in 1872, liberal dictator Justo Rufino Barrios secularized the national university, prohibited religious processions, prevented priests from using clerical garb in public, and expelled some religious orders. The Archbishop responded by excommunicating Barrios. Not to be outdone, Barrios expelled the Archbishop. The Liberal party newspaper declared that the new state religion was the "religion of duty, the religion of work."[4]

In 1882, President Barrios personally invited the first Protestant missionary to Guatemala. Presbyterian missionary Rev. John Clark Hill arrived in Guatemala on November 2, 1882 as part of Barrios' personal entourage when the President returned from a visit to New York. He then deeded the Presbyterians a piece of land just across from the Roman Catholic cathedral in Guatemala City. This plot became the site of Central Presbyterian Church. As one might expect, relations between Catholics and Protestants in Central America have been strained since the Presbyterians arrived. Not only have the two churches been associated with competing political parties, but Central American evangelicals have historically dismissed Catholics as quasi-pagans mired in syncretism and idolatry. Protestant evangelistic efforts are still directed principally toward the Catholic community. Indeed, many Central American Protestants use "Christian" as a synonym for "evangelical."

Evangelicals interpreted the anticlericalism of the liberals as a special sign of God's blessing. They even viewed the relative freedom granted them by the liberals to organize churches, worship publicly, proselytize, and administer religious institutions, despite conservative Catholic opposition, as a sign of divine intervention on their behalf. These Protestants also overlooked the social injustice, corruption, and violence upon which the liberal dictators built their rule. Describing themselves as being apolitical, they emphasized the saving of souls. This tendency was reinforced when those local church leaders who ran for public office frequently were contaminated by the reigning structure. Since the system was based on corruption, violence, and injustice, many church leaders who dabbled in politics abused their authority and forsook the evangelicals' pietistic moral code; such was the accepted route to political success and personal gain.

Since World War II, Central American Protestants have added a hearty dose of McCarthyist anticommunism to their political convictions. This tendency was reinforced when China was closed to Christian missions after Mao Tse-tung rose to power in 1949. Most evangelicals still sense no inherent contradiction between being rabidly anticommunist and claiming to be apolitical. In more recent years, especially since the Sandinistas came to power in Nicaragua in 1979, some Central American evangelicals have said that silence in the midst of violence, oppression, and injustice is hardly apolitical. The historic quid pro quo with the liberals, they argue, expresses a very clear political option.

EVANGELICALISM DIVIDED

The basic divisions among Central American evangelicals are more style than substance: most evangelicals accept the basic tenets of fundamentalist doctrine; most are fascinated with doomsday eschatology; most consider themselves to be both anticommunist and apolitical; most are more concerned with "pie-in-the-sky by-and-by" than with "the nasty now-and-now," although many now recognize that curative medicine, education, and even rural development projects can be useful proselytizing tools.

However, there are important differences in belief about the Holy Spirit. Traditional evangelicals don't trust the emotional catharsis associated with Pentecostalism. This division goes back to the early 1930s when one of the Primitive Methodist missionaries in the western highlands of Guatemala turned out to be a Pentecostal. He began what is now one of the region's largest and most influential denominations, the Iglesia de Dios - Evangélio Completo (related to the Church of God, Cleveland, Tenn.). Today church and denominational schisms occur over such apparently superficial issues as hand-clapping and guitars—especially electric ones. Traditionalists consider these to be clear steps on the path to faith healing, shouted sermons, and glossolalia. Such issues are often only the surface justification given for splits generated by power struggles and personality clashes. While evangelicalism has achieved a remarkable following in the region, the movement has always been plagued with the factionalism generated by a strong emphasis on individualism and authoritarian leadership.

Pentecostals are divided between traditional Pentecostals and neo-pentecostals. Informed observers note a variety of differences between the two:[5] (1) Traditional Pentecostals tend to have a significant presence in the rural areas while neo-pentecostals are more concentrated in population centers. (2) Traditional Pentecostals are concentrated among the poorer sectors of the population, whereas the neo-pentecostals have made significant inroads among middle-class professionals and working-class people who are struggling to be upwardly mobile. (3) Traditional Pentecostals deny the ultimate importance of their material existence, while neo-pentecostals tend to be highly materialistic. (4) Traditional Pentecostals form traditionally organized denominations, whereas neo-pentecostals organize around strong charismatic leaders. (5) Traditional Pentecostals train their leaders in local Bible institutes, which are frequently directed by nationals, whereas neo-pentecostals frequently depend on outsiders, especially from the U.S., for doctrinal orientation. (6) Traditional Pentecostals proselytize chiefly among Catholics, whereas neo-pentecostals frequently proselytize among other evangelical groups. (7) Traditional Pentecostal worship, although frequently emotional, seldom reaches such exotic realms as "dancing in the spirit" and "holy laughter" explored by the neo-pentecostals. (8) Traditional Pentecostals are significantly more open to ecumenical relationships with other evangelical denominations.

Neo-pentecostals have been heavily influenced by the "health-and-wealth" gospel from the United States that claims that God wants all people to be healthy and wealthy. Those who are not, they say, lack faith or live in sin. This theology apparently comforts middle-class believers and legitimizes their privileged position in a desperately polarized society. It also stimulates upwardly mobile evangelicals as they battle to survive in an intensely competitive and unforgiving economic environment. As I will show, religious broadcasting is an important influence on the development of such popular theology. As in the United States, public expressions of religious faith shape private belief.

The evangelical presence in Central America is statistically significant, although data are not thoroughly reliable. As of July, 1987, 31.6 percent of the Guatemalan population was evangelical. For Honduras, the 1985 estimate was 11.7 percent. In Costa Rica, one-fifth of the population was evangelical in 1988. The most recently published data for the remaining countries, which go back to the late seventies, credit Nicaragua with 2.5 percent and El Salvador with 6.5 percent. Both countries are now believed to be in the 10–15 percent range.[6] No one is quite sure just how many evangelical denominations currently exist in Central America. At latest count, Guatemala had about three hundred. Some one hundred of those had one thousand or more members. About two hundred had one thousand or fewer members. I would guess that about 20 percent of Central American evangelicals are historic traditionalists, 40 percent traditional Pentecostals, and 40 percent neopentecostals. Included with the traditionalists are a few liturgical and ecumenically oriented Protestants such as the Anglicans and Lutherans.

THE ARRIVAL OF RELIGIOUS BROADCASTERS

Evangelical religious broadcasting began in Central America shortly after World War II. Radio Station TIFC in San José, Costa Rica (Radio *Faro del Caribe*) was established in 1948 by the Latin American Mission. Station TGN in Guatemala (Radio *Cultural*) was established in 1950 by the Central American Mission. Then came Radio *Ondas de Luz* in Managua in 1959, *La Voz Evangélica de Honduras* in Tegucigalpa in 1960, and Radio *Progreso* in San Salvador in 1963. There are about eighteen evangelical radio stations in Central America, plus an undetermined number of commercial stations with largely evangelical programming.

A pressing reason for evangelical investment in the broadcast media was to create a new platform from which to battle with the Catholics. For example, Radio *Ondas de Luz* in Managua, Nicaragua opens the book honoring its twenty-fifth anniversary by stating,

Since the Gospel came to Nicaragua, it has suffered great persecution, principally from the Roman Catholic Church:

calumnies, offenses, assaults against persons and churches, etc. The spoken and written press have not lost an occasion to launch improprieties and calumnies against the Cause of Christ; but we had no means of defense, for, although we protested or wrote, no one attended to us. The broadcast media were closed to us; but were always open to our detractors.[7]

But the principal motive for religious broadcasting was highly practical: radio might reach more individuals with the gospel than would ever be possible through traditional missionary work. And in a region where illiteracy was (and is) the norm, radio could reach people inaccessible through the printed word and people into whose language the Bible had not yet been translated. Today the vast majority of Central Americans listen to radio. Most town and city dwellers, rich and poor, also watch television. Consequently, evangelists believe that religious media programming is the most cost-effective way to reach the population. In this context, evangelism is viewed largely as an engineering problem and the electronic media are viewed as God-given gadgets uniquely equipped to provide a technical solution. Here, too, the influence of the United States is unmistakable. Schultze's description of the situation in the United States mirrors later developments in Central America.

> Largely because of their theological commitments, especially their eschatology and proselytism, evangelicals frequently attributed great spiritual significance to broadcasting technologies. If the Second Coming of Jesus Christ were imminent, as conservative Protestants increasingly believed. . . , there was no time to waste and no technology to overlook in the task of global evangelism; millions of unsaved souls would soon perish. Evangelicals projected American technological optimism onto their view of radio and later television.[8]

Following the tradition of North American mass evangelists, Central American religious broadcasters defined religious conversion in technical, marketing-oriented terms. Evangelism became little more than getting individuals to respond to a short theological laundry list similar to the following: (1) Do you believe you are a sinner? (2) Do you believe God loves you and wants to save you? (3) Do you believe that Jesus is God's Son and that He died for your sins? (4) Are you willing to confess your sin, ask God for forgiveness, and ask Jesus to be your Lord and Savior? If the listener or viewer understood the questions and was able to respond, either affirmatively or negatively, he was considered evangelized. If the person who responded affirmatively also repeated a short prayer, he was considered saved.

Thus, in Central America the religious media, as well as the general media, have been organized according to the model established in the United States. The principal purpose of the media is to propagate a consumerist mentality. The media are organized vertically, with those who transmit messages exercising almost complete control over programming, and the receiving public left with the limited choice of whether or not to tune in or, if they do, whether to accept or reject the program content. These media do not promote a critical or communal consciousness in the audience, regardless of whether they are religious or strictly commercial media. On the contrary, they praise individualism, unquestioning obedience to authority, and conspicuous consumption.

In recent years a variety of critics have begun to question whether the broadcast media as currently organized in both the U.S. and Central America can faithfully transmit the gospel message. Baptist theologian Harvey Cox observes,

> God comes (to humankind) in weakness, vulnerability and impotence. The very organization of the mass media makes them powerful, virtually immune to response and frightfully capable of weaving a world of deceit and triviality around the heads of their victims. . . . A gospel presented in a context that contradicts the Gospel ceases to be the Gospel. One can't speak to a person of Christ (although many have done so) when that person is threatened at the point of a sword. One can't communicate a message of love and reciprocity while talking to someone who can't answer.[9]

Brazilian sociologist and theologian Hugo Assman takes the criticism a step further by noting the apparent ideological ties between religious broadcasting and civil religion in a consumer society.

> In general media programming, religion is often alluded to or invoked explicitly. . . . This persuasive religion, which penetrates all the moments of life, must be taken seriously and analyzed critically. We suspect that a strange interventionist god is at work here: a Destiny god; an "It is God's Will" god; a Lottery god, a god of the arbitrary. Could it not be possible that religious programs actually work in complicity with this god who helps score goals for the local football team?

. . . .When a distorted Christianity penetrates into the pores of an oppressive system and becomes part of that system's glands, to speak of religion is a very risky and dangerous business. We may suddenly find ourselves having become allies with that which we had wanted to change.[10]

CONTEMPORARY RELIGIOUS BROADCASTING IN CENTRAL AMERICA

Beginning in the 1960s Central American evangelicalism grew rapidly. U.S. evangelists such as Billy Graham, Luis Palau, and Paul Finkenbinder began organizing mass evangelistic campaigns supplemented extensively by radio, television, and film. As in the U.S., these evangelists adapted the gospel to the dominant characteristics of the media. They attractively and persuasively packaged the gospel like a consumer product, assuming that the Christian faith could be reduced to a simple formula and that evangelism consisted of persuading individuals to repeat and accept that formula. The result was an explosion of people who considered themselves evangelicals. But as in the case of brand loyalty in mass marketing, it was not altogether clear whether the new converts were really committed to the faith. Evangelical pastors generally agree that relatively few converts actually become regular church members as a result of evangelistic crusades, radio, or television. In fact, the vast majority of the audiences, perhaps over 90 percent, are already evangelicals. Thus, the media function religiously largely as revivalism, not evangelism. However, the media have increased the general public's awareness of evangelicalism, perhaps making it a more socially acceptable personal belief system.

More recently, though, radio revivalism has created a boomerang effect as the general public responds negatively to a new genre of aspiring evangelists. The vast majority of radio programs now aired in the region are not produced by United States–sponsored evangelists, but by local preachers with little or no technical training. These instant radio evangelists either broadcast live or produce their shows at home with poor quality portable cassette recorders. Scripts are virtually unknown. Rehearsal is frowned upon since it might quench the spontaneous leading of the Holy Spirit. At least half of a typical program is devoted to greeting donors by name or reviewing the preacher's past or future speaking schedule. The format then settles down to a predictable sequence of hymn-prayer-sermon-hymn. Sermons are often vitriolic attacks on Catholics and especially charismatics, who are characterized as Catholics slyly pretending to be evangelicals. Competing radio preachers or rival denominations are also frequent targets. Since the programs are often live, many of the amateur orators preach about the theme presented in the preceding show, forcefully correcting the so-called doctrinal errors of their predecessor on the same station. The climax almost always includes an extended altar call, which may not have anything to do with the theme of the day, supposing there was a theme. The conclusion usually includes an urgent appeal for funds.

Amazingly, such radio revivalists justify their shows to the local evangelical community as evangelism. Not so surprisingly, few nonevangelicals tune in to these programs. One dubious achievement is that "The Evangelical Radio Preacher" now forms as much a part of the region's humorous folklore as "The Peasant Who Visits the Big City" and "The Lascivious Priest." There is, for instance, the Nicaraguan evangelist who declared to his radio audience that at his upcoming evangelistic campaign women would be allowed in only if they were not wearing pants. Yet religious and commercial stations continue to air these programs by the dozen, back-to-back and at all hours. Commercial stations have found them to be a lucrative way to fill the pre-dawn hours.

The radio stations operated by the traditional evangelical sector, especially Radio *Faro del Caribe* in San José, Costa Rica and Radio *Cultural* in Guatemala, are important exceptions to the above characterization. These stations have relatively high technical standards and dedicate large blocks of their program schedule to easy-listening music interspaced with short evangelistic and pre-evangelistic programs such as those produced by Hermano Pablo and Luis Palau. This low-profile program approach is targeted mostly toward the urban middle-class audience. Creative and technical interchange between the traditionalists and the new revivalists has been minimal, largely due to the deep divisions within the evangelical community.

The influences of U.S. evangelicalism and the U.S. broadcasting system on the local radio zealots is unmistakable. First, the local radio preachers are clearly entrepreneurs following the U.S. tradition of strong, charismatic, male-dominated religious programming. Second, the programs do not question the political or economic status quo. God is presented as being far more concerned with eschatology than with present human suffering or injustice. Third, the radio preachers are naïvely fascinated with technology as a means of gaining access to a broader audience. They give little thought to the medium's impact upon the message. Fourth, funds are raised by justifying the broadcasts as evangelistic tools despite the fact that little critical thought is given to what evangelism means, especially when most of the audience is evangelical.

In 1984 the Latin America-Caribbean region of the World Association for Christian Communication held a conference in Conocoto, Ecuador, to analyze the content of religious radio programs from throughout Latin America. The programs studied were technically superior to those produced by the revivalists described above, but their content was similar. The conference participants identified the following program characteristics:

1. Most programs seem to be directed toward middle-class urban adults who are already familiar with evangelical jargon.

2. They usually present a "magician Christ" who solves all the problems of those who have faith in him.

3. The shows emphasize death more than life, the individual more than the community, the spiritual world more than the material world.

4. Christians and the church are treated in an idealized way that tends to disregard the fact that they have not yet attained perfection.

5. Programs frequently propagandize for the sponsoring institution more than they evangelize.

6. Programs frequently attempt to manipulate the audience through constant references to personal conflict, sickness, loneliness, and other crisis situations.

7. Most programs ignore the daily context of the listening audience.

8. Many programs are more concerned with style and form than with substance.

9. Most programs are modeled on imported formats alien to the local context, negating local cultural values and national identity.

10. The church is usually presented as a hierarchical and paternalistic institution concerned mostly with fundraising.

Central American evangelicals have little experience in religious television broadcasting. Production and program-time costs, as well as limited access to technical training, have restricted religious television in the region largely to programs produced by U.S. televangelists who buy time on commercial stations for their U.S.–produced shows. Guatemala City and San Jose, Costa Rica have the region's only evangelical television station. Guatemala City's Channel 21 relies heavily on the Trinity Broadcasting System in Southern California for funding and programming. Since most Guatemala City TV viewers lack the necessary loop antenna to pick up a UHF signal, Channel 21's viewing audience is limited almost exclusively to the evangelical community; the station's daily program schedule is not even carried in the local newspapers with all the others. San Jose's evangelical TV station is new, but it appears to be based on the same type of model. Similar evangelical TV projects are reportedly planned for El Salvador and Honduras.

The only locally based Central American TV preacher to establish a following in the region is Guatemalan Catholic lay evangelist Salvador Gómez. Gómez began as a Catholic seminarian, left the Roman church for one of the large neo-pentecostal groups (Elim) for a few years, and was eventually wooed back to the Catholic Church where he began his "*Ministerio Trigo.*" His enthusiastic style and fervent affirmation of Catholic doctrine are apparently designed to keep Catholics from taking the leap into Pentecostal pastures. Although his program is not yet available throughout the region, he is becoming widely known and travels throughout Central America.

THE IMPACT OF U.S. MEDIA EVANGELISTS

Despite the scandals in 1987 and 1988 involving U.S. televangelists Jim Bakker and Jimmy Swaggart, North American evangelists still command an important following in the region. The amateurish content and production quality of most of the local programs make the U.S. imports especially attractive, despite the "peccadilloes" of their stars. Swaggart's widely broadcast public confession, in which he tearfully asked God and his followers for forgiveness for unspecified sins, maintained the marketability of his programs in the region though without the same popularity.

Prior to the scandals, in 1985, the Latin American Evangelical Center for Pastoral Studies, known by its Spanish acronym as CELEP, coordinated a study of the impact of religious programming in the electronic media on the active Christian population in Central America. They asked 1,188 Christians from four Central American countries how they felt about selected evangelical programs broadcast on radio and TV. The two radio programs studied were "Luis Palau Responds" and "A Message to the Conscience" with Hermano Pablo. The TV programs were the Spanish versions of "PTL Club" and "Jimmy Swaggart." The sample of active church-goers was about two-thirds Protestant and one-third Catholic; 79 percent of those interviewed attended church at least once a week. In the sample, 94 percent had access to local radio and 35 percent had access to shortwave radio. Nearly 79 percent had access to a television set.

The results of the study suggest much about the popularity and significance of the religious broadcasting celebrities in Central America. Almost three-quarters of the Central American Christians had watched or listened to Jimmy Swaggart— more than any other media evangelist. Hermano Pablo was next (65%) followed by Luis Palau (59%) and the "PTL Club" (52%). Swaggart also had the highest weekly audience (37% of the sample), followed by Pablo (35%), the "PTL Club" (33%), and Palau (30%). Central American Christians generally felt that the media celebrities merited their trust; about 40 percent said so for Swaggart, Pablo, and Palau. Only the "PTL Club" elicited a significantly lower trust level (24%).

Most revealing, perhaps, was the perceived usefulness of the programs in the daily lives of Central American Christians. In all four countries, Swaggart's teachings are perceived by 70 percent of the sample as being more useful than those received in the local church. On the other hand, only 9 percent said the same for Pablo, 7 percent for Palau, and 5 percent for "PTL Club." Moreover, the viewers and listeners clearly felt that the selected programs had positive impact on their lives: Swaggart (41%), Pablo (41%), Palau (35%), and the "PTL Club" (22%). The vast majority of these people characterized the positive impact as pastoral support, using such terms as "spiritual blessing," "consolation," "advice," "healing" and "family life." Only 4 percent of the sample (48 out of 1,188) claimed to have been converted as a result of the programs.

Especially notable in the CELEP study is that Swaggart, despite his clear Pentecostalism, had penetrated not only the traditional Pentecostal and neo-pentecostal sectors, but also the traditional evangelicals and Roman Catholics. This is especially interesting in the light of the continued bitter rejection of Pentecostal liturgy by traditional evangelicals and the Roman Catholic preaching against the TV preachers. Although the Roman Catholic Church has even countered Swaggart's broadcasts with its own locally produced charismatic-style TV programs, there is little evidence that the Catholic media efforts are stemming Swaggart's tide. No single Catholic radio or television program is transmitted throughout the region, so a comparative study is not possible. Salvador Gómez's TV program might become the first Catholic show available throughout Central America.

The disparity in the CELEP study between the *usefulness* of the programs and the *trustworthiness* of the media evangelists suggests that this programming is not fundamentally religious instruction or worship, but entertainment. Because most active churchgoers in Central America are poor, their daily existence is devoted almost entirely to the struggle to produce enough to survive. They have very limited time and resources to invest in entertainment. Evangelicals are at an added disadvantage since their rigid pietism frequently excludes many ordinary diversions such as movie-going, dancing, playing soccer, and drinking alcoholic beverages. Even watching TV is a suspect, although universally practiced, diversion. Swaggart, being both a rousing preacher and a master showman, permits a rather strait-laced audience to feel good about feeling good. Swaggart is simply more entertaining than most Central American clergy; on top of that, his programs legitimize TV viewing.

Compared with most Central American worship services, Swaggart's program is very impressive. Most local evangelical pastors have less than a secondary education, and their wages are usually below subsistence levels, leaving them little choice but to seek outside employment to supplement their meager income. Few churches can offer dramatic charisma and carefully honed homilies. Since most preachers are responsible for at least three sermons and several Bible classes each week, on top of other employment, they cannot compete with the carefully crafted, visually stunning, highly engaging programs of someone such as Swaggart. Even in the relatively affluent churches with trained pastors, the worship service cannot be approached with the care and precision of a television program with a multi-million dollar budget. In a real local church, the faithful are exposed to all the human foibles of their pastors and of each other. Such is not the case on television. In Central America, many local churches and pastors are losing the entertainment war with Swaggart & Co in spite of the scandals. The market has such broadcasts solidly established regardless of what happens to any particular radio or television evangelist.

Beyond the entertainment battle, however, lies a deeper and more distressing reality: many of the churches in Central America are simply not meeting the pastoral needs of the people. The electronic church is partially filling a void created by the local churches. As already mentioned, pastors lack training and resources. Also, Christians are deeply and bitterly divided between evangelicals and Catholics, Pentecostals and traditional evangelicals, traditional Pentecostals and neo-pentecostals. Strangest of all, in a bizarre twist of ecclesiastical history, evangelicals are falling into a kind of pre–Vatican II clericalism and superstition. Once they made a career out of accusing pre–Vatican II priests of hiding the Bible from the common people and replacing it with distorted teaching and superstition. Now many evangelicals, in spite of their high regard for the Bible as the exclusive, unquestioned, and literally interpreted guide to faith, are increasingly reticent to interpret the Scriptures without specific guidelines provided by some authority figure. They look to pastors, media preachers, or *gringo* missionaries to tell them what the Bible means, for fear of falling into doctrinal error. In many evangelical homes the Bible is essentially a prominently displayed fetish believed to have quasi-magical powers. The book is often open to a Psalm or other passage that has been recommended by an authority figure as being especially effective in attracting blessing to the home. On the other hand, Roman Catholics, especially those organized in Base Ecclesial Communities, are more likely to engage in contextualized biblical reflection. Such reflection is usually dismissed by evangelicals as being a politicized distortion of the true faith.

After Vatican II, Latin America's Roman Catholic bishops returned from Rome to try to implement profound reforms in one of the world's most conservative, oppressive, and authoritarian ecclesiastical structures. As they met in Medellin, Colombia, in 1968 to map out their task, they came to a very disturbing conclusion. Somewhere in the shuffle of five centuries of ministry, their church had lost the essence of the gospel. Their task, then, was to re-evangelize their church with the gospel of Jesus. Perhaps evangelicalism in Central America will have to undergo a similarly painful process.

After one hundred years of Protestant mission activity and forty years of evangelical religious broadcasting, Central America now has a large number of people who identify themselves as evangelicals. Many sincere people point to transformed personal lives, miraculous healing and material blessings as the fruits of the gospel. But not all the fruits have been sweet. Bitter sectarianism, isolationism, individualism, crass materialism, and alienation from the historical processes at work in society are also characteristic of Central American evangelicals.

What responsibility do evangelical broadcasters bear for these bitter fruits? Some, certainly, but I suspect that broadcasters have mostly exacerbated tendencies already built into the ideological superstructure. The best that can be said is that evangelical broadcasters in Central America have been an unreflective part of the problem, not part of the solution.

NOTES

[1]Echeverria and Castillo, "Elementos para la teoria de la ideologia" in *Ideologia y Medios de Comunicación*, ed. Martinez (Buenos Aires: Amorrotu Editores, 1973–74), 14–15.

[2]J. P. Siméon, "Penseé et idéologie," *Esprit* 1 (1972): 31, quoted by Henri Mottu in *The Bible and Liberation: Political and Social Hermeneutics* ed. Norman K. Gottwald (New York: Orbis Books, 1983), 239.

[3]C. I. Scofield, ed., *The New Scofield Reference Bible* (New York: Oxford University Press, 1967), 3.

[4]Jim Handy, *Gift of the Devil: A History of Guatemala* (Boston: South End Press, 1984), 61–63.

[5]Rev. Gilberto Flores (Interview by author, 1 September 1988. Tape recording, Conference of Evangelical Churches of Guatemala [CIEDEG], Guatemala City).

[6]Cliff Holland (Telephone interview by author, *Instituto Misionlógico de las Americas* [IMDELA], San José, Costa Rica, 2 September 1988).

[7]Agustin Ruiz, *Bodas de plata: 25 años en el aire y en el corazón*, trans. Dennis Smith (Managua, Nicaragua: Radio YNOL, 1983), 5.

[8]Quentin J. Schultze, "The Mythos of the Electronic Church," *Critical Studies in Mass Communication*, 4 (1987): 248.

[9]Harvey Cox, "Can the Mass Media Communicate the Gospel?" *The American Baptist* and *Canadian Baptist* joint anniversary issue, retrans., Dennis Smith, 1980.

[10]Hugo Assman, *La iglesia electrónica y su impacto en América Latina*, trans. Dennis Smith (San José, Costa Rica: Editorial DEI, 1987), 127–28.

14

SAVING THE WORLD? AMERICAN EVANGELICALS AND TRANSNATIONAL BROADCASTING

ROBERT S. FORTNER

It is not entirely clear when international radio broadcasting began. The Soviet Union began a domestic shortwave service, for instance, in 1917, which could be heard in central Europe. The Belgians apparently put "wireless concerts" on shortwave as early as 1914, but the experiment was cut short by the outbreak of World War I. The Soviets also intentionally broadcast to other countries in 1927, during the tenth celebration of the Russian Revolution, but these broadcasts, which were aired in foreign languages, ceased at the end of the scheduled events. The Dutch began the first regularly scheduled noninterrupted international radio program in 1927, and were soon joined by Germany (1929), France (1931), the United Kingdom (1932), and Japan (1934). International religious and commercial broadcasters also got an early start, with American commercial broadcasters beginning in 1923, and religious broadcasters in 1931.

Radio Vatican was the first international religious broadcasting operation to take to the air, inaugurating its service on transmitters provided by Guglielmo Marconi in February 1931. Evangelical and missionary radio began a few months later when HCJB, the "Voice of the Andes," began operating from Quito, Ecuador, in December. The Far East Broadcasting Company, Inc., was established in 1945. In 1951 missionaries began the Pacific Broadcasting Association to evangelize the

Japanese. Three years later Dr. Paul Freed began The Voice of Tangier, which developed into Trans World Radio.[1]

During their nearly six decades of operation, religious broadcasters have become the largest single category of international radio users, broadcasting more hours per week in more languages than any other transnational services. In addition to HCJB, operated by the World Radio Missionary Fellowship, Inc., Trans World Radio (TWR) operates transmitters in Monte Carlo, Cyprus, Netherlands Antilles, Swaziland, Sri Lanka, Guam, and Uruguay. Two sister organizations, Far East Broadcasting Association (UK) and Far East Broadcasting Company, Inc. (USA), operate facilities in the Seychelles (FEBA) and the Philippines, South Korea, Mariana Islands, and the United States (FEBC). Other smaller broadcasters or program-producing organizations include the Pacific Broadcasting Association (Japan), various "national partners" of TWR, including *Evangeliums-Rundfunk* (West Germany) and Norea Radio (Norway), IBRA Radio AB (Sweden), Radio ELWA (USA, operating in Liberia), CAM International (USA, operating in Guatemala), the Evangelical Alliance Mission (USA, operating in South Korea and Peru), World Radio Bible Broadcasts (USA), World Christian Broadcasting Corporation (USA), and LeSea Broadcasting Corporation, Inc. (USA).[2] Even this list does not include all the evangelical or national program producers, or operators of stations within individual countries. These organizations together produce and transmit over twenty thousand hours per month of evangelical Christian radio programs worldwide in over 125 languages.

Table 1

Comparison of Major International Radio Services

Service	Number of Languages	Hours per Month
Voice of America	42	9,644
FEBA/FEBC	106	9,000
Radio Moscow	82	8,916
TWR	80	4,000
British Broadcasting Corporation	37	2,932
HCJB	14	2,130

The "Big Five" international radio organizations—ELWA,

FEBA, FEBC, TWR, and HCJB—engage in many cooperative ventures, often airing each other's programs, participating in or purchasing audience research data from other organizations, such as the British Broadcasting Corporation (BBC) World Service, and joining forces in major evangelistic efforts, such as the current goal to deliver the Gospel by radio in every major world language by the year 2000.

THE DIFFICULTIES OF CROSS-CULTURAL BROADCASTING

It seems fairly simple to many evangelicals to proclaim the Gospel on radio. Believing that there is power in the Word of God, many undoubtedly assume that evangelism will succeed simply if the Word is proclaimed in languages appropriate to a particular country or region. One TWR pamphlet proclaims, for instance, that

> radio is vital to mission work. Ever since Christ instructed his people to reach the uttermost part of the earth, the challenge has become greater and greater. . . . Broadcasting the Good News of Jesus Christ, Trans World Radio penetrates with its programmes into areas that would have been otherwise inaccessible. When creating the universe, God provided for this possibility. Reaching the world with the gospel requires radio.[3]

Such technological optimism has long been a staple in missionary work dependent on media. Unfortunately, it is not that simple. A variety of constraints can influence the rooting of the Gospel cross-culturally, regardless of the "power" assumed to inhere within "God-given" technologies. Although evangelicals dominate international broadcasting in terms of hours broadcast and the number of languages used, the size of their audiences is remarkably small, particularly when compared with commercial, state-run, and independent international broadcasters. Constraints on missionary proclamation include technical, cultural, politico-economic, and missiological limitations.

TECHNICAL CONSTRAINTS TO CROSS-CULTURAL RADIO EVANGELISM

Perhaps the most obvious, yet least well understood, technical impediment to radio evangelism outside the industrial

West is the availability of appropriate reception apparatus. Although radio evangelism can use any wave band (medium frequency or very high frequency bands being those in common use in the United Sates), most international radio uses high frequency, or shortwave, bands. FEBC, for instance, operates thirty-seven separate radio transmitters, thirteen of which are shortwave. Total broadcasting power for these shortwave transmitters is twelve hundred kilowatts, which, by comparison, is twenty-four times as much power as the largest U.S. clear channel AM radio stations produce.[4] Trans World Radio's Monte Carlo transmitters alone generate over two million watts of power. Power of this magnitude (the largest shortwave transmitters now generate 500 kw) allows signals to be carried great distances, crossing oceans and continents to seek audiences in specified target areas.

The shortwave bands, however, are subject to a large amount of natural and man-made interference, and their ability to carry (or propagate) radio signals depends on the time of day, the season of the year, and the sunspot cycle. People's ability to receive shortwave signals also depends on the amount of atmospheric noise the signals must travel through, and the man-made interference and natural noise present in their area. Thus, many international broadcasters, such as the Voice of America (VOA) and the BBC, use multiple frequencies to carry their signals into designated target areas, because engineers can never be sure precisely which frequency or propagation path will provide the best quality signal to the potential listener. International religious broadcasters (IRBs) do not typically use this approach, however, as they seek to maximize audiences by broadcasting in as many languages as possible, rather than covering given audiences with multiple signals.* It is thus more difficult for potential listeners to locate IRB signals than those of say, VOA or the BBC.

Also, the shortwave bands have grown increasingly crowded since the end of World War II as not only religious broadcasters, but a growing number of governments have used these frequencies for either domestic or international services.

---

*For the sake of economy, I will refer to international religious broadcasters as IRBs. The reader should understand that this acronym refers only to transmitting organizations, the most prominent being ELWA, FEBA, FEBC, HCJB, and TWR.

Many of the national domestic radio services in sub-Saharan Africa still use shortwave, since its propagation characteristics allow them to provide national coverage with a minimum of capital investment in transmitters and antennas. Lack of multiple-frequency coverage, atmospheric interference, and crowding of the shortwave bands thus complicates the task of IRBs and their listeners. IRB signals may simply not be sufficiently powerful to overcome the propagation obstacles.

Perhaps even more basic, the distribution of radio receivers with shortwave capability is uneven, and not all shortwave-capable sets can detect all shortwave frequencies. In India, for instance, only about 10 percent of all households have radios of any kind. In South Africa, the white government has established local VHF (FM) radio stations for the majority black population, so few blacks own shortwave receivers. In some countries, such as Zimbabwe, domestic shortwave services are being phased out in favor of VHF (FM), which will result in even fewer shortwave receivers in that country a decade from now. A study completed by the Voice of America research department showed that not all shortwave sets include all shortwave bands, which means that the size of the potential audience for a program depends on the frequency used to deliver the signal.[5] Also, because of international debt problems, many countries in South America and Africa have been unable to import the quantities of radio receivers needed to replace aging sets, so the numbers available for use have been dwindling since 1982. This problem will probably get worse if the debt crisis does not ease, because the rapid population growth in these regions suggests that the number of households in these countries will increase much more rapidly than the ability of countries to import consumer technology. This will make it more difficult for international broadcasters to maintain their current levels of household penetration.[6]

A related technical impediment is the competitive milieu within which international radio services function. When shortwave began its rapid growth after World War II, it had little competition, even from domestic radio services, in many parts of the world. In the United States, for instance, there were only 1,005 radio stations on the air (including fifty-seven FM stations) in 1946, compared with over ten thousand today. Television barely existed, with only six American stations operational in 1946, compared with the current total of over twelve hundred.[7]

Gradually the newly independent countries of Africa, the Middle East, and Asia established radio and, sometimes, television systems, requiring international radio broadcasters to provide more competitive programming to encourage people to listen. This was not difficult in areas where people owned shortwave radios and where domestic services offered only limited coverage, weak signals, or dull programming (as it often was). The BBC's external services consistently attracted large audiences to its news and current–affairs–based programs, particularly in countries where people did not trust their own media.

The record of IRBs in responding to the new milieu has been uneven. FEBA has perhaps responded most appropriately, altering its programming in response to audience change in its target broadcasting areas, adding news and even a program on computers. FEBA and FEBC jointly established a Manila-based news center to provide Asian news to their stations. But most evangelical programming is still preaching.

During the past decade, however, the competition faced by international radio has become increasingly keen. In addition to new domestic and international radio services, more and more countries have established television services, satellites have made foreign television programs easier to obtain, and many people have acquired audio and video cassette recorders, automobile radios with audio playback systems, boom boxes, rack-mounted high-fidelity systems, Walkman radio/cassettes, and, more recently, compact disk players. Both high–fidelity audio and the moving images of video/television have developed as realistic alternatives for people around the globe. In the most–developed countries, cable television, direct broadcast satellites, and digital satellite audio systems are also developing. This trend will likely accelerate, too, if the serious debt problems of many countries in sub–Saharan Africa and Latin America abate, allowing them to import greater quantities of these consumer goods.[8]

The implications of this trend for international religious services is that the technical quality of their programs must be consistently high, and their content must provide incentive for people to tune in. Many evangelicals, however, assume that merely preaching from scripture is sufficient. Production quality is secondary to them, audience analysis an expensive luxury. But even Jesus was consistently misunderstood, misinterpreted, and mistaken for someone else. Those evangelizing over radio today should therefore pay more attention to the scanty audience research figures available; they demonstrate the mistake of assuming that preaching the Word is enough to attract listeners.

A third technical problem is program scheduling. International broadcasters do not have the luxury enjoyed by their domestic counterparts to program in a few languages (or even a single language) and to cultivate an audience with programs designed to attract and hold it. International program schedules typically include multiple languages, each of which may be broadcast for as little as fifteen minutes at a time. For example, TWR's transmitter in the 41 meter band from Monte Carlo, beginning in September 1988, carried English programs from 0625 hours UTC to 1145 hours, but then (depending on the day of the week) provided programs in German, Russian, Crotian, Serbian, Macedonian, Slovenian, Belorussian, Ukrainian, and Romanian from 1145 to 1930 hours UTC. Between 1515 and 1845 hours UTC its 25-meter-band transmitter carried programs in Tadzhik, Kasakh, Kirghiz, Usbek, Farsi, Kurdish, Turkish, Czech, Hungarian, Bulgarian, and Russian. Audiences had to know not only the proper frequency, but the specific times when programs in their own languages would be aired. Those who knew such things were those who could maintain contact with the broadcasters, since frequencies typically change four times each year.

This obviously creates difficulties for presenting the Gospel in detail. But this is not the only problem. Even in languages in which IRBs provide multiple programs for lengthy periods of time, other facts intervene. International religious broadcasters typically air programs from a variety of program producers, each of whom has his/her own ministerial agenda. In such an environment production policies, which all religious broadcasters have, cannot assure that language services are actually meeting their avowed goals, whether that be to provide the "whole counsel of God" or merely to avoid airing confusing alternative explanations—or even unintentional contradictory statements.

The last technical problem for cross-cultural broadcasting is the technical skill of indigenous producers. Many international religious radio broadcasters rely on Christians recruited from the target nations themselves to translate and produce programming for audiences. It is unusual, however, particularly in developing countries, for these recruits to have had formal radio training sufficient enough to allow them to make the best use of the medium. Also, they may not have the equipment or resources to produce high-quality products, even when they have content provided by the broadcaster or other producers. But training such producers is not typically a high priority with broadcast organizations, often for lack of appropriate training facilities, funds, or will.

CULTURAL CONSTRAINTS TO CROSS-CULTURAL RADIO EVANGELISM

Religion is not easily communicated across cultural divides. David J. Hesselgrave wrote, "There is a very real danger that, as our technology advances and enables us to cross geographical and national boundaries with singular ease and increasing frequency, we may forget that it is the cultural barriers which are the most formidable."[9]

There are several cultural problems associated with international broadcasting. The problem for international religious broadcasters is especially difficult, however, because there is an additional barrier to overcome: that of religion itself. Whereas people may see organizations such as the BBC or Radio Moscow as representing political systems at variance with a country's own declared preference, and may jam it (as has been done to the BBC by various countries), religious programming may be seen not only as politically subversive, but culturally subversive as well.

People apprehend information entering their cultural environment through cultural screens: they may accept, reject, or alter it as they attempt to make sense of it. Religious programming, therefore, will be accepted "at face value" only if it conforms to a culture's prevailing sense-making activities; if at variance, it will be ignored or rejected, or altered to bring it into conformity. The Word, then, may not arrive as intended by those who produce programs including it. "The most important reason why we seem unable to penetrate other cultures," as Merrie Goddard puts it, "is that our theology of the cross and our understanding of Jesus are tightly wrapped in our American cultural application of Christianity."[10] That understanding should be assumed to be irrelevant to people in other cultures.

Successful evangelists must know the culture of the audience, whether animated by Animism or Islam, whether responding to political oppression or freedom, abundance or poverty, whether matriarchal or patriarchal. If the Word is not speaking to these basic conditions of life, it is *impractical*. People do not know what to do with it. If Jean Stromberg is correct, that, "the good news has always needed, from the very beginning, to be incarnated in human cultures" then that message must be perceived as newsworthy by those to whom it would speak.[11] But, as Temba L. J. Mafico has warned, "Christianity is implicitly regarded [in Africa] as a western religion with limited relevance to practical problems confronting African believers."[12] This is not a warning that many who provide programs to IRBs have heeded.

For example, since most programming aired by IRBs originates in Western countries, it typically uses either traditional/classical sacred music, or American gospel/spiritual music. This music is readily available, is free of copyright restrictions and expense, and is familiar to program producers. It is part of Western cultural life. But it is not necessarily appropriate in a developing country. So the ethnocentric bias of international evangelical programs originating in the United States is evident in their Americanized content.

It is difficult, however, to determine precisely where some programs do originate. Although some are clearly produced by U.S. organizations, others are co-produced by Christians in two or more countries, and still others involve producers in target countries who are hired by Western evangelical organizations to produce the content. Some programs, therefore, are more sensitive to cultural differences than others, even though their source may appear to be the United States.

In the 1988 Monte Carlo schedule of TWR over 38 percent of programs appeared to originate in the United States. Other significant program origination countries included West Germany (33%), TWR (a U.S. organization 8%), the United Kingdom (8%), Finland (4%), Austria (2%), and Norway (2%). Other production countries included Australia, Canada, the Faroe Islands, the Netherlands, Spain, and Switzerland.

If scheduled programs are broken down by language, then American organizations provided the percentages found in Table 2. In addition, TWR and its West German partner, *Evangeliums Rundfunk*, provided another 21 percent of Arabic programming, the remainder of Armenian, 33 percent of Bulgarian, 61 percent of Croatian, 36 percent of Czech, 18 percent of English, the remainder of Farsi, all the German and Greek, 36 percent of Hungarian, 25 percent of Italian, all the

Kazakh, Kurdish, and Lithuanian, 50 percent of Kirghiz and Macedonian, 37 percent of Polish, 8 percent of Romanian, 37 percent of Russian, all the Serbian, Slovak, Spanish, and Tadzhik, 82 percent of Slovenian, and 8 percent of Turkish programming.[13]

Table 2

**Percent of Programming by TWR Monte Carlo
Provided by American Evangelical Organizations**

Albanian	43%	French	46%
Arabic	60	Hebrew	100
Armenian	32	Hungarian	45
Berber	50	Italian	68
Bulgarian	67	Polish	47
Croatian	38	Romanian	92
Czech	50	Russian	44
English	51	Turkish	78
Farsi	63	Ukbelo	100

A major reason for such dominance is that IRBs air many programs produced in multiple languages. "Through the Bible," as the most obvious case, is produced in Armenian, Arabic, Croatian, Czech, English, Farsi, French, Hebrew, Hungarian, Italian, Polish, Russian, and Turkish. It is produced, as are many others, in English and simply translated into other languages. "Words of Hope" is produced in Albanian, Arabic, Bulgarian, Czech, English, and Russian. Many others, including the "Back to God Hour," the "Children's Program," "Christ Liveth," the "Family Bible Hour," "Good News," "Hour of Decision," "Living Word," "Radas," and "Youth" are produced in at least three languages for TWR. These programs are all produced in the West, although some of them involve producers who construct programs specifically for particular audiences, rather than merely translating them. These special programs carry the same name, but contain different content. In either case, however, the majority are produced by American evangelical organizations who may be converting people to American culture as much as to Christianity.

Obviously related to this specific problem of program

content is the more general one of U.S. evangelical dominance. The figures speak for themselves. As Rene Padilla emphasized at the Laussane Congress on World Evangelization over ten years ago, "We have equated 'Americanism' with Christianity to such an extent that we are tempted to believe that people in other cultures must adopt American institutional patterns when they are converted. We are led through natural psychological processes to an unconscious belief that the essence of our American Way of Life is basically, if not entirely, Christian." Padilla went on to criticize approaches to evangelism, based in such assumptions, which reduced the Gospel "to a formula for success and equates the triumph of Christ with obtaining the highest number of 'conversions.'"[14] Stanley J. Samartha even claims that IRBs and local missionaries have been viewed by their audiences as being "mixed up" with "military conquest, political domination and economic exploitation," and "racial arrogance." That, at least, is the perception in India, where both Christianity and Islam "came with claims of exclusiveness, seeking to overcome and displace other religions and cultures in the world that provided spiritual sustenance, theological direction and ethical guidance for millions of people for a few thousand years. They brought in entirely new beliefs, doctrines and ways of life."[15] Such perceptions are a major cultural difficulty faced by evangelism, and particularly by those who practice it from afar.

One place to begin examining evangelical approaches is with the audience itself. What assumptions are being made about the audience by programmers? Assumptions can often be teased out by close examination of program texts. The nature of the language used there, for instance, can suggest what producers assume (perhaps unconsciously) about the audience's knowledge, its culture, even its humanity. Even language itself can be a clue. There is a different perception of the audience, for instance, in IRBs or program producers that make programs in colloquial Arabic and those that make them in classical Arabic. Likewise, the assumption of producers who work in lingua franca (such as Swahili) as opposed to imperial languages (English in East Africa, for instance) are different. It is not merely a question of asking what languages people speak, for many speak imperial tongues for trade, business, and political reasons who would choose to avoid it in family or tribal life and worship. If languages are chosen merely because they are most efficient in target areas, closer examination of cultural reality may show that such choices were wrong: they neither deliver audiences nor portray Christ appropriately. Instead, language choice makes him out as prophet for the powerful.

Due to scheduling difficulties and the number of languages used, IRBs may also air programs at inappropriate times, failing to take account of the fact that each culture has its own routines and rhythms of life. Many are not "clock cultures" like those of industrial countries. They follow the natural rhythm of daylight and darkness, climate and season. People in countries with hot climates are active at different times of day than those in more temperate climates. Extreme northern and southern peoples' routines differ with the variation in length of days and nights created by the seasonal tilt of the earth. Nomadic tribes move to follow animal herds or to find new forage for livestock. Many cultures celebrate particular rituals according to when particular natural phenomena occur.

But IRB broadcast schedulers not only have to make "tradeoffs" based on the number of transmitters available and the number of programs and languages used, but they also must change their frequencies and schedules four times per year in response to changing atmospheric conditions, and renegotiate contracts and air times with program producer-suppliers who have their own agendas that are responsive to the expectations of financial contributors. The result is a changing potpourri of programs, some of which necessarily will not be broadcast at optimal times for potential listeners.

Cultural sensitivity requires that producers be intimate with such routines, rhythms, and rituals. Otherwise, the Word may be seen as irrelevant, impractical, even laughable. The problem persists: producing programming in one culture assuming that the power of the Word itself (as interpreted and framed in that culture) will cross into foreign contexts with its potency undiminished is naïve. Programs focusing on material-ism, for instance, or the stresses of urban life, or those using illustrations from American day-to-day activities, are largely (if not entirely) irrelevant to nomadic peoples, subsistence farmers, or villagers in most areas of Africa, Latin America, and Asia.

POLITICAL-ECONOMIC CONSTRAINTS TO CROSS-CULTURAL RADIO EVANGELISM

IRBs depend on contributions for their economic survival, both directly and indirectly. They benefit directly from donations that support their own costs, and they benefit indirectly from the donations made to program producers who purchase airtime on their transmitters. Both IRBs and program producers, then, must satisfy their financial patrons, rather than the audiences they seek to evangelize, in order to function. They are concerned about audience response to their programming, to be sure, but their primary concern must be to those who fund their activities. This patronage system affects both the relationship between broadcaster/evangelist and audience, and the choices of research strategies used to determine the success of broadcast activities.

The financial underpinning of IRBs are the American and British evangelical communities, which contribute both directly and indirectly to keep international religious radio on the air. Direct support comes in the form of contributions to organizations such as FEBA, FEBC, HCJB, and TWR. Indirect support comes in two forms. First is the commitment made to individual radio missionaries to provide the necessary financial support for them to work with these organizations. Second is the commitment made to individual program producers who, in turn, purchase air time from these organizations. Since station operators do not produce all the programs they air, they depend on program providers to fill their air schedules and to pay for the time they use. In this activity they function as "time brokers," providing air time to other users who are themselves responsible for filling the spots provided.

In general, the expectations of financial contributors to IRBs (and their program providers/purchasers) are that the Gospel will be proclaimed, that evangelism will be accomplished. But the methods by which this can be accomplished are much less direct than financial backers recognize. Also, the context within which evangelical messages should be expressed for target audiences may require program producers to grapple with difficult indigenous issues outside the framework of traditional missiological practice or with issues that may be perceived as threatening by target populations or their political elites. For instance, IRBs remove politically sensitive remarks, negative comments about other religions or alternative Christian doctrines, and critical comments about specific people. The necessity of practicing such care is obvious, given the experience of Radio Voice of the Gospel (RVOG), a Lutheran broadcaster that was shut down in Addis Adaba in 1977 (after fifteen years of operation) by the new revolutionary government, which objected to its programming content.[16] But such cultural and political constraints are often subtle, confounding the avowed intent to evangelize even while they remain unrecognized by program producers. When letters from listeners indicate that conversions occur, producers often draw conclusions that their efforts are successful, rather than wondering what may have prevented a larger response.

Also, the Gospel itself is not always easy to depoliticize. Dealing with social justice, for instance, may have political overtones that are difficult to avoid. Social justice may be an issue that, if dealt with sensitively, may make the Gospel practical within a particular culture. But its practicality may also be seen as a threat by the powerful members of a society.

Such an issue may also raise other questions in the minds of an audience not intimately knowledgeable about the situation in the producing country (if known). Listeners to IRBs probably also listen to other international services. They hear of situations that, if not addressed by the programmer appropriately, may result in charges of hypocrisy. Even themes of brotherhood or equality before God could lead to wrong conclusions if others provide information about racism, sexism, or favoritism to the same listeners.

The point is that IRBs do not alone determine the context for their operations. The political context (and the economic, cultural, and technical context) affects interpretations of their programming. People do not live in vacuums and IRBs do not provide an entire diet of information about, and interpretation of, daily world events.

In addition, IRB dependence on American and British patrons leads to the necessity of claiming program effectiveness. Research is expensive; field work to determine the response of an audience even in a single country may cost over $75,000. Purchasing research from other organizations can cost from five to ten thousand dollars, even when the data provided may not address issues of primary concern to IRBs. Such research also typically shows how small IRB audiences are, compared with those of many other shortwave broadcasters. The BBC, VOA, Radio *Deutsche Welle* (West Germany),

Radio France International, Radio Netherlands, Radio Liberty, and Radio Free Europe all attempt to determine, by one mechanism or another, how large their audiences are, how often people listen to their programs, and what kinds of programs their audiences prefer. Their research shows that regular audiences (defined as listening at least once per week) for IRBs usually range between 1 and 3 percent, while audiences in the same areas for international services (such as the BBC or VOA) will more likely be 15 percent or more. Where international commercial services are available (such as West Africa), their audiences may be as high as 78 percent of the population.

Two notable exceptions to this generalization exist. The first was RVOG which, when it was operational, would draw regular audiences in East and North Africa of about 15 percent. HCJB also does well in Central and northern South America. In both cases programming included not only obvious evangelical material, but also news, health and agricultural information programs, and the like.

Therefore, because of costs, IRBs do little audience research and rely on letters from listeners to determine the impact of their broadcasts. Letters provide good insight into one segment of the audience: the literate, motivated, and grateful listeners. They provide little to no information, however, about nonliterate or unmotivated listeners, or—in some countries—individuals who cannot respond (such as women, nomadic populations, or those without reliable postal service). Even more troublesome, letters cannot represent those who are not listening, perhaps the most important audience for IRBs, given their evangelical intent. While letters may provide pithy anecdotes useful in fund-raising appeals, newsletters, and missionary presentations, their value as indicators of ministry effectiveness in reaching the unchurched, or non-Christian populations, is limited. (See Table 3.)

It is unlikely that IRBs can pursue such research vigorously, however, unless their financial patrons recognize its value and are willing to support it appropriately. IRBs understand well the necessity of responding to patrons' expectations. They also recognize their own financial limitations. But IRBs and program producer patrons actively *devalue* audience research when they remain satisfied with letters that depict individual stories of salvation or dramatic responses to calls for repentance.

Table 3

Comparison of Audiences, IRBs, BBC, and VOA

Radio Service	Letters per Year	Estimated Regular Audience
BBC	452,000	130 million
VOA	400,000	130 million
FEBC/FEBA	600,000	Unknown
HCJB	120,000	Unknown
TWR	500,000	Unknown

MISSIOLOGICAL CONSTRAINTS ON CROSS-CULTURAL RADIO EVANGELISM

IRBs are missionary organizations, dedicated to proclaiming the Gospel. The three goals of World Radio Gospel Broadcasts (W. Monroe, Louisiana), for instance, are to allow as many people as possible to hear the Gospel in their own language, to acquaint new areas of the world with the church of Jesus Christ, and to enhance mission work. FEBC's programming goals are to make the Gospel known to people who otherwise might never know of it and to strengthen Christians who do not have other means of strengthening themselves in the faith. The Pacific Broadcasting Association sees its mission as using broadcasting to evangelize the Japanese. TWR's philosophy of ministry has two primary elements: to preach and teach the Word of God, and to reach people. These are missionary statements.

Dialogue is the essence of evangelization, dialogue that "indicates our resolve to rid our minds of the prejudices and caricatures we may entertain about the other man; to struggle to listen through his ears and see through his eyes so as to grasp what prevents him from hearing the Gospel and seeing Christ."[17] This is perhaps the fundamental cross-cultural problem of IRBs: to make a medium of communication designed for one-way mass distribution of information into one that provides for dialogue.

IRBs and their program providers will not accomplish this, however, until they pay closer attention to the audience than they have done in the past and ground their messages in the cultural realities of this audience. That is unlikely, too, until IRBs pay less attention to the expectations of financial donors and more attention to those of their audiences.

Yet it is the evangelistic goals themselves that ultimately encourage (or require) IRBs to produce programs filled more with conversion calls than sensitive "inductively based" programming.[18] Most evangelical radio is little more than sermonizing. Content analyses of TWR's English-language Bonaire transmissions to the United States and Russian-language Monte Carlo transmissions both show the sermon to be the most prevalent form of radio programming. As TWR's own research staff put it, "Overall, this would seem to indicate a definite tilt toward rather heavy, information-loaded programming which is not a strong use of the radio medium."[19]

A contrast to the sermon emphasis of missionary radio is provided by the BBC's overseas religious broadcasting. It consciously avoids religious jargon, such as "salvation," "redemption," "atonement," etc., which audiences may not understand. David Craig, organizer of Overseas Religious Broadcasting, says he thinks of religious programming as being like the opera *Parsifal*, which is full of religious symbols and meanings, but only to those who are familiar with them. Otherwise, he says, the opera is seen in an entirely different way, but still understood. Approaching religious radio in a similar fashion, however, would require that producers and IRBs redefine their missiology to encourage more use of program formats other than the sermon, and to allow less "sacred" language to be seen as religious.[20]

The problem here is a basic missiological one: what is the ultimate purpose of missionary radio? The answer may seem obvious: it is evangelism. Clearly this is supported by IRBs' own goals. However, IRBs make a further claim of discipleship. They take the Great Commission of Jesus seriously: "Go and make disciples." Pacific Broadcasting Association stationery carries the slogan "the great commission . . . using radio and television." One of FEBC's goals—strengthening Christians— implies use of the Great Commission as well. TWR's analysis of Russian-language programming concluded that it had more than twice as many programs directed to believers as to nonbelievers.[21] Thus discipleship appears to be an ultimate missiological goal.

These stated goals make it unlikely that the approach of the BBC would find fertile soil in the activities of IRBs or evangelical program producers. But the failure of the IRBs to attract audiences on the scale of the BBC or other international broadcasters, even while transmitting more hours of programming in more languages than their secular competitors, leads to the conclusion that different program strategies—or goals— may be in order. Although IRBs have no accurate estimates about their regular listening audiences (defined by secular organizations as people who listen at least once a week), they do estimate that their signal can be heard by 80 percent (TWR), or 67 percent (FEBA/FEBC) of the world's population, thus providing "potential" listeners on the order of between two and two and a half billion people.

IRBs are already efficient, when compared to their secular counterparts, even though their audiences are much smaller. They may fairly be judged as good stewards, then, at least when judged on the basis of annual cost per letter received. (See Table 4.) But the opportunities for audience growth are enormous, when their audiences are compared with other international broadcasters.

Table 4

Measures of Efficiency—BBC, VOA, and IRBs

Service	Annual Budget	Cost Per Regular Listener	Cost Per Letter Received
BBC	$115 million	.88	$254
VOA	$150 million	1.15	$375
FEBA/FEBC	Not Available		
HCJB	$ 10 million	unknown	$ 83
TWR	$ 18 million	unknown	$ 36

THE FUTURE OF CROSS-CULTURAL RADIO EVANGELISM

New technologies are changing the nature of international communication transactions. Already the Japanese are using direct-broadcast satellites for television delivery, fiber optics are supplementing undersea coaxial cables and satellite links, and the number of facsimile and telex terminals is mushrooming. In

Western Europe the French and West Germans are planning digital transmission radio delivery to apartment complexes. The Voice of America is examining possibilities for international direct broadcast satellite (DBS) audio delivery. The Cable News Network is rapidly expanding into a global television system and entertainment programs are now available across international boundaries in the Americas, Europe, the Arab states of the Middle East, and Asia.

None of this activity, however, will usurp the role of international radio (medium wave or shortwave) over the next three or more decades, particularly in the developing world. Most southern hemisphere countries are unlikely to reverse their economic fortunes to allow for massive investments in such new technology. Only combinations of countries—and, more likely, partnerships with developed countries—will allow such systems to become practical alternative methods of communication in most of the world.

These new systems will have an impact on international radio broadcasting, however, particularly when they are coupled with computers that allow machine-to-machine communication, access to massive international data bases, and new forms of electronic surveillance. Perhaps the most significant impact will be on the way in which people in specific cultures will define their identities. The more information available to a person, the wider the context within which that person defines himself or herself. As new types of information become available, people will understand themselves differently.

For instance, information about the use of chemical weapons in the Iran-Iraq war, or about the Bhopal disaster involving toxic chemical fumes, or the Cameroonian lake disaster, or the dumping of toxic industrial wastes in West Africa, may all combine in the consciousness and cause people to wonder how and why such substances could be created, and why they should be so carelessly shipped to countries where other humans are subjected to their toxicity.

Thus, new information provides both new opportunities and new dangers for radio evangelism. The opportunities are perhaps obvious: How does the Bible explain the nature of humanity, man's inhumanity to man, and so on. The dangers are more subtle and will depend on the circumstances of the information—whether it taints the message, or the messenger. But the context must be taken into account, and the more paths that information can follow, the more difficult it will be to know the context and respond to it appropriately. Otherwise, the evolving understanding that people have about their identities, and even about the nature of human dignity itself, will be missed, and the message of faith will become irrelevant.

Another impact of these new technologies and the information they bring will be on the style of religious programming and information. As different styles of reporting, of diversion and entertainment, of live linkages between newsmakers and ordinary people, of persona creation and celebration become globalized, the expectations for presentation and explanation of information will also change. Commanding attention will require greater attention to creative expression of religion and higher levels of technical expertise by program producers—whether working for IRBs or independent organizations. It will also require that IRBs pay greater attention to achieving message consistency in their programming and that they judge the place each program has in cultivating an audience in a particular language. The "planned spontaneity" of media will begin to have a more severe impact on the practices of IRBs in regard to program suppliers and their own production activities.

Such changes will complicate the relationship between IRBs and their patrons. If patrons' expectations remain constant—fixed on evangelism—the ability of IRBs to respond to these changes will be diminished and their audiences more difficult to reach. But if their programming does change, their patrons' expectations will have to be reoriented, or IRBs will likely have difficulty raising the funds necessary to continue operation.

CONCLUSION

The changes in the environment for international religious broadcasting is rapidly altering the context within which IRBs and other missionary organizations perform their work. But the changes have not been reflected so far in most of the transmitted programming. Some changes, however, have occurred. FEBA, for instance, airs a weekly program on computers into Southeast Asia. For the most part, however, the daily pressures of filling broadcasting schedules, raising funds, recruiting and training staff, and maintaining producer contacts occupy the staff time that might be more profitably spent. Too often IRBs fail to avail themselves of opportunities to step back from these activities to assess them or to choose new approaches to meet their evangelical objectives. The need to satisfy financial patrons often saps the energy that might be devoted to program or audience research.

The developing technological context of international communication increases the stakes for IRBs to perform longer-range analyses, however. When producers and broadcasters fail to make the case for research and program review and experimentation to their patrons and to fund such activities adequately, then their activities are likely to become increasingly irrelevant to the people they attempt to reach. This necessity is made more poignant by the announced intention to provide the Gospel to all peoples by the year 2000. This goal, while perhaps admirable, is at root a message-centered goal. The needs for the remainder of this century, however, and the first quarter of the next, are more audience-centered, requiring that both independent program producers and IRBs know their audience and its socio-cultural and technological context intimately—as Jesus did when he spoke to those he brought to new faith out of the despair of their daily lives.

Change, of course, is difficult. Shifting from patron-centered to audience-centered operations itself would entail risks of financial failure. Ignoring the problems and the changing context for their activities, however, would be equally fatal. Although the funds might continue to flow, the value of the activity would likely be increasingly difficult to demonstrate.

NOTES

[1]Paul Freed's account of the beginnings of Trans World Radio can be read in *Towers to Eternity* (Chatham, N.J.: Trans World Radio, 1979).

[2]See *World Radio TV Handbook* (New York: Billboard Publications 1988), 45–48.

[3]Trans World Radio, "Reaching the World Requires Radio." (Hilversum, The Netherlands, n.d.).

[4]Information provided by the Far East Broadcasting Company, Inc.

[5]Elehie N. Skoczylas, "Audiences and Frequency Use: VOA Broadcasting Options" (Unpublished Report, Washington, DC: Office of Research, United States Information Agency, May 1984, 34, 35.

[6]See Robert S. Fortner and Dona A. Durham, *A Worldwide Radio Receiver Population Analysis* (Washington, DC: Academy for Educational Development, USIA Contract No. IA–22188–23, May 15, 1986).

[7]Christopher H. Sterling, *Electronic Media: A Guide to Trends in Broadcasting and Newer Technologies 1920–1983* (New York: Praeger, 1984), 5, 18.

[8]Information on trends can be found in Robert S. Fortner, and Dona A. Durham. *A Worldwide Radio Receiver Population Analysis.* See also Robert S. Fortner, "The Prospects for DBS-Audio in International Communication: Technological, Political and Economic Realities," *Journal of Broadcasting and Electronic Media* 32 (1988): 183–95.

[9]David J. Hesselgrave, "The Role of Culture in Communication" in Ralph D. Winer and Steven C. Hawthorne, eds., *Perspectives on the World Christian Movement: A Reader* (Pasadena, Calif.: William Carey Library. 1981), 391, 395.

[10]"Putting the Cross back in Cross-Cultural Ministry," *Evangelical Missions Quarterly* 24 (January 1988): 52.

[11]"Communicating in Mission: What Word for Today?" *International Review of Mission* 77 (January 1988): 82.

[12]"The Old Testament and Effective Evangelism in Africa," *International Review of Mission* 75 (October 1986): 400.

[13]These percentages are based on TWR's September 1988 program schedule.

[14]"Evangelism and the World," in J. D. Douglas, ed., *Let the Earth Hear His Voice: International Congress on World Evangelization.* Lausanne, Switzerland. Official Reference Volume: Papers and Responses. Minneapolis: World Wide Publications, 1975, 125, 126. Padilla was quoting David O. Moberg *The Great Reversal* (1972), in his first statement.

[15]"Mission in a Religiously Plural World: Looking Beyond Tambaram 1938," *International Review of Mission* 78 (July 1988): 321.

[16]See Manfred Lundgren *Proclaiming Christ to His World: The Experience of Radio Voice of the Gospel, 1957–1977* (Geneva: The Lutheran World Federation, circa 1983).

[17]John Stott, "The Biblical Basis of Evangelism" in J. D. Douglas, ed., *Let the Earth Hear His Voice.* 72.

[18]See Michael Green's comments in "Methods and Strategy in the Evangelism of the Early Church," Douglas, J. D. (ed.) *Let the Earth Hear His Voice.* 162.

[19]Don van den Akker and Gillian Hogg "Content Analysis: Russian Language Broadcasts," (Unpublished Paper, Bussum, The Netherlands: TWR Intracare, April 1987), 10.

[20]Interview with David Craig at the BBC, Bush House, London (July 15, 1988). Further information on "formats" of missionary radio can be found in J. Harold Ellens *Models of Religious Broadcasting* (Grand Rapids: Eerdmans, 1974).

[21]van den Akker and Hogg "Content Analysis," 8.

Part VI

ASSESSING THE EVANGELICAL MEDIA LEGACY

15

REDEMPTIVE MEDIA AS THE EVANGELICAL'S CULTURAL TASK

CLIFFORD G. CHRISTIANS

> . . . *The falcon cannot hear the falconer;*
> *Things fall apart; the center cannot hold.* . . .
> *The ceremony of innocence is drowned;*
> *The best lack all conviction, while the worst*
> *Are full of passionate intensity.*
> —*William Butler Yeats*
> *"The Second Coming" (1924)*

Without a coherent philosophy of culture, evangelicals and their popular culture drift along on imaginary clouds. Yeats' apocalyptic warning about social anarchy speaks in microcosm to today's volatile situation: Without a cultural center, articulated from an evangelical worldview, communication falls apart, driven largely by "passionate intensity."

The media are agents of acculturation, and to the degree we understand culture we understand communication as well. Devoid of a theory of culture, evangelicals attach communication technologies exclusively to the Great Commission and celebrate their alleged cost-effectiveness in winning souls. Inarticulate about the symbolic character of cultural forms, they allow unacceptable splits between reality and fantasy. Malcolm Muggeridge, for example, grounds his heavy-handed critique of television on a misdirected dualism between the "truth" of the printed word and the inherent deception of the televised image.[1] With an underdeveloped notion of culture—failing to recognize cultures as value-laden human constructions—evangelicals mainly perpetuate a sacred-secular dichotomy, glibly labeling religious broadcasting "sacred" and, by default, the remainder "secular."

The result has been disastrous for evangelicalism. While claiming to save the world through mass communication, evangelicals have merely adopted the techniques of the "secular" culture they so deplore. Ironically, it is the Bible—or at least their reading of it—that has led evangelicals astray in their media use. Overlooking their own roots in the entire Scriptures, they locate their calling merely in the New Testament command to preach the Gospel to the world. As a result, evangelicals lack a theory of culture that would powerfully animate their media efforts and provide them an intellectual home for critiquing media institutions. Hoping to convert others, they are reshaped themselves by the marketing ethos and stimulus-response mentality of the commercial broadcasting industry.

CULTURAL MANDATE

In the biblical account largely ignored by contemporary evangelicals, the human species was given the cultural mandate at the time of creation. God commanded the first parents to be fruitful, to replenish the earth, and to subdue it (Gen. 1:26–28). The Creator God commissioned human beings as his vice-gerents over creation, giving only them the intelligence and creative power to be his agents. In this "world-and-life view" Christians historically have found the rationale for studying chemistry and mathematics, producing literature and the arts, redirecting the mass media as cultural institutions, and entering government and economics.

Enhancing creation's beauty and excellence has remained the Christian mandate, though fractured and disrupted since the Fall. With the earth "full of violence" (Gen. 6:11), God sent the Deluge and devastated all cultural achievements born of hubris; but afterward the cultural mandate (Gen. 9:1–11) was renewed forever. Recognizing the overwhelming secularization of the present technological era, God's kingdom builders today often appear to be aliens in a strange land. Like the people of Israel in Babylonian exile, few believers hear the prophetic injunction to form culture:

This is what the Lord Almighty, the God of Israel, says to all those I carried into exile from Jerusalem to Babylon: "Build houses and settle down; plant gardens and eat what they produce. Marry and have sons and daughters. . . . Increase in number there and do not decrease. Also seek the peace and prosperity of the city to which I have carried you into exile. Pray to the Lord for it, because if it prospers, you too will prosper. . . . For I know the plans I have for you," declares the Lord, "plans to prosper you and not to harm you, plans to give you hope and a future." (Jer. 29:4–7, 11)

In this biblical scenario, culture is fallen totally in its extent but not absolutely without redeeming value. Human creations are corrupted—warped, twisted, and misdirected. This cultural mandate enjoins God's children to convert cultural forms, not to eliminate them wholesale. The fall into sin is radical but is not of the same life-giving quality as the creation. Believers are obliged to demonstrate signs of Christ's kingdom, rather than unmercifully condemn human cultural accomplishments. The apostle Paul expresses the full significance of God's covenant with the created order: "The creation waits in eager expectation . . . that [it] will be liberated from its bondage to decay" (Rom. 8:19, 21 NIV).

Captive to their own narrowly construed theology of conversion, evangelicals have lacked a theology of culture. They have failed to see that culture is a secondary environment built from God's created order by people's creative effort. It stands distinct from nature because it is a human achievement. Culture is human heritage in time, place, and civilization, the total of purposeful servanthood. And communication is the catalytic agent, the driving force in cultural formation, not merely the sending of messages or calls to conversion. In Scripture, humankind stands in a creaturely relation to their Maker while having dominion over their own creations. As a sign of his unique responsibility, Adam names the animals and communicates with God in the garden, giving an account of his activities.

Jacob Bronowski tells the story of the Sherpas in his spectacular book *Science and Human Values*.[2] The Sherpas know intimately the face of Mount Everest seen from their home valley. When shown another side by Western climbers, they refuse at first to believe. How could it possibly be the same mountain from a different angle? But they are moved emotionally, and their disbelief turns to amazement at the revelation that their time-worn mountain can open to them in a new way. So it is with all culture, driven by both belief and disbelief. American evangelical culture sees only one side of the mountain. From the other, more holistically biblical side, the mass media are not merely purveyors of information but more importantly creators and shapers of culture. Within the cultural paradigm, communication is the symbolic process expressing human creativity and grounding cultural formation. Culture is the womb in which symbols are born, and communication is the connective tissue in culture building. Thus released from transmission views of communication rooted in either positivism or engineering, evangelicals are enabled within a cultural paradigm to illuminate the communicative dimension of God's universe in categories faithful to biblical anthropology.

COMMUNICATIONS TECHNOLOGY

The implications of this cultural view of human communication for the religious use of mass media technologies are momentous. While everyday nomenclature reduces technology to tools or products, a more comprehensive view refers to the technological process as a cultural activity involving design, fabrication, and use. From this perspective, technology is a distinct cultural enterprise in which human beings exercise their God-given freedom and responsibility by forming and transforming the natural creation aided by tools and processes for practical ends. This definition reiterates the general argument so far—without a philosophy of culture there is no philosophy of technology. While the mass media are cultural institutions, the mass communication system is technological in character; therefore, evangelicals need a philosophy of technology in order to construct a normative framework for articulating the direction in which media technologies ought to proceed if they are not to be anticultural.

Jacques Ellul developed the contention that technology is decisive though not exclusive in defining twentieth-century culture. As an explanatory element, he argues, it plays the role of capital in Marx's interpretation of the nineteenth century. That does not mean that technology has the same function as capital or that the capitalist system is a thing of the past. It still exists, but capital no longer fulfills the role Marx claimed for it. Whereas work creates value for Marx, in extremely technological societies the determining factor is *la technique*.[3] This generates value now and is not peculiar to capitalism. The characters have changed. We can no longer divide society into capitalists and workers; the phenomenon is completely different and more abstract. We now have technological organizations on one side and all humanity on the other—the former driven by necessity and human beings demanding freedom. Ellul concludes that we must read the world in which we live, not in terms of capitalist structures, but in terms of technology. While this analysis privileges the industrial order, even the three-fourths world that is nontechnological finds itself defined in terms of technological parameters. And, as Hans Jonas has clarified in his compelling book *The Imperative of Responsibility*, today's global age dialectically has the technological sophistication to destroy all humanity, and simultaneously communication technologies exist to bind all nations of the world into a unified information network.[4]

From Ellul's perspective, a technological civilization has emerged in the late twentieth century. Technology is not merely one more arena for philosophers and sociologists to investigate, but a new foundation for understanding the self, human institutions, and ultimate reality. A society is technological, Ellul argues, not because of its machines, but from the pursuit of efficient techniques in every arena of human endeavor. Whereas in previous eras techniques were ordered into a larger complex of social values, the pervasiveness and sophistication of modern techniques reorganize society in conformity with efficiency. Mechanistic techniques are applied not just to nature, but to social organizations and our understanding of personhood. A technological society separates itself from previous ones—including industrial civilizations— "through its historical consciousness that society is not fixed and given with the order of nature, but is an artificial human creation."[5] Because of their extraordinary power, modern techniques tend to subordinate all other, less–efficient values to their requirements. As a result, all appearance of change created by *la technique* remains fundamentally an illusion. In this sense, for Ellul, finding freedom in a technological civilization is in essence a religious problem. Unable to establish a meaningful life outside the artificial ambience of a technological culture, human beings place their ultimate hope in it. Seeing no other source of security and failing to recognize the illusoriness of their technical freedom, they become slaves to the exacting determinations of efficiency.

Whereas previous social orders operated with a triad—
humans/tools/nature—in technological societies nature recedes
and humans perceive themselves as living in a technical artifice.
We have become aware that we do not exist in nature but in
culture.

> Man does not any longer live in a natural environment but
> rather in a milieu composed of the products of his technol-
> ogy. . . . He can no longer take any significant action
> without technological intermediation. Technology consti-
> tutes an engulfing universe for man, who finds himself in it
> as in a cocoon.[6]

Culture is now dominated by technological structures. Thus we
use labels such as the information age, the telematic society, the
communications revolution, and the television generation. In
Ellul's framework, communications media represent the meaning-edge of the technological system, the arena where the
latter's soul is most clearly exposed. While exhibiting the
structural elements of all technical artifacts, their particular
identity as a technology inheres in their function as bearers of
symbols. Information technologies thus incarnate the properties of technology while serving as the agent for interpreting the
meaning of the very phenomenon it embodies. Ellul calls our
communication systems the "innermost, and most elusive
manifestation" of human technological activity.[7] All artifacts
communicate meaning in an important sense, but media
instruments carry that role exclusively. Thus, as the media
sketch out our world for us, organize our conversations,
determine our decisions, and influence our self-identity, they
do so with a technological cadence, massaging in our soul a
technological rhythm and predisposition.

Jean Baudrillard established that modern society has
become less a consumption of material objects than a consumption of symbols.[8] We purchase not to meet needs but to gain the
status indicative of power and wealth. We consume symbols
that cohere with technological production. In the process we
sterilize symbolic patterns in order to facilitate our adaptation to
technology and leave in disarray those symbolic forms that
enable us to situate ourselves critically in our new technological
environment and even to master it. Ellul appropriately calls
modern mass media "sociological propaganda." In his scheme,
the principle of efficiency that characterizes the technological
enterprise as a whole also dominates the communications

apparatus; the media do not transmit neutral stimuli, but they integrate us into the system. Like the fish's perfect adaptation to its water environment, we are enveloped in data, absorbed in a mono-dimensional world of stereotypes and slogans, and integrated into a homogeneous whole by the "propaganda of conformity." The mass media have become so powerful, Ellul argues, that congruity with the system is considered normal—even desirable—and we ironically declare that new ideas or alternative worldviews are ideologies or "just propaganda."[9]

Those with a well-articulated philosophy of culture contribute to the critical discourse regarding the technological system. Unfortunately, the evangelical community has remained virtually silent, trapped in the reductionism of technological objects as neutral. While a blindspot regarding technology may not have been devastating for evangelicals in the nineteenth and early twentieth centuries, when technological products were less determinative, it leads to wholesale misjudgments in today's technological culture. Evangelicals wrongly presume the commonplace assumption of industrialized countries that technology is merely a tool open to proper or improper use. As Oxford's R. A. Buchanan has expressed it, "Technology is essentially amoral, a thing apart from values, an instrument which can be used for good or ill."[10] A knife in a surgeon's hands saves a life; in the hands of a murderer a knife destroys life. The same projector shows pornography and National Geographic Specials. One is reminded of the familiar slogan, "Guns don't kill people, people do." In Arnold Pacey's example, in Swedish Lapland snowmobiles are used for reindeer herding, among Canada's Eskimos for trapping, and in Wisconsin for leisure.[11] Technological products are independent, we are told; they can be used to support completely different cultures and lifestyles. In the hands of evangelicals the media are life-giving, while in the hands of secular broadcasters they are demonic. Devoid of a philosophy of technology, as well as a theory of culture, conservative American Protestants have adopted this truncated notion from the popular mythology. As Quentin Schultze has convincingly documented, presuming technologies to be neutral instruments, American evangelicals have blithely integrated media technology with a doctrine of progress and millenarian theology. As a result, they unreflectively incant for electronic communications the mythos of the technological sublime and invest them with divine significance.[12]

The presumption of neutrality has been very costly to evangelicals and the wider society. It has led to an exaggerated, unbalanced emphasis on magnitude, control, uniformity, and integration—what Pacey calls the virtuosity values.[13] In its heaviest form, it has promoted a version of technological determinism in which technology's own inner logic appears mysteriously to drive its development. This narrow view fosters the working rule that "if it can be done, it should be," eradicating other significant dimensions from our decision-making. In religious broadcasting, for instance, the church's ministries of *koinonia* (fellowship) and *diakonia* (serving) are replaced by numerical expansion.

The sheer numbers of broadcasts, stations, and listeners are taken naïvely as evidence of evangelical power. Not surprisingly, evangelicals typically focus on hardware, tools, and mechanical artifacts while largely ignoring the values embedded in the technological process. Contrary to popular opinion, technological products are particular, combining specific resources into distinctive entities with unique properties and capabilities. Technological objects embody decisions to develop one kind of knowledge and not another, to use certain resources and not others, to release energy of a specific form and quantity and not some other. There is no purely neutral or technical justification for all these decisions. Instead they arise from implicit conceptions of permissible practices, good stewardship, and justice.

Contrary to contemporary slogans, technological objects do impose constraints upon their users. Clearly there is latitude in function, but never complete freedom. Nuclear bombs, for example, condition modern warfare. A simple technological product such as a can opener must be utilized in a certain way to be effective. Air travel opens up several options, but it closes others, such as schedule and destination flexibility or the chance to stop and enjoy the scenery. The unique entity we call the computer embodies specific capabilities and restrictions. As George Grant elaborates,

> Abstracting facts so that they may be stored as "information" is achieved by classification, and it is the very nature of any classifying to homogenize what may be heterogeneous. Where classification rules, identities and differences can only appear in its terms.

This means, he concludes, "that computers increase the tempo of the homogenizing process in society."[14] Available choices are not randomly susceptible to unlimited genius, but depend on the regimen of technology's structure. Each technological artifact embodies particular values in spite of how or by whom it is used.

Harold Innis, the Canadian communication theorist, has introduced an influential line of scholarship based on this truism. Using the history of communications media as his laboratory, Innis documented a bias—tendency, propensity, impulse—regarding space and time. Oral communication systems, he argued, are biased toward time, rendering time continuous while making space discontinuous. In tribal societies, for example, culture is preserved through generations while cultural differences are accentuated from one geographic region to the next. Print systems, by contrast, are biased toward space, making geography continuous and breaking time into distinct units; nations spread their geographic empires while generational differences are accelerated. As his minor premise, Innis argued that one form of communication tends to monopolize others, rendering them residual; communications media do not exist innocently and neutrally alongside one another.

Innis' work on communication technology has been elaborated further by Marshall McLuhan, Eric Havelock, Elizabeth Eisenstein, Walter Ong, and James Carey. Together they represent the thesis that the history of communications is central to the history of civilization, that social change results from media transformations, that changes in communicative forms alter the structure of consciousness, including religious faith. Thus from the introduction of the telegraph to today's fiber optics, electronic technologies have attracted considerable attention—scholars in the Innis tradition examining all significant shifts in technological form, presuming from them subsequent alternations in culture and in perception.

TELEVISION

Within this paradigm of bias in communication systems, the significance of particular media technologies such as books, cinema, radio, and satellites can be elaborated in depth. The intellectual challenge is to identify the distinguishing properties of a technology such as television. With only shadowy notions of the cultural mandate, however, evangelicals have not delved deeply into television's technological and dramatic properties. Like the technocrat or the futurist, they have pronounced the presumed benefits of the medium without reflectively analyzing its peculiar potential and limits. But neither have the secular broadcasters nor the TV critics made such analysis. Traditional aesthetics, for example, is based on the contemplation of solid materials. Television is geared to electrical energy, peculiar pulsations of brightness and shade, vibrations of sound and light that die away even as they come into being. Aesthetics often result in unhelpful distinctions—Shakespeare as high culture and "Miami Vice" as low culture, for example—remnants of a long–standing but unproductive debate between Bernard Rosenberg and David Manning White.[15]

The other error is viewing television in terms of its siblings, film and radio, and call it picture radio or home theatre. We give television names such as "cinema made private," or see it as a bland version of theatre film. TV grew out of the womb of radio, in the sense that television was poured into radio's programming frames and network patterns. But this close connection ought not beguile us into wasteful misunderstandings of it as picture sound, small-screen film, or electronic book. Admittedly, four decades are a scant period for coming to terms with television's character, but it retains to this day a peculiar rootlessness born of our reluctance to take it seriously as a communication technology in its own right.

Every medium has its own grammar, that is, the elements enabling it to communicate. Even in the hands of evangelicals, there is no changing the inherent biases of a medium. The technology of each medium must be evaluated according to its own aesthetic features. Inspired by a sophisticated philosophy of technology, the first step is identifying the artistic laws and relationships that characterize each medium. And two medium-specific properties of television, for example, are intimacy and visual immediacy—depth regarding private space and simultaneity regarding time. These properties of the tube have shaped the evangelical message just as they have formed the contours of commercial television. Unfortunately, evangelicals have not thoroughly come to terms with their impact.

Intimacy. Television provides a fresh capacity for the penetration of character, which neither theatre, nor cinema possesses. On the TV set the visual foreground becomes a critical element. The iconography of rooms, for example, is far more determinative of television than exterior location. Expansiveness is inappropriate and no more than 3 or 4 actors can appear on the screen at once; everyone else becomes part of the studio audience, the congregation, or the "extras." Camera distance is defined by the actor's size and movements. The constraints of the screen's boundaries forces producers to develop the drama by concentrating it in the faces of the characters and entrusting them to unfold the complexity, beauty, and depth of the human personality—even when such personality is pathological.

Television's essential artistic resource is the actor's performance. Far more decisively than movie-actors, the television-actor controls the meaning. Television's visual scale grants a privacy unavailable elsewhere and thereby demands a believable performance. As David Thorburn suggests, "When an actor . . . causes us to acknowledge that what he is doing is true to the tangled potency of real experience, not simply impressive or clever, but true—what happens then is art." Vivid and highly professional acting over the history of TV accounts for nearly all those series most highly rated for quality—"Hill Street Blues," "Gunsmoke," "Twilight Zone," "Cade's County," "The Name of the Game," and "Mary Tyler Moore," for example. But they also account for the powerful personality cults created around televangelists whose cameras communicate entertainingly and effectively their own histrionics.

Visual immediacy. The lavish moments in television programming often have been live transmissions—the Kennedy assassination and funeral, the 1968 Democratic convention, Vietnam, the moonwalk, the Olympics. To a degree no other instrument can match, television captures immediacy and eventfulness; its representations coincide with the time of origination. John F. Kennedy's burial did not take place in Arlington Cemetery alone, but in the living rooms, bus terminals, and town squares of the world. Because of television, his "casket did not ride down Pennsylvania Avenue only. It rode down Main Street."[16] Television made the land mines in Vietnam explode in our own back yard.

Television is an immediate communication mode; the moment of creation is simultaneous with that of showing. The time element is the same for the director as it is for the spectator. Television broadcasters realize they have no later stage at which they can change the story line. In other words, one difference from cinema is the immediate, spontaneous, and topical nature of televised communication. TV has the tremendous advantage of enabling us to participate, as it were, in events as they occur. Television gives spectators the gift of ubiquity. And the roughness and unpredictability that are the spice of events as they unfold give great television an incomparable interest. Aesthetically mature television exhibits these qualities and attracts viewers by the real and immediate character of the picture. But in the hands of religious communicators, this capacity for greatness can be narrowed to the mendacities of TV faith healers and false prophets. The tube creates the sense of visual immediacy even when it is not intended, communicating televangelists as power brokers over empires, for example. Sometimes television's immediacy is co-opted purposely to fulfill the immediate needs of producers and celebrities for increased viewership or contributions.

Immanence. Technological bias can also be understood, not just in terms of one medium, but across a media category. Visual media, for example, share immanence as a common property. Pitirim Sorokin correctly defined sensate culture as that arena where reality is considered equal to the senses.[17] In this paradigm, no meaningful transcendent vision exists beyond the time and space accessible to the senses. Life is located only within the universe we see and hear, and not in some referent beyond immediate experience. In this secular version of the world, the supernatural—realities higher and deeper beyond the immediate—is excluded. Visual media such as television, cinema, and photography encourage a sensate worldview. They promote a closed, nontranscendent universe where an upper story does not exist. In a simplistic sense, that is what it means to be popular—television's tactile world corresponds to our society as a whole, neither tolerating the nonmaterial. Television art is largely a series of variations on a windowless immanence. Critics typically acquiesce and insist that film and videotape as media are hospitable only to realism. By immersing us in life's action and color, visual media are usually thought intractable to the supernatural.

Television shares the constraints of other photographic media. Picture-making is not based on synthesis but reduction. By contrast, paintings are constructed from a storehouse of skills, attitudes, and materials. Pictures are merely "taken." It has always been a concern to artists since photography's invention in the nineteenth century how this mechanical, selective process can produce clarity, coherence, and perspective—how it can add rather than relentlessly subtract. Picasso, for instance, explained the difference by comparing the painter to children who keep distance between themselves and reality by playing with it. For Picasso, the photographer resembles a surgeon who operates directly on the tissues of reality. The painter's image is total; he or she *creates* in a useful sense of the term, whereas the photographer penetrates through to a detail and concentrates there. On television, the religious communicator similarly replicates *real* images bound by the limits of the medium. Few evangelical broadcasters struggle to explore the limits of TV's windowless immanence. Instead, they often baptize a sensate worldview with the trappings of popular religious culture through so-called health-and-wealth theologies.

These examples of television's technological properties illustrate, but do not exhaust, the potency of a culture-embedded philosophy of technology. They are sufficient, however, to establish the thesis that each medium ought to be enabled to reach the limits of its symbolic capacity. As modern purveyors of the latest communications technologies, evangelicals are remarkably naïve about the cultural impact of the very media they appear to use so effectively. They have not aimed to discover strategies for working creatively within the boundaries that define each technological form. Therefore evangelicals have not contributed as meaningfully as possible to our social discourse or enhanced the symbolic theatre in which we live. If evangelicals could demonstrate how a medium's expressive scope is maximized—or, in other terms, how a medium's biases are overcome creatively—they would be subduing it for the kingdom of God and showing leadership in the artistic arena at the same time.

MORAL LITERACY

Mass-media technologies as cultural agents provide a common body of symbols for enabling our public rituals. To reiterate Ellul's formulation, communication technologies represent the meaning-edge of our cultural habitat. If evangelicals have a particular strength for enhancing contemporary culture, it is the articulation of a moral order. Evangelicals could help redeem popular art by engendering moral literacy; to the extent they stimulate the moral imagination, they fulfill a transformative purpose. We have heard this language in a sanitized sense: "Do these films have any redeeming social value?" Evangelicals should seek not unlimited religious broadcasting or abundant sacred media, but redemptive programming. While redemption with a small "r" cannot be equated with the Atonement, a richer concept of redemptiveness insists on Christian agency over culture as a whole and a symbolically mature popular art.

Neo-Marxists often speak of a message's dominant or preferred interpretation, which serves the ideological interests of the socioeconomic elite. Indeed, the media ordinarily engage in language practices that legitimize existing structures of power. While not acquiescing in Jean Lyotard's claims, for example, about the media weaving a fabric of repression, they ought to become sites of struggle against continuities and consensus. Using this nomenclature, redemptive media would communicate alternative discourses or offer subversive texts. At that epiphanal moment when the taken-for-granted world is made problematic and the moral contours illuminated, the media could serve as signifiers of justice, peace, and harmony.

Technological culture is an amoral environment, measuring values in terms of technique, efficiency, and the mystique of machineness. Moral norms are thus precluded, since efficiency values and judgments about rightness or wrongness are mutually exclusive. *La technique* acts tyrannically as a spiritual guillotine, decapitating other values and thus depriving them of cultural power. A civilization engrossed in means eliminates all moral obstructions to its ascendency, as "in ancient days men put out the eyes of nightingales in order to make them sing better."[18] *La technique* characterizes contemporary life to such an extent that moral judgment lies ruined within it. A "mean-sified" civilization converges on itself so relentlessly that, in principle, all necessities for moral decision are obviated; an alternative center of interest is congenitally inconceivable. Moreover, a technicized morality replaces ethical imperatives with averages and probabilities mathematically computed. Ellul foresaw already in 1948 that as the world of technics expands, our concerns will increasingly diminish to cost and time effectiveness, to administrative niceties, and become devoid of the moral dimension.[19] Thus the motifs of greatness and power receive virtually automatic justification. Everything that succeeds is declared good; results become the amoral criterion of contemporary activity.

In that climate, the theoretical rationale for privileging moral literacy ought to be obvious. Assuming that culture is the container of the human symbolic capacity, the constituent parts of such containers are a society's values. As to ordering relations, values direct the ends of social practice and provide implicit standards for selecting courses of action. With standards inherent in the concept of symbolic forms, indicating what authentic social existence involves is a theoretical imperative. Defining culture as "the symbolic-expressive aspect of social behavior," Robert Wuthnow correctly identifies the moral order as a set of cultural elements with a distinguishable symbolic structure. Moral codes, therefore, are necessary cultural constructions that articulate "the nature of commitment to a particular course of behavior."[20] As a sign of our distinctive humanness, we create symbolic patterns along the boundaries between moral norms and actual behavior, the deepest self and our roles, the intentional and the inevitable. These constructs are the moral code that plays a role in human life comparable to that of instinct in the lower organisms. As instinct keeps animals on target, so moral codes orient human beings. Freedom from instinct constitutes the ground for our radical inner freedom, the liberation of the human will. The ultimate menace occurs when our symbol systems start disintegrating, since ironically no one knows freedom without goals worth pursuing. If we read Jacques Derrida as a warning rather than a *fait accompli*, the self and public life may come to exist only in the text; our humanity faces the threat of surviving merely in our language and even when we seek it there, it is gone. Therefore, in cultures aligned toward normlessness and illusive centers of textuality, the media's prophetic task is calling communication technologies to their appropriate role in opening windows on the moral landscape by engaging the conscience. Evangelicals have much to offer here, but a viewer would never discern it from their typically moralistic programming that closes windows.

Glimmers of moral literacy appear at times. Among them are reenactments of purposeful history and justice among women and men, news reports that serve as instruments not of accommodation but of critique and social change. Documentaries, columnists, commentators, opinion journals, *Consumer Reports*, public broadcasting, and mass-market paperbacks often resonate with a redemptive accent, stir the human conscience, and liberate their viewers or readers from the dominant text. For example, Ken Auletta's *Underclass* represents the redemptive motif. He succeeds in demonstrating that next to war and peace—and perhaps the economy—the underclass is "the most momentous story in America."[21] It shows a redemptive glow in a professional world encumbered by snippets of unrepresentative events. Auletta's book-length reporting engages the will of careful readers and enhances their political insight.

The close observer certainly celebrates the achievements. The Arizona *Daily Star* once provided a sensitive and intelligent twenty-eight-page section on life in the Chicano ghettos entitled "Tucson's Barrios: A View from Inside." When Chet Huntley retired from NBC news, he recalled his proudest moments—and rightly so—as NBC's crusader for the Latino migrants in the groves of Florida. Over mass-media history, some papers and stations and reporters have refused the arrogance of power and sought to awaken the public conscience with the vigor of Jeremiah. Pulitzer prizes are still awarded, by and large, to professionals who distinguish themselves for community service and who shun careerism and mega-dollars. In public broadcasting, the "MacNeil/Lehrer Newshour" and National Public Radio's "Morning Edition" and "All Things Considered" frequently engender moral literacy by probing deeply and sensitively into events. Ted Koppel's "Nightline" and the ethnic press often provide a subversive reading. Sometimes local papers rise to the occasion and produce a penetrating examination of a local problem, as the *Chicago Tribune* illustrated with its award-winning "American Millstone" series in 1985. *Time*'s Lance Morrow wrote a penetrating account of the pope's visit to his would-be assassin, under the subhead: "A Pardon from the Pontiff; Lesson in Forgiveness for a Troubled World" (9 January 1984). In this lead news story, Morrow quoted biblical teaching on forgiveness, probed the psychological impact of this highly publicized encounter, and then concluded with a redemptive accent.

> Forgiveness is not an impulse much in favor. The prevalent style in the world runs more to the hard, cold eye of the avenger. Forgiveness does not look much like a tool for survival in a bad world. But that is what it is.

Roger Rosenblatt's "Children of War" (*Time*, 11 January 1982) and Richard Ostling's "Who Was Jesus?" (*Time*, 15 August 1988) demonstrate the redeemed mind as well, communicating truth in a public medium that cuts away the commonplaces and engages the affective roots of human personality.

Where are the evangelical attempts to broaden the moral landscape of a modern highly technological age? Contemporary televangelism often appears benign and innocuous before the society it allegedly seeks to redeem. Much evangelical mass communication simply reinforces the amorality of technology: it claims large audiences and converted sinners while ignoring the articulation of an explicit moral order.

But I do not insist on a dogged documentary seriousness. Humans can obviously be aided in moral literacy through drama as much as through news and public affairs.[22] Woody Allen's *Manhattan*, Antonioni's *Blow-Up*, Fellini, and Bergman often penetrate to our ultimate values. The classics *Loneliness of the Long Distance Runner*, *Charly*, and *The Silence* explore the crannies deep within the human spirit. National Geographic's "Incredible Machine" sounds a redeeming note as it celebrates the wonder and polyphony of life. *Chariots of Fire*, Horton Foote's *Tender Mercies*, and *Ordinary People* offer a healing voice without being Pollyannaish. Mel Brooks' *Elephant Man* wrestles with that immense theme, the apparent arbitrariness of life, its seeming unreason against our yearning for an explanation. John Merrick, the world's ugliest man who dies at age twenty-seven in 1890, is the historical setting for a tale of redemption in which the monstrous deformity cannot crush a heart of gold and the delicate humanity underneath. In Aristotle's profound understanding of artistic tragedy, great dramatists do not merely arouse pity or fear but "effect proper purgation."[23] Through the tears of Mrs. Treves, the spire of St. Philip's cathedral across the street, Merrick's astonishing recitation of Psalm 23, his boyish prayers as he lies down to sleep for the last time—*The Elephant Man* resists moral chaos and purges our human fear of capricious suffering. The tragedy of evangelical media is that they have rarely captured the moral and spiritual spaciousness of the historic Christian faith. Instead they are interpreted by their audiences as accommodating themselves to the latest production fads.

REDEMPTIVE TELEVISION

These intimations of redemptiveness are drawn from various media of popular culture: paperbacks, film, comics, television, general circulation magazines, and the newspaper. But television, as the major mass medium in the United States, deserves special attention. Moreover, as the reigning champion among evangelical media, television begs for analysis and critique. Can each of television's defining features—intimacy, immediacy, and immanence—be shaped by biblical givens? The question is whether evangelicals can present television as a redemptive artistic form, or will they relegate this technology to secular moralists?

First, television's peculiar capacity to exhibit and penetrate human character typically tends to erode the mystery of humanity. The Scriptures shed light on the numberless dimensions of humanity—the whole person, the full person, image-bearers of the Creator living in a dependent relationship with him. By contrast, so-called Christian programs sometimes degrade human beings as objects to be propagandized. Like much popular art, evangelical shows predominantly imbibe a naturalistic worldview in which women and men are bundles of biological drives and physical senses. There are few strong and complicated people; there are mostly caricatures of born-again believers. Only a limited range of human emotions and motivations comes through. On balance, no genuine longing for spiritual fulfillment nor authentic religious doubts are expressed. Evangelical programming is virtually destitute of deep moral discernment, preferring instead to rail against personal sin while overlooking institutional corruption. The sharp edges of life disappear, and fundamental conflict dissolves into grayness. In this sense the televangelists and most TV drama prefer visual sensation over normative reflection.

Television redeems its peculiar capacity for intimacy when it seriously wrestles with our humanness, provides glimpses of mature realism, and pushes toward greater variety and sagacity. Occasionally the small screen opens an outsized window on credible people; cut against naturalism, some programming illuminates the complications of choosing between righteousness and evil, with people held morally culpable for the alternative selected. At various points this symbolic form is used to confront ultimate human problems—not just this war, but "why any war?" not just this loneliness, but "why any forsakenness in the midst of multitudes?" Even "M*A*S*H*" raised occasionally the permanent questions about life's logic and God's involvement that escape the televangelists. Compared to "Dragnet," "Cagney and Lacey" seriously probes issues about authority, punishment, and patriarchy that the earliest shows in the law-and-order genre never confronted. Cagney and Lacey themselves often become instances of what

Jean Paul Sartre in *The Family Idiot* called the "universal singular," that is, particular embodiments of broad historical struggles and achievements.[24] "Hill Street Blues," a critics' favorite until it waned toward predictability in its later years, made forgiveness integral to the storyline, and developed a "rich texture of human relationships."[25] But none of these were evangelical programs.

And within the aesthetic history of crime fiction, highly sensationalized "Dallas" deserves a closer analysis than it ordinarily receives. In spite of its contrived characterization, as Mary Mander has argued convincingly, "Dallas" examines the morality of organizations rather than that of individuals. "Dallas" mirrors correctly our deepening realization that individualism no longer explains the social order. Using the melodramatic formula, the show contends that only in the collective—the corporation or the family—do individuals survive. "Dallas" enters the domain of power, beliefs, and hidden struggles through the family—a symbol that may have replaced the impassioned image of the frontier in its national appeal. Or stated differently, "Dallas" works off a contradiction between two sets of values: the ruthless, cutthroat world of the corporation, and the domain of nurture represented by the family. As such, this television series has redemptively located the collective search for moral order within the context of family and corporation. Televised communication has this capacity to penetrate character but does not allow us to grasp visually the corporate and macroscopic. "Dallas"—and "Knot's Landing" less successfully—represents a significant attempt to reverse that deficiency.

Robert Bellah's *Habits of the Heart* documents today's social fragmentation; and to the extent that postmodernism's "Death of Man" speaks for our age, a medium taking humanity seriously provides a significant counterforce. But sophisticated responses in evangelical programming have been minuscule to date. Ironically, the programs criticized by evangelicals may be approximating the right questions and illuminating in a gross fashion the real bewilderment of the human soul. Yet it will take the redeemed mind in cultural production before television can compellingly represent the human condition on this side of a historical fall.

Second, regarding immediacy, what view of history emerges from television? How does it treat human society in space and time? Does the historical tempo on the screen match the biblical one? Television technology makes the living moment brilliant; to be redemptive, the vividly immediate cannot contradict the elaborate realities of purposive history. However, with the exception of soap operas, occasional mini-series, or made-for-television movies, each episode on television is typically self-contained. "Little House on the Prairie," "The Waltons," and "Bonanza" rested somewhere in a historical period, yet their structural pattern was an enclosed hour and not the perplexing arena of space-time history. Television tends to insulate audiences from history and create a texture commensurate with its own electronic dynamics. In Ellul's terminology, television creates a punctilliar canvas, whose momentary flashes and kamikaze dives into our temporality do not register moral sensitivity. Evangelical programming, from pulpit to variety and talk shows, is no exception.

As Protestant reformer John Calvin put it, God is constantly vigilant, efficacious, operative, continually engaged, and edging history toward a climax.[26] His God, and presumably the God of evangelicals generally, controls history in his providence; thus, however obscurely seen, nothing is aimless or circular, or curved in upon itself, or unremittingly destructive. In this view, things do not merely happen; they are brought about and shaped by the God who resides at the center of a meaningful universe. Programs that purge the narrowness of modern humankind's ahistorical understanding of itself rightly and provocatively open the movement of time to a fresh and sometimes chilling view. They introduce more complexity into our speech about morality by seeing human fallenness as both judged and overcome. NBC's nine-and-a-half-hour docudrama, "Holocaust," re-enacted a historic event through the story of two German families from 1935 to 1945. Legitimate critics scorned NBC for exploiting such serious material for commercial gain, and the enormous complexity of the moral issues was inevitably trivialized. Despite the shortcomings, however, "Holocaust" raised the consciousness of millions about the dangers of anti-Semitism by embedding its own event-character within the flow of history. It moved beyond mere candor to engage the public scruples. "Roots" also combined historical circumstances with dramatic intensity, in spite of predictable plots and stereotyped characters. The apocalypticism of "The Day After" tended to weaken at times its redemptive impact; however, it nudged its seventy million viewers away from hysteria or indifference, and thus toward heightened moral awareness about their own fate in history.

In many respects, Bill Moyers' "CBS Reports: People Like Us" serves as a model of the type of news story coveted by the redeemed mind. Moyers gave a voice to Larry Ham, Frances Dorta, and Cathy Dixon—powerless people who had fallen through the government's safety net. Television became an instrument for those being hurt—though often unintentionally—by social policies poorly designed or ineptly administered, and in some cases blatantly unfair. Consistent with the canons of acceptable news practice, Moyers gave no moralistic preachments. He sought only to make the faces of the poor as distinct and their voices as clear as audiences typically hear and see from agents of the establishment. The result was redemptive programming anchoring its immediacy in the currents of purposive history and honoring the cause of social justice. Evangelicals, by contrast, tend to produce moralistic tirades about the dangers of liberal governments and devilish social programs, without serving as a positive instrument of justice.

Third, television—as with other visual media—does not easily communicate the nonmaterial. Its technological structure tends to equate truth with immediate sensory impressions and remove mystery from life. Television's various symbolic patterns together sustain a monistic, senses-bound fictional frame called by Alfred Schutz "ordinary-commonsense reality."[27] Some dramatic styles regularly assert self-transcendence, the necessity of bettering one's lot by moving beyond personal and social circumstances. They are not content with the visual and material; they do not superficialize human trauma. The modern age, they declare in effect, must discover higher levels of consciousness. Sometimes humanistic psychology, Eastern mysticism, and Castenadan lore are mined for techniques to present that heightened awareness. Nevertheless, prime-time television is categorically sensate. All such pointings are metaphors only; they do not communicate genuine transcendence, that is, as a category on its now terms with unique configurations.

"The Incredible Hulk," as did "The Six Million Dollar Man," and "Wonder Woman" earlier, demonstrated the same theme of self-transcendence but this time premised on an ultimate faith in human ability to surmount limitations by technological creativity or larger-than-life comic-strip heroes. Complex negative forces, we were assured, can be subdued by engineering or mystical force. The original "Superman" contained these elements, and "Planet of the Apes," "Buck Rogers in the 25th Century," "Battleship Galactica," and "The Night Stalker" contained some of them. These series presumed that humans may ultimately exercise absolute command over their environment, but they did not verify the supernatural. Meanwhile, mysteries such as "Star Trek," "Twilight Zone," "Space 1999," "Project UFO," and "Mission Impossible" were really only a game, a challenge to the organized mind. Since logic and craftiness solved each episode, this genre did not promote genuine transcendence. As with self-transcendent emphases generally, mysteries in popular art do no more than express deep-rooted faith in the human faculty for authenticating our species-superiority by acts of the will and genius.

Regardless of the different artistic forms that comprise the kaleidoscope we call television entertainment, the sensate mentality is a fundamental, generic theme. Obviously immanence cannot be presented as mass entertainment's total meaning, but television formulae are firmly anchored in nontranscendence regardless of differences in setting, stylistic structures, fictional characterization, episodic touches, religious intent, and an enormous range in artistic quality. TV creates a monodimensional cosmos with an unmistakable terrain—what Levi Strauss calls the narrative's deep structure.[28] All the while, there is little point in speaking contemptuously of artistic thinness on prime-time American television; that aesthetic matter is related, but is essentially another issue. Even solid entertainment that mixes poignancy and humor may fail to establish transcendence.

In spite of the visual media's bias against an ineffable realm, Paul Schrader marshals convincing evidence in his *Transcendental Style in Film* that video art can express transcendence.[29] By freezing a view that transcends the disunity of human existence, we are nudged toward the invisible through the visible itself. Another reality is established alongside sense reality. A world that refuses to be constrained within ordinary patterns of explanation can open up. Perhaps this transcendent possibility should be enough to call evangelicals to the medium of television. Instead, evangelicals have been called to "preach the Word," an activity that is increasingly problematic in a medium designed largely to arouse sensations through images. How does one *hear* the voice of God through a technological process that naturally promotes the material while obfuscating the transcendent message? If Schrader is right, television as well as film could do so through visual storytelling. But evangelicals are suspicious of much entertainment, let alone metaphoric televised transcendence. As a result, evangelical broadcasters have typically based their scripts on straightforward, propositional claims about God and humankind. Nothing could be less effective on the small TV screen for communicating transcendence.

Evangelicals should do more than issue tedious reports and siren warnings about the mass media's part in our modern malaise. They should let their worldview, with all of its moral and spiritual depth, shape their media products and establish a healthy but critical moral climate. Popular culture sorely needs its Charles Williams reminding this secular age of a spiritual realm, and its C. S. Lewis dramatizing the moral contest within that realm. Courageous executives and creative producers are scattered among the evangelical media enterprise, but it needs more distinctive artistry, not more technology, to overcome its pusillanimity and orient its structure toward cultural transformation. For television to be redemptive, symbolizing an authentic, transcendental realm warrants our serious aesthetic attention. Evangelicals can assist television in becoming a distinctive form of popular art by producing ambitious examples of the transcendental style.

Whenever one sees conscientious insight into humankind as a moral species; whenever there are concerted efforts toward purposeful history; whenever the vast reaches of the supernatural are symbolized, there one sees the hand of God. Such popular culture with a redemptive bearing fulfills the cultural mandate. "All truth," Arthur Holmes declares in another context, "is God's Truth."[30]

CONCLUSION

Over the longer term, the success of evangelical mass communications systems may destroy the cultural fabric of the local church in particular and the evangelical community in general. The realities of global politics or national economics may necessitate using the electronic media, as an automobile can haul sand like a pickup when necessary or a wrench can pound nails when no hammer is available. But presenting the gospel of grace is still fundamentally the province of orality, and missionary broadcasting cannot substitute for personal evangelism. All cultural institutions—including the mass media—serve a range of human interests, while designed around a fundamental core. In evangelicalism, that core has obviously become the Great Commission. But the Great Commission has not abrogated the cultural mandate. The question that evangelicals will increasingly ask themselves is whether a technological enterprise for saving souls can actually serve as the basis for establishing and maintaining any social institution—including the church.

The Bible sees the church's critical task as empowering the laity to become transformers of culture for the good of humankind. In this scenario, the media's role in moral literacy might be analogous to public health; for all its spectacular importance, however, experts in medicine and surgery are still needed to run a hospital. Popular culture that enhances moral literacy plays a vital part in developing a public philosophy. As Ellul wrote,

> Day after day the wind blows away the pages of our calendars, our newspapers, and our political regimes, and we glide along the stream of time without any spiritual framework, without a memory, without a judgment, carried about by "all winds of doctrine" on the currents of history. . . . Now we ought to react vigorously against this slackness, this tendency to drift. If we are to live in this world, we need to know it far more profoundly; we need to rediscover the meaning of events, and the spiritual framework which our contemporaries have lost.[31]

A laity mobilized to know this world profoundly could use redemptive mass communications for the good of all. So far the evangelical community has exalted the mass media for outreach, but has had little positive impact on their contribution to the overall flow of cultural history.

NOTES

[1]Malcolm Muggeridge, *Christ and the Media* (Grand Rapids: Eerdmans, 1977).
[2]Jacob Bronowski, *Science and Human Values*, rev. ed. (New York: Harper & Row, 1965).
[3]Jacques Ellul, *Perspectives on Our Age*, trans. Joachim Neugroschel (New York: Seabury, 1981), ch. 2.

[4]Hans Jonas, *The Imperative of Responsibility* (Chicago: University of Chicago Press, 1984), ix–xi, ch. 1.

[5]Darrell J. Fasching, "Theology, Technology and Transcendence: Reflections on Bernard Lonergan and Jacques Ellul" (Unpublished paper, University of South Florida, Tampa, n.d.).

[6]Jacques Ellul, "Symbolic Function, Technology and Society," *Journal of Social and Biological Structures*, October 1978, 216.

[7]Jacques Ellul, *Propaganda* (New York: Knopf, 1969), xvii.

[8]Jean Baudrillard, *For a Critique of the Political Economy of the Sign*, trans. Charles Levin (St. Louis: Telos, 1981), ch. 9.

[9]Ellul, *Propaganda*, 166; cf. 30, 64, 77.

[10]R. A. Buchanan, *Technology and Social Progress* (Oxford: Pergamon, 1965), 163.

[11]Arnold Pacey, *The Culture of Technology* (Cambridge, Mass.: The MIT Press, 1983), 1–3.

[12]Quentin J. Schultze, "The Mythos of the Electronic Church," *Critical Studies in Mass Communication*, September 1987, 245–61.

[13]Pacey, *Culture of Technology*, 102.

[14]George Grant, "The Computer Does Not Impose on Us the Way It Should Be Used," *Beyond Industrial Growth*, ed. A. Rotstein (Toronto: University of Toronto Press, 1976), 125–26.

[15]Bernard Rosenberg and David Manning White, eds., *Mass Culture Revisited* (New York: Van Nostrand Reinhold, 1971), 3–21.

[16]*Newsweek*, 9 December 1963.

[17]Pitirim A. Sorokin, *Social and Cultural Dynamics*, 4 vols. (New York: American Book Co., 1937–1941). Cf. Clifford Christians, "The Sensate in Sorokin and in Primetime Television," *Et cetera: A Review of General Semantics*, Summer 1981, 189–201.

[18]Jacques Ellul, *Presence of the Kingdom* (New York: Seabury, [1948] 1967), 75.

[19]Other sociologists now confirm what Ellul anticipated 40 years ago in *Presence of the Kingdom*. Kevin P. Philips writes, for example: "There is a worrisome truth in the analysis that morality and postindustrial-cum-communications technology do not easily co-exist," in his *Mediacracy* (Garden City, N.Y.: Doubleday, 1975), ix. Claus Mueller argues that the central problem of advanced capitalist societies has shifted from the economic sphere to that of moral values and beliefs in his *Politics of Communication* (New York: Oxford University Press, 1973).

[20]Robert Wuthnow, *Meaning and Moral Order: Explorations in Cultural Analysis* (Berkeley: University of California Press, 1987), 4, 66, 71–75.

[21]Ken Auletta, *The Underclass* (New York: Random House, 1982), xviii.

[22]Cf. Johan Huizinga, *Homo Ludens: A Study of the Play Element in Culture* (Boston: Beacon, 1955) and Josef Pieper, *Leisure: The Basis of Culture*. (New York: Random House, 1963), chs. 1–5.

[23]Aristotle, "De Poetca," in *Introduction to Aristotle*, ed. Richard McKeon, trans. I. Bywater (New York: Modern Library, 1947), 1449b, 630–31.

[24]Jean Paul Sartre, *The Family Idiot: Gustave Flaubert, 1821–1857*, vol. 1 (Chicago: University of Chicago Press, 1981), ix.

[25]Mark Fackler and Stephen Darling, "Forgiveness on Prime-Time Television—A Case Study: Hill Street Blues," *Studies in Popular Culture*, 10:1 (1987), 64–73.

[26]John Calvin, *Institutes of the Christian Religion*, ed. John T. McNeill (Philadelphia: Westminister, 1960).

[27]Alfred Schutz and Thomas Luckman, *The Structures of the Life-World* (Evanston, Ill.: Northwestern University Press, 1973).

[28]Claude Levi-Strauss, *Structural Anthropology* (New York: Basic Books, 1963).

[29]Paul Schrader, *Transcendental Style in Film: Ozu, Bresson, Dreyer* (Berkeley: University of California Press, 1972), 3–13.

[30]Arthur Holmes, *All Truth Is God's Truth* (Grand Rapids: Eerdmans, 1977).

[31]Ellul, *Presence of the Kingdom*, 138.

16

A SHORT STORY OF EVANGELICAL SCHOLARSHIP IN COMMUNICATIONS STUDIES

MARK FACKLER

The essays in this volume are compelling evidence of the kind of spirit Daniel Boorstin has typified as the "go-getter" mentality—the spirit of American entrepreneurs who tamed a continent by presence of will and forceful ingenuity, who paid a considerable price in suffering and risk yet established institutions and transformed cultures to fit their unformed visions of the good, true, and beautiful. They did it, Boorstin claimed in his series on the Americans, largely because it was there to be done.[1]

For American evangelicals who used, manipulated, debased, and built mission enterprises with the technologies of mass media, questions of motivations and *mentalities* are at the center of the historical account. These go-getters had to explain their entrepreneurship in theological categories that both blessed and cursed their manifold works. The commonwealth of Christians who supported their efforts had to be made to want the product and be convinced that it represented a legitimate extension of the Bible's mandate to make disciples of all nations. Not without forceful personalities blind to their own weaknesses was the evangelical media establishment built. Not also without a sense of mission that Boorstin could only allude to, but never isolate. Why did they do it, these evangelicals? What heavenly visions prompted their embrace of all the modern megaphones we call media? Is the product of their work a series of Babels, or as one radio entrepreneur titled his book, "towers to eternity"?[2]

The printing press and the Reformation are inventions indelibly linked in the evangelical consciousness. How the new press helped transform religion from centralized system to fragmented diversity, at the same time placing the "means of grace" into every believer's hands, is articulately described in Elizabeth Eisenstein's formidable work *The Printing Press as an Agent of Change: Communications and Cultural Transformations in Early- Modern Europe* (1979). Nathan Hatch carries that historical search into colonial America in *The Democratization of American Christianity* (1989) and David Paul Nord shows how revivalism and the printing press worked together to create a common culture of mutual, same-day reading ("The Evangelical Origins of Mass Media in America, 1815–1835" *Journalism Monographs,* May 1984), as the pamphlet and booklet replaced the chalice as a central symbol of Christian unity.[3]

Fascination with technology was all the more pronounced with the invention of radio. Quentin Schultze has expanded on James Carey's work to describe the sacralizing of ether and Audion in "The Mythos of the Electronic Church" (*Critical Studies in Mass Communication* 4:1987), an essay that takes to task the kind of grandiose claims by religious broadcasters satirized in Joseph Bayly's farce *The Gospel Blimp.* Schultze has also contributed an accessible and important analysis (from an evangelical and Reformed perspective) of commercial broadcasting in *Television: Manna from Hollywood* (1986), which updates and expands Paul Borgman's 1979 book directed to parents worried about children in front of the tube, *Television: Friend or Foe?* William Fore is perhaps mainstream Protestantism's most prolific commentator on religious media, though James Walls' many essays in the *Christian Century* (and his 1971 *Church and Cinema*) are equally as penetrating. Fore contributed *Image and Impact: How Man Comes Through the Mass Media* in 1970 and most recently *Television and Religion* (1987). Students of media must begin with these scholars, none of them broadcasters but each identifying the key questions of cultural change and technological artifact that define this diverse field.[4]

Yet for an introduction to religious media, the story must include at least a brief search of the handbooks and theologies that began to establish a literature in print and broadcast. One can hear echoes of the "mythos" in Charles Stelzle's *Principles of Successful Church Advertising* (1908) and Christian Reisner's

Church Publicity: The Modern Way to Compel Them to Come In (1913). As if transfixed by scientism, Clarence Barbour edited *Making Religion Efficient* in 1912 and Wendell Loveless collected his experience and knowledge in the first textbook for Christian radio, *Manual of Gospel Broadcasting* (1946), which includes a fascinating chapter on broadcast ethics. Bruce Barton's well-known book *The Man Nobody Knows* (1924) is not a text on broadcasting, but public relations in its most astounding religious analogy. For insights on church use of media just before the world changed in the 1960s, see Sue Nichols *Words on Target: For Better Christian Communication*; William Leidt, *Publicity Goes to Church*; and James Kimsey, *How to Conduct Religious Radio Programs*. The gist of Leidt's manual was transported into evangelical circles by William Lessel's *Church Publicity* (1970) when addressographs were still standard equipment in every church office. A more up-to-date book on church publicity is James Vitti's *Publicity Handbook for Churches and Christian Organizations* (1987).[5]

With an eye to the Payne Fund studies of 1929–32, Edward John Carnell began to probe the impact of television, even in its infancy, in *Television: Servant or Master?* (1950) while the Hollywood-based, Neibuhr-inspired Episcopal churchman Malcolm Boyd expanded on questions of impact and symbol in *Crisis in Communication: A Christian Examination of the Mass Media* (1957) and *Christ and Celebrity Gods: The Church in Mass Culture* (1958), where the discussion turns to Hollywood's religious films. Eugene Nida's *Message and Mission: The Communication of the Christian Faith* (1960) took an international perspective the same year that John Bachman issued the first of his writings, a reflection of the 1958 National Council of Churches' Study Commission on the Role of Radio-Television and Film titled *The Church in the World of Radio-Television*. Bachman's 1980 *Media: Wasteland or Wonderland* is one of the few thoughtful Christian critiques of commercial broadcasting. From London came F. W. Dillistone's *Christianity and Communication* (1956). Yet these cultural analyses were precursors and agenda setters. In the history and criticism of specific media (nonbroadcast especially), much waits to be done.[6]

The short shelf of monographs on religious print media must rank as a modern anomaly, given the impressive development of the religious book industry, if not evangelicalism's reverence for the book. Until Marvin Olasky's recent work, students of the religious press had John Gill's compelling biography of Elijah Lovejoy, *Tide Without Turning* (n.d.), and Judith Duke's atlas and survey, *Religious Publishing and Communications* (1981). Wesley Norton's area study, *Religious Newspapers in the Old Northwest to 1861* (1977) should have inspired similar projects, but did not. John Ferré's *Social Gospel for Millions: The Religious Bestsellers of Charles Sheldon, Charles Gordon, and Harold Bell Wright* (1988) provides much–needed background and analysis in a style consonant with popular culture studies. Scholars should not let Ferré's inspiration slip away.[7]

It may be significant, at least interesting, that two recent books on religious publishing were both brought out by a publishing house fundamentalist in origin and entrepreneurial (though strongly conservative) today. Crossway Books in Westchester, Illinois, issued Cal Thomas' *Book Burning* in 1983 and Olasky's *Prodigal Press* in 1988. Each argues that an anti-Christian bias in American culture has suppressed the evangelical presence in book and newspaper publishing. Thomas is ostensibly worried about first-amendment freedoms for Christians, while Olasky, a media historian who is editing a major series for Crossway on a full range of cultural crises, uncovers important background on the evangelical moorings of daily journalism in colonial America up to the Jacksonian era. Where does one go beyond these sources? The University of North Carolina Press has just issued a collection of papers in black history that includes much correspondence on the black antebellum press, a story that cannot be told apart from its religious dimension. The Wheaton Seminar in Religious Book Publishing has given a forum for the beginning of a history of evangelical book publishing, but much work remains in gathering the complex story of a subindustry now celebrated in two competing trade magazines.[8]

On the topic of religious magazines, we can only note that the essay by Stephen Board in this volume cites not a single monograph on his topic. All of his material is drawn from personal interviews, occasional isolated articles, biographies, shop talk, and portions of chapters in books devoted to broader, loftier themes. Evangelical presses have produced a veritable feast of books and magazines on every facet of spirituality and Christian life, church history and sectarian aberration, social action and better parenting, not to mention Bible products, but on its own history those same presses have been silent. Perhaps the work begun in this volume will inspire more research in this elder mass medium.

When one turns from print to broadcast, however, the parched desert of scholarship becomes instantly a brimming oasis of refreshment and activity. It would be impossible here to comprehensively note the growing literature. Individual scholars keep such bibliographies up to date on their hard disks, but our purposes will be served, we trust, by isolating the leading lights and attempting to point to polar opposites that, read with judgment, articulate the perennial questions and draw their respective tentative conclusions.

Known in Britain for his wartime radio talks as much as for his dramatic conversion from Marxism to Christianity, Malcolm Muggeridge, journalist and humorist, is still the most uncompromising evangelical opponent of doing anything righteous on television. His *Christ and the Media* (1977) offers an either-or to readers, much as Jacques Ellul's *Humiliation of the World* (1985) argues that capturing reality in photograph or moving image is an oxymoron of the most subtle and pervasive kind. What good can come of television, they ask? The nature of the medium itself violates the intensely personal and spiritual nature of genuine revelation. Believers who place hope of sustenance or evangelistic growth in this medium have been duped by idols, they claim. Virginia Stem Owens joins that chorus in her stinging critique of telephilia, *The Total Image: Selling Jesus in the Modern Age* (1980), an argument that Bruce Barton would have found incomprehensible.[9]

Quite the opposite portrait is given in Ben Armstrong's *Electric Church* (1979), a book not intended to be controversial but made so by its unrelenting optimism on the presence and future of broadcast religion. That Armstrong directed for many years the National Religious Broadcasters should signal the inevitability of blue-sky over this book eternally. If ever a mythos can be found in evangelicalism's embrace of technology, it is here. As an elixir to the dismal future advanced by Muggeridge and Ellul, Armstrong has no equal.[10]

Scholarship in televangelism (as opposed to evangelical research on commercial television) dates from the mid-1950s and Everett Parker, the former director of the Office of Communication of the United Church of Christ who led the civil rights charge against station WLBT in the 1960s and still represents the pro-Fairness Doctrine viewpoint as forcefully as ever. Parker's *Religious Radio* (1957), *Religious Television* (1961), and (with D. W. Barry and Dallas Smythe) *The Television-Radio Audience and Religion* (1955) were initial efforts to describe and prescribe a phenomenon that had not yet broken free of network constraints. In those days, televangelism was as restless as independent film producers in the early 1900s, and just as migrations to Hollywood broke apart the film trust, so independent religious program producers were soon to overtake mainline denominations in airtime and audience ratings. Peter Horsfield's *Religious Television* (1984) traces that history again and provides the most current booklength analysis of the impact of paid-time, vis-à-vis sustaining-time, religious programs.[11]

Between Parker and Horsfield, with pens as sharp as swords, stand J. Harold Ellens and Donald Oberdorfer, both churchmen who care personally about trendiness in Christian programming and seek to assist our understanding of it. Ellens developed an intriguing typology in his *Models of Religious Broadcasting* (1974), concluding that the discursive, doctrinal, and explicitly evangelistic thrust of most religious programs was wrong-headed both in terms of desired outcomes and in use of the medium's natural strengths. His own church was devoted to stand-up television preaching at the time. Sympathetic readers can get the other side of Ellens' viewpoint in David DeGroot's *Worlds Beyond: The Story of the Back to God Hour* and Peter Eldersveld's *Nothing but the Gospel*. Oberdorfer's prognosis is more moderate and hopeful (*Electronic Christianity: Myth or Ministry*, 1982), a point of view taken a decade earlier by Dennis Benson in *Electronic Evangelism*. Stewart Hoover's *Mass Media Religion: the Social Sources of the Electronic Church* (1988) expands his earlier book, *Electronic Giant*, with a Protestant mainliner's sympathetic call to a more socially responsible and self-conscious telechurch. Hoover also provides the latest statistical studies on telechurch audiences, which should be read along with George Gerbner, et al., *Religion and Television* (1984).[12]

The dethronings on moral grounds of televangelists Jim and Tammy Bakker in 1987 and Jimmy Swaggart in 1988, and the setback of presidential candidate (and CBN Network founder) Pat Robertson, have been rehearsed in several accounts. Jeffrey Hadden and Charles Swann signaled the potential for such abuse of privilege (Bakker and Swaggart) and ambition (Robertson) in *Prime-Time Preachers: The Rising of Televangelism* (1981). Hadden joined Anson Shupe in updating the story in 1988 (*Televangelism: Power and Politics on God's Frontier*), a book that added to Razelle Frankl's more cursory *Televangelism: The Marketing of Popular Religion* (1988) as a not-so-sympathetic expose of the not-always-admirable fellows who command personal allegiance and precious cash from a surprisingly large and gullible constituency. No reader need wonder about the slant of Larry Martz's *Ministry of Greed: The Inside Story of the Televangelists and Their Holy Wars* (1988), or Jerry Sholes' *Give Me That Prime-Time Religion* (1979). The editors of Moody Press took a genuine step of faith with (editor) Michael Horton's *Agony of Deceit* (1990), a substantive and controversial critique of televangelist theology that *Time* magazine featured in a full-page review. Untold pages are yet to be consumed in rejoinders and rebuttals, but the issues are now engaged. Absent from the fray but still one of the most visible of television preachers, Billy Graham survives as an evangelist crafted for stadium pulpits and untouched by innovations in television programming. Old films of his crusades in New York, for example, are not much different in form from contemporary telecasts. Michael Real (*Mass-Mediated Culture*, ch. 4) analyzes the crusade event while John Pollock (*Crusades: 20 Years With Billy Graham*, 1969; *Billy Graham: Highlights of the Story*, 1984) and other biographers (Paul Westman, George Burnham, John Capon) confirm Graham's abilities at using television as a tool, a conduit, a neutral sender of high-impact signals, as if hypodermic-needle theories may yet have some relevance.[13]

Concerning missionary radio, which evangelicals prize as one of their great monuments to taming technology, the story is largely told by insider histories, now dated and in need of revision both as to information and triumphalism. The "big three" in missionary radio are HCJB-Quito (*Seeds in the Wind*, 1961), Trans World Radio (*Towers to Eternity*, 1968), and Far East Broadcasting (*Sky Waves*, 1963). Other radio biographies tell of ELWA (*Voice Under Every Palm*, 1972), worldwide programming (*Slim Fingers*, 1976), and East Africa (*Proclaiming Christ to the World: The Experience of Radio Voice of the Gospel*, 1983). In nearly every account, the blessing of God is seen in the height of towers, scope of signals, mail response of listeners, fragile broadcasting agreements with yet more fragile foreign governments, and continuing and timely support of U.S. donors. The clear message is that radio has begun to do what the typical foot-soldier missionary cannot: get everywhere with the same and single story of Jesus. This important aspect of the evangelical presence desperately needs a von Rankian for the next generation of biographies and institutional histories.[14]

A broadcast shelf not directly addressed in this volume is church handbooks, the broadcast texts, and program catalogs prepared with the pastor and church education director foremost in mind. It is ironic to note that all the authors cited here represent mainline denominations, not independent evangelicals. Clayton Griswold and Charles Schmitz produced a 1957 handbook for the National Council of Churches (*How You Can Broadcast Religion*). Holland, Nickerson, and Vaughan declared the arrival of small video technology in *Using Nonbroadcast Video in the Church* (1980). Jaberg and Wargo added to that drama in *The Video Pencil: Cable Communications for Church and Community* (1980). Edward McNulty's popular books (*Television: A Guide for Christians*, 1976; *When TV Is a Member of the Family*, 1981) move media strategy toward Ellen's fourth (unevangelical–like) model, and Tom Neufer Emswiler has honed his thinking at a state university ministry (*A Complete Guide to Making the Most of Video in Religious Settings*, 1985). All handbooks must bow, however, to B. F. Jackson's three-volume *Communication for Churchmen*, which covers, successively, learning theory, TV-radio-film, and equipment (1968–70). Implicit in all these user guides is a friendly vision of balanced media presence effectively employed by religious and lay professionals semi-skilled in camera work, lighting, sound, and scripting. One does not need a Ph.D. in video to know that video is a tool for spiritual learning and development, the European critics notwithstanding.[15]

Much of the same debate is found in the literature surrounding contemporary Christian music, from Bob Larson's diatribe (*Rock and the Church*, 1971) to Steve Lawhead's appeals for balance (*Rock Reconsidered*, 1981). The researcher can find histories of the industry, stories of the great artists, theologies expounding the difference between lyric and beat, and a storehouse of thoughtful magazine articles ranging from the work of John Guest in *The Banner* to Al Menconi (*Rock Music: A Window to Your Child's Soul*, 1990) in his organization's newsletter *Media Update* to the ever-present journal *Contemporary Christian Music*. Beyond these few references, I defer to Bill Romanowski's excellent essay and to the sources he carefully cites. The question remains: Can a medium so admired and in quarters so flagrantly anti-Christian still be a source of God-ward inspiration? I am encouraged to find evangelicals both at the forefront of religious music and actively researching what is probably the most powerful medium—secular rock—for shaping the values of adolescents and young adults.[16]

What can be said about the need for systematic historical and economic research on the religious motion picture business? Here is an industry using a medium vilified by the devout, cherished by the young, historically attacked by the churches, once nearly imprisoned by Catholic morality (with strong Protestant support), and now as free to explore the widest ranges of subject and themes as any medium in the known history of communications technologies. It was a motion picture case that challenged and dismantled America's anti-blasphemy laws. It was film attendance that became sufficient warrant for withholding the church's sacraments in several communions. Only film has been assigned the scarlet "C." Concerning religious film (that is, film produced explicitly for religious instructional purposes) we face such idiosyncracies as a converted theater in Philadelphia with altar calls after each showing, a radio psychologist (James Dobson) who commands the overwhelming share of church film rentals, and an upstart company that hires a Hollywood producer to do a "moral movie" and without script or concept ballyhoos support and finances from people who forbid their children to enter a movie house. Here is a patchwork of companies and artists struggling to adapt to a video-centric culture, fearful that its meager 16mm viewer base is in certain jeopardy, largely unwilling to reveal its story and thin-skinned about people who ask from whence it came and to what purpose it is directed.[17]

Terry Lindvall's work at Regent University has created an academic home where research on the evangelical film industry may bear fruit. Evangelical film currently has a weak and protective trade group, no journal, and no independent review since the *Christian Film and Video* newsletter ceased publication in May 1989. Imagine a film like *Thief in the Night* (a past best renter in church circles and still wildly popular in foreign markets) being foisted upon a Christian public without a word of critique or interpretation. Spirituality and dogma in evangelical films remain as unanalyzed as the viewer-user-budget information hidden within private corporate files or simply unknown. Recent work at Baylor University by Michael Korpi and Judith Saxton is an important beginning, but the surface is barely scratched. To my knowledge, no research library of any size has an articulated mandate to collect religious films.[18]

To shift from media studies to broader questions of communications, technology, and public discourse requires that the orbit of typical evangelical concerns expand exponentially from strategic problems of message conveyance to semiotics, social theory, rhetoric, orality-literacy, and revelation. Charles Kraft's *Communication Theory for Christian Witness* (1983) and Theodore Baehr's *Getting the Word Out* (1986) synthesize relevant theories to serve purposes of persuasion and mission. James F. Engel and Wil Norton, Sr., have contributed at a popular level (*How Can I Get Them to Listen?*, 1977) and in concert with Kraft's strategic concerns (Engel, *Contemporary Christian Communications*, 1979). Philip Yancey (*Open Windows*, 1982) and Douglas Frank (*Less Than Conquerors*, 1986) have raised important questions about blindsidedness in evangelicalism—questions that surely interface with concerns expressed in these essays and at institutions where religious communications is given the agenda it needs. David Augsburger's *Communicating Good News* (1972) implies a substantial theological critique of media manipulation, while Carl Henry addresses media issues in theological context in various parts of his densely reasoned, six-volume *God, Revelation, and Authority* (1976–79). Franky Schaeffer rightly badgers Christians to use media thoughtfully (*Addicted to Mediocrity*, 1981) but his own ghoulish film ("Wired to Kill," 1986) challenges his book's thesis and hence its credibility. Donald Drew (*Images of Man*, 1974), Dorothy Sayers (*The Mind of the Maker*, 1941), and Nicholas Wolterstorff (*Art in Action*, 1980) all provide philosophical and literary stimuli to approach media as stewards, crafting from its rough rock the shapes and textures that reveal the Creator's character. Robert Webber is the only evangelical theologian in recent years to produce a book for the communications field. *God Still Speaks* (1980) grew out of his original courses at Wheaton College, generated by an appeal to make the required master's-degree theology work salient to communication students who needed encouragement to think Christianly about their field. Such needs embrace all of us. Ronald Falconer's *Message, Media, Mission* (1977) and John Poulton's *Christian Communicator's Questions* (1970) remind us that British scholarship offers a perspective that can only sharpen American minds and pens.[19]

By these few citations we must admit that evangelical

scholarship in communications, grounded in theological substance and energized by historical studies and social theory, has only begun. We can be grateful that in fields such as literature and history, evangelical scholarship is strong and research collections abundant. We can also be grateful for thoughtful Christian writings formally outside the evangelical camp but ecumenical in their reach and interests. Walter Ong's *Presence of the Word* (1967, reprint 1981) signals the importance of dialogue across the Reformation. Jacques Ellul's prolific writings, some already mentioned but *Propaganda* (1965) and *The Technological Society* (1964) too important not to cite, compel American evangelicals toward dialogue across the Atlantic and frequently in Ellul's later books into Marx, Kierkegaard, and Barth for background. Paul Tillich pitches his tent as far from the evangelical camp as a Protestant theologian can get, yet his *Theology of Culture* (1964) remains at the intersection of the two disciplines, wedded as they are by shared questions of how meanings are conveyed and what differences those meanings make.[20]

My own ruminations on the theological center of communications studies began during a late-night reading of Clifford Christians' seminal essay in *Christian Scholar's Review* (7:1977): "A Cultural View of Mass Communication." I had sprained a shoulder playing racquetball against a superior opponent earlier that day, could not sleep, so pulled out Christians' essay sent to me by a friend. His argument made sense; I went to study the field under him. That's why I am particularly pleased that his essay concludes this volume—not because he has the last word, but because his keen sense of biblical warrant catapults us to the heart of the questions that need a generation of reflection and writing. It is not surprising that his ISAE (Institute for the Study of American Evangelicals) conference presentation, given on a Saturday afternoon as the last paper to only half the registered delegates, sparked the most heated debate, provoked the most emotional and intellectual rejoinders, unsettled the entire crowd, and gave all of us the feeling that the entire conference needed to reconvene soon. At the risk of pointing a spotlight at an unsuspecting player, I must recommend at least Christians' writings in *Jacques Ellul: Interpretive Essays* (1981); "The News Profession and the Powerless," *Calvin Theological Journal* (20:1985); and "Prophetic Witness to a Technicistic Society" and "Technology and Mutual Responsibility" in *Responsible Technology* (1986). An insider has told me that he is working on a major statement on press theory and public responsibility that a year from now will have to be added to the list. But for now, there is enough to get the reader started.[21]

NOTES

[1]Daniel Boorstin, *The Americans: The Democratic Experience* (New York: Vintage, 1973), 3.

[2]Paul E. Freed, *Towers to Eternity* (Waco, Tex.: Word, 1968).

[3]Elizabeth Eisenstein, *The Printing Press as an Agent of Change: Communications and Cultural Transformations in Early-Modern Europe* (New York: Cambridge University Press, 1979); Nathan Hatch, *The Democratization of American Christianity* (New Haven, Conn.: Yale University Press, 1989); David Paul Nord, "The Evangelical Origins of Mass Media in America, 1815–1835," *Journalism Monographs*, May 1984.

[4]Quentin Schultze, "The Mythos of the Electronic Church," *Critical Studies in Mass Communication*, April 1987, 245; Joseph Bayly, *The Gospel Blimp* (Havertown, Pa.: Windward, 1960); Quentin Schultze, *Television: Manna From Hollywood* (Grand Rapids: Zondervan, 1986); Paul Borgman, *Television: Friend or Foe?* (Elgin, Ill.: David C. Cook, 1979); William Fore, *Image and Impact: How Man Comes Through the Mass Media* (New York: Friendship, 1970), and *Television and Religion: The Shaping of Faith, Values, and Culture* (Minneapolis: Augsburg, 1987).

[5]Charles Stelzle, *Principles of Successful Church Advertising* (New York: Revell, 1908); Christian F. Reisner, *Church Publicity: The Modern Way to Compel Them to Come In* (New York: The Methodist Book Concern, 1913); Clarence Barbour, *Making Religion Efficient* (New York: Association Press, 1912); Wendell Loveless, *Manual of Gospel Broadcasting* (Chicago: Moody, 1946); Bruce Barton, *The Man Nobody Knows: A Discovery of the Real Jesus* (Indianapolis: Bobbs-Merrill, 1925); Sue Nichols, *Words on Target: For Better Christian Communication* (Richmond, Va.: John Knox, 1963); William E. Leidt, *Publicity Goes to Church* (Greenwich, Conn.: Seabury, 1959); James Kimsey, *How to Conduct Religious Radio Programs* (St. Louis: Bethany, 1958); William M. Lessel, *Church Publicity: Basic Principles and Practices for Churches and Church-Related Organizations* (Camden, N.J.: Nelson, 1970); James A. Vitti, *Publicity Handbook for Churches and Christian Organizations* (Grand Rapids: Zondervan, 1987).

[6]Edward John Carnell, *Television: Servant or Master?* (Grand Rapids: Eerdmans, 1950); Malcolm Boyd, *Crisis in Communication: A Christian Examination of the Mass Media* (Garden City, N.Y.: Doubleday, 1957); Malcolm Boyd, *Christ and Celebrity Gods: The Church in Mass Culture* (Greenwich, Conn.: Seabury, 1958); Eugene Nida, *Message and Mission: The Communication of the Christian Faith* (New York: Harper & Row, 1960); John W. Bachman, *The Church in the World of Radio-Television* (New York: Association Press, 1960), and *Media: Wasteland or Wonderland: Opportunities and Dangers for Christians in the Electronic Age*, foreword by Martin E. Marty (Minneapolis: Augsburg, 1984); F. W. Dillistone, *Christianity and Communication* (London: Collins, 1956).

[7]John Gill, *Tide Without Turning: Elijah P. Lovejoy and Freedom of the Press* (Boston: Starr King, 1958); Judith S. Duke, *Religious Publishing and Communications* (White Plains, N.Y.: Knowledge Industry, 1980); Wesley Norton, *Religious Newspapers in the Old Northwest to 1861: A History, Bibliography and Record of*

Opinion (Athens: Ohio University Press, 1977); John Ferré, *A Social Gospel for Millions: The Religious Bestsellers of Charles Sheldon, Charles Gordon, and Harold Bell Wright* (Bowling Green, Ohio: Bowling Green State University Popular Press, 1988).

[8]Cal Thomas, *Book Burning* (Westchester, Ill.: Crossway, 1983); Marvin N. Olasky, *The Prodigal Press: The Anti-Christian Bias of the American News Media* (Westchester, Ill.: Crossway, 1988); Allan Fisher (Unpublished papers on the history of religious publishing).

[9]Malcolm Muggeridge, *Christ and the Media*, 1st American ed. (Grand Rapids: Eerdmans, 1977); Jacques Ellul, *Humiliation of the Word*, trans. Joyce Main Hanks (Grand Rapids: Eerdmans, 1985); Virginia Stem Owens, *The Total Image: Or Selling Jesus in the Modern Age* (Grand Rapids: Eerdmans, 1980).

[10]Ben Armstrong, *The Electric Church* (New York: Thomas Nelson, 1979).

[11]Everett C. Parker, Elinor Iman, and Ross Snyder, *Religious Radio: What to Do and How* (New York: Harper & Brothers, 1948), and *Religious Television: What to Do and How* (New York: Harper, 1961); Everett C. Parker, David W. Barry, and Dallas W. Smythe, *The Television-Radio Audience and Religion* (New York: Harper & Brothers, 1955); Peter G. Horsfield, *Religious Television: The American Experience* (New York: Longman, 1984).

[12]J. Harold Ellens, *Models of Religious Broadcasting* (Grand Rapids: Eerdmans, 1974); David DeGroot, *Worlds Beyond: The Story of the Back to God Hour, 1939–1979* (Palos Heights, Ill.: Back to God Hour, 1979); Peter H. Eldersveld, *Nothing But the Gospel: Radio Messages Presented by Peter H. Eldersveld*, collected by the Radio Committee of the Christian Reformed Church (Grand Rapids: Eerdmans, 1966); Donald N. Oberdorfer, *Electronic Christianity: Myth or ministry* (Taylor Falls, Minn.: Brekke & Sons, 1982); Dennis C. Benson, *Electronic Evangelism* (Nashville: Abingdon, 1973); Stewart M. Hoover, *Mass Media Religion: The Social Sources of the Electronic Church* (Newbury Park, Calif.: Sage, 1988), and *The Electronic Giant: A Critique of the Telecommunications Revolution from a Christian Perspective* (Elgin, Ill.: Brethren, 1982); George Gerbner, *Religion and Television* (Philadelphia: Annenberg School of Communications, University of Pennsylvania, 1984).

[13]Jeffrey K. Hadden and Charles E. Swann, *Prime-Time Preachers: The Rising of Televangelism* (Reading, Mass.: Addison-Wesley, 1981); Jeffrey K. Hadden, and Anson Shupe, *Televangelism, Power and Politics on God's Frontier* (New York: Holt, 1988); Razelle Frankl, *Televangelism: The Marketing of Popular Religion* (Carbondale: Southern Illinois University Press, 1987); Larry Martz, *Ministry of Greed: The Inside Story of the Televangelists and Their Holy Wars* (New York: Weidenfeld & Nicolson, 1988); Jerry Sholes, *Give Me That Prime-Time Religion; An Insider's Report on the Oral Roberts Evangelistic Association* (New York: Hawthorn, 1979); Michael Real, *Mass-Mediated Culture* (Englewood Cliffs, N.J.: Prentice Hall, 1977); John Pollock, *Crusades: 20 Years with Billy Graham*, special Billy Graham Crusade ed. (Minneapolis: World Wide Publications, 1969), and *Billy Graham: Highlights of the Story* (Basingstoke, England: Marshall Pickering, 1984); see also Paul Westman, *Billy Graham: Reaching Out to the World* (Minneapolis: Dillon Press, 1981); George Burnham, *Billy Graham: A Mission Accomplished* (Westwood, N.J.: Revell, 1955), and John Capon and Derek Williams, *Billy Graham: The Man and His Mission* (Moor Park, Northwood, Middx.: Creative, 1984).

[14]Frank S. Cook, *Seeds in the Wind: The Story of the Voice of the Andes, Radio Station HCJB, Quito, Ecuador*, rev. ed. (Miami, Fla.: World Radio Missionary Fellowship, n.d.); Paul E. Freed, *Towers to Eternity* (Waco, Tex.: Word, 1968);

Jane Reed and Jim Grant, *Voice Under Every Palm* (Grand Rapids: Zondervan, 1970); Kay Landers, *Antenna Country* (Chicago: Moody, 1972); Philip A. Booth, *Slim Fingers* (Fort Washington, Pa.: Christian Literature Crusade, 1976); *Proclaiming Christ to the World: The Experience of Radio Voice of the Gospel*.

[15]Clayton T. Griswold and Charles Schmitz, *How You Can Broadcast Religion* (New York: National Council of the Churches of Christ in the United States of America, Broadcasting and Film Commission, 1957); Daniel W. Holland, J. Ashton Nickerson, and Terry Vaughan, *Using Nonbroadcast Video in the Church* (Valley Forge, Pa.: Judson, 1980); Gene Jaberg and Louis G. Wargo, *The Video Pencil: Cable Communications for Church and Community* (Washington, D.C.: University Press of America, 1980); Edward McNulty, *Television: A Guide for Christians* (Nashville: Abingdon, 1976); Thomas Neufer Emswiler, *A Complete Guide to Making the Most of Video in Religious Settings: How to Produce, Find, Use, and Distribute Video in the Church and Synagogue* (Normal, Ill.: Wesley Foundation, 1985); B. F. Jackson, Jr., ed., *Communication for Churchmen* (Nashville: Abingdon, 1968).

[16]Bob Larson, *Rock and the Church* (Carol Stream, Ill.: Creation House, 1971); Steve Lawhead, *Rock Reconsidered: A Christian Looks at Contemporary Music* (Downers Grove, Ill.: InterVarsity, 1981); Al Menconi, *Rock Music: A Window to Your Child's Soul*, (Elgin, Ill.: David C. Cook, 1990).

[17]"The Miracle Decision," Burstyn v. Wilson, 434 v.s. 495 (1952); see for example, "The Church and the Film Arts," Acts of Synod, 1966, Christian Reformed Church, Supplement 32; Tim Stafford, "His Father's Son: The Drive Behind James Dobson, Jr.," *Christianity Today*, 22 April, 1988, 16; Lyn Cryderman, "The Players: Jim Kennedy's Humble Empire," *Christianity Today*, 18 March, 1988, 38.

[18]Terry Lindvall, "Cinematic Dogma: The Evangelical Response to Hollywood" (Unpublished paper, 1985); Michael Korpi and Judith Saxton, "Supporting the Status Quo: Film and Video Use in Protestant Churches" (Unpublished paper, 1988).

[19]Charles Kraft, *Communication Theory for Christian Witness* (Nashville: Abingdon, 1983); Theodore Baehr, *Getting the Word Out: How to Communicate the Gospel in Today's World* (San Francisco: Harper & Row, 1986); James F. Engel, *How Can I Get Them to Listen?* (Grand Rapids: Zondervan, 1977), and *Contemporary Christian Communications, Its Theory and Practice* (Nashville: Nelson, 1979); Philip Yancey, *Open Windows* (Westchester, Ill.: Crossway, 1982); Yancey also deserves credit for some of the most perceptive sociology of evangelical industries to appear in print. His method is interview and participant observation, and he gets to the heart of his case with Weberian instincts. For an example, see "The Ironies and Impact of PTL," *Christianity Today*, 21 September 1979; Douglas Frank, *Less Than Conquerors: How Evangelicals Entered the Twentieth Century* (Grand Rapids: Eerdmans, 1986); David W. Augsburger, *Communicating Good News* (Scottdale, Pa.: Mennonite Publishing House, 1972); Carl Henry, *God, Revelation, and Authority* (Waco, Tex.: Word, 1976) v. 1–6; Franky Schaeffer, *Addicted to Mediocrity: 20th Century Christians and the Arts* (Westchester, Ill.: Cornerstone [Crossway], 1981); Donald J. Drew, *Images of Man: A Critique of the Contemporary Cinema* (Downers Grove, Ill.: InterVarsity, 1974); Dorothy L. Sayers, *The Mind of the Maker* (New York: Harcourt, Brace and Company, 1941); Nicholas Wolterstorff, *Art in Action: Toward a Christian Aesthetic* (Grand Rapids: Eerdmans, 1980); Robert E. Webber, *God Still Speaks* (Nashville: Nelson, 1980); Ronald Falconer, *Message, Media, Mission* (Edinburg, Scotland: St. Andrew Press, 1977); John Poulton, *The Christian Communicator's Questions: A*

Study of Where Research Stands in Christian Communication, and a Look Ahead (London: World Association for Christian Communication, 1970).

[20]Walter J. Ong, *The Presence of the Word: Some Prolegomena for Cultural and Religious History* (Minneapolis: University of Minnesota Press, 1981; previous ed. New Haven: Yale University Press, 1967); Jacques Ellul, *Propaganda: The Formation of Men's Attitudes* (New York: Knopf, 1965), and *The Technological Society*, trans. John Wilkinson, (New York: Vintage, 1964); Paul Tillich, *Theology of Culture*, (New York: Oxford University Press, 1964).

[21]Clifford Christians, ed. *Jacques Ellul: Interpretive Essays* (Urbana: University of Illinois Press, 1981); Stephen V. Monsma, et al., *Responsible Technology: A Christian Perspective*, by the fellows of the Calvin Center for Christian Scholarship (Grand Rapids: Eerdmans, 1986).

NAME INDEX

SUBJECT INDEX

A & M Records, 161, 162, 163, 164
ABC, 84–85, 89, 103, 159
Abingdon Press: highly regarded evangelical publisher, 102, 105
Abundant Life: Oral Roberts periodical, 121, 124
Age to Age: first CCM million-copy album (Amy Grant), 143, 157, 160
American Bible Society Record: organization-focused periodical, 121, 124
American Broadcasting Company; *See* ABC.
American Protestantism, 69, 72, 76, 81, 82, 85–86, 88
Angels: God's Secret Agents: best-selling book by Billy Graham, 99
Approaching Hoofbeats: The Four Horsemen of the Apocalypse: on secular best-seller
    lists, 111
Assemblies of God, 101, 125, 132
Association of Logos Bookstores, 107, 109
Audience: composition of; books, 105–6, 113–14, 115; magazines, 135–36;
    radio, 172, 176–78, 183, 192, 268, 300, 301; television, 200, 231: size of;
    books, 111, 114–15; magazines, 135–36; radio, 15, 79, 81, 172, 176–79, 309,
    321, 324; television, 27, 222, 231–32, 233–35, 236, 246, 268
Augsburg, 105

Baby boomers, 100, 143–44, 145–47
"Back to God Hour, The": early national radio program, 79, 87
"Back to the Bible": Theodore Epp's early national radio program, 79, 86
Baptist, 72, 85, 89, 102, 125, 269
Barbour and Company, Inc.: parent company of Book Bargains, 108
BFC; *See* Broadcasting and Film Commission.
"Bible Fellowship Hour, The": T. Myron Webb's early national radio program,
    79
Bible, the: versions published, 103, 104
Book Bargains: the major wholesaler of evangelical remainders, 108
Book distribution: evangelical; growing dominance of wholesalers, 106–8:
    remainders; 108
Book publishing: evangelical 14–15, 99–106; as reflecting conservative trends in
    American culture, 100; audience, 105–6, 113–15; boom-and-bust cycle in
    1970s and 1980s, 99–102, 114–15; compromised literary and intellectual
    integrity, 105; concern about secular "gatekeeping" of evangelical books,
    111, 112; increased emphasis on the bottom line, 104, 105; reliance on
    marketing techniques, 114–15; tendency for "gatekeeping," control of
    ideas, 109–11, 112, 113: religious; now dominated by denominational
    houses, 102
Book Supply Company: early mail-order publisher, 102
Books: evangelical, 31; criticized as simplistic and mediocre, 106; questionable
    evangelistic effect, 105–6, 115
Bookstores: evangelical, 108–9, 110–11, 112, 113; as primary sellers of Christian
    records, 152, 158, 173, 181; tendency for "gatekeeping," control of ideas,
    109, 110–11, 113: religious; most dominated by evangelical preferences,
    111

American Evangelicals and the Mass Media was typeset by the Photocomposition Department of Zondervan Publishing House, Grand Rapids, Michigan on a Mergenthaler Linotron 202/N.
Compositor: Susan A. Koppenol
Editor: Jan M. Ortiz
Designed by: Jan M. Ortiz

The text was set in 10 point Palatino, a face designed by Hermann Zapf in Germany in 1948. Palatino is probably one of the two most highly regarded typefaces of this century. This book was printed on 50-pound Husky Vellum paper by Color House Graphics, Grand Rapids, Michigan.

practical/successful 100
critics of publishers 105 F
pluralism 111
media evangelists 13